Anishinabe

Anishinabe
6 Studies of Modern Chippewa

J. Anthony Paredes, *Editor*
Michael A. Rynkiewich
Stuart Berde
Barbara D. Jackson
Timothy Roufs
Gretel H. Pelto

A Florida State University Book

University Presses of Florida

Tallahassee

cop. 2

University Presses of Florida is the central agency for scholarly publishing of the State of Florida's university system. Its offices are located at 15 NW 15th Street, Gainesville, FL 32603. Works published by University Presses of Florida are evaluated and selected for publication by a faculty editorial committee of any one of Florida's nine public universities: Florida A&M University (Tallahassee), Florida Atlantic University (Boca Raton), Florida International University (Miami), Florida State University (Tallahassee), University of Central Florida (Orlando), University of Florida (Gainesville), University of North Florida (Jacksonville), University of South Florida (Tampa), University of West Florida (Pensacola).

Some of the material in Chapter 7 of this volume has appeared previously in *Anthropological Quarterly* (October 1971).

Library of Congress Cataloging in Publication Data
Main entry under title:

Anishinabe : 6 studies of modern Chippewa.

   "A Florida State University book."
   Bibliography: p.
   Includes index.
   1. Chippewa Indians—Addresses, essays, lectures.
I. Paredes, James Anthony, 1939–
E99.C6A45   970'.004'97   79-20091
ISBN 0–8130–0625–2

Typography by American Graphics Corporation
Fort Lauderdale, Florida

Printed by Thomson–Shore, Inc.
Dexter, Michigan

Contents

Foreword

Ruth Landes

This volume gives reports of certain Minnesota Indians' adoption of American social systems on reservations and in a "white man's" town. The contributors combine their observations of the public behavior of the Indians with references to related discussions in older ethnographic accounts. The Indians' participation in the political and economic systems controlling much of their behavior has been grossly handicapped by historic prejudices against all aboriginal Americans. The psychological and sociocultural dynamics shaping the behavior of a community under such relentless pressures are difficult to appraise, and the persistence of ancestral native tradition in the conduct of individuals and in the community's ethos under these circumstances is an extraordinary phenomenon.

The research presented here, which describes the changing ways of the native people, was conducted in the mid-1960s. I come to the published results from the background of my own intensive studies among the same people in Minnesota and in Ontario during the 1930s. I find similarity in the behavior, values, and interests of the Indians then and now, despite the passage of time and the myriad intrusions of modern influences.

Since before the 1920s, ethnologists have been attracted to the Ojibwa-Chippewa because they are accessible. They talk readily and to the point. They are zestful and wicked survivors, extremely alert to the possibilities of an ungenerous environment. Their wit is cruel and startling to the white middle-class outsider, at whom it is often directed. Their celebrated pursuit of spiritual protectors, through visions induced deliberately by starvation and thirst, has produced fierce and remarkable sorcerers.

Acculturated to modernity as the Minnesota Ojibwa of the present work appear to be, they must yet resemble psychoculturally their forebears, who pushed others around to get land and to win war games with a favorite foe, the Dakota, and who accommodated strategically to the hard encounters with Europeans and Americans. Their shamanistic forebears became subordinate partners of the Europeans as voyageurs, trappers, interpreters, even Christian missionaries; and the partners liked each other, according to the records. That the Indian people have not penetrated further into the modern world suggests to me active preference for ancestral ways, besides the brute hindrances of the ruling society's prejudices. The personalities I knew and wrote about understood exactly what life meted out to them and they were not intimidated. Their individualistic values made them self-respecting and brave and reliable in their undertakings.

The Ojibwa-Chippewa of this book no longer seem unusual in their modern ways and purposes. They know, however, that they are sons and daughters of dreamers, sorcerers, tellers of tales, bold hunters and warriors — once bent on glory. We must watch for their quality to emerge.

Preface

The studies in this book originated under the auspices of the Upper Mississippi Research Project, a general study of the people of north central Minnesota. Because our work was done in the 1960s, it does not portray truly contemporary Chippewa; nonetheless it provides small but important pieces of the immediate historical background of the Indian activism of the 1970s.

More important, the studies remain to date the only thoroughgoing anthropological descriptions of modern Chippewa people of northern Minnesota. I emphasize "modern people," for we were not so much concerned with ferreting out remnants of Chippewa *culture* as with producing a balanced description of a broad spectrum of the lifeways of Chippewa *people* — the mundane as well as the exotic, the synthetic as well as the traditional, the ordinary as well as the unusual, the nondistinctive as well as the distinctive. In pursuit of these aims we combined "old-fashioned" ethnographic and ethnohistorical techniques with sampling and quantitative data in the methodological style of Pertti Pelto, the senior anthropologist in the Upper Mississippi Research Project. In the course of our analyses we addressed a variety of issues, some of interest primarily to Ojibwa specialists, others of broader relevance for understanding contemporary American Indians and for the anthropology of complex societies in general. Finally, though the several authors have given careful attention to variations among modern

Ojibwa, in the end we have tried to show how these variations fit together into a complex whole, the Chippewa people, in the context of the larger society.

In early 1964 the Upper Mississippi Research Project was organized as a 3-year study of the sociocultural and psychological characteristics of 5 counties served by a local mental health center in northern Minnesota. The general idea for the project was conceived by Dr. Howard Reid, director of the center; he obtained funds from the George W. Nielson Foundation of Minneapolis to support the research and enlisted the collaboration of the Department of Anthropology at the University of Minnesota. In June, 1964, I became the resident research coordinator of the project. From the outset the Chippewa Indians of the area were to be included, but the bulk of our research involved the local white population, who were in the majority. It is perhaps ironic — but understandable, given the predilections of anthropologists — that the first book to emerge from the Upper Mississippi Research Project should be this volume on the Chippewa.

Several students received their first fieldwork experience in the project. A number of them began thesis studies within the project, studies which in some cases lasted well beyond the project. In this book the contributions by Jackson, Pelto, Roufs, and Rynkiewich began as master's theses at the University of Minnesota. The first version of Berde's chapter was an undergraduate honors thesis at the University of Minnesota. Paredes's study, the last to be completed, was first prepared as a doctoral dissertation at the University of New Mexico in 1969.

In 1970 I began the task of editing the studies and framing them with introductory and concluding chapters. In the preparation of Chapter 1 I borrowed liberally from the original versions of some of the later chapters. The original version of the concluding chapter was not completed until the fall of 1972. After acceptance of the manuscript by the Florida State University Press in the spring of 1973, fiscal, editorial, and institutional difficulties combined to delay its publication till now.

This book is thus the product of unusual patience and endeavor. While we take full responsibility for our work, we owe much to many people and organizations that have aided us along the way. All of us are indebted to the George W. Nielson Foundation, Mrs. Katherine Cram, the staff of the mental health center, and the University of Minnesota Department of Anthropology for their support during the active stage of research. Additional assistance for Jackson, Roufs, and Rynkiewich was provided by a National Institute of General Medical Sciences Graduate Training Grant (#GM 01164), and Jackson also received funding from the University of South Dakota American Indian Oral History Project. Paredes's work was further supported by a National Institute of Mental Health Fellowship (#MH 41898-0181). A succession of capable typists in the Department of Anthropology at Florida State University prepared the final manuscript.

We are greatly indebted to Pertti J. Pelto and to Frank C. Miller for their intellectual leadership. Each of the authors has indicated a desire to acknowledge fellow contributors; of particular importance is the appreciation we all extend to Timothy Roufs for his aid in the field and afterwards. All of us, too, owe a very special thanks to Anna Paredes, the tireless hostess, dispassionate critic, and ever-patient confidante in the field.

Various contributors wish to acknowledge, for advice and assistance, Philip Bock, Robert Byles, Richard Carter, Cecilie Crosby, Nancie González, Peter Hackett, Michael Haralambos, Robert Lynch, Harold Maier, Dale McCullough, Katharine Salter, Stephen and Jay Schensul, the VISTA volunteers of "Wicket," and Douglas White.

The people to whom we are most indebted must remain anonymous. Without the tolerance and cooperation of the Chippewa people of the "Deer Lake" Band and the Minnesota Chippewa Tribe, this volume would not have been possible. In addition there are many specific individuals — both Chippewa and white — of "Deer Lake," "James Lake," "North City," "Rice Village," and "Wicket" to whom we are especially indebted, but to identify them by name would be a breach of our pledges of anonymity. We trust that they will know who they are and will realize how sincerely grateful we are for their guidance and help. *Migwéch* — thank you.

As editor of this volume I use my prerogative to pay special tribute to Harry W. Basehart and the late W. W. "Nibs" Hill for their patient guidance and encouragement and faith in me over many years. I wish to express my heartfelt thanks to the other contributors for their extraordinarily patient forbearance over the years that this book has been in the making. Finally, I thank my parents, Antonio and Mildred, for getting me started, and my wife, Anna, and children — Anthony, Teresa, and Sara — for keeping me going.

J. Anthony Paredes
Tallahassee 1980

1
The Setting and the Research

By the shores of Gitche Gumee,
By the shining Big-Sea-Water...

Longfellow's romantic tale of Hiawatha, based on Schoolcraft's Chippewa materials, did much to popularize bits and pieces of Chippewa history and culture. In many ways, the Chippewa, or Ojibwa, indirectly have been a source for stereotypes of the American Indian. Among the images conjured by the romantics, the Indian brave in his birchbark canoe silently slipping through "sky blue waters" against a backdrop of towering pines (with appropriate melodies from *Rose Marie* softly playing in the distance) is second only to that of the war-bonneted horseman of the Plains. While, as Barnouw (1950) argues, the Chippewa may have readily acquiesced to white domination, their native culture has left an indelible mark on the language and folklore of the United States. (The Ojibwa of the United States often have been termed "Chippewa" in the literature. "Chippewa" also remains the official designation of reservations and tribal governments. Because of this usage, the term "Chippewa" will be encountered throughout this book despite the increased sentiment among the U.S. Ojibwa for the use of "Ojibwa" and even "Anishinabe," the name they call themselves.)

In American anthropology, the Ojibwa are in the company of the Iroquois, Zuni, Crow, and Kwakiutl as perennially favorite "ethnographic examples." The Chippewa have had an enduring and illustrious role in the development of American anthropology. It was Schoolcraft's work among these people, in the 1820s and '30s, that inspired at least one historian of anthropology to term him "America's first social anthropologist and the first genuine field anthropologist in the world" (Hays 1958:5). Morgan's monumental work on kinship was prompted by his discovery of similarities in the terminological systems of the Iroquois and Chippewa (Hays 1958:22–23, Eggan 1966:78). From the Chippewa word *dodaim,* for example, the ever popular subject of totemism derives its name. Since Schoolcraft's time, important additions to knowledge of traditional Chippewa culture have been made by a series of distinguished ethnographers, including Jenks (1900), Densmore (1929), Hilger (1951), and Landes (1937, 1968). Hallowell's comparisons (1942, 1950, 1952) of several Ojibwa groups are regarded as classics in culture and personality studies. The work done by Caudill (1949), Barnouw (1950), Boggs (1958), Friedl (1956), and James (1961) has further contributed to the prominence of the Ojibwa in the literature of acculturational psychology. In his general book on culture and personality, Barnouw (1963), for example, devotes an entire chapter to the Chippewa and their analysts. Notwithstanding the apparent confusion in the literature between social organization and personality, the Ojibwa have often been taken as the type case of an individualistic society, and they have been used as a comparative referent for such diverse peoples as the Skolt Lapps of Finland (Pelto 1962) and Mexican-Americans in a Texas city (Rubel 1966). Social atomism among the Ojibwa, as well as other northeastern Algonquians, has continued to be a subject of considerable ethnohistorical debate (e.g., see Hickerson [1967] and accompanying comments).

Although James (1961) has described the "poor white" type of culture of a contemporary Wisconsin Chippewa reservation, the lifeways of thousands of modern Chippewa living in scores of communities scattered across the Upper Great Lakes states still remain relatively obscure in the anthropological literature. This is particularly true in the case of the Minnesota Chippewa, despite several anthropologists who were doing salvage ethnography on the Minnesota reservations in the earlier decades of the 20th century. Although Miller has reported on modern political developments (1966, 1967) and adolescent behavior (with Caulkins 1964) on one of these reservations, much remains to be done to provide a well-rounded account of the contemporary Minnesota Chippewa. For a more recent, semipopular account of the Minnesota Chippewa, see Roufs (1975), and for a recent bibliographic survey, see Tanner (1976).

As anthropology quickens its pace toward the study of complex societies, a more attentive examination is needed of Indian cultures and societies as they exist at present. Of course, vast numbers of acculturational studies have been devoted to the American Indians, but, in general, these works have not attempted to describe these societies as ongoing concerns. Rather, they have emphasized the exotic elements and have given short shrift to the more mundane aspects of Indian life shared with other Americans. For example, one often loses sight of Indians as people who live in a world of television, hard rock music, nuclear energy, national politics, and Kentucky Fried Chicken (even long-haired Navajos at Window Rock are greeted by the smiling Colonel), in addition to whatever elements of an aboriginal past they have inherited. There also appears to have been a general tendency for analysts to focus on cultural loss and social disorganization rather than on positive elements of change like addition, substitution, and recombination in the structure and dynamics of contemporary Indian communities as operating sociocultural systems. The emphasis in acculturation studies has, for good reason, been based on the cultural modification of *tribal* peoples rather than on the synchronic analysis of American Indians as *moderns*.

Fortunately, for some time efforts have been made to describe and analyze systematically the complicated (and often confusing) lifeways of the 20th-century descendants of aboriginal Americans. Margaret Mead's study of the "Antlers" (1932) was one of the first contributions to the "ethnography of the present" in American Indian studies. Other examples of early researches of this kind have included studies of modern American Indians by Spicer (1940), Noon (1949), and Mac-Gregor (1946). In recent years, the numerous papers and monographs covering specifically the contemporary social and cultural patterns in present-day American Indian communities have included works such as those by Sasaki (1960), Kupferer (1966), Kluckhohn (1966), Woodward (1968), Spindler (1955), Polgar (1960), Shimony (1961), Bock (1966), and Wolcott (1967), to mention but a few. Several of the *Case Studies in Cultural Anthropology* (Downs 1966, Chance 1966, Basso 1970, Rohner and Rohner 1970) are indicative of an increased interest in the study of contemporary American Indian (and Eskimo) communities as a legitimate area of ethnographic research. Any discussion of studies of modern American Indians must also acknowledge the contribution of Adair and Vogt (1949) and Aberle (1966), among others, in bringing a measure of modernity to the anthropological study of the Southwest. New directions in American Indian research have been pursued by Hurt (1961–62), Frielich (1958), Ablon (1964), Hodge (1969), Graves (1970), and others in their studies of the adaptation of American Indians to urban life. Increased anthropological interest in contemporary Indian problems is clearly reflected in such general works as *The American Indian Today* (Levine and Lurie 1968). Finally, McFee's (1968) demonstration of the inadequacies of simple levels of acculturation schemes for describing the present-day Blackfeet, as well as Boissevain's (1963, 1965) excellent accounts of the maintenance of Indian identity in contemporary New England, help to document the emergent anthropological view of American Indians as "ethnics" in a national context rather than as merely scattered remnants of the aboriginal past. Although Bushnell's felicitous transposition "Indian American" (1968) failed to gain popular currency, the phrase "native American" (for a while, at least) achieved popularity—even among some American Indians themselves.

Given the extreme economic deprivation of many American Indian communities, it is somewhat surprising that they have not figured more prominently in the surge of interest in poverty research. Perhaps it is a consequence of a continuing emphasis in American Indian studies on acculturation rather than adaptation that, while economic difficulties are seldom unmentioned, the full potential of materials from modern American Indian societies in discussions of "the culture of poverty" (e.g., Lewis 1961, Finney 1969) has yet to be realized. Alexander Leighton and his associates, for example, in their study of "Stirling County" Nova Scotians (1959) attempted to relate psychiatric disorder to social disintegration. It is rather perplexing that community mental health research of this type has not been employed more often on Indian reservations. Nonetheless, James (1970) has raised the issue of "Indian poverty culture" as a primary determinant of contemporary Indian behavior, and he has attacked proponents of the persistence of traditional culture among the Ojibwa. James's arguments, though oriented to the Ojibwa, have much broader implications. But his paper is only a beginning, with much remaining to be done to assess objectively the role of poverty variables in modern Indian society and behavior.

Purposes of the work

More than any other single factor, the characterization of the American Indians as impoverished in the midst of American affluence has placed continuing study of American Indians in the forefront of the concerns of social anthropologists attempting to probe the complex problems, both theoretical and practical, of modern humankind's industrialized and electronically controlled world.

The purposes of the present work are three: the first is to add still another chapter to the continuing anthropological story of the Ojibwa; the second, to contribute to the general knowledge of modern American Indian life; and the third, to examine a number of issues with broad implications for improving our understanding of human behavior in present-day complex societies.

The studies in this book were initiated under the auspices of the Upper Mississippi Research Project, a general cultural, social, and psychological research program in northern Minnesota during 1964–66 (see Pelto 1970a). (These investigations were undertaken jointly by the Department of Anthropology, University of Minnesota, and the local mental health center serving the research area under a grant from the George W. Nielson Foundation of Minneapolis.) Some preliminary findings on a series of non-Indian (white) communities in the 5-county research area have been reported (Schensul et al. 1968). This volume is intended as the first in a projected series, to be followed by a similar book on the white communities, and one of a more psychological nature dealing with both Indians and whites.

Since it has been over 10 years since the completion of the research reported in this volume, many particulars of communities and situations described have changed, and perhaps some longstanding social trends have even begun to reverse. Because of the specialized nature of Pelto's analysis of specific, brief historical events, she has written mostly in the past tense. The other authors have often adopted the convention of the "ethnographic present," but they recognize that in an era of fast-paced change, even brilliant insights into contemporary Indian affairs may be outdated before they can appear in print. Nonetheless, these studies, in depicting a variety of Chippewa situations as they were in the 1960s, reveal the social and cultural roots of many ongoing processes.

This research provides important baseline data for present and future studies of the northern Minnesota Chippewa. Likewise, it is now evident that the time period of the studies, covering the latter half of the 1960s, is a critical one in modern American Indian history. The research thus stands as a small but significant element in the background of the much publicized Indian activism of the 1970s.

Since researchers frequently assured informants, both Indian and white, that the identity of places as well as of individuals would be disguised in publication, the consistent use of pseudonyms throughout this volume should not be taken as evidence for a dehumanizing or "people-as-objects" view on the part of the authors. Quite the contrary: given the disagreement among some anthropologists over the use of pseudonyms for groups and communities, the rationale offered for the adoption of identity-concealing pseudonyms by Margaret Mead in her pioneering study of the "Antlers" bears repeating.

> Why I realized from the beginning that I would want to protect the identity not only of the individuals (as I had done in my Samoan study) but also of the tribe, I am not sure. But this is a decision I have never regretted and to which I still adhere. Any ethnologist can, of course, place the "Antlers," and interested members of the tribe have known about the book for many years. But where pride in group identity enters into a picture that also includes disintegration, demoralization, and despair, the group as well as the individual must be shielded from casual reproach. (1966:xx)

History

Although each of the authors has presented background materials directly pertinent to his or her particular research, an introductory historical and descriptive overview of the research area may clarify for the reader the general context of these related studies.

When Europeans first explored northern Minnesota in the 17th century, they found the region inhabited by Siouan-speaking peoples. Under the impetus of trade with French and British fur companies, the Ojibwa, first encountered in the area of Sault Ste. Marie, began to expand their territory. By the beginning of the 19th century the Chippewa occupied a vast and diverse territory, including almost the entire region between the lower peninsula of Michigan and the plains of eastern Saskatchewan. In the United States, the Chippewa were occupying lands adjacent to the northern parts of the Upper Great Lakes, as well as the entire region of the headwaters of the Mississippi.

The Indians occupying this vast area were not a politically united or even a culturally homogeneous population as the single general term Chippewa might imply. But within the area, 4 geographic divisions (with concomitant cultural variations) have been distinguished among the Chippewa. The Plains Ojibwa of this period closely resembled other northern Plains tribes in their bison-hunting economy and in features of their social and ceremonial organization. The northern Chippewa, located in the Laurentian uplands north of the Great Lakes, came to bear a resemblance to other historical subarctic Algonquian hunters. The southeastern Chippewa, occupying lower Michigan and adjacent parts of Ontario, coupled horticulture with their hunting and fishing activities. The inhabitants of the fourth division, labeled the southwestern Chippewa, were chiefly hunters and trappers. They occupied territory along the southwestern shores of Lake Superior, as well as land to the interior of Minnesota and Wisconsin.

In 1679 the fur trade in the Upper Great Lakes region experienced a period of considerable expansion. Through the efforts of the French, a peace was effected between the Chippewa and the Dakota, who were living in the interior of the area to the south and southwest of western Lake Superior. This activity soon developed into a full-scale Chippewa-Dakota commercial alliance, resulting in the movement westward along the shores of Lake Superior by Chippewa who had previously resided at Saulte Ste. Marie. (A few Chippewa may have begun this movement even earlier [Roufs 1976:46].) These Chippewa settled mainly in 2 villages, the larger located on the Chequamegon Peninsula and the smaller on the Keweenaw Peninsula. These villages were apparently founded on commercial relations with the Dakota, and Hickerson notes that the Chippewa "carried on hunting in Dakota country and undoubtedly aided their friends, who were notoriously poor trappers, in taking of furred game, to the great benefit of both" (1962:66).

Chequamegon apparently then became of great importance as a Chippewa center. It was a home base for hunting excursions into Dakota territory, as well as for local sedentary activities, such as farming and fishing. The population of Chequamegon is estimated to have been between 750 and 1,050 by 1736 (Hickerson 1962:67). At this time, since the French expansion of trade to the south and west had effectively eliminated the commercial foundation of Chequamegon and the advantages of the alliance with the Dakota, the stage was set for the Chippewa domination and settlement of Dakota territory in Minnesota.

French expansion, from Lake Superior to Lake Winnipeg—by way of the border lakes region, and then beyond, along the Saskatchewan—was dependent on establishing direct trade with the Cree and Assiniboin, who had long been enemies of the Dakota. By way of conciliating the Dakota, the French initiated a direct line of trade with these groups by forming a large trading post and mission on the Mississippi at Lake Pepin. In establishing this post, the French specified that no trade would be conducted in the direction of Chequamegon. Since the Dakota who at that time traded at Lake Pepin were the same as those who had been trading with the Chippewa, the Chequamegon Chippewa found the market for their trade commodities greatly reduced (Hickerson 1962:69); the amiable relationship between the Chippewa and the Dakota likewise suffered. The Chippewa were thus in the position of competition with the Dakota for the game and furs of Dakota territory.

In order to maintain their use of Dakota territory, the Chippewa allied themselves with the Cree and Assiniboin to the west, engaging in bitter warfare against the Dakota between 1736 and 1765. The Chippewa met with success and gradually came to extend their domain over northern Wisconsin, Minnesota, and even beyond. The Chippewa had succeeded in driving the Dakota out of northern Minnesota by the last quarter of the 18th century, even though minor skirmishes continued between the 2 groups. In 1825, the Treaty of Prairie du Chien set a line of demarcation between the tribes that essentially assigned the northern part of the territory to the Chippewa and the southwestern portion of Minnesota to the Dakota. Despite this division of territory by treaty, however, minor hostilities continued for another 25 years (Minnesota Governor's Human Rights Committee 1965). Hickerson has emphasized that this constant threat of military engagement with the Dakota contributed to the maintenance of relatively stable villages among the southwestern Chippewa (1962:12–64).

In 1837, however, the competition with the Dakota for trapping territories was suddenly no longer significant because the fur trade collapsed after the Panic of 1837. The American Fur Company abolished its credit system, and traders could no longer provide credit to the Indian hunters and trappers in the form of equipment and supplies (Hickerson 1962:89). On the other hand, wild rice (*Zizania aquatica*), which had been important to the Chippewa for subsistence and as a trading item during the prosperous days of the fur trade, probably achieved even greater importance in the Chippewa economy.

Following the collapse of the fur market, the Minnesota bands of Chippewa entered into 9 treaties with the United States government during the period 1837–67. Under the terms of these treaties, they ceded virtually all of their lands in return for annuities, goods, and the establishment of reservations. Only the Deer Lake Band retained title to sizable tracts of "aboriginal lands." Today, the Deer Lake Reservation represents the only Minnesota Indian lands not ceded to the federal government (U.S. Bureau of Indian Affairs 1965a:8). These 19th-century treaties established the reservation boundaries in approximately their present location.

With the passage of the Dawes Act of 1887—and even earlier in Minnesota—Indian lands were allotted in severality. As an indirect result, the Chippewa of the upper Mississippi lost most of their remaining land to white settlers and timber interests that were moving rapidly into the region. The Deer Lake Band, however, continued to resist the allotment plan successfully and they still hold their lands in common. Under the provisions of an act of 1889, all the Minnesota Chippewa, with the exception of the Deer Lake Band, were supposed to be induced to move to one reservation—Beaver Pelt—where they were to be given allotments (U.S. Bureau of Indian Affairs 1965a:3). While many of the Chippewa did go to Beaver Pelt, others elected to remain in their original reservation areas. After 1905, when provisions were made for the sale of many of the Beaver Pelt lands to whites (U.S. Bureau of Indian Affairs 1965a:3), most of this reservation area was alienated from Indian ownership altogether. Through all this, however, the Deer Lake Band, who were able to retain their lands, were rapidly becoming politically distinct from the other Minnesota Chippewa.

From the 1880s onward, the Indians slipped into the background as a poor racial minority and the region's history rapidly became dominated by the whites as they settled the area. The present situation of the northern Minnesota Chippewa must therefore be viewed in the context of the wider developments affecting the white majority in the region as a whole.

North central Minnesota: the research area

In Minnesota, the 3 largest, most populous Indian reservations lie in close proximity in the north central portion of the state. Central to these reservations is the small but important urban center, North City. It is the major administrative, educational, and commercial center both for the Indians on the 3 reservations and for the whites in several surrounding counties. Research activities for the studies in this volume were conducted on 2 of the reservations, Broken Reed and Deer Lake, and in North City. Although this volume includes no studies made in the Beaver Pelt area specifically, this reservation has important connections to the Broken Reed Reservation and many of the Chippewa of North City originated from Beaver Pelt. Accordingly, Beaver Pelt is included in this general description (see Figure 1.1).

Once provisions had been made for whites to acquire Indian lands,

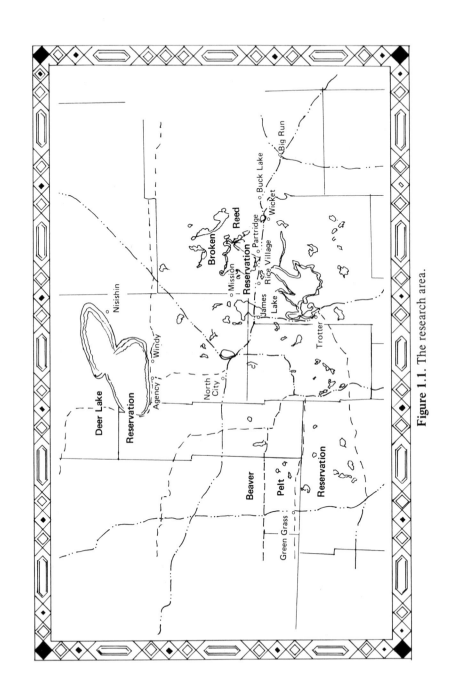

Figure 1.1. The research area.

the timber companies and the settlers began to establish villages and towns in north central Minnesota. Many of these communities were being located within the boundaries of the Broken Reed and Beaver Pelt reservations. The Deer Lake Reservation remained closed to whites except for one minor settlement. Nearly all the white communities in the area were established during the period 1880–1910. Since the early growth of these communities was closely linked to the expansion of the timber industry, many settlements were essentially boom towns. Old-timers delight in tales about when "there were 10,000 lumberjacks in Draketon on a Saturday night." Draketon now has a population of fewer than 800. As forests were depleted, most of the towns dwindled in population and wealth, some disappearing completely. Even now, the big-timber myth of Paul Bunyan continues to be perpetuated enthusiastically by local citizens—primarily for the benefit of tourists.

Homesteaders followed the lumberjacks and the timber companies. Homesteading continued in some areas as late as the 1920s. With the population increasing, prospects seemed good for continuing development and economic growth in the area. But the dislocations of World War II and major technological and social changes after the war altered the pattern.

By the decade of the 1960s, state and federal agencies had designated most of the counties in the Minnesota research area as economically depressed. The total tax evaluation of the counties was low, partly because of the large acreages—forests, game refuges, and Indian lands—under state and federal control. Rates of unemployment in the area were high compared to the state as a whole. The 1965 12-months average unemployment rates for counties in the region are shown in Table 1.1. Unemployment rates tend to fluctuate greatly over the year, revealing rates which are relatively low during summer and fall but high in winter and spring. During times of high employment, many workers

Table 1.1. Unemployment rates (12-month average, 1965)

Cramton County	8.0%
Deep River County	11.9
James County	7.4
Motherwell County	9.3
Nebish County	15.0
State of Minnesota	4.1

Adapted from Hunter 1966.

Table 1.2. Population trends

Census year	1890	1900	1910	1920	1930	1940	1950	1960
Cramton County	312	11,030	19,337	27,079	20,707	26,107	24,962	23,425
Deep River County	n.a.	n.a.	6,870	8,569	9,546	11,153	10,204	8,864
James County	1,247	7,777	11,620	15,897	15,591	20,646	19,468	16,720
Motherwell County	1,412	6,578	9,831	10,136	9,596	11,085	11,085	9,962
Nebish County	n.a.	n.a.	3,249	6,197	6,153	8,054	7,059	6,341
Truehead County	743	4,573	17,208	23,876	27,224	32,996	33,321	38,006
Zecker County	9,401	14,375	18,840	22,851	22,503	26,562	24,836	23,959

n.a.: Figures not available since these counties did not exist as political units during these census years.

Adapted from U. S. Bureau of the Census 1921:111-12.

_____ 1943:43-51.

_____ 1952:43.

_____ 1961:161-72.

are actually out of the region working in more prosperous areas to the east, west, and south. Welfare recipiency was also found to be high in these counties (e.g., in 1964, the percentage of the population receiving Aid to Dependent Children was approximately twice that for nonmetropolitan Minnesota as a whole).

The major demographic trends in the region are displayed in Table 1.2. The period of rapid white settlement of the area is clearly marked by the sharp rise in population between 1890 and 1910. The major trend shown thereafter is one of gradual increase for the decades 1910–40, followed by a decrease for the 1940–60 period. Truehead County proved exceptional because of prosperous mining towns of the Giant Iron Range located in its eastern section. On the whole, the postwar population decline appeared to be the result of young adults emigrating in search of employment and greater economic opportunity. The resultant population distribution reveals disproportionately large numbers of dependent children and aged persons. The Indian segments of the population of these counties have followed essentially the same trends. Only the Cramton County Indian population, which includes virtually all those residing on the Deer Lake Reservation, has continued to increase (see Table 1.3). Since 1950, increasing numbers of these Minnesota Indians have migrated to the Minneapolis–St. Paul area.

Table 1.3. Indian population trends

Census year	1920	1930	1940	1950	1960
Cramton County	1,580	1,961	2,521	2,673	2,959
Deep River County	357	461	399	331	319
James County	1,022	1,304	1,757	1,814	1,542
Nebish County	1,405	1,612	1,414	1,009	789
Truehead County	448	490	666	526	770
Zecker County	1,694	1,880	2,138	1,527	1,236
Total	6,506	7,708	8,895	7,880	7,615

Adapted from Minnesota Governor's Human Rights Committee 1965:42.

In contrast to the decline of population in surrounding rural areas, the population in North City rose from 2,183 in 1900 to 10,000 in 1950, its then all-time high. In 1960, the recorded population was 9,958 (U.S. Bureau of the Census 1961). This slight decline is perhaps partially attributable to suburbanization as affluent persons moved beyond the enumeration boundaries of the city.

The major economic activities of the region also changed. The big-timber days had effectively disappeared by 1920, with agriculture rising in importance as the major industry. However, even the agricultural production generally declined after World War II, following the same pattern as the population.

Lack of conservation during the early part of the 20th century resulted in a rapid depletion of the originally rich timber resources. Since that time, the region has often been characterized as the "cut-over country." Where once there were magnificent stands of white and Norway pine, in the forested areas today there are only jack pine, birch, aspen, and other second-growth trees. Many of the nonforest areas, of course, still contain small farms and pastures cleared by the settlers. Recently, the second-growth forests have had considerable economic value as pulp and pole wood. Harvesting these smaller trees ("cutting pulp," in local parlance) has become one of the main occupations of the region. Even though, for the average operator, this is an unstable source of marginal income, the extraction of forest resources is still one of the major industries of the region.

Aside from agriculture and forestry, tourism and recreation constitute the only other major industry in the immediate area, which has considerable natural beauty, with its trees, streams, and thousands of lakes. The plentiful fish and game have made it one of the best fishing and hunting regions in the nation. North City's main entrances are lined with motels, while the surrounding countryside is dotted with summer resorts. The major recreation areas include a national forest, covering much of the Broken Reed Reservation area, and a state park of national prominence. Small businessmen in the towns and villages are quick to say, "If it weren't for the tourists, I'd be out of business."

The Chippewa Indians themselves provide an attraction for tourists. Many local shops sell Indian curios. Hundreds of tourists view summer Indian dances at North City, Trotter, and Wicket, and on the Deer Lake Reservation. The Deer Lake Tribal Council has also developed some recreation areas for vacationers on the reservation. A summer program sponsored jointly by the Deer Lake Band and by state and county agencies has used Deer Lake teenagers as reservation tour guides for North City visitors. The Indian leaders at Wicket would also like to attract tourists to their traditional powwow, but tourism is mainly a white people's concern.

The tourist industry of the region has grown considerably since the 1940s, but in the late 1960s local leaders were becoming increasingly aware of competition from the recreational centers in other parts of the United States. They recognized that the area's natural resources alone are insufficient attractions; major capital investments and adequate planning are needed to develop fully the recreation industry's economic potential. For instance, efforts were being made to stretch the short tourist season beyond the summer into winter. A small ski area was developed north of North City (although its slopes probably cannot compete very well with hilly areas toward Lake Superior). Frozen lakes provide ice fishing, long a locally favored winter sport, as well as an added attraction for enthusiasts of a new sport, snowmobiling. Increasing numbers of snowmobilers from the southern part of the state are making weekend vacation trips to the area.

The natural environment, however, also has its economic disadvantages. The terrain is generally wooded and rough, the last glaciation having left its mark in the forms of many sand and gravel deposits and erratic boulders. The southern shore of glacial Lake Agassiz crosses the northern part of Cramton County. Such natural conditions, plus a short growing season, limit the ability of local farmers to compete with the larger, more mechanized farms of the Great Plains, which begin less than a hundred miles to the west of North City. In fall and winter, work in the forests is sometimes slowed by deep snows. In spring, lumbering is halted for several weeks as melting snow turns thawing ground to mud.

Because of its economic difficulties, the area has received relatively large amounts of state and federal aid. The local education, public welfare, and health agencies receive the largest legally allowable proportions of their financial support from the state to augment meager local revenues. After 1964, several poverty projects in both Indian and white communities obtained federal funds under the Economic Opportunity Act. In addition to these directly funded programs, the area receives income from government-supported agencies such as the Bureau of Indian Affairs, Public Health Service, and a state college at North City and from government-supplied services to parks, forests, and highways.

The region as a whole clearly was experiencing economic difficulties in the 1960s, but the situation for Indians was especially severe. The median family income in 1960 for Cramton County was $3,949, compared to $5,573 for the state as a whole, while the median income for nonwhite families (almost all Chippewa) in the county was $2,928 (U.S. Bureau of the Census 1961). Similarly, the median family income for the total James County population was $3,020 compared to $2,198 for nonwhite families (U.S. Bureau of the Census 1961).

In general, little regular employment is available in the area for unskilled and semiskilled workers. For many Indians, the only opportunities are seasonal "woods work" and occasional manual labor jobs. Partly for geographical reasons and partly for social reasons, the Indians ordinarily have less access than the whites to the few available salaried positions in retail trade, manufacturing, and services. One major exception is work in the various governmental agencies that serve Indians primarily, but even these positions often require advanced training or formal education.

The reservations in the 1960s

Beaver Pelt and Broken Reed are 2 of the 6 reservations comprising the Minnesota Chippewa Tribe established under Section 16 of the Indian Reorganization Act of 1934. (The Deer Lake Reservation is a separate political entity.) According to the Constitution, the tribe's purpose and function are "to conserve and develop tribal resources and to promote the conservation and development of individual Indian trust property; to promote the general welfare of the members of the tribe; to preserve and maintain justice for its members and otherwise exercise all powers granted and provided the Indians and take advantage of the privileges afforded by the Act of June 18,1934..." (Minnesota Chippewa Tribe, Constitution and Bylaws, Article 1, Section 4).

In 1937, the tribe requested and received a corporate charter. Since 1964, a new constitution has given a great responsibility for tribal business to the local reservation governments (U.S. Bureau of Indian Affairs 1965b:2). Each of these local governments is called a "Reservation Business Committee," with one established for each of the component reservations of the tribe. The committee members, elected for staggered 4-year terms, are chosen by tribal members living in the respective reservation areas. The chairmen and secretary-treasurers from the 6 comprise the Tribal Executive Committee. The members of the executive committee elect their own officers, who serve 2-year terms. In some of the separate communities within the Broken Reed and Beaver Pelt reservations, there are also local Indian councils.

Reservations comprising the Minnesota Chippewa Tribe are widely scattered throughout the northern half of the state. These reservations, along with three small Sioux communities in the southern part of the state, are administered by a Bureau of Indian Affairs agency in North City.

Deer Lake Reservation

The Deer Lake Reservation has its own agency of the Bureau of Indian Affairs in addition to a tribal government separate from that of the Minnesota Chippewa Tribe. In 1954, the Deer Lake agency and the James Lake agency for the Minnesota Chippewa Tribe were consolidated in North City. In 1962, however, the separate Deer Lake agency was reestablished on the reservation.

The membership of the Deer Lake Band of Chippewa Indians is composed primarily of the descendants of the bands living in the vicinity of Deer Lake during the 19th century. Historically, the "Deer Lakers" have successfully resisted allotment of lands and have continued communal ownership of all their lands. Deer Lake is thus a "closed reservation," to use a local expression.

In response to internal and external pressures for allotment and to claims on Deer Lake resources by other Chippewa groups and by timber interests, the Deer Lake Indians órganized a centralized, constitutional government in 1918. Under this constitution, the governing body consisted of a tribal council of 7 hereditary chiefs, 5 representatives selected by each chief, and 2 officers (a chairman and a secretary-treasurer) selected by the entire council. The prime organizer of this government was a highly educated "mixed-blood," who was selected as the first secretary-treasurer, serving in that post for 39 years. In time, his influence became so great that he was able to assume almost complete control over the major decisions of the council. The death of this secretary-treasurer in 1957 resulted in a year of factional disputes over control of the council. The dispute was resolved in 1958, however, with the formation of a new constitutional government which achieved recognition by the U.S. Department of the Interior (Miller 1966:174–82). The new constitution provided for the first time a representative government on the reservation. The new tribal council consists of 10 councilmen (representing the several districts of the reservation) and a chairman elected at large. The 7 hereditary chiefs now serve only as an advisory body. The main organizer of the 1958 government, who was elected as the first chairman, continued in that capacity during the 1960s.

The Deer Lake Reservation consists of 2 types of holdings, a major block of 407,000 areas of nonceded land and 157,363 acres of restored land (U.S. Bureau of Indian Affairs 1965a:7) scattered to the north of the main body of the reservation. Though there are a few farms on the western end of the reservation, most of the land is heavily forested. In the past, members of the band engaged in more gardening and farming. Some of the old-timers attribute the decline of horticulture and animal husbandry following World War I to the competitive appeal of commercial fishing, which is currently controlled by a tribal cooperative. During recent years, the 200-member cooperative has had an average annual income of $300,000 (Minnesota Governor's Human Rights Committee 1965:47). In addition to the opportunity for commercial fishing, members of the band can fish and hunt for home consumption the year round, since reservation territory is not subject to state game regulations. Despite the presence of some wild rice beds, "ricing" is not an important activity on the Deer Lake Reservation, although some members do gather rice outside reservation boundaries.

The few shops on the reservation are either Indian-owned or operated by whites under permit. However, with prices generally high, selection limited, and important items of clothing and furniture not available, members of this reservation do much of their shopping elsewhere, usually in nearby white communities, especially North City. Electricity and television reception are available to nearly all parts of the reservation. Fuel (mainly wood) and water still must be hauled to many houses. In recent years, however, a cooperative housing project has provided some families with running water and gas heat.

Of approximately 3,000 people who live on this reservation, most live south of Lower Deer Lake. In addition to the homes which are generally scattered along the highway and its side roads, the 2 main population centers are Agency and Windy. A third community, Nisishin, is situated on the spit of land separating Lower Deer Lake from Upper Deer Lake.

The Agency community includes the Bureau of Indian Affairs office, a Public Health Service hospital, the tribal office, the Forest Service, the State Highway Department garage, an elementary school, the high school, the tribal police station, and the headquarters for various antipoverty programs. Also at Agency are a few stores and filling stations, a post office, a Roman Catholic mission and elementary school, and an Episcopal church. Windy has a tribally owned sawmill, a fishing cooperative (packing house and office), 2 small wood-products plants, a few stores, a post office, a movie theater, and churches of several denominations. This community is the only place on the reservation where there are non-Indian-owned lands, which were alienated from the reservation when a half-section of land was sold to a railway company in 1906 (Vandersluis 1963:8). Much of this tract, however, has now been restored to tribal ownership.

The Nisishin community is the center of Chippewa conservatism on the Deer Lake Reservation. Located here are an elementary school, a post office, 2 small grocery stores, housing for teachers, and a number of abandoned buildings. A fundamentalist sect maintains a mission in the village, but proselytizing activity has been unsuccessful on the whole, because most of the 500 or so people at Nisishin are adherents of traditional Chippewa religious beliefs and practices. It is here that the Grand Medicine Society survives and the chief shaman lives and practices his arts. Funerals and wakes usually are conducted with "Indian rites," and grave houses are clearly visible in family yards. Nearly all the people on the south of the lake are Christian (at least nominally), mainly Roman Catholic and Episcopalian. However, some elements of traditional religious beliefs and practices can still be found among these groups also. In recent years, the proselytizing carried on by the Church of Jesus Christ of the Latter Day Saints has been generally unsuccessful on the Deer Lake Reservation.

This reservation has its own tribal courts and police. Although residents of the reservation may vote in the Cramton County elections, the county has no jurisdiction over the reservation except for the nontribal lands at Windy. The schools on the reservation, except for the Catholic mission school, are operated by an organized independent Minnesota school district, which has a school board elected from among reservation members and funds supplied by state, federal, and tribal sources.

Each summer the 3 major community celebrations on this reservation are the Fourth of July festivities at Agency and Nisishin, lasting for several days, and a tribal fair at Agency during August. The main activities at these celebrations are powwow singing and dancing. During these events, many members of the band who have moved away will return for a visit. In addition, the festivities are regularly attended by Indians from other reservations in Minnesota, other states, and Canada. At Agency, scores of white tourists usually come in for the Fourth of July, but otherwise these events are primarily Indian celebrations.

Beaver Pelt Reservation

The Beaver Pelt Reservation had been intended as the home for all Minnesota Chippewa, with the exception of the Deer Lake Band. For this reason, the present-day Indian population of the reservation is composed of the descendants of Chippewa from many parts of the state. The reservation encloses a sizable area, completely encompassing one county and parts of 2 others. Only a small portion of this land is actually Indian owned, however; 25,382 acres of tribal land and 2,099 acres of allotted lands (U.S. Bureau of Indian Affairs 1965a:4) are widely dispersed throughout the reservation area. The majority of people living in the reservation area are non-Indians (see Tables 1.2 and 1.3, under Nebish, Deep River, and Zecker counties).

Unlike the Deer Lake and Broken Reed reservations, much of the Beaver Pelt land, though heavily timbered in some places, is suitable for farming. In the past, many of the Indians (particularly those of mixed blood) were relatively successful in agriculture, though only a few now operate farms. Employment is principally in forestry and in agricultural manual labor. The economic conditions of the population—especially the Indians—are particularly poor, with very high rates of welfare recipiency as a consequence.

To deal with these significant economic problems, the 1968 chairman of the Beaver Pelt Business Committee attempted to attract small industries to the reservation. He used as one selling point to prospective industrial developers the availability of several buildings suitable for small manufacturers. These tax-exempt properties, which are located on a former dairy farm on the reservation, are owned by the Minnesota Chippewa Tribe.

At the Beaver Pelt community of Green Grass there is a Public Health Service day clinic as well as the headquarters for the reservation Community Action Program. The program has not been as generously supported by federal grants as have similar programs at Deer Lake and Broken Reed.

Most of the Indians on this reservation profess Christianity, as either Episcopalians or Roman Catholics. Although there are no communities of practitioners of the traditional Chippewa religion, elements of native belief and practice survive, and certain Christian rites as practiced on the reservation have a distinctly Chippewa quality. One of these rites found on all the reservations is the wake for the dead, which continues over 3 to 4 nights. The wake, usually performed in a private home, is characterized by singing songs in Chippewa and feasting. One of the predominantly Indian communities on the Beaver Pelt Reservation has a fundamentalist church whose minister (also a school bus driver) is a local Indian.

Until about 25 years ago, some of the large secular celebrations on this reservation sometimes had *Midéwiwin* ceremonies as adjuncts. Although in 1966 the Community Action Program tried to revive the old Flag Day powwow at Green Grass, the attempt was unsuccessful in attracting enough singers and dancers, and as of 1968 no Indian community celebrations were being held on the reservation.

Broken Reed Reservation

The perimeter of the Broken Reed Reservation transects the boundaries of 4 different counties and encompasses hundreds of thousands of acres. However, as in the case of Beaver Pelt, only a portion of the area is actually Indian-owned. Only 12,320 acres belong to the tribe, and another 13,922 acres are in individual Indian allotments (U.S. Bureau of Indian Affairs 1965a:4). The boundaries of the reservation coincide almost exactly with those of the Ojibway National Forest, to which much of the non-Indian land belongs, with whites constituting the majority of persons living within the reservation area. Just as on the Beaver Pelt Reservation, the casual motorist sees little to suggest a reservation. Yet, in most of the several villages within the reservation there are concentrations of Chippewa. Trotter, the county seat of James County, is an important shopping community for many Indians in the area, although relatively few Indians actually live there. The Chippewa also occupy several small settlements isolated in the forests, one of which, Mission, is located less than 15 miles from North City. This little settlement appears to be one of the most traditional and conservative on the reservation, one evidence being a so-called pagan graveyard in which several people have been buried within the past few years.

The Broken Reed Reservation, in the heart of the lake country, is an area of intensive tourist activity, although timber work, in the woods and at the several sawmills, provides the major portion of the livelihood of residents in the reservation area. Shops adequate for ordinary needs are to be found in the reservation's small towns, but for significant purchases, many people make fairly frequent trips to nearby larger communities such as North City and Big Run.

Although the white residents of the community of James Lake constitute a slight majority, it is the most important Indian community on the reservation, and the Chippewa living there constitute the largest residential concentration of Indians on the reservation. The Public Health Service Hospital for all members of the Minnesota Chippewa Tribe is located here, as well as the headquarters for the Broken Reed Community Action Program (Office of Economic Opportunity). The funds for the program were secured by the Reservation Business Committee, even though it is supposed to provide assistance to both the low-income whites and the Indians who reside within the reservation's boundaries. Following some charges by the local Indians of discrimination by village police and officials, James Lake was the scene of Federal Bureau of Investigation inquiries in 1964. Despite the inconclusive findings of the investigation, James Lake became the location in the late 1960s of a federally funded legal services program—the only one of its kind on Minnesota Indian reservations. The project was designed to increase Indian awareness of legal rights and to correct any prejudicial treatment in local village and county courts that might occur. These legal services were also extended to Indians on other reservations.

The religious situation among the Chippewa on this reservation is complex. There are enclaves of traditionalists in some areas who may occasionally enlist the services of a shaman elsewhere, at Nisishin on the Deer Lake Reservation, for example. However, like the Beaver Pelt Chippewa, most of the Broken Reed Indians are Roman Catholic or Episcopalian. Christianity as observed on the Broken Reed Reservation has some distinctly Indian elements, as it does on the other reservations. Although the Episcopal vicar at James Lake is an Indian who was originally from the Beaver Pelt Reservation, most of his active parishioners are whites. At James Lake, the Mormons, who have been relatively successful in winning Indian converts, now have their own meeting hall. Several miles east of James Lake is Rice Village, the only community of Chippewa peyotists in the state.

At Broken Reed there are no longer any reservation-wide celebrations. Nor do many Indians usually participate in the community celebrations of the predominantly white communities on the reservation (e.g., the Water Carnival at James Lake). The Indian community of Wicket, however, sponsors a 4-day powwow celebration on the 3rd weekend in July of each year. The celebration is a focus of local community organization and pride, also providing a tourist attraction visited by the many travelers using the federal highway which passes through the village. During the summer, the Trotter Chamber of Commerce sponsors weekly powwows. Although primarily for the benefit of the many tourists in the immediate vicinity, the activities of Trotter powwows are attractive to Indians as well. The Chippewa attend not only from nearby communities on the Broken Reed Reservation but also from Deer Lake and Beaver Pelt reservations. A local white master of ceremonies for the powwows executes his duties with dignity and taste—even using a few phrases in Ojibwa occasionally. These Indian dances at Trotter are much more successful than comparable ones sponsored by the North City Chamber of Commerce. One of the Trotter powwows each summer features the open selection of an Indian princess, while the Deer Lake Reservation selects its own princess at its tribal fair. Indian girls from Deer Lake may enter the Trotter competition, but only the girls of the local band may enter the Deer Lake contest.

Unlike Deer Lake, there are no tribal police or courts on either the Broken Reed or Beaver Pelt reservations. Law enforcement is the responsibility of village, county, and state governments. Except for about 120 pupils at a mission school in Green Grass, the children of Broken Reed and Beaver Pelt attend public schools, most of which are in predominantly white communities. At Deer Lake, however, other than children of government service personnel and the few whites at Windy, the student bodies are entirely Indian. Likewise, several elementary schools at Beaver Pelt are attended mainly by Indian children, who frequently experience adjustment difficulties when they transfer to the predominantly white high schools.

The collection of wild rice is an important source of income on both the Broken Reed and Beaver Pelt reservations. The Indians now gather relatively little of the rice for their own consumption; most of it is sold, unprocessed, to white buyers and dealers. Wild rice harvesting has come under the control of the Minnesota Department of Conservation. The department prescribes the days and hours on different lakes for legal collection of rice during the few weeks in the early fall when the grain ripens. Therefore, the Indians no longer establish rice camps for intensive gathering on a single lake throughout the season. Instead, with the aid of automobiles, they may go to several different lakes during the season, and perhaps to the same lake on several occasions. Despite regulation by the state, an expert pair of ricers—one to pole a boat and one to knock the rice into it—during the 1960s could earn $2,000 in a good season since the price paid for "green" (unprocessed) rice might rise to as much as $1.75 per pound. The wholesale processing, buying, and selling of rice is effectively controlled by white entrepreneurs, some of whom own flotillas of boats available for rent to Indians who have no equipment. Also, much to the consternation of the Indians, a number of whites have began gathering the wild rice themselves.

On the Broken Reed Reservation, according to 19th-century treaties, some wild rice beds were to be restricted to Indian use. However, since the entire lakes are not controlled by Indians, limiting the access to these restricted areas is difficult. It is possible to control one relatively large and abundant rice lake in the northeastern corner of the Beaver Pelt Reservation because it is completely encircled by tribally owned land. The lake is harvested by both Beaver Pelt and Broken Reed wild rice gatherers, with the latter also gathering from lakes in their own reservation area.

On the Beaver Pelt and Broken Reed reservations, the members of the tribe are supposed to have treaty guarantees to hunt and fish on tribal lands without being subject to state game and fish laws. In practice, however, since the tribal lands on these 2 reservations are only tiny patches in the midst of vast areas of non-Indian land, an Indian who takes game or fish on tribal land will usually have to cross non-Indian land to get it home, thus becoming subject to the state laws. (*Editor's note*: Since completion of the original manuscript for this chapter, the Indian people of the Broken Reed Reservation have not only regained the right to hunt for their own consumption but also the imposition of special licenses required for non-Indians to hunt within the reservation perimeters.)

On all 3 of the reservations, some subsistence is provided by the gathering of wild berries and maple sugar, but the maple sugar is not collected so often as it was in the 1940s. Now, both maple sugar and berries are relatively unimportant sources of income on the reservations. By contrast, the traditional staple, wild rice, has been transformed into an important cash crop. However, for many Chippewa, gathering wild rice represents more than just an economic activity—it is tinged with the nostalgia of "the Indian way of life."

About these studies

The fieldwork for all the studies in this volume was conducted during the period 1965–68. All the authors were in communication in the field and, to a large extent, they coordinated their efforts with the general aims of the Upper Mississippi Research Project. However, the studies by Jackson, Roufs, Pelto, and Paredes may be distinguished from the specialized studies by Rynkiewich and Berde by their high degree of comparability and continuity.

Rynkiewich's study of powwows on the Deer Lake Reservation and at Wicket establishes an important link between the ethnographic past and contemporary Chippewa life. In keeping with the ethnological approach of earlier American Indian studies, Rynkiewich traces the sources and development of modern powwows, pointing to significant ethnohistorical differences in this important institution among the neighboring Chippewa groups. Having established the historical context, he examines contemporary forms of powwow organization in meticulous detail, also exploring the psychological and social functions of the powwow in modern Chippewa life. This activity is shown by Rynkiewich to be not only a crucial element of Indian identity and community involvement in northern Minnesota but also one of the primary cultural institutions articulating the Chippewa to the wider Indian community of modern North America.

Wild rice in the native cultures of the Upper Great Lakes was the subject of an extensive early study by Jenks (1900). Berde's chapter reviews that study and presents much-needed complementary materials on the role of wild rice in modern Chippewa life. The quantitative data from James Lake suggest variables attendant upon individual variation in involvement in wild rice collection under present circumstances. These 2 studies—on powwows and on wild rice—deal with perhaps the most important, and certainly most easily discernible, elements of "Indianness" in present-day northern Minnesota. They provide useful background for the 4 studies which follow.

Jackson, Roufs, Pelto, and Paredes address themselves to some of the same problems in the communities where they worked, utilized similar research strategies, and employed much the same methodology throughout the research project. Although each of the authors describes his or her own research methods in detail, certain methodological features common to the 4 studies warrant discussion here.

In gathering their basic ethnographic data, Jackson, Roufs, Pelto, and Paredes all employed the traditional anthropological field techniques of participant observation, casual interviewing, and key-informant interviews. Beyond this, however, each of the researchers was concerned with matters of representativeness, operationalization of concepts, intracommunity variation, and quantification of results. To these ends, all 4 authors gave careful attention to the sampling of households and to the development and use of standardized interview schedules within each community. The schedules used in the several communities, while not identical, were very similar and employed many of the same questions, thus facilitating close intercommunity as well as intracommunity comparisons. Likewise, these studies reflect some similarity in their use of scales, indices, and statistical tests of association in the analysis of sample data. In each case, moreover, the quantitative analysis is meshed with general description and discussion derived from participant observation and other informal methods. Thus, these studies exemplify what Pertti Pelto has called the "quantitative-qualitative mix" of sound research in modern anthropology (1970b:368). Despite the attempts to utilize similar methodological approaches, the important differences in emphasis and focus which emerge among the 4 studies are partly a function of the fundamental demographic, geographic, social, and cultural differences among the communities themselves.

The 4 communities are located along a 50-mile stretch of a heavily traveled major federal highway connecting the grain fields of the West with an important Lake Superior port and also serving frequently as a route for Wisconsin and Illinois vacationers seeking the wonders of the "North Woods" and the "Great American West." Three of the 4 communities are situated within the boundaries of the Broken Reed Reservation (see Figure 1.1). Despite its distinction as an urban center and its location less than 15 miles from the western boundary of the Broken Reed Reservation, North City is in closer proximity to the Beaver Pelt and Deer Lake reservations than are the Broken Reed communities. On the other hand, the Wicket community is distinguished by its close economic connections with the iron mines and the large white towns just beyond the eastern edge of the reservation, as well as its closer relationships with the Chippewa of the Hook Lake Reservation to the northeast.

Within this small sample of communities in which Chippewa live are wide variations along important social and cultural dimensions. Some of the major differences among the communities are displayed in Table 1.4. Beginning at North City, the other 3 communities are arranged eastward from this urban center at regular intervals of about 15 miles, with Wicket the most distant. A smaller urban center, Big Run, lies only 22 miles east of Wicket. Thus, of the 3 communities, Rice Village is situated at the greatest distance from an urban center. Similarly, the communities range in population from a low of 41 persons in the tiny hamlet of Rice Village to the urban concentration of 10,000 in North City. The percentages of Chippewa in the 4 communities range from the nearly 100 percent Indian composition of Rice Village to the small minority in North City of only 3 percent Indians. Wicket has a small but significant white minority; James Lake has the largest number of Indians of all the communities, but within its total population Indians are still outnumbered by whites.

In geographic territorial distribution, the Indian population and total community are isomorphic at Rice Village. At the other extreme,

Table 1.4. General characteristics of communities

	North City	James Lake	Wicket	Rice Village
1. Distance from North City	–	13 miles	55 miles	35 miles
2. Total population (whites and Indians)	10,000	1,500	450	41
3. Indian percentage of population (approximate)	3%	45%	85%	100%
4. Territorial concentration of Indian population within community	Dispersed through-out white areas	2 major concentra-tions with enclaves in white areas	Pockets of whites	Coterminous
5. Exposure of Chippewa to whites within community	Constant	Regular	Regular but limited	None
6. Composition of Chippewa popula-tion (place of origin and religion)	Very heterogeneous	Heterogeneous	Homogeneous	Very homogeneous
7. Community awareness and solidarity	Virtually none	Moderate	High	Acute
8. Maximum form of Indian community organization	Interconnecting personal networks	Weak local Indian council	Active and effective village council	Kin-based religious congregation and village council
9. Involvement in reservation-wide affairs	Generally marginal	Central	Central but quasi-autonomous	Marginal

the Indian population of North City not only is small but is widely dispersed throughout white areas of habitation. In the large town of James Lake, there are clearly identifiable concentrations of Indian households in the community, with one of these on a tribally owned tract near the Indian hospital. In general, it may be stated that within the community of residence the Rice Villagers have little or no contact with the whites, the North City Chippewa are in a situation of nearly constant exposure to the whites, while the James Lake and Wicket Indians occupy intermediate positions in this respect.

The 4 Indian populations per se exhibit important internal differences. Rice Village constitutes a kin-based settlement of families, all members of the Native American Church. Even though such religious and familial homogeneity may make Rice Village more traditional in some ways than the other communities, the practice of Peyotism by Rice Villagers very sharply departs from contemporary and historic Minnesota Chippewa cultural traditions. The Wicket community also is characterized by a relatively high degree of social homogeneity and community solidarity. Even though Wicket has a sizable percentage of Chippewa who have in-married from other communities, the vast majority of Wicket Indians were born on the Broken Reed Reservation. Only about 20 percent of the Wicket Indian population are not at least nominal members of the local Roman Catholic church. Finally, despite certain factional disputes, Wicket is recognized locally for its outstanding community development.

In comparison to Wicket, the James Lake Chippewa group includes a slightly higher percentage of in-marrying persons originating from other reservations. Likewise the religious affiliations of James Lake Indians are quite mixed, particularly since the recent success of Mormon proselytizing. Also in contrast to Wicket, the official local Indian council at James Lake ordinarily rallies little support from its constituency. The James Lake community, however, through its several government offices and services, as well as the size of its Indian population, provides centrality to Indian affairs on the Broken Reed Reservation. (Since completion of these studies, James Lake has become the administrative center for the entire Minnesota Chippewa Tribe and has acquired a modern tribal office complex with an annual budget of several million dollars.) Although Wicket has supplied a number of effective leaders in reservation and tribal politics, it has retained and strengthened a kind of quasi-autonomy within the reservation.

The Chippewa population of North City, by contrast, is extremely heterogeneous, having virtually no sense of group identity. Religious affiliations vary. The percentages of North City Chippewa born on Deer Lake, Beaver Pelt, and Broken Reed reservations are proportionate to the populations of those reservations. With no formal political or voluntary associations, the social organization among these urban Chippewa, beyond the household level, consists only of overlapping personal networks. In general, North City Chippewa are peripheral to reservation affairs, as are Rice Villagers—although for different reasons. However, a few North City Chippewa individuals have achieved important roles in the regional social structure of northern Minnesota Indian affairs.

It is tempting to develop a kind of Redfieldian folk-urban continuum on the basis of these 4 communities. But, realistically, it is best to characterize them simply as representing a sample of the range of variation among modern Minnesota Chippewa communities in religious affiliation, solidarity, local homogeneity, and interracial relationships.

The study of Rice Village deals with the social, geographic, and religious factors that have contributed to the solidarity and distinctiveness of that community. In a systematic comparison with the James Lake Chippewa materials, Jackson describes acculturative differences between the 2 groups and analyzes those circumstances that have insulated Rice Villagers from whites and the wider reservation community, yet have provided them with a unique set of ties to other, distant Indian groups. The description of the religious life of this isolated group is also an important addition to the anthropological literature on Peyotism.

Roufs was first attracted to a study of Wicket by its local reputation for success in community development. His study documents the course of this success, assessing factors to which it may be attributed. In addition to its merits as an account of another "village that chose progress" (Redfield 1950), Roufs suggests general conditions which must be met before success can be anticipated in similar efforts to achieve "community development."

The history and racial composition of James Lake provided an excellent setting for an updated study of patterns of Chippewa relationships with Euro-Americans—a subject of enduring interest to Algonquianists. Already in the early 1960s Indian-white relations in James Lake had begun to take on the cast of the "civil rights struggle," with obvious signs of the mobilization of an ordinarily dormant Indian polity. It is in this context that Pelto describes the Indian-white status differential in James Lake and reexamines the problem of Chippewa individualism in the light of developments in "Indian politics."

By virtue of its small size and its proximity to the reservations, North City provides a kind of microcosm for the study of Chippewa urban adaptation. Comparative materials from the Broken Reed communities are also used by Paredes in attempting to identify features by which the North City Indian population may be distinguished from its reservation counterparts. Patterns of variation among individuals in their adaptation to the urban-reservation milieu are described quantitatively, and the social ecology of the North City Chippewa is discussed.

The studies in this book thus explore a wide range of topics—powwows, wild rice gathering, religion, community development, acculturation, interethnic relations, Indian politics, urban adaptation. The settings for these studies are as varied as the topics—an isolated settlement of kinsmen, an Indian village, a "closed" reservation, a white-dominated reservation town, an urban center. Furthermore, careful attention is given in all the studies to the variation among individuals and small groups within each of these settings. From these different explorations, a picture begins to emerge, reflecting the complexity of the present-day Chippewa and of their position in the modern world.

2

Chippewa Powwows

Michael A. Rynkiewich

The structures and functions of contemporary Chippewa powwows, particularly the 2 largest annual celebrations of northern Minnesota, are examined in this chapter. The stages of their historical development are traced, with emphasis on the changing form of dance events on the 2 reservations and the diffusion of associated traits.

Powwows described here basically include drumming and singing, dancing in costume, speech making, communal eating, and formal gift giving. Central features of each powwow are a dance contest for men and another for women. This complex of activities, conducted at specially prepared grounds, is coordinated by a planning committee. The Fourth of July celebration at the community of Agency on Deer Lake Reservation is held July 1 through July 4 or 5. The *Mi-Gwitch Mah-Nomen* (Wild Rice Thanksgiving) Days powwow at Wicket on Broken Reed Reservation is held on the second or third weekend in July. In addition to these larger and more elaborate annual events, the term powwow also refers to several similar but smaller and more simple events, which occur as often as twice a month throughout the year. The smaller celebrations may be held either at the powwow grounds, in a building in winter, or near the site of another ceremonial or social event, such as a building dedication or a church bazaar. The less elaborate powwows include some of the basic characteristics of the major annual celebration but not the full range.

The ethnohistorical and structural-functional methodologies employed here were once thought of as opposing schools in anthropology.
However, Bennett (1944) has succinctly summarized the nature of these
schools, noting that the more formal distributional studies of the 1920s
gave rise to studies such as those by Opler (1941) and Hoebel (1941),
which focus on limited problems. This study, which is of the latter type,
focuses on a particular area and examines particular problems of cultural
dynamics. Change is analyzed by reconstructing the history of the
development of the powwow on 2 adjacent reservations, comparing the
resulting institution in both, and examining the role of the powwow in
community life. Two groups of people with the same cultural background are settled in a similar environment. Both have developed
powwows that have formal similarities but are significantly different in
their organization and function. This study attempts to identify some
specific conditions contributing to this divergent development.

Ethnohistory can be partially defined as the reconstruction of
institutions and events derived from oral and written accounts. The
historical sections in this chapter can thus be considered a type of
ethnohistory based mainly on descriptions gathered in the field and on
ethnographic literature about the Chippewa, Dakota, and Menomini.
The study is not concerned with ultimate origins and does not attempt a
complete analysis of the distribution and diffusion of traits.

In the functional examination of the powwow, motives are distinguished from results—just as Merton differentiates between subjective
dispositions and objective consequences as functional explanations
(1949:513). Statements of subjective disposition take the form that an
event occurs because a participant has a particular function in mind.
Such explanations of powwow events will be avoided because they
presuppose knowledge of the participants' attitudes and values. Instead,
statements about the functions of events will be based on observed
results or *consequences*. The participants' interpretations of the powwow
will be reported explicitly in order to maintain this distinction. Since this
analysis is not concerned with the whole societal system, it does not
postulate the functional unity or disunity of the society. Even though the
powwow is analyzed in relation to community integration, no assumption is made about the extent to which the powwow contributes to such
integration. Finally, the study does not assume that the powwow is the
only institution that does or could serve its present functions.

This study, then, is a comparative one, small in scale and limited in data, that attempts to combine "the sound anthropological concepts of structure and function with the ethnological concepts of process and history" (Eggan 1954:758–59).

Fieldwork

Field observation of powwows in northern Minnesota was included in the Upper Mississippi Research Project (UMRP). Anthropologists involved in this project and in the University of Minnesota's Summer Ethnological Training Session collected data during 1964, 1965, and 1966, through observations of, and conversations with, spectators and participants at powwows. My introduction to the powwow came in 1966 when I was a field-worker for the UMRP, and my fieldwork on powwows was conducted during the summer of 1967. From June 30 to July 4, I camped at Agency, observing the Deer Lake Band's Fourth of July powwow, taping songs, and making appointments for later interviews. From July 14 through 16, I camped at Wicket, on Broken Reed Reservation, where I made the same kinds of observations at the Wicket powwow that I had made at Agency. I stayed on in Wicket another 8 days to interview 6 people involved in the powwow. Reactions to my presence in the community were largely favorable. The attitudes of the Wicket respondents ranged from indifference to great concern that the interview questions be answered well. While no one refused to be interviewed about the powwow, I was unable to make contact with all of those I wished to interview.

From Wicket I returned to Agency, on the Deer Lake Reservation. I camped there from July 26 through August 3 and conducted 7 interviews with Agency powwow participants. The community reaction to my presence was indifference, but the informants responded carefully to my questions and were enthusiastic in teaching me about the powwow.

In both Agency and Wicket the respondents constituted a purposive sample. Some informants were chosen because they had planning or leadership roles in their respective powwows. Others were selected as prominent dancers or singers. Still others were chosen for a combination of their advanced age and their ability to remember the dancing that had occurred in their youth. For the period preceding that of these elderly informants' earliest recollections, it was necessary to rely on the ethnographic literature on dances for the Great Lakes region and the adjacent Plains area.

Early dance associations of the Plains

The military and ceremonial organizations of the Plains tribes have been
well described, particularly in the classic collection by Lowie and
Wissler (1916). In addition, as Wissler observed, "There are still a
number of ceremonials of a more or less social character which because
of their loose organization we have designated as dance associations"
(1916b:451). All of the Plains tribes had in their social and ceremonial
life a variety of dance associations, varying not only in form and content
but also in tightness of organization. Thus, some tribes marginal to the
Plains were able to assimilate some dance associations and integrate
them into their social and ceremonial life. The origin and diffusion of
certain traits connected with Plains dance associations became a major
interest of the anthropologists of the historical reconstruction era of the
1920s. Thanks to this work, it is now possible to trace, in part, the origin
and diffusion of some aspects significant in the development of the
modern powwow.

The 3 complexes outlined below were selected because of their
relevance to Chippewa dance associations. The Chippewa speak of the
War Dance, Squaw Dance, and Dream Dance as precursors of their
contemporary powwow. In addition, the ethnographic literature on
adjacent areas presents these generalized ceremonial complexes as
related or antecedent to modern powwows.

War Dance

The War Dance (*bwasinimidin*), also called the Sioux Dance or Grass
Dance by the Chippewa, is often referred to as the Omaha Dance in the
ethnographic literature. Fletcher and La Flesche claimed that this dance
association originated among the Omaha in connection with the
Hethushka dance society (1911:460–61). Wissler, however, contended
that the Dakota obtained the dance from the Omaha, who in turn obtained it from the Pawnee (1916a:48). Howard, on the other hand, agreed
that the Hethushka "complex is very likely Pawnee in origin" and that
"the Dakota secured their Omaha or Grass Dance from the Omaha and
Ponca" (1965:156). Howard estimated further that the dance spread to
the Teton Dakota about 1860, though there is some evidence to indicate
that the eastern Dakota divisions received the dance somewhat earlier
(1951:83). Among the Pawnee and Omaha, the War Dance originally
was associated with a sodality, ultimately being diffused to the Dakota in

that form (Howard 1951:83). The Dakota thus were the center of dispersal for the northern Plains tribes. By the end of the 19th century, the War Dance had spread not only to all the Plains tribes but to those on the plateau and in the northern woodlands as well. Even though the particular traits accepted by each tribe varied, each ceremonial association being organized differently, the theme of war as well as a particular type of drumming, singing, and dancing persisted as common traits.

The dance was structured around a group of officials and a set of ceremonial acts. Usually 8 braves or dancing chiefs led the dancing and directed the ceremonies. Other officials included pipe keepers, food servers, a whistle bearer, whippers, heralds (or messengers), singer and drummers, and drum keepers (Wissler 1916c:862–68). Ceremonies and customs peculiar to the complex included a feast of dog meat for the braves and old warriors, counting coup on a fallen costume ornament, and making speeches about bravery and war. Wallis's description of the War Dance of the Canadian Dakota is a typical example. As leaders, he included a male dance leader, a male assistant leader for men, a male leader for women, a female leader for women, male drummers and singers, a male policeman for men, a male policeman for women, female strikers (or whippers), male heralds (or announcers), and female singers (1947:42).

In areas on the margins of the Great Plains, the dance associations were not so tightly or elaborately organized. Merriam noted that "the Plains Grass Dance, described by a number of ethnographers, is a much more formalized and structured performance than the Flathead War Dance apparently ever was, and certainly than it is today" (1967:97). Among the Chippewa, the dances and formal feasts characteristic of the Plains War Dance have similarly been modified and are less formally structured.

In these marginal areas, traits from the complex were adopted selectively and integrated into the indigenous ceremonial life of the tribe. The syncretic forms of the War Dance that developed were much less distinct and less formally structured than the antecedent Plains War Dance forms.

Contemporary traits of the War Dance that appear to be ancestral include the dance itself and some principles of organization, the type of drumming and singing, aspects of the costume and paraphernalia, gift giving, feasting, and speech making. For example, the deer and porcupine hair headdress worn by the Chippewa can be linked to the headdress worn by the Omaha (Fletcher and La Flesche 1911).

Squaw Dance

Although much less is known about the origin and organization of the
Squaw Dance, it is often mentioned in connection with the War Dance
and Dream Dance. Because women had been prohibited from dancing in
the War and Dream dances, the Squaw Dance proved a significant social
event in which they could participate fully. Around 1900, although the
dance apparently had been interspersed with the War dances at a single
event, a separate and distinct association also held Squaw dances at
times and places apart from the War Dance, with the Round and Giveaway dances as related forms.

The Squaw Dance is probably as old as the War Dance. Teit noted
that the Squaw, or Round, Dance was introduced to the Flathead by
visiting Cree or Ojibwa about 1895 or 1900 (1930:389). Barrett's account
of the Menomini Dream Dance reported that a Squaw Dance was held at
the conclusion of the 10-day ceremony (1911:350). Howard saw a relationship between the Squaw, or Round, Dance and the older Scalp and
Soldier dances among the Ponca and Omaha, with the latter dating to the
late 1800s (1965:133). These accounts suggested that the Squaw Dance
has several closely related prototypes dating from the middle 1800s and
that the form or forms have spread from the Central Plains area, first to
the north and thence to the east.

The Squaw Dance was normally held on separate grounds from the
War or Dream dances, and separate drums and songs were used. In
contrast to the seriousness and individuality of the Dream Dance, the
Squaw Dance was characterized by couple dancing and a light, group-
focused atmosphere (Barrett 1911:350). The main recurring event was a
formal invitation to dance given by one person to another, usually along
with a gift. Both the invitation and the gift were customarily reciprocated
later. The gifts varied in value from buttons to horses; the degree of
ceremony associated with the presentation and invitation was dependent
on the value of the gift. An announcer often shouted out whatever
valuable gifts had been given. A formal speech was supposed to accompany the presentation of a gift, representing the bestowal of an honor in
addition to the usual invitation to dance.

The singers and their drummers sat in the center of a circle of
dancers, who faced them. After the couples joined hands, the whole
circle moved in one direction, with the dancers stepping sideways to
alternating loud and soft drumbeats. A leader reversed the direction of
the dancing every few minutes. While the men sometimes wore cos-

tumes, the women seldom did. The dance event might last from several hours to several days. In the latter case, food was distributed, and communal eating was enjoyed. The main legacies to the contemporary powwow from the Squaw Dance are the dance step and the songs.

Dream Dance

The origin of the Dream Dance, more recent than the others, is better known. Basically, it was "a variant of the ceremonial Grass Dance which has been modified into a religion" (Howard 1966:117). In fact, the Grass Dance is often called the Drum Religion. Skinner stated, "I suspect that it is related more closely to the Omaha or Grass Dance of the Dakota than to any other ceremony" (1923:428). Among the Chippewa and related groups the origin of the Dream Dance is usually attributed to a Sioux woman, who, according to the legend, was fleeing from soldiers and hid behind some reeds in a lake. Presently, a *manido* ("spirit") appeared to the woman, and he taught her the paraphernalia and songs of the Drum Religion. After instructing her own tribe, the Sioux woman carried out the *manido*'s orders by taking the drum and teaching the religion to other tribes. Even though the drum, songs, officers, dance, and paraphernalia for the Dream Dance were all similar to those of the War Dance, the theme differed in emphasizing peace instead of war. The central aspects of the Dream Dance thus included the presentation of a drum to another tribe or group, with speeches exhorting peaceful coexistence with other Indians and with whites, together with a ceremonial feast.

   Although there seems to have been a Sioux woman who traveled around spreading this religion, the date of its origin, and thus the time of diffusion, is not clear. Skinner (1923, 1925) and Michelson (1923, 1924, 1926), in a series of exchanges in the 1920s, gave full treatment to the premises of the argument. Michelson accepted B.J.G. Armstrong's word that he had interviewed the Sioux girl in 1878 and had found that the battle in the legend was the massacre of a band by General George A. Custer in 1876. On the other hand, Skinner was convinced by the assertions of his Menomini informants that the ceremony had been introduced to them by the Prairie Potawatomi as early as 1862. Hoffman, however, claimed that the dance "became known to the Menomini in the autumn of 1880, through the Potawatomi of the Prairie, or those living in Indian territory and Kansas" (1896:157). Slotkin maintained that the Dream Dance reached the Chippewa and Menomini of Wisconsin in 1878 and 1879, with the former receiving it from the Sioux woman and the latter from the Chippewa or the Potawatomi (1957:16–17). Ritzenthaler suggested an earlier date, indicating that the Dream Dance "spread to the Wisconsin Chippewa around 1876, and thence to the Potawatomi" (1953:159). The Drum Religion thus seems to have emanated from the Dakota to the Chippewa sometime in the late '60s or early '70s and thence to the Potawatomi and the Menomini. The Dakota themselves, however, seem not to have adopted the ceremony, although ultimately the religion was accepted by "the Minnesota, Wisconsin, Ontario, and Michigan (Upper Peninsula only) Ojibway; the Menominee and Forest band Potawatomi of Wisconsin; the Prairie band Potawatomi of Kansas; the Citizens band Potawatomi of Oklahoma; the Meskwaki or Fox of Iowa; the Roseau River band of Plains-Ojibway in Manitoba; the Iowa of Nebraska and Oklahoma; the Absentee Shawnee of Oklahoma; the Wisconsin and Nebraska Winnebago; and (some say) the Osage" (Howard 1966:188).

The Dream Dance drums, the central symbols of the Drum Religion, were owned by individual members of a tribe. The drums might be acquired from other tribes through drum presentation ceremonies, or they could be manufactured according to supernatural dream instructions. A drum owner usually appointed the other members of the drum organization. Membership varied, but usually 8 singers and 8 male dancers were appointed, with each group having a head man called *nimiwe-winini-wug,* or "dancing man" (Barrett 1911:304); see Table 2.1. Other members included 8 women dancers, braves (4 male and 4 female), a cook, and a herald.

At the beginning of a Dream Dance ceremony, as the drum owner's song was sung, he entered and danced solo. Then, one at a time, each male dancer entered the dancing circle to dance to his own song. Next, the 8 women dancers entered one at a time, continuing to dance in the circle until all the women's songs had been sung. The braves, usually 4, then danced in to their own songs. According to Ritzenthaler, *ogicidan* was the Potawatomi name for braves in their Dream Dance (1953:153). These braves controlled the oral tradition of the ceremony. Barrett identified *ogitcida-ogima* as the term for the Wisconsin Chippewa braves who were "directors or masters of ceremony" (1911:304). Next entered 4 women braves dancing, and these were called *okitcitakwe* by the Plains-Ojibwa (Skinner 1914:482) and *okeceta-wkwe-wak* by the Menomini (Slotkin 1957:51). These women braves helped to guide the other women dancers. After these male and female "officials" were all introduced, other men could dance and sing if there was room at the drum, but no women other than the officials were allowed to dance.

Table 2.1. Native terms for Dream Dance drum members

Broken Reed informants	Menomini & Chippewa (Barrett)	Chippewa (Densmore)	Menomini (Slotkin)	Plains-Ojibwa (Skinner)
nemeiwe wininiwak *"dancers"*	nimiwe-winini-wug *"dancing men"*			
ogicidan *"braves" (male)*	ogicida-ogima *"directors of ceremony"*	ogitcida *"brave"*	okeceta *"warriors"*	okitcitak *"strong-hearted men"*
ogicidakwek *"braves" (female)*			okeceta-wkwe-wak *"warriors' women"*	okitcitakwe *"okitcita woman"*
uskabiwis *"helper"*	skabewis *"messenger"*	ockabewis *"aide"*	skapawes *"waiter"*	
ahgwaisekwe winini *"bull cook"*	ugwasekwe-winini *"food consecrator"*			
ahbikisike wanini *"drum tightener"*				

The head cook, or "bull cook," who was called *ugwasekwe-winini* in Chippewa (Barrett 1911:313), danced alone to his song before he elaborately consecrated the food for the feast, which he then supervised. The herald, or messenger, was called *skabewis* (Barrett 1911:304), and the Minnesota Chippewa called him *ockabewis* (Densmore 1913:147) or *oskkabewis* (Rohrl 1967:99). In describing the herald's function, Rohrl noted that he "not only invites the people, but also prepares the dance lodge, fetches water, and distributes the ceremonial repast. At the appropriate point in the ceremonial dance he passes the pipe around to the men" (1967:99).

When the bull cook was called, he and the aides placed the head of a steer, pig, or dog in the center of the dancing area. The braves, or one old brave, then took up a knife or hatchet and danced in front of the head, advancing and retreating until finally a brave struck the head. At this point, the rest of the food could be served. This ceremony also had a counterpart in the War Dance.

Summary

Prior to 1900, the 3 related dance associations—War Dance, Squaw Dance, and Dream Dance—had diffused through the Plains and into marginal areas. The dances described above are ideal types and were not always practiced by the tribes as discretely as the separate names for the dances might suggest. The difficulty in separating these dance forms may be seen in Skinner's comments on the dances of the Plains Ojibwa and also on the Plains Cree dance as "a modification of the Sioux 'Omaha' and Central Algonkin 'Dream' or 'Religion' dance.... The dance is called 'powwowing' by the Whites ..." (1914:508–532). As the war theme declined and the dance associations decreased in social importance, the War, Squaw, and Dream dances lost their distinctiveness. By the 1930s, many of the early traits of these dance associations had disappeared and the separate forms had merged. The earliest memories of the informants I interviewed about these dances reflected this more amorphous, fluid state.

Dances on the Broken Reed Reservation from 1915 to 1930

Historical data on the dances were collected from 6 informants on the Broken Reed Reservation in order to reconstruct in part the development of the powwow there. The birth years of informants were 1905, 1905, 1912, 1913, 1916, and 1920. The period before 1920 was generally regarded by the informants as the traditional and almost ideal past. The

War, Squaw, and Dream dance complexes—along with the Grand Medicine Dance, or *Midéwiwin,* an indigenous religious dance connected with healing—all seem to have been fairly distinct until the early 1930s, when they began to decline. Since the Grand Medicine Dance differs from the others in theme, songs, and dance pattern, it is not considered in this study (see Hoffman 1891; Densmore 1913).

In the early 1930s, the War and Squaw dances tended to merge. Subsequently, the Dream Dance disappeared altogether from the Broken Reed Reservation, and the other 2 or a synthesis of them showed decline in frequency, complexity, and number of participants. During World War II and through the early 1950s, few if any War-Squaw dances were held on the Broken Reed Reservation. The informants' description of the earliest powwows they had seen suggest an event resembling both the War and Dream dances as they are described in the ethnographic literature. Often the informants included a description of the Squaw Dance. In fact, it was difficult to determine which of the 3 dances was being described by the informants, if indeed they were describing separate events.

This lack of precise distinction can be explained on several bases. The War and Dream dances were very much alike in form, and they were also often accompanied by the Squaw Dance. In addition, by 1920, all 3 dances were on the decline. Informant data reveal that the same person might belong to 2 drums and that many drums on the reservation were lacking a full complement of officers, suggesting that a decrease in personnel contributed to the decline of these dance complexes.

It would appear that most of the dances on the Broken Reed Reservation, whatever their type, were executed by a single group of individuals. That fact no doubt contributed to the similarity of the dances as the informants recalled them from their youth. All dance events, however, were times of gathering to dance, eat, and enjoy social interaction.

Around 1920, there were at least 5 dance halls on the Broken Reed Reservation. Two were at Townsite, 2 miles north of Wicket, one about 100 feet in diameter with board sides and a log floor, and the other, smaller, with log sides and only bare ground for a floor; 2 halls were needed to hold the War and Squaw dances separately. Near Buck Lake was an octagonal hall with big log walls, a cement floor, one row of seats around the perimeter, and, in the winter, 4 or 5 stoves. Most of the dance halls were of similar construction, such as those at Mide and Maple Point. (See Densmore 1929, Plate 5, for a picture of a log dance hall at Mille Lacs.)

In the summer, dances were occasionally held outside. Then the dance site could be any open place where the drummers could sit with the dancers circling around them. In some cases, permanent outdoor grounds were prepared, with seats or a shelter or both provided for the singers. The perimeter of such grounds was marked by a fence, possibly built on a low mound.

One informant reported that there were many Indian drums, each handled somewhat differently. Although drums were made and owned by individuals, each drum had a group of members who prepared and presented dances. Only men would use the War Dance drum, *inine dawayegan*. Densmore, who referred to this drum as *ogitcida deweigun*, or "warrior drum" (1913:145), described it as the Broken Reed informants did. According to both, the drum was from 20 to 30 inches in diameter, with the top larger than the bottom, and from 10 to 20 inches thick. A wooden washtub was often used for the body, with heads constructed of untanned deer or moose hide. Often the drum was suspended by rings placed over notches on 4 decorated stakes. The top head, and often the bottom one, would be painted half blue and half red, with either a yellow stripe or a multi-colored red, blue, and yellow stripe down the middle. Other drum decorations used include pieces of flannel, beadwork, metal ornaments, ribbons, and pieces of fur. During storage, several types of tobacco would be placed on the drum.

Women could view, but not participate in, the War Dance, or *bwasinimidin*, which was explicitly initiated by and for men. The Broken Reed informants described both the slow and fast versions of the War Dance in which each participant danced in place or circled the drum with his side to the singers; the step is a toe-heel alternation with each foot. Central features of this gathering included both the speeches given by braves and a ritual feast. In the formal speeches, the braves (*ogicidan*) would tell of their exploits in war, or their prowess over other men.

The Squaw Dance, on the other hand, was reported as the most common dance, providing the most frequent occasion for a social gathering. Densmore calls it *ikwenimiwin* (1913:45); Barrett, *kweinimitiwin* (1911:350); and one of the Broken Reed informants, *kwenimidim*. According to another of the informants, the drum is called *ikwe dawayegan*. The informants stated that about once a month, the members of the drum would plan a dance, with people dancing in the evening and through the night. In summer, a dance might last a week or more, depending on the number of drums and the amount of food available. Gifts would range from horses, furniture, blankets, quilts, and dress goods to a piece of calico, a handkerchief, a coin, or tobacco.

One informant stated that the Squaw Dance provided a great opportunity to meet girls. He recalled that he often noticed a girl across the hall and went over to give her a gift—a button or a coin, but nothing very extravagant. The girl then was obliged to dance with him and they became acquainted. Since, by custom, she had to reciprocate, he would get to dance with her twice. The informant noted that he met and talked with many girls in this way.

After a few Squaw dances, the singers would break into the song for the Cow, or Buffalo, Dance. (The Chippewa word for both cow and buffalo is *bajiki*.) In this free dance performed by one man, the dancer bends his knees and jumps twice in one direction; then, turning at about a 75-degree angle, he jumps twice the other way, all the time imitating a buffalo with his torso and head movements.

Next, the singers would perform several War Dance songs, with only the men dancing. Four or 5 free couple dances then follow, usually the Two Step, or Pheasant, Dance. In this dance, couples hold each other around the waist while standing side by side, and, stepping forward, take 2 steps with each foot before switching to the other.

At this point, the Squaw Dance was resumed, together with the giving of gifts. In the Squaw Dance couples' step, the man and woman face the drum and step to the side with one foot, then pull the other foot to it with the second or fourth beat. The circle moves first in one direction, then in the other, alternating several times per dance. One informant described a step which involves flexing the knees, rotating on the toes, and then on the heels, indicating that this step was perhaps used earlier than the couples' step described here.

Fried bread and wild rice mixed with blueberries or raisins were the foods normally provided by the members of the women's drum and others from the dance community. The singers would sing a special song for a man to dance a fast War Dance alone, after which he would serve the food. Other members of the drum group included the drum tightener, braves, women braves, and singers.

The Dream Dance as practiced at Broken Reed was quite similar to the Dream Dance as described elsewhere. For example, the names of dance members given by the Broken Reed informants and those given in the ethnographic literature are quite similar (see Table 2.1). At Broken Reed, the Dream Dance, although religious in character, did not replace the *Midéwiwin* because the *Midé* is dedicated to obtaining health and long life, whereas the Dream Dance has peace as its central theme. The emphasis of the Dream Dance thus rests on broad responsibilities, including an inflexible adherence to the moral law of living justly and wronging no one (see Densmore 1913:142).

According to the Broken Reed informants, games were often played on the periphery of a Dream Dance performance. Lacrosse (*papasikawen*) and a similar game, *bagaduwan*, would be played in open fields or on sandy beaches. The moccasin game was a favorite game of deception. Young men would also engage in foot and pony races and other more quiet games such as *pagese,* or the dish game, which Densmore termed *bugesewin* (1929:115).

Dances on the Broken Reed Reservation from 1930 to 1950

All forms of dancing declined rapidly on Broken Reed Reservation during the decade 1930–40. One informant said that he quit dancing in 1933 because others were causing trouble for him in the ring. Another related that "there was too much drinking. The sheriff's deputies came and made them quit. This was before World War II. For a while there was no dancing. Everybody forgot the old way." Of the 6 Broken Reed informants only 2 could remember dances during the late 1930s and early 1940s. One, who was living on the Beaver Pelt Reservation at the time, traveled to South Dakota to dance, and the other was living in Mide, the most traditional community on the reservation, where even now there is an old handmade drum. But no one remembered going to dances anywhere else on the reservation.

By 1930, the interest in the War Dance had declined, since there were no old braves left who had fought the Dakota. One informant recalled a man from Anemaji, a Broken Reed community, who during a War Dance remembered earlier days: "In my younger days there was no man I was afraid of. I never used a club on a man then; I only used my hands. A man really had to be something to be a brave then." (One of Paul Radin's Winnebago informants, S. B., told of a train trip he and several of his friends took to kill and count coup on a Potawatomi in order to wear feathers as war honors at a War Dance [1963:35–37].) When the motivating theme loses social force, its ceremonial representation also begins to fade. However, the War Dance step remained a favorite among the men, who would dance it at any gathering.

The Squaw Dance also declined, losing its drum and membership. By World War II, the practice of giving gifts as an invitation to dance had almost disappeared. The informants differ on the date, but either just before World War II or around 1950, when dancing was revived, women started dancing to war songs with men, who were adopting a less vigorous variation of their steps. Thus, as in the case of the Squaw and couples' dances from 1900 on, the war songs were incorporated as part of the social dances.

The Dream Dance, however, suffered the greatest decline during this period. By World War II, with few members left, the meetings gradually ceased. One informant reports the replacement of handmade drums in the late 1930s by the big army bass drum. Densmore also mentions a "modern bass drum" being used as early as 1929 in northern Minnesota (1929:165). While the incorporation of this drum into all 3 dances probably contributed to their disorganization, it is as much a symptom as a cause. The only documented case of the Dream Dance in Minnesota after World War II is at Mille Lacs (see Howard 1966; Rohrl 1967).

Even though some dance steps and traits of the Squaw and War dances survive, their full assemblage of paraphernalia and ceremony have not been continued. During World War II, dances were infrequent, usually being celebrated to send a young man off to the army properly. Although some dances were held for returning veterans at other places after World War II, none occurred on the Broken Reed Reservation. Consequently, up to the early 1950s the Broken Reed Ojibwa either danced outside their own reservation or they did not dance.

Continuity of dance traits

The continuities between the early dances and the contemporary pow-wow at Broken Reed are illustrated in Figure 2.1. An attempt is made to identify each dance with a collection of traits and then to trace the continuity of these traits over time. This approach admittedly simplifies data for comparison. In some aspects, continuity and discontinuity have been based intuitively on the participants' views of development which emerged during the interviews.

The solid lines in Figure 2.1 indicate when a trait was vigorous, as judged by the imprint of that trait on the memories of informants. Conversely, broken lines represent a relatively weak trait. Lines, or the lack of them, between pre– and post–World War II traits also indicate the degree of continuity, solid lines indicating a high degree of continuity; a broken line, some continuity; and no line, little or no continuity.

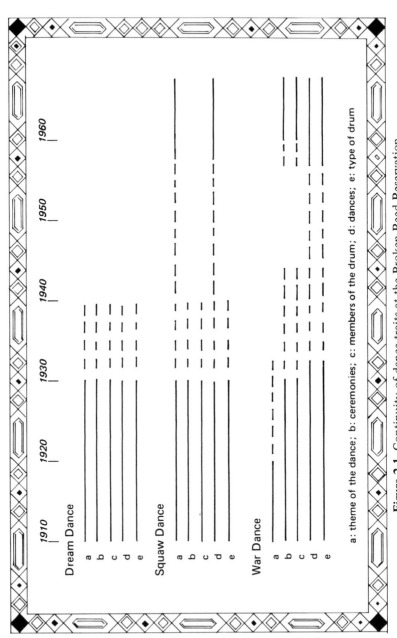

Figure 2.1. Continuity of dance traits at the Broken Reed Reservation.

The War Dance, as an event and as a coherent collection of traits, finally disappeared in the late 1930s. The theme (a) had been irrelevant since tribal wars had become a thing of the distant past and fighting had been repressed by both tribal and civil governments. Since the ceremonies (b) and members of the drum (c) were functionally related to the expression of the theme, the social structure of the War Dance and its associated ritual patterns also disintegrated. The revival of dancing and the organization of powwow celebrations in the late 1950s provided new structures to carry out some of the functions formerly a part of the ceremonies and the drum organization. For example, just as the ceremony of the feast for braves has a contemporary counterpart in the free meals given to dancers and singers, the organizational tasks of the drum owner currently are the responsibility of the powwow committee chairman. The braves' job as masters of ceremony is now carried out by an announcer, while the jobs of the head singer, lead dancer, and cook have been assumed by the corresponding powwow activity committee heads.

The War Dance (or Grass Dance) step, as simply a choreographic form (d), shows the most continuity of any trait in the 3 dances compared in Figure 2.1. Here the behavior remains almost unaltered, but the changes in the intent do parallel the theme changes. As in the past, the dancers and singers participate for their own enjoyment. This intrinsic pleasure in dancing, as well as the use of the War Dance step as part of the Squaw Dance and the Dream Dance, helps account for the continuance of this particular dance form.

The traditional war drum itself (e), as indicated above, has been replaced by a modern army bass drum. Despite the decrease in dance activity, the new drum continued to be used for dance gatherings and its use became widespread in the dance revival in the 1950s.

The Squaw Dance lost continuity first in part of its theme and then in number of officials. Perhaps because of the Great Depression, gift giving ceased to be a common practice during the 1930s. The convivial social interaction portion of the theme has continued to the present. Although in the past, everyone at the Squaw Dance was served food in a more or less ceremonious fashion, today's dancers are provided with free meals in the community hall as a special service of the council. Nevertheless, the male orientation of the powwow tends to support the view that modern similarities probably derive more from the War Dance than from the Squaw Dance, even though the boundaries between the War and Squaw dances became so vague after 1930 that variants of either could be said to include enough parallel traits to resemble the contemporary powwow. As it developed on the Broken Reed Reservation, the powwow can be described as a complex of traits derived in large part from the War Dance and the Squaw Dance, which began to merge in the 1930s. By the 1950s, the powwow had evolved into its present form, replacing both of the earlier dance forms.

Development of *Mi-Gwitch Mah-Nomen* Days at Wicket

The Wicket Local Indian Council, formally organized in 1963, began with the very concrete objectives of building a community center, laying out a baseball diamond and a powwow ring, developing a housing program, and encouraging the development of a tourist trade for Wicket (see also Roufs, Chapter 5 in this volume).

The first meetings were held in the homes and business establishments of members. A strong sense of unity in moving toward clearly articulated goals was expressed in the resolutions and newspaper articles that chronicled the council's struggle in the first year. After raising a thousand dollars the council proudly requested aid from the government in the name of the people of Wicket. Just before their second powwow, an article in the Port City *News-Tribune* stated that "the 300 inhabitants of the village on Highway 2, near James Lake, hope their festival will bring in much of the cash they need for purchase of building material." Another issue reported: "'We hope to raise enough money to give our building fund a hearty boost,' said the council chairman. Under the leadership of the council, residents are in the midst of a self-help project which embraces construction of a community hall, public picnic grounds, baseball field, and Indian dance ground."

The organizational and financial success of the 1964 powwow and the community's cooperation in its production prompted the following glowing comment from the Bureau of Indian Affairs adult education specialist for the area:

> This unusual cooperative effort by the [Wicket] Local Indian Council not only grossed over $2,000 (with an anticipated net profit of around $1,300), but also served as a source of inspiration to many other communities. The comments of visitors from neighboring reservations and communities point out the value and achievement of the festival. The Local Indian Council can be justifiably proud of its achievements, and can look forward to becoming a major and central attraction for Indian people and tourists in the years to come.

The community hall was built the following year and dedicated with a powwow in May, 1965; the baseball field and celebration grounds had also been completed by this time. The council then turned its attention to the problem of better housing. A United States senator broke ground for this project at the 1966 powwow, and the homes were completed for occupancy by the time of the 1967 celebration.

Inception of the celebration

Although locally organized dancing had disappeared in Wicket after World War II, certain other external forms had been instituted. In the middle 1950s, the merchants of Buck Lake, a town of about a thousand inhabitants located 7 miles east of Wicket, began to invite people from the Broken Reed Indian communities to dance and sing there at night on weekends. These "powwows" were sponsored in order to attract tourists. Much of the encouragement for the Indians to dance came from the Catholic priest, who took up church collections for the participants each weekend. A similar phenomenon occurred in James Lake, 40 miles to the west of Buck Lake. Some Indians had, of course, continued dancing but were traveling to other reservations and other states in order to participate. White-sponsored events and the traveling dancers gave some continuity and provided extra impetus for the inception of the Wicket celebration.

The first *Mi-Gwitch Mah-Nomen* Days celebration was held on August 24 and 25, 1963, at the opening of the wild rice season, only 4 months after the organization of the Wicket Local Indian Council. The first formal mention of planning for the celebration is found in the council minutes for June 24, 1963, although clearly some general plans had been made before then. The 3 problems facing the council included publicity for the celebration to ensure attendance, locating a place to hold the celebration, and, most important of all, determining how to make a profit—a crucial consideration, because the initial cost would deplete the council's earnings from bingo games and dinners. The council members demonstrated an enthusiastic desire to cooperate, but their decisions revealed caution and an experimental approach in making selections among both traditional and modern celebration activities.

The council made imaginative efforts to publicize the celebration. It sent invitations to each local Indian council and reservation in Minnesota. In addition, it entered a float in the Wild Rice Festival parade at Buck Lake a few weeks before the Wicket celebration. In the regional newspapers appeared pictures of princess candidates riding on the chairman's pickup truck beside a birchbark wigwam.

The Wicket council appointed the chairman of the Broken Reed Reservation Business Committee, a Wicket resident, to head the entertainment committee. The powwow was held on his property. Other committees were appointed to build the powwow ring, concession stands, and drummers' stand. Records of council meetings reveal careful deliberations on such questions as whether a log fence or a commercial lathe snow-fence should be used to bound the dancing circle and whether the drummers' stand should be covered with boards or branches of leaves. In both of these cases, the committees decided in favor of the more traditional structure—a log fence and a bough roof.

The initial outlay of money was eased by council members' donations of food for concession stands and by contributions collected at the powwow to defray the travel expenses of visiting dancers and singers. While the food concession stands showed some profit, the total was small (especially in comparison to the costs of materials that had not been donated). A bingo stand yielded some income, particularly since merchants of Buck Lake and Big Run had donated merchandise for prizes. However, the largest return was from the raffle of a beaded leather jacket. To ensure an adequate sale of raffle tickets, the council decided to name as princess the candidate with the most ticket sales.

The first day of the powwow, Saturday, August 24, was also the opening day of the ricing season; and since the structures for the evening's activities had been prepared, most of the town went "ricing." Two people were delegated to finish the last-minute preparations. The lack of workers proved to be a problem in conducting the events, but shifts of workers were eventually coordinated, and the 2-day event was a modest financial success.

Although the council netted $1,000 on the celebration, they were far from satisfied. No more than 12 dancers were present either day, and the participants felt that the whole powwow had been somewhat limited by the concurrent ricing. The chairman, on the other hand, felt the powwow activities were not fully developed because of vagueness about responsibilities. Though pleased by the powwow's moderate success, the council also carefully appraised the overall problems of the celebration.

When results of the 1963 celebration were discussed at the February, 1964, council meeting, the following guidelines were suggested for the next powwow:

(1) Changing the *Mi-Gwach Mahnomin* [*sic*] days, from the third week in August to July some time. (2) Cashier for each stand. (3) Toilets for the grounds (at least 4). (4) Leveling grounds for pow-wow ring. (5) Have R.E.A. [Rural Electric Association] put pole and transformer in on grounds. (6) Have police protection at all times. (7) Having a float for parades. (8) Speakers for the day of the festival. (9) PA system. (10) Have [the Bureau of Indian Affairs adult education specialist] plan this with us. (11) Committees to be appointed, best suited for them, for the stands, that they carry through their duties. (12) Closing in the hamburger stand, to be out of the wind, and purchasing hamburger from one grocer, and bread from the other, that way giving business to each store. And each member of the community to donate at least $2.00 toward the meats and bread. (13) Raffle prizes about the same as last year's, or seeing [a merchant] about making up prizes for us. (14) Paying the dancers. (Wicket Local Indian Council, February 28, 1964)

Of the 20 meetings held before the 1964 powwow, 2 were special celebration-planning meetings, and 17 of the 18 other meetings were devoted primarily to discussions of plans and problems. The 8 additional 1964 meetings held after the celebration included 2 reviewing the 1964 celebration and planning for the one in 1965. The significance of the powwow event and the general concern for careful preparation are clearly reflected in the minutes of council meetings.

The March, 1964, meetings of the council were concerned with improving the organizational effectiveness in arranging and producing the powwow. The planning committee divided responsibilities among various subcommittees. Major activities included inviting dancers and singers, the printing of tickets and posters, looking for new modes of advertising, asking area merchants for donations, acquiring bingo equipment, preparing to feed the dancers and singers, building and equipping the food stands, ensuring police protection, and organizing a crew for cutting brush from the grounds.

In the April meetings leading up to the 1964 celebration, the list of jobs lengthened as new suggestions widened the range of possible activities. The new suggestions included an Indian master of cere-monies, a Squaw (or Giveaway) Dance, a handicraft stand, and a cleanup committee. By May, the list of donations was impressive. An arts-and-crafts merchant from Big Run offered to make a crown and loan the council a buckskin dress for the princess, sell raffle tickets in his store, and provide several prizes for the bingo stand. A paper company in Big Run donated paper for posters, while 4 Wicket families donated the use of 2 stoves and refrigerators for the hamburger stand.

The cooperation among the Wicket council members, as well as between the council and the wider community, provided significant reinforcement in the formulation of council plans for the 1964 celebration. That the council was aware of this situation is evident in their decision to rent space only to those concessionaires whose merchandise was not in competition with either council-owned stands or stores in Wicket (see minutes of the Wicket local council, May 22, 1964). For example, on July 8, the council rejected an application for concession space on the grounds that the sales would hurt local merchants. On the other hand, a local businessman turned away the women who were asking for donations with the statement that "the council should donate to us." Later, the merchant apologized and offered money to the council, but the response from the council was, "It is too little, too late" (Wicket Local Indian Council, 1964). The owner sold his business within a year.

Although the celebration date was set for July 18–19, little work had been done on the grounds by early June. A bulldozer requested by the council from the Bureau of Indian Affairs (BIA) finally cleared and leveled the grounds. The BIA superintendent for the Minnesota Chippewa Tribe also promised 4 to 6 picnic tables and 2 toilets. In order to complete the work remaining, the council decided to form work crews on Saturdays and Sundays with the women preparing picnic lunches. During this last month before the 1964 powwow, the fence and the drummers' stand were built and the ring was sodded. The committees were busy building stands and signing up workers to work on the 2 celebration days.

By July 15, the major preparations were completed. A public address system had to be rented when none was donated, and the U.S. senator invited to speak announced that he was unable to appear. Yet newspaper articles and a BIA report attest to the powwow's success. Articles and pictures from the newspapers show dancers not only from other communities on the Broken Reed Reservation but also from the Deer Lake, Beaver Pelt, Mille Lacs, and Hook Lake reservations in Minnesota, as well as participants from other states, including North Dakota, South Dakota, Wisconsin, and Oklahoma.

The names and places mentioned in records and media reports of the powwow and the preparations for it indicate the broader social significance of the Wicket powwow. Traditional factionalism was temporarily overridden, as evidenced by the appearance of family names from all potential factions plus several white families. Also, intercommunity ties were strengthened, as seen in the frequent mention of merchants from Big Run and Buck Lake. The powwow thus helped not only to open up new relationships but also to reinforce old ones. On the larger scale, the presence of Indian visitors from other Minnesota reservations, as well as from out of state, signaled Wicket's entry into the widespread "powwow circuit" which extends over the United States and Canada.

In the development of *Mi-Gwitch Mah-Nomen* Days there is a relationship between the pre–World War II dances and the modern Wicket powwow. Obviously the old people remembered what the old dances were like and fashioned the present events on the basis of their recollections. In addition, some local dancers and singers had never ceased to participate in powwows elsewhere, both in and out of state. However, other influences are also possible. A note in the council minutes states that a Big Run merchant had shown some movies of the ceremonial at Gallup, New Mexico, and of other powwows in northern Minnesota. The effects of these external factors are difficult to determine. Certainly they had some influence, but more likely on external aspects than on the basic organization of the Wicket celebration. Analysis of the Wicket powwow reveals affinities with modern white and Indian celebrations, while its organization and division of labor show continuity with the pre–World War II dances described earlier in this chapter.

Mi-Gwitch Mah-Nomen Days: 1965–67

Mi-Gwitch Mah-Nomen Days, as celebrated in 1965, 1966, and 1967, can be described anthropologically on the basis of my notes and those gathered by field-workers from the University of Minnesota and the UMRP who were at the celebrations each year.

The sponsoring group for the powwow is the Wicket Local Indian Council, which serves as a general planning committee with the chairman as director. The powwow planning is carried out both as part of regular council meetings and at specially called meetings. The organization of committees has tended to follow precedents set by the 1964 powwow while making improvements on previous operations and exploiting new possibilities. Thus, up to half of the year's council meetings are devoted to powwow planning, including committee appointments, committee reports, complaints, and problem solving.

During the first 4 months of the year, planning activities are not considered urgent. Although some discussion takes place, all major activity is delayed until May. At this time, the council reorganizes its priorities somewhat and urges committee chairmen to begin their assigned activities. After the initial planning in May, however, little is accomplished until early July. In the interim, the work assignments are reviewed and queried, with most of the participants apparently satisfied that since "things are organized, things are getting done."

About 2 weeks prior to the celebration, an organizational meeting is held to report on activities and to finalize plans, with committee chairmen reporting progress and projecting dates for the completion of their work. In 1966, the following committees reported during this early July meeting: handicraft stand, lunch stand, pop stand, bingo stand, popcorn stand, meals for the participants, advertising, car parkers, grounds preparation, and sheriff's deputies. Together with the other committees, these made a full complement of more than a dozen separate groups. Some groups have multiple duties; but some responsibilities, such as publicity, may be shared by several committees.

After this early July meeting, committee chairmen invariably encounter problems. A week later, only a few days before the celebration is to begin, another meeting is held during which committee chairmen report their successes, complain about their problems, or sidestep a lack of success by projecting a new completion date—the day of the celebration. Most of the work in preparing the grounds and readying the concession stands is accomplished in this last week.

Although the committee organization may vary from year to year as new ideas are tried and old ones dropped, more or less the same committees are retained. The dance committee, headed by a man sometimes called the "dance chief," makes contacts with singers and dancers from other reservations to ensure a steady supply of performers during the 2 days. In addition, the committeemen arrange for the use of several drums, have a sufficient number of drumsticks made, and obtain housing for the performers. During the celebration proper, the dance committee provides water and soft drinks for the singers, and sees that all performers are reimbursed for travel expenses. The dance chief has the responsibility of making sure that there are dancers and singers in the ring throughout the celebration; he also organizes and directs the dance contest.

Preparing meals and readying the community hall are the responsibilities of the food committee. In 1965, council members made or secured food donations of at least 24 pounds of coffee, 25 pounds of sugar, 5 cases of corn, 25 pounds of cheese, and 8 dozen eggs. In 1966, the food donations for the meals and the lunch stand totaled 40 pounds of wieners, 40 pounds of hamburger, 9 pounds of butter, one case of canned milk, 5 dishes of baked beans, and 5 pounds of onions.

Each stand around the powwow ring is the responsibility of a particular committee. The committee responsible for the soft drink or hamburger stand must build or repair its stand, obtain facilities for storing and serving food, and schedule the workers needed for the full 2 days and nights. The handicraft stand is run by one woman and a helper. Materials such as headdresses, necklaces, chokers, bracelets, war clubs, drums, beaded aprons, birchbark toy canoes and birdhouses, baskets, purses, rugs, earrings, and potholders are either donated by women in the community or obtained on consignment from women in the area or from a souvenir shop in Big Run.

Although the Teen Council attempted to sponsor the popcorn stand in 1965, they were forced to close early because of low interest and shortage of materials. In 1966, a popcorn concession was imported from a town on the Sleeping Giant Iron Range. The following year, a concession from a white town in the northwestern part of the state was permitted to sell popcorn, snow cones, and cotton candy. The council's policy during this period allowed outside white concessionaires to operate for a fee of 25 dollars as long as they were not in competition with either the council or local businesses, but Indians from other reservations could set up noncompetitive stands without paying a fee.

The games of chance, such as bingo, are in another class. A local council committee operated these stands during the 1965 and 1966 powwows; in 1967 the local Volunteers in Service to America ran them for the council. Part of the preliminary activity for these stands had been to persuade local merchants and council members to donate the prizes needed. These committee members also had to locate a public address system, erect and repair the temporary stand, and arrange for the full 2 days of the event. During the various powwows, concessions featuring other games of chance have been tried—a dunking tank and turtle race in 1965, a dart toss and penny pitch in 1966, and a penny pitch and baseball throw in 1967. These stands were sponsored by the Teen Council for its own profit. The only other game committee arranges baseball and girls' softball games for the 2 days.

The advertising committee provides signs for the highways around Wicket, has posters printed for distribution to stores, gas stations, and other powwows, and prepares news releases for the area newspapers, radio stations, and television station. Two committees are responsible for grounds maintenance. One group prepares the grounds beforehand, and the other cleans up the area afterward. The speaker's stand, drummers' pavilion, fence, benches, electrical wiring, and turf must all be rebuilt, repaired, or refurbished. For the present site, the original structures were built in 1964, the ring sodded and wired electrically in 1965. In 1966, the structures were repaired, but by 1967, most of the structures had to be rebuilt, the ring resodded, and the wiring revamped. During the 1967 alterations, however, much of the work was done by a crew working under a federal government program provided by the Nelson Amendment. This assistance was particularly valuable since it was always difficult to find helpers, especially for the cleanup; since 1967, the Nelson Amendment crew has performed the policing job in addition to dismantling, storing, and painting the structures.

Finally, one of the appointed committees is responsible for managing cars; the other manages people. The first group, which has been called the traffic committee or the car-parking committee, consists of 3 or 4 men who direct the parking of cars. The members of the second committee are deputized by the county sheriff for the 2 days. Their primary task is to keep out of the dance ring any participants who have drunk so much as to be unable to keep the drum beat, follow requests from the announcer, or dance in a decorous manner. Inebriates are not only a menace to other performers but also an unpleasant distraction to spectators. Several times each evening one or 2 deputies may be seen walking into the ring and quietly leading someone out. Other duties include finding lost children or lost parents, stopping fights, and preventing theft or malicious mischief late at night. A night watchman or 2 may be appointed for the latter job.

The organization of the committees is relatively loose. New committee chairmen may be appointed yearly, or the previous year's chairmen may retain their positions. Someone may volunteer to do a job, and in such cases others on the council rarely object openly. The chairmen are expected to recruit committee members if there are not enough volunteers. Although the structures and functions of the committees overlap, the organization overall is sufficiently integrated and the involvement of the council chairman powerful and extensive enough to make the celebration a cooperative success every year, even if last-minute preparations continue well into the powwow's first day, as was the case in 1967.

Powwow grounds

The Wicket powwow grounds, on tribal land adjacent to a secondary road some 500 yards off the main highway, consist of a powwow ring and its structures, the community hall, and the ball field. The ball field is farthest from the road, on a gentle slope; it requires the least amount of upkeep since grass rarely grows on the sandy soil, and the only permanent features are a backstop, several benches, and the bases.

The community hall is the first structure visible from the highway. A 2-story, white frame building about 40 by 60 feet, the hall requires little special preparation in advance of the celebration because one of the celebration's main purposes is to provide money for year-round maintenance of the hall. Although free meals served to dancers and singers are prepared and eaten in the hall and the teen dance is held in its basement, it is otherwise not used for the powwow. Even the restrooms are kept locked to prevent vandalism.

The focal point of the powwow grounds is the ring and its related structures (see Figure 2.2). The ring, about 100 feet in diameter, is a circular log fence with 6-inch-thick uprights placed 5 to 8 feet apart to support horizontal logs at 2.5-foot and 4.5-foot levels. A single row of benches inside the fence seats about 300 spectators; the fence itself holds another 300 or so. There are 2 6-foot gateways at approximately the north and south points on the circle. At 2 points on the fence are sets of bleacher seats, and built into the fence on the south is the speaker's stand. An elevated platform about 5 feet high, the stand is boarded beneath and fenced above to a height of 4 feet and is equipped with microphone, public address system, and record player. A 15-foot-high board roof protects the stand and equipment.

The drummers' stand located in the middle of the ring was until 1967 a square frame of pine logs, roofed over with branches at the appropriate time to give the stand an authentic rustic appearance. For the 1967 powwow, a 6-sided frame structure, 20 feet across and reminiscent in shape of the old dance houses, was built. Benches were placed outside it for the dancers and folding chairs inside for the singers. The top of this new stand was boarded over and shingled, a flag pole rising from one corner. It can hold from one to 4 drums at a time, with as many as 2 to 10 drummers on any drum. Between the fence and the drummers' stand is the open area in which the dancers perform. Though maintained by frequent leveling and sodding, this area becomes quite dusty after 2 days of dancing.

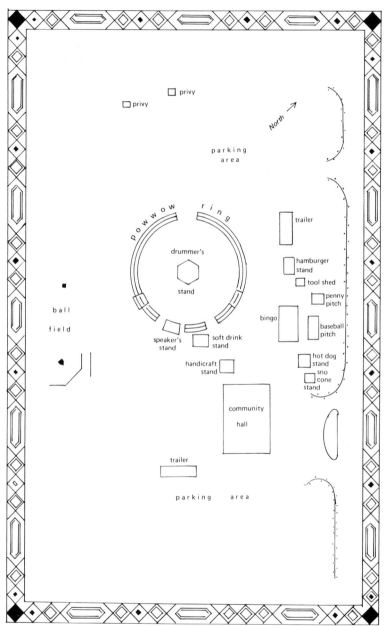

Figure 2.2. Wicket powwow grounds, 1967.

The soft-drink stand, a permanent structure about 8 by 12 feet, which abuts the fence to the south between the gate and speaker's stand, faces away from the ring toward the 8-foot-square handicraft stand and the community hall, both of which are also permanent structures. The remaining stands, lying to the northeast of these, are bunched together between the ring and the road. Closer to the ring are the bingo and hamburger stands. The latter, a permanent building about 10 feet square, has an 8-by-10-foot temporary addition framed with logs and benches and roofed over with canvas. For bingo, the prizes are set up in the middle of a 15-by-25-foot enclosure; numbers are called on a public address system. Between the hamburger and bingo stands is a permanent tool shed, usually used during the celebration to store drums and chairs for the singers.

The stands behind the hamburger and bingo stands are all temporary structures. Beginning at the north end is the penny pitch, an 8-foot-square stand bounded by a log fence 4 feet high. Adjacent to the south is the baseball pitch, which is outlined by an 8-by-20-foot light timber fence. The remaining outside concessions are 6-foot-square stands. Two other semipermanent structures on the grounds are trailers, neither of which is related to the powwow. One houses the local Community Action Program office, the other a local teacher.

Directly north and south of the ring the council has laid out parking lots, the larger to the north, where there are a few trees, 2 outhouses, and a pine forest beyond. Across the road from the grounds to the east the council has completed a housing project; several hundred feet south of it is the former schoolhouse, now a tavern.

Groups

The social organization of the powwow itself may be described in terms of the various groups of people and the settings in which they interact during the course of the celebration. The most easily recognized and most tightly knit groups are the singers.

Each reservation (and sometimes communities within reservations) has a group of singers who normally sing and drum together, both at powwows and locally in practice sessions. Consequently, each group of singers has a particular repertoire of songs that it knows and sings well. Since these songs are kept only in the minds of the singers, both melodies and words are susceptible to variations. While singers from different reservations can sing together easily, singers from different areas will show variations in the renditions of the same songs. Accordingly, groups will form at the singers' stand, differentiated from one another by reservation or by such alternatives as old/new songs, fast/slow songs, high/low singing, high/flat tones (drums), and even drunk/sober singers. There is not necessarily any consensus among the singers about which is the best group to belong to. So a singer's choice of drum group may be based on a wide variety of factors.

Although the singers will group by drums, they do not form completely isolated groups. No 2 drums play at the same time, and attention is thus focused on only one group at a time. When a song is finished, for example, comments and jokes pass between singers at different drums as often as between those at the same drum. Among the groups there is usually no pattern of dominant and subordinate positions except during the dance contest. The group from Nisishin on the Deer Lake Reservation, for example, are widely acclaimed as having the best singers. They sang all the songs for the men's and women's contests in 1967, while the other drum groups sang only the "breather" songs in between the contest songs.

Each group has a lead singer for each song. One man begins the song, the others join in on the second and third rounds. Although the man beginning a song is called the leader, it is only because of his decision to initiate a song. Generally, only one or 2 men will lead a group, but any man may lead a song if he is able to sing well enough and loud enough and knows the entire song. The man who is leading can also direct the singers. For example, pointing the index finger down means "lengthen the phrase," while holding the hand out palm up means "get a higher pitch on the singing," and holding the hand palm down means "cut down on the drum."

After each song, the singers usually converse in Chippewa. Their speech is slow, quiet, and low-toned, their laughter low and deliberate. The singers generally ignore the usual events outside their stand. The benches for the dancers form a boundary. Communication with nonsingers, even with the dancers, is rare. Occasionally the announcer or deputies may force their attention on the singers but never physically.

The dancers, who form the next group, isolate the singers by surrounding them. The group of dancers is divided only according to sex, the men and women dancing and resting separately. Only rarely in the War Dance or in the infrequent couples' dances, do the men and women break this division to dance together. When their group is resting, the women gravitate toward the benches around the drummers' stand; the men during their periods of rest move nearer to the spectators' benches. The men and women do not regroup by reservation except when the announcer requests the dancers from a single reservation to dance a special dance.

On the benches of the drummers' stand the dancers sit with their backs to the singers. The women in this group usually tell jokes, talk about another dancer's performance, or recognize other women dancers going by with a chuckle that makes the passing dancer feel self-conscious. The dancer, in turn, stops to coax those who laughed to come out to dance with her. The men dancers, on the other hand, stand in a row facing the singers, waiting quietly for another song; they speak now and then, but they do not converse.

Dancers wait until a song is going well and the rhythm is well established before beginning to dance. During War Dance songs they move alongside others of their own sex. Hands and arms are not joined except on certain occasions, as when a novice tries his feet, when an elderly parent dances with an adult offspring, or when young girls dance together.

Another center of social interaction is the speaker's stand. It is the antithesis of the isolated drummers' stand. Spirited or heated interactions frequently take place on the speaker's stand or between the announcer and the dancers, the spectators, or the singers. What formal direction there is to the sequence of events is controlled at the speaker's stand either by the chairman of the council or by one of the announcers. An announcer may request special solo or group dances or a special type of dance, ask for applause after songs, announce or comment on the dancing and the singing, repeat the general schedule of events, tell jokes (in Chippewa and in English), poke fun at particular individuals, or give a running commentary on activities under way, such as the dance contest.

A variety of people may use the microphone at the speaker's stand. The council chairman and the dance committee chairman are permitted unlimited use of the microphone, although the council chairman usually does little announcing. Several men who are well known both on and off the reservation as masters of ceremonies for powwows are given frequent access to the microphone. Other council members may have limited use without permission, but they usually prefer to ask the person with the microphone to speak for them.

Until 1967, the announcers were always Chippewa. That year, the director of the reservation's Community Action Program provided the public address system. Since he had previously worked with country and western music groups, he did much of the announcing. The privilege of making announcements seemed to depend on several factors in 1967, including one's relationship with the council and degree of forwardness.

If the speaker is Chippewa, up to half of the announcing will be in Chippewa. Often this is done to convey a joke, perhaps to keep it from the whites. For example, the master of ceremonies from Mille Lacs once said, "The police have just informed me that there will be no drinking. If you go into the ring, you will be weeded out." Then he followed with a few words in Chippewa and the Indians laughed. Later, while drinking from a 7-Up can, "I'd better watch it or the police'll get me. This is really 7-Up." Other statements in Chippewa are often made to recall former customs and former dances.

For a special presentation, someone other than the persons already mentioned may serve as announcer. In 1967, for example, 6 Mormon missionaries asked permission to present a special show of their own native dances. There were three from Hawaii, one from New Zealand, a Ute from Utah, and a Pima from Arizona.

In 1966, a special introduction was made by a woman from Nisishin presenting 2 girls scheduled to perform the Corn and Eagle dances, which are imported from the western tribes. In restrained tones, the woman said to the audience, "I'm sorry that we forgot her headpiece, but tonight she'll have to use a headdress. I know our good Lord up there will know there was a reason why we forgot this headpiece, so I hope you'll excuse us tonight. Tomorrow night she'll have her headpiece." In introducing the second dance, the woman continued, "We are happy to perform for you. You filled our tummies and our gas tank and we are thankful. My sister goes to school in Salt Lake City and has performed there. We are proud of her. The song represents a Sioux praying at corn planting time and giving thanks to the Great Spirit for a good season."

Tense situations often develop at the speaker's stand. Several times during the 1967 powwow there was trouble over the use of the microphone when the announcer wanted the singers to stop while a special program was being presented. The singers continued to pound the drum. Although a few were drunk, even the sober ones objected to being preempted. At one point, the announcer called for the head deputy to restore order. Also in 1967, when a white announcer noticed that a VISTA volunteer was dancing, he announced that anyone could dance without a costume. The council chairman, who had just refused to permit 2 drunk white boys to dance by explaining that the Indians took pride in their dance, quickly corrected the announcer and required him to withdraw his earlier invitation. After the dance contest one evening, a disgruntled loser complained about how the contest had been run, arguing fruitlessly with the announcer. Such incidents, not uncommon, simply form part of the overall fabric of the celebration activity.

Most persons attending the powwow celebrations, whether Indian or white, are spectators. The only locations not open to the spectator groups are the areas within the ring and the speaker's stand. The spectators sit on the benches around the edge of the ring, cluster around its perimeter, and scatter out beyond these points for as far as a quarter of a mile. The spectators form temporary groups in a number of ways. Those watching the dancing may join friends and acquaintances or engage strangers in casual conversation. The spectators in the area immediately adjacent to the ring continually move from one conversation group to another. Beyond the ring itself, groups are constantly shifting from one stand or activity to another. In the ring, the focus is on the dancers and singers; elsewhere the focal points include the game and concession stands, the community hall, and the ball game.

The entire celebration is divided into 3 main settings for group interaction: the dance ring, the ball-playing area, and the community hall. The game stands and parking lot may be considered less important areas of focus within the powwow area (see Figure 2.3).

Groups form only temporarily around the concession stands. Despite the activity there, the music still dominates the scene, and one's gaze constantly shifts back to the ring during any conversational lag. Persons waiting at food stands to be served usually do not form groups but order food and depart as quickly as possible. Groups are more likely to form around the handicraft stand, where people stop to discuss the wares. Frequently, more stable groups are formed around the bingo stand, which thus becomes an area of minor focus during the powwow; groups often stay for hours playing and conversing there.

In the parking lot, 2 types of groups form. Both are focused on the powwow, but their involvement is not as great as that of participants and spectators in the ring area. One kind of group consists of persons who arrive together in one car, drive up close to the ring, and sit in their car to watch, thus interacting within their initial group only. Another kind of group is formed by people who arrive in separate cars, get out, and sit around in the parking lot, talking to others. A variation of the second type clusters around dancers who are donning their costumes. It takes a dancer from 15 to 45 minutes to dress. Though he uses a mirror and his family helps him, the dancer is usually in no hurry, occupying a good

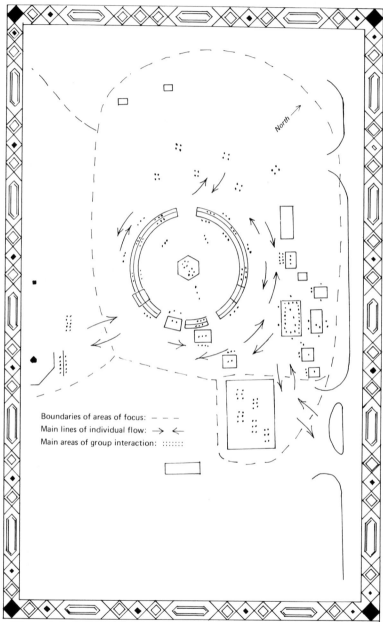

North

Boundaries of areas of focus: — — —
Main lines of individual flow: → ←
Main areas of group interaction: ::::::::

Figure 2.3. Individual flow and group interaction at Wicket powwow.

part of the time spent dressing with small talk and joking with spectators standing nearby.

Spectators usually gather around the baseball field and the ball players. Here the behavior of both players and spectators resembles what is seen at any smalltown ball game—except for unique comments such as "Too much *waboose!*" which may be heard when a player swings hard and misses or throws a wild ball.

The women who prepare meals and clean up after the diners form a stable group in the community hall, a group more or less permanent throughout the 2-day celebration. The diners are also a distinct group within which interaction subgroups are formed on the same bases as those that develop around the dance ring.

Schedule of events

In contrast to the relatively precise schedules associated with white American culture, and the frustrations apparent when such schedules are not followed, the Wicket people operate on "moccasin time," having little concern for timetables. For instance, a council meeting set for 8:00 a.m. might not start until 10:00, even though a quorum would usually be present by 8:30 or 9:00. Little or nothing is said to late arrivers, indicating that the white concept of "late" is not an Indian viewpoint. Likewise, in scheduling events for the powwow, only very general time designations are specified. If a time is actually set, its purpose is usually to reassure the spectators that a particular event will take place. Since the Indians are generally content with the dancing and singing being presented, they do not react negatively when an event is overdue.

The following chronology of events should be regarded as an ethnographic construct based on events of the 1965, 1966, and 1967 celebrations. Men on the grounds preparation committee arrive about 8:00 a.m. on Saturday to finish their work and to give a final cleanup. About 9:00 the women begin work in the kitchen. At this point, only a few youths and old men are standing around talking, and there is no hustle and bustle, even when the soft drinks are delivered from Big Run or when the public address system is installed. By 11:00 the final preparations at the various stands are being completed prior to opening for business; tape recordings of Indian songs are now being played over the loudspeaker. Few visitors arrive before noon, and little activity develops until after 2:00 p.m. By this time, the bingo stand has attracted a few players, and some of the singers are thinking about getting the powwow started at the dance ring. At first the singers may not be enthusiastic, and if no new singers and no dancers appear, the first group leaves the ring for a while.

Shortly after 2:00, the announcer starts his continual appeals for singers and dancers. The announcer's opening statement at the 1967 powwow began: "Welcome visitors! The drummers from [Nisishin] will be here and dancers who have been dancing for many years. [Statement in Chippewa.] The drummers are really getting going, so dancers, come on in. We are expecting a lot of dancers from Mille Lacs, [Hook Lake], and [Deer Lake]."

Five minutes later, he commented: "If you're hungry or thirsty, we have refreshment stands here on the grounds. I see ———— from [Deer Lake] is out here, but he hasn't gotten his feet wet yet. We'd like to announce another powwow in the area July 30, at the [Wicket] mission. This is our annual church bazaar and powwow, and you're all invited to come."

About 2:30 the baseball game is started, even though there are only 20 to 30 spectators in the bleachers. At this time, nearly 250 people on the grounds are involved in various activities, including playing ball or watching, bingo playing, cooking, tending stands, singing and dancing (or considering it), or conversing quietly. A dozen or more participants or spectators may take time out to go across the road for a beer. By mid-afternoon, unless some participants have been instructed specifically to be singing and dancing at this time, there is a lull in activities in the ring. Recorded music is again played through the loudspeaker, while the announcer tries to fill the void by previewing the forthcoming activities. Continual pleas for singers and dancers punctuate his announcements, revealing his concern.

From 10 to 20 singers and dancers in all may go into the ring between 3:00 and 5:00 p.m., after which they break for supper. The baseball game has ended, the amusement stands close, and most spectators either leave the grounds or go into the community hall for supper. During the supper break, which may continue until 7:00, the announcer is particularly active in repeating information about coming attractions interspersed with joking comments. His plea for performers starts again about 6:30 and continues until a sufficient number have been coaxed into the ring. Paraphrased below are the dance committee chairman's remarks between 5:15 and 6:45 p.m. on Saturday evening of the 1966 *Mi-Gwitch Mah-Nomen* Days, followed by the sequence of events in that celebration.

There will be a break now for about an hour. The dancers have run out of gas and need to replenish. All the Indians here are Minnesota Chippewa and Deer Lake Band. They come from Mille Lacs, Broken Reed, Deep Lake, Hook Lake, and Deer Lake. We even have a singer-dancer combination from Deep Lake to give us an Indian watusi after supper.

[Statement in Chippewa.]

We have a lot of dancers and singers here—a lot of talent—a lot of performers. They will be getting dressed after supper. Some dancers will do specialties later. There'll be beautiful costumes and beadwork—all authentic Chippewa-made.

Tomorrow afternoon we have a groundbreaking ceremony scheduled. Senator ——— will be here at 2:00 p.m. We are expecting a large crowd and want a fine reception for the senator.

Will all the dancers and singers eat their meal right away so we don't keep the cooks too long.

Tomorrow we will have a men's and women's dance contest with prizes of $25 and $15 for the men and $15 and $10 for the women.

[Several sentences in Chippewa, response of laugher.]

——— wants to sing a song. I'd better not let him—he might chase the crowd away.

[Several sentences in Chippewa.]

Will the visitors please get their meal tickets and get fed?

There are people here from Agency, Nisishin, and Windy.

Will the Twin Lakes girls' softball team get out there—the other team is waiting.

At dusk, the Stars and Stripes are lowered to the accompaniment of an Indian flag song. The announcer then calls for a few special dances (for example, a Round Dance for everyone), or for a solo by a well-known performer. At 8:00 p.m., the teen dance begins in the community hall with a band from North City. In the ring, participation builds from 8:00 until 10:00 or 11:00. At 9:00, after the princess candidates are presented, the winner is announced. She thanks the audience briefly and performs a solo dance once around the ring. By this time, there are 2 or 3 drums on the stand, 25 to 30 dancers in the ring, and about 500 spectators ranged around the ring's periphery.

At 9:30 an aged Chippewa is asked to come up and say a few words in Chippewa about the old way of life. The singers then resume but stop at 10:00 so that the 2 girls from Nisishin can do their Corn and Eagle dances to taped music. After about half an hour, the singers and dancers return to War Dance songs. Although all the cleanup work in the community hall has been finished by this time, the bingo and teen dance activities are still in full swing.

After another specialty dance (performed by a visitor) and a couples' dance, it is 11:00 p.m. and the deputies are walking drunk participants out of the ring. Their tactics are often well disguised. For example, a deputy spots a man dancing rather erratically. The deputy starts across the ring, greets the man from about 5 feet away, says a few words to him as he passes, and goes to sit down on a bench inside the ring. Within half a minute, the drunk stops dancing, walks over to where the deputy is sitting, and sits down with him. As midnight draws near, the work of the deputies increases.

Between 11:00 and midnight the 500 or so spectators dwindle to as few as 200. The lights are turned off at midnight, but the singers are usually reluctant to stop. As the deputies pressure them, they decide to sing one more song. When only a few dancers are left, the singers leave the ring but regroup in the parking lot, continuing to sing and talk until as late as 3:00 a.m.

The cleanup committee has a bigger job on Sunday morning than on Saturday. The women begin preparing their final 2 meals at 10:00 a.m. About 11:00, when the drums and chairs are brought out of storage, there is still little activity. The announcer soon begins to call participants, announcing in both Chippewa and English that the noon meal is ready. After the meal, drummers go out to sing a few leisurely songs, and some dancers may perform a few rounds if the temperature is agreeable. At 1:30 p.m., the 250 or so spectators on the grounds converge to watch the baseball game. If a speaker or performing group is scheduled, the first half of the afternoon is spent waiting for him. But if the program has not started by about 3:00, the singers and dancers resume their performances.

By mid-afternoon the parking-lot attendants have their hands full. Several drums are brought into the stand, and except for occasional interruptions, the singing and dancing increase in vigor and intensity. Many Indian visitors come from Minneapolis and nearer towns, and many local whites stop by. Just before supper, activity on the grounds reaches a peak; but during the supper break, all activity subsides just as it did on Saturday. After supper, the announcer tries to spark interest and force participation by calling on a number of individuals and groups of dancers to perform their specialties. After the flag song and the dances by the Nisishin girls, there is a brief pause for the raffle ticket drawing.

The dance committee chairman begins about 9:30 p.m. to line up singers and judges for the final dance contest. To forestall any accusation of favoritism, both local and visiting judges are selected. From a half-hour to one and a half hours are needed to get all the participants prepared, but finally the Nisishin drummers are at one drum, the judges have their instructions, and the dancers are numbered. The judges first choose 3, then 2, then one dancer. The process may take as long as 45 minutes, since each contest song is followed by at least one "everybody dance" song so that the contestants may rest and the judges may confer. In the women's contest which follows, a similar schedule is followed. By this time, most of the stands have closed for the night because all attention is focused on the contests. After the winners in both contests have been chosen, they are each asked to dance a solo for the spectators. (In 1967, the second-place winners presented the council with a blanket and a quilt in appreciation of the honor given them.)

After the contest, which is over by midnight, the crowd rapidly disperses as the announcer continues to thank all the reservations and the people of Wicket for a successful celebration. (See Figure 2.4, a graph of attendance and participation levels at the 1966 powwow.) Even though a few of the dancers and singers want to continue the celebration, by 1:00 a.m. the area is relatively quiet, with perhaps a couple of teenagers strolling around or the woman at the handicraft stand trying to finish loading her remaining material. Deputies are still trying to help the drunk and the lost, and some of the visiting dancers and singers may be looking for someone to fill out their gas money tickets. The dust settling over the ring diffuses the artificial lights so that the stands and the fence seem to blur and fade. When the lights are turned off, the quiet in contrast to all the recent activity seems like a hush. The few remaining people quietly depart.

The next morning and most of the next week are devoted to clearing the powwow area of trash, dismantling the temporary structures, cleaning up the permanent stands, and repairing damage. This process is carried out by the cleanup committee or by the Nelson Amendment crew. The other council members are glad to stay home and recuperate from a successful celebration.

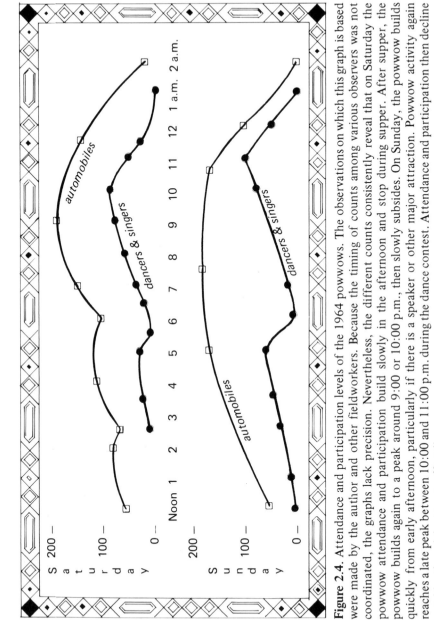

Figure 2.4. Attendance and participation levels of the 1964 powwows. The observations on which this graph is based were made by the author and other fieldworkers. Because the timing of counts among various observers was not coordinated, the graphs lack precision. Nevertheless, the different counts consistently reveal that on Saturday the powwow attendance and participation build slowly in the afternoon and stop during supper. After supper, the powwow builds again to a peak around 9:00 or 10:00 p.m., then slowly subsides. On Sunday, the powwow builds quickly from early afternoon, particularly if there is a speaker or other major attraction. Powwow activity again reaches a late peak between 10:00 and 11:00 p.m. during the dance contest. Attendance and participation then decline quickly; the celebration is officially over.

Dances on the Deer Lake Reservation from 1900 to 1940

Seven dancers and singers were interviewed informally on the Deer Lake Reservation. The interview schedule and techniques were the same as those used with the Broken Reed Reservation informants. The sample developed as one informant recommended another. Their birth years were 1887, 1911, 1917, 1923, 1926, 1927, and 1933.

The oldest informant was a local historian and keeper of oral literature for the band. He provided information reinforcing the view that the War Dance spread from the Dakota in the northern Plains, that the Chippewa and Dakota concluded a treaty in northern Minnesota in the late 1840s, and that the diffusion of the War Dance included many traits of the complex in addition to the dance step itself. Although the first series of events occurred before this informant's birth, the basic story is not a legend handed down over countless generations. This man had heard the account from the mother of a well-known Minnesota Chippewa. She died in 1927 at the age of 90. At the beginning of the diffusion process she was 10 or 11 years old. The events she described appear to have occurred in the late 1840s and early 1850s. The informant tried to relate the story as he originally heard it from the old woman:

> This story that I am telling this man is not a story that is handed down. The last war path the [Deer Lake] Indians went on against the Sioux was before 1840. This was heard from 2 members of the last war party of [Deer Lake] Indians against their enemies. After that, a peace treaty was made between the Sioux and the Chippewa.
>
> It was rumored for a long time that these people were going to come to make peace. A lot of people didn't believe it. Finally, as it went on, the [Nisishin] Indians came and gathered all the people to go to the west part of [Agency]. There was no [Agency] then, and the area west is now called Little Rock. They came to the spot where they were supposed to meet. There they were, *ogicidan*. All had round clubs. (That's just what she said.) There were people who were going to do something when they came. There were no roads then, just trails. They were all lined up along the trail looking west. Several *ogicidan* walked up and down. They said, "If anybody does anything to start or do anything, you will be bludgeoned to death." (The teller said they meant what they said.)
>
> The people were tired of war, always living in fear as long as the tribes have been hostile. This was long before the missionaries

came. So the old lady said, all it was we could hear was singing from the west. There was a turn in the path. We could hear a voice higher than the other voices that were singing. Everybody noticed that high voice. Here they came! (That's just what she said.) Here they came walking along. This voice above all the others was a man riding on a horse. He had braids on each side of his head. Here they came, they sang right along the path among the people.

The whole reservation was there. (The old woman didn't mention the other reservations, so I can't say anything about them.) Of course, we worked with [another Chippewa band]. They were not mentioned, but we fought the Sioux with them. As the Sioux approached, the song that they sang was kept until a few years ago as the Brave Song. They sang the song to the credit of the people who had met for peace. It is a song of bravery. It was kept as a song by itself and only the braves could dance it. All who took part in the treaty were privileged.

There they were; as far as I know, there was no Grass Dance [War Dance] at that time. The peace pipe was there, and they used it to make peace. (I wouldn't add on what I don't know to be true, but they must have had an interpreter. They had those for many years because I remember them.) Now the next year, or not too long after that, the [Deer Lake] Indians returned the visit to the Dakotas, and everything went all right. Now comes the powwow. I don't know the exact time, but it wasn't far away, that the Sioux came again and gave the Chippewa the Grass Dance. It was one they could do all the time. Now, the Chippewa were told, "This dance is given to the Chippewa. You have the right to give this dance to any other group of people you wish, and they will have the privilege to pass it on to any group." The Chippewa were told if anything new comes in, they will get it.

This teller was careful to relate all that was told to him without adding anything of his own. Two days later he took me to another old man who had often heard the story from the same woman. When the second informant had read the transcription, with intermittent smiles, he said, "That was the way it was told, just like that." Although the story is rich in historical detail, the most important point is that the War, or Grass, Dance diffused from the Dakota in the 1850s or early 1860s as the 2 tribes made peace, in the course of which the Chippewa acceptance of the songs and dance proved significant.

Another event described by the first historian-informant supports this significance. He recalled that it was just before 1900 that

they had a Feast of the Seasons. In the ceremony, they had a pig's head and a performance with it. When they finally finished it, the old people would sit and eat; then anyone could eat.

First, they would have a regular powwow. Then, when the time comes, they sing a special song, the Feast Dance Song. Then everybody knows what's coming up. Then, the interpreter (we'll call him the interpreter) walks up to the drum. He says, "What is this, what is going to be?" The drummer says, "We're going to start singing the 10 songs." Now, they only sang the first verse, though each Indian powwow song has 2 verses. They sang one right after another for 10 songs. Anyone could dance then. If the singers lingered and didn't pick up a song right away, they were fined.

After that, the pig's head was brought out in a pot covered with a cloth. There was a special decorated stick in the pail. It was like a sharp arrow and was stuck in the pail. Then a special man (we'll call him the ceremonial dancer for this feast) danced around once. Then he picked up the stick. He danced around approaching and retreating from the head, but always facing it. There was a special song for this. Then he danced around and came back to tease again. People kept thinking, "He's going to stick it now. No!" Finally, when he's tired probably, he puts it through. Then the drum goes to pieces; it is hit by all the drummers out of time. Then the older men, those with a record of bravery, squat and eat. They carried their own knives and there were a lot of braves. Then the others could eat. The powwow paused while they ate, then continued.

I'm not telling you a story handed down from one person to another. I wouldn't do that because I don't trust it. I've seen this happen.

Like the War Dance, the Squaw Dance also seems to have been a pre-1900 dance on the reservation. Since it apparently did not come from the Dakota, it was most likely introduced from elsewhere in the Plains area. The Squaw Dance was probably already on the decline in 1915 because it does not seem to be prominent in the memory of any of the Deer Lake informants.

The Dream Dance, which presumably came from the Dakota and which was prominent at Broken Reed, was not mentioned by any of the Deer Lake informants. Perhaps, like the Dakota themselves, the Deer Lake Band did not absorb the dance into their ceremonial life. Even though there is evidence from the informants that dreams were considered important in the making of drums and in the creation of songs, the Dream Dance complex as a whole, with its organization and structured ceremony, apparently did not occur at Deer Lake. The Two Step and Rabbit dances were assimilated from the Dakota in the late 1800s, which may be interpreted as part of the Dakota promise to send along any new dances that were developed.

About 1900, several domed log dance halls existed near Agency, and a few near Nisishin (see Densmore 1913, Plates 44 and 45, for powwow at Wabacing Village [Nisishin]). One of the dance halls in Nisishin was reported to be in use as late as 1953. Also being used were powwow rings (with fences, benches, and drummers' stands covered with leafy boughs). The drum tightener, or drum warmer, was a common but not special figure at all dances. The braves, the interpreter, or spokesman, and the consecrator of the feast were common at a War Dance, but the membership structure was informal; for example, there was no exclusive group of drummers. At events that included both the Squaw Dance and the War Dance, gift giving was common. The gift, as usual, represented an invitation to dance. When visitors came to a dance celebration lasting several days, on one night the spokesman would make a speech asking for gifts to express appreciation for the sacrifices their friends had made to attend. A blanket was spread, and gifts for visitors were piled on it; the leaders of the visitors distributed the gifts to their people. The last known occurrence of such gift giving reported by the informants at Deer Lake was during World War II.

The older informants indicated a decline in interest and in the number of dances in the late 1920s and early 1930s. At Deer Lake the decline was not so great as it was at Broken Reed. The economic stresses of the Great Depression, coupled with the loss of the old braves, resulted in the formal War Dance disappearing by the 1940s. One informant stated that in the late '30s there were only 2 people on Deer Lake Reservation with costumes and there was no drum. Since 1940, however, interest has steadily grown and the powwows have become larger and more frequent. The War Dance seems to be the immediate precursor to the contemporary powwow at Deer Lake.

Dances on the Deer Lake Reservation from 1940 to 1964

During World War II, powwows were held for Indian soldiers as they departed from or returned to the reservation, and also for those who died in the war. These sometimes lasted through each night for a week or more. Often an old man would rise to reminisce about the War Dances of old, comparing the bravery of warriors then and now. Speeches also occasioned gift giving, since this custom was no longer associated exclusively with the Squaw Dance, which had disappeared in the 1930s. The powwows of the 1940s also included the Round Dance, Rabbit Dance, Two Step, and Shake Dance—a fast dance for men which was a gift from the Dakota and was used particularly in contests. Although the army bass drum had replaced the traditional drum, it was (and is) still treated respectfully as a symbol; the singers maintain the custom of walking out of the ring with the drum as they sing the last song.

On the Deer Lake Reservation, the Fourth of July celebration was in existence prior to 1900. The oldest informant, aged 13 in 1900, said he could not remember when there was *not* a Fourth of July celebration there. Densmore stated that she attended such a celebration at Wabacing [Nisishin], in 1910 (1913:251). Another informant postulated that the long existence of this particular event is probably the result of its early association with the aboriginal midsummer celebration (*abitanebin*). Mittleholtz's history (1957) contains an illustration of a Fourth of July celebration in the early 1900s depicting men on horses and a number of tepees surrounding the ring. This evidence suggests the antiquity of the celebration and of camping at the grounds.

During the 1940s at Deer Lake, a loosely organized "committee" was responsible for the Fourth of July celebration and for any other dancing on the reservation. Although the committee had a leader and other individuals were appointed to particular jobs, the bulk of the preparation was accomplished by the community collectively. Costs for food were low since the men hunted and the women cooked for pow-wows. Because most of the work in those years was volunteer, the celebration did not cost more than $500.

This same type of organization for the event continued in the 1950s, although by this time the committee was elected at an annual meeting of reservation members. Volunteer work continued to be important in the preparation and execution of this celebration and of other powwows. When the council was reorganized in 1959 (Miller 1966), the celebration committee was also restructured. Though still elected, the committee members began to be paid for their work. Volunteer assistance from the community has declined. In recent years the committee has been reelected as a whole instead of individually. Since some nonproductive members have thus been reelected, the committee itself has been forced to drop some of its members and make new appointments.

During the early 1950s, after being located at Windy for 5 years, the celebration site was moved back to Agency. Several powwow rings were then in use on the reservation. The site at Agency, however, has been changed 3 times, and there are now at least 3 permanent rings on the reservation. One is at Agency, where the Fourth of July celebration and other, smaller powwows are held. A site at Nisishin is sometimes used for a separate Fourth of July powwow as well as for other powwows held throughout the year. In a recreation area at the southwest end of Lower Deer Lake, a third ring, not now in use, was built several years ago to provide dancing facilities where tourists might congregate. In the early 1900s the concession stands maintained on these sites for Fourth of July powwows were just lemonade stands; since World War II, however, hamburger, soft drink, coffee, lunch, and bingo stands have been added.

At the Deer Lake Reservation, where the Fourth of July celebration continues to be the biggest event of the year, powwows are held as often as every 2 weeks in some parts of the year. In the winter, the celebrations are held in the community hall at Agency. A powwow may be held for various reasons: to honor soldiers leaving or returning, to commemorate holidays, to recognize a person's years of service at his retirement, to greet persons coming to Deer Lake to work in government offices, to remember someone who has died. A powwow may be organized simply because it has been a long time since the last one. Traditions also govern the times for holding powwows; for example, one is held just before but none during Lent.

Visitors to the Fourth of July celebration most often come from the Dakota reservations in North and South Dakota, from the Dakota, Chippewa, Cree, and Assiniboin reservations in Manitoba and Saskatchewan, and from Minnesota Chippewa Broken Reed, Beaver Pelt, Hook Lake, and Mille Lacs reservations. The order in which these reservations are listed here reflects the intensity of friendships and the number and frequency of reciprocal visits between Deer Lake Indians and the others. One informant pointed out that in 1967 a particular singer from Fort Totten, North Dakota, was attending his 36th Fourth of July celebration at Agency. Another informant indicated that during a winter season these visitors may attend several of the smaller powwows. A number of singers and dancers from Portage-la-Prairie, Manitoba, have been coming as a group to the Deer Lake Fourth of July celebration for more than 10 years. Lines of communication between the Deer Lake powwow and other powwows seem to run west and north rather than east and south toward the rest of the Minnesota Chippewa.

The Fourth of July celebration at Agency

My fieldwork in 1966 and 1967, together with notes by field-workers of the Upper Mississippi Research Project made in 1964 and 1965, supplied the data for this section.

At Agency both the Fourth of July celebration and the other pow-wows held throughout the year are planned and prepared by a celebration committee. This committee, which is distinct from the governing council, is chosen by general elections. The committee organizes itself according to the various tasks to be performed. The Fourth of July celebration requires the most complex committee structure and demands the maximum preparation in a great variety of jobs.

The basic celebration committee is composed of 10 to 13 men, including a chairman, vice-chairman, secretary, and treasurer. Although the tribal councilmen are honorary members, they do not take an active part. The committee chairman, who functions as coordinator, calls meetings whenever necessary. During these meetings, a simple majority vote controls the delegation of jobs and adoption of policies, the chairman voting only to break a tie. Since the committee is divided into several task-oriented subcommittees which are not mutually exclusive, a man may be on several committees. Several of the major tasks require the attention of all committeemen. Other men are hired to serve as ring policemen, ticket collectors, and night watchmen. During the celebration itself, the committeemen will be paid at the rate of 15 dollars per day for being on the grounds attending the celebration instead of working at their regular jobs. While on the grounds, each committeeman wears a piece of red ribbon pinned to his clothing as an identification badge.

A head drummer, head dancer, and head singer are appointed from the celebration committee to assure that there are enough performers present for continuous dancing and singing during the first stages of the celebration and in the early afternoon each day. Four other men see that everything is ready for dancing and attract other performers to participate. Since one of the 3 official announcers belongs to this group, he will use the public address system to entice dancers to enter the ring each afternoon. The head announcer is responsible for planning with the committee chairman for each day's program and for directing the program over the microphone. The other announcers relieve the master of ceremonies from time to time, and all may embellish their spiels with stories about the old days in order to highlight each event.

Members of these subcommittees organize all of the dance contests. This entails selecting the judges for the local and visitors' divisions, as well as scheduling the events. The Little Chief ceremony is also their responsibility; committeemen must ensure that the sponsors are ready, and the announcer must explain the ceremony and call the names of the recipients of gifts.

The welfare of visitors is also the concern of the committee. During the Fourth of July celebration the camping area just south of the ring is filled with tents and trailers. Visitors are registered, and the committee makes food rations available free to all participating campers. Densmore (1913:25) recorded a distribution of food during the dancing in 1910, where moose meat, venison, and fresh fish were provided. Each morning the committee chairman travels 30 miles to North City to buy groceries. Campers receive about 3 dollars worth of groceries a day and 5 dollars for gas money at the end of the Fourth of July celebration. All the committeemen, in a sense, are responsible for providing sufficient rations.

Since the celebration committee does not build or operate the concession stands, no subcommittee is assigned to these tasks. A subcommittee does rent space to local and off-reservation concessionaires, at rates of about 14 dollars for the 4 days or 10 dollars a day.

Each year the committee tries to hold a parade, and a subcommittee organizes and leads it through the town. The weather, and local interest, determine whether there will be a parade. Bad weather in 1967 caused postponement of the parade for 3 days, but finally several flatbed trucks of singers and dancers, and several cars bearing the Deer Lake princess and her court (selected annually during the August Fair), left the powwow grounds and toured the Agency community.

A cleanup committee is organized, and its members are individually and collectively responsible for the condition of the grounds. One man leads a group to clean up the grounds each morning, but other persons often have to be hired to complete the job.

The Fourth of July celebration is not intended to make a profit. In fact, it costs the celebration committee each year between $2,500 and $3,000 more than the revenues of about $600 from the concessions and admissions charges. The unrecovered expenses are met with cash from several sources: bingo games held weekly throughout the year, teen dances and raffles, contributions from the tribal recreation fund, and private donations. In 1967 the celebration committee's funds were so low that money was appropriated from the tribal treasury. The treasurer of the celebration committee handles all bills, itemizes his transactions, and sends a full report to the council for review.

The committee functions year-round in planning for powwows on Memorial Day, Labor Day, Veterans' Day, and New Year's Day, and in connection with the August Fair. It may organize other powwows as well. The organization of work in conducting a powwow, though more formal than it was before World War II, is still relatively loose in terms of assigning specific tasks to specific persons. Because responsibilities are broadly defined, the scope of the completed tasks varies according to the ardor with which each man does his job.

Powwow grounds

The grounds are about half a mile east of Agency, north of the highway, and 500 yards south of Lower Deer Lake. The surrounding area is empty of other structures. The grounds area is bounded by forest on the south and east and by open grassland on the north and west. A large, permanent sign marks the entrance to the grounds, and a dirt road curves for 200 yards from the highway to the powwow ring area (see Figure 2.5).

Around the ring are 10 to 15 stands—3 permanent, one semipermanent, the rest temporary. In 1967, from the southeast side of the ring northward, there were a lunch stand supervised by local people; a converted, immobile bus serving as a lunch stand managed by a local family; a root beer stand brought in from Iowa in 2 parts; a hamburger stand in the charge of local people; another hamburger stand run by Deer Lake people; a bingo tent and bus managed by people from southern Minnesota; a lunch stand run by local people; a popcorn and candied apple stand, including a truck, run by whites; 3 small stands and a truck, all from off the reservation, selling hot dogs, ice cream, and cotton candy; an operable bus converted to a lunch stand managed by the owners of a local grocery store; and last, due south of the ring, a popcorn truck brought in by a white concessionaire.

Made of unfinished lumber, the 3 permanent stands each have a large window for a serving area and space inside for a refrigerator and a range. The converted bus, a wreck and presumably semipermanent, is storage place for foodstuffs; an adjacent framework of boards functions

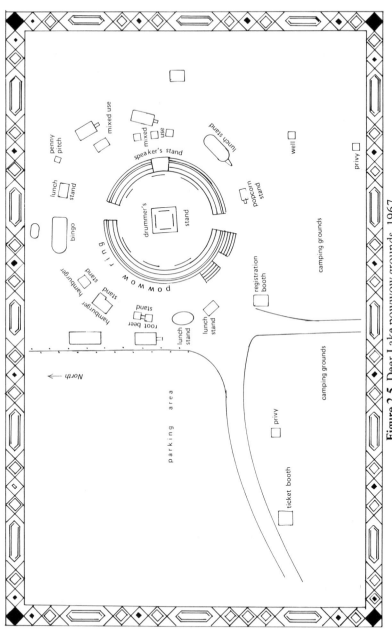

Figure 2.5. Deer Lake powwow grounds, 1967.

as a serving area. In contrast, the bus on the opposite side of the ring is driven onto the grounds on the first day, holes are dug for its wheels, and it is literally driven into the ground for the duration of the Fourth of July celebration. Inside, the seats have been cleared out to store soft drinks and candy, and one of the sides is lowered to form a serving area. The other local lunch stand, an 8-foot-square building on wheels, is temporary.

The stands erected by outsiders of prefabricated metal and glass are similar to those in small carnivals. The 20-foot-high bingo tent is about 50 by 30 feet on a side; the bingo operator's bus sits right behind the tent, ready to take on all the equipment when the celebration ends. In 1967 a traveling circus set up behind the bingo stand and offered attractions ranging from a frightfully thin elephant to a roller coaster ride.

The powwow ring is about 75 feet in diameter. It consists of an 8-foot-high fence; rows of seats made of 2-by-8-inch boards laid side by side at 6-, 4-, and 2-foot levels; 2 10-seat bleacher units built by the Neighborhood Youth Corps; and, about 5 feet inside all these seats, a segmented circle of single-board benches used mainly by the audience but occasionally by dancers. Telephone poles encircle the ring bringing electric power lines to the concession stands.

The drummers' stand is a square, flat-roofed pavilion. It has 2 rows of benches, one inside the other outside the 4 corner posts. Lights are hung from poles rising from the floor, and 2 loudspeakers are placed on the roof. A microphone is hung within the stand, and all announcements are thus given from the center of the ring. There is space for 2 drums in the center of the stand.

A speaker's stand, built into the east side of the ring, rises 8 feet above it. Essentially a platform boarded on the front and covered overhead only with a framework of boards, the speaker's stand is shaded by leafy boughs on special occasions. On the Fourth of July the featured guest speaker, with accompanying dignitaries, uses the speaker's stand.

Groups

Groups form at several places on the grounds; personal interactions vary with the locations and interests of the groups (see Figure 2.6). Most permanent are the camping units composed of kin and friends. Fifty to 75 camping units occupy the area south and southwest of the ring. In 1967, in addition to tents, there were one trailer and several small camper trailers. Some visitors stay with local relatives on the reservation, but most who are staying for the whole celebration camp on the grounds. The

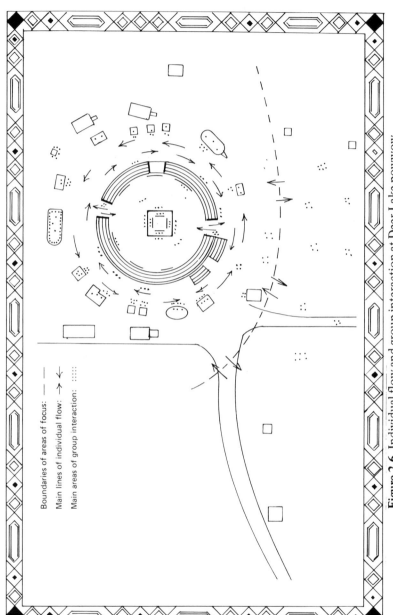

Boundaries of areas of focus: ——
Main lines of individual flow: →
Main areas of group interaction: ⋮⋮⋮

Figure 2.6. Individual flow and group interaction at Deer Lake powwow.

camping units are usually nuclear families plus or minus one other relative or 2 nuclear families who are related. Most camping groups are formed before they come to Agency.

Interaction among 2 or more of these groups can be constant and intense. The women share food and gossip; children join in play; men gather to talk about the weather, the dancing and singing, or about other powwows, recent or anticipated. Activities range from trading newly learned songs to discussing recent federal legislation affecting the Indian peoples. Others at the celebration, both reservation residents and visitors, often have friends camping there whom they join when retiring from the ring for rest and relaxation.

The outside (nonlocal) concessionaires form groups that are permanent for the duration of the powwow. Most of them sleep and eat in their vehicles beside their stands. The groups of concessionaires are relatively separate and are not nearly so involved with the powwow or with other people as are the campers. The operators of the bingo concession, who have been coming to Agency for the Fourth of July celebration for 15 years, are an exception because they know some of the local families.

Groups that are less permanent, but more integrated into the celebration, are formed around the locally owned concession stands. A family with a few helpers usually makes up the labor force for a concession stand, and, of course, they know the other people who live on the reservation. Little groups are always forming around these stands, to buy refreshments or to converse.

For the close-knit group of singers, the drummers' stand is a focal point. Since the microphone is there, it is also the center of attraction of the ring and surrounding area. The microphone is not used to give a running account of the powwow or to banter with the audience. It is used to coax dancers and singers into the ring, to announce special events such as a contest, and to explain a particular custom. Singers are not controlled by the announcer except during the contests; they sing what they like and move at their own speed. Usually a single drum, with 3 to 10 drummers, is used. Since the singing is usually continuous from 1:00 p.m. to 1:00 a.m. each day for 4 or 5 days, all singers have ample opportunity to participate.

Early each afternoon the group at the drum is a conglomeration of local and visiting singers ranging in age from 15 to 90. Committeemen in charge of starting the singing are there along with visitors from North Dakota and Canada. Instead of one singer taking the lead, several leaders may emerge, taking turns. As the afternoon passes into evening, the group is likely to become more homogeneous, with the singers usually all from a single area and accustomed to singing together. By early evening they are intensely involved in their songs and do not usually respond to events outside the drummers' stand. They act as a closed group, admitting others only if they join in the drumming and singing. If a singer wants to talk to someone outside the group, he will leave it, if only to walk 2 or 3 feet away.

Dancers sit on benches around the drummers' stand with their backs to the singers; ordinarily they do not talk to the singers. Or they sit on benches just inside those around the ring; or they stand at the outer edge of the dancing area. Women are more likely to sit and men to stand. Dancers from one reservation tend to stay together and apart from other groups unless one of their members has a friend from another reservation in another group; in that case the 2 groups may interact freely. Frequently 2, 3, or 4 dancers from the same reservation dance and rest together throughout the Fourth of July celebration.

Short-lived groups may form anywhere on the grounds, primarily around the ring but also in the camping areas and the parking lot. The spectators include a wide variety of individuals. Indians greatly outnumber whites, who tend to be under 25 or over 50 years of age, perhaps because the celebration takes place in part on work days. Indians of all ages are present. Children dance or play in groups throughout the grounds. There are few teenagers, and they rarely dance; most small groups, all male or all female, circle the ring or sit in the parking lot. Couples sometime pair off, usually only temporarily. There are few men in their early twenties. Young wives with small children are seen, as well as men and women in their thirties or older. Persons in their fifties form the largest age group among the spectators; they can be seen sitting around the ring watching the action intently or talking among themselves, or perhaps slowly circling the ring, moving from one conversation to another or finding friends to visit elsewhere in the camp.

Schedule of events

The generalized description of the powwow that follows incorporates data collected at celebrations over a 4-year period. Times given indicate the sequence and approximate duration of activities, not formally established times.

The celebration generally starts on July 1 and continues through July 5. In the preceding week the celebration committee or the Neighborhood Youth Corps or both will clean up the grounds and repair the ring and other public structures. The local concessionaires repair their stands, equip them with stoves and refrigerators, and store provisions. The committee has already provided the public relations needed, by sending posters with invitations to other reservations, even though most of the Indians within 500 miles would already know that the Deer Lake Reservation has an annual powwow on the Fourth of July.

On the evening of June 30, several of the local concessions receive some final touches; a few of the outside concessionaires arrive, but few stands are ready for business. Only a few workers are visible; a committeeman is watching things, and one or 2 visitors are pitching their tents. Except for a few teenagers passing through the grounds, there may be little other sign of the coming festivity. If the weather is good and several visitors appear on the night before the first day, the committeeman may set out a drum for singing and dancing.

About 9 a.m. on July 1 the committeemen arrive to finish the last-minute preparations of the grounds. By noon, several carloads of concession workers usually have arrived and are at work. By afternoon, the popcorn truck, which has been parked south of the ring, is preparing a few batches for the evening trade. The lunch bus reaches the grounds about mid-afternoon. Several men dig holes for the wheels, drive the bus into them, and get ready for their business. By late afternoon there are 5 tents in the camping area. Little groups of children are running about the grounds as their mothers cook supper near their tents. The few picnic tables on the grounds are quickly claimed. The committeemen have the loudspeakers set up and the lights and electricity checked out. At suppertime, the local people go home to eat, while the outside concessionaires stop work and go to their trucks or trailers for supper. After a 2-day trip, the couple with the bingo stand usually arrives late and postpones setting up until the next day.

Shortly after supper, local men and campers haul out a drum and begin to practice in the camp. Since their voices are a bit rusty, good-humored laughter follows each man's song. Although each singer is embarrassed at his own mistakes, he thoroughly enjoys those made by others. Around 7:00 p.m. the participants move out to the ring. The announcer then walks out, and even though there are probably not more than 100 people on the grounds, including concessionaires, he begins to call for singers and dancers. Participants include an Indian visitor from Canada who has brought his tape recorder into the ring to pick up some new songs. Around 8:30 several dancers casually walk into the ring dressed in black outfits with extensive beadwork.

One of these men's outfits is typically Chippewa despite being exceedingly elaborate. Although the costume is basically a black cotton shirt and pants, the pants legs have tufts of feathers, beaded discs, and a beaded chevron at the calf. A beaded black apron with fringes along the sides hangs front and back, with a 1-inch-wide beaded strip running the full seam of each leg, the bottoms of which cover sheep bells tied around the ankle just above fully beaded moccasins. In addition to an exquisite 4-inch-wide belt with flower and other woodland designs in bead embroidery, he wears a fully beaded harness, much like the suspenders of lederhosen, as well as beaded armbands and wrist cuffs. A few tufts of feathers at his shoulders and a beaded neckband complete his suit. The headdress consists of a porcupine and deer tail hair roach attached to a beaded headband, with a strand of beads crossing the cheekbones, connecting to the headband above the nose and ears and falling down to his shoulders at the outer edge. Two lengths of guitar string or speedometer cable with feather tufts on their ends stand erect from the headpiece.

In the dance, he leans forward from the waist, throws his chest out, bending both arms slightly and then drawing them back and holding them back. His motion derives mainly from turning and twisting at the waist, with a constant toe-heel alternation with his feet. He keeps his head up while concentrating on the beat of the drum. In the dance contest, the ability to concentrate will be crucial for winning. Since this is not a commercial exhibition, his attitude is one of restraint, not display.

Two hundred people are on the grounds by 9:00 p.m. A squad car of the Deer Lake Police Department arrives. The announcer jokes that the dancers had better get dressed and get in the ring before there is no more room. At this point, there are 5 singers and 4 dancers, including women and children. From the group, the oldest dancer moves to take the microphone, saying, "I'd like to say a few words." He welcomes a friend who has just arrived for the celebration, extolling the virtues of the man and the good he did while he lived on the reservation.

As the sun sets, the announcer calls for the flag song. All present stand as the singers beat out the rhythm while 2 men slowly lower the flag, which is then folded in a triangle and quietly carried out of the ring. The peak attendance and participation are at about 10:30 p.m., when 500 people are present. The singers sing a Round Dance song, and some women sing along as they are circling the drummers' stand. The announcer calls for the singers from Nisishin, outlines the coming activities, and finally tells a few jokes in Chippewa. Several drunks find their way into the ring, but committeemen quickly lead them out.

The announcer introduces a "white boy" (an Indian "hobbyist") from Chicago who does a solo dance, after which people begin to leave for home or for their tents. A cold wind blowing light rain off Lower Deer Lake forces the remaining people to huddle around the drummers' stand or the refreshment stands. The stands soon close down, and the dancers retreat rather than get their outfits wet. Since the singers are not costumed and are sheltered in their stand, they continue until the lights go out at 1:00 a.m.

By 10:00 a.m. the next morning, there are cars from Iowa, North and South Dakota, and Canada in the camping grounds, with about 30 tents pitched. At 10:30 a committeeman announces the distribution of rations for the day. When the campers who are participating as dancers or singers line up, they are given coffee, sugar, flour, canned vegetables, and either fresh or canned meat and fish, whichever is available. Although there is no activity in the ring yet, the bingo tent is being erected. While all other stands are completed, they will not open until the afternoon. Because it is cold, the parade is postponed, but the announcer promises that the day's activities will start at 1:00 p.m. But only after an hour or so of pleading and cajoling do some of the singers brave the weather to sing a few songs, and a half-hour later not one dancer has followed the singers into the ring. Spectator attendance increases slowly.

An old committeeman takes the microphone and says, "I'd like to say a few words to the people from Minneapolis, about tunes. The tunes differ just like white songs. If you people stay a few hours, you'll see dancing like our forefathers did many years ago."

The singing is only sporadic throughout the rest of the afternoon. By suppertime fewer than 10 singers and dancers have performed at any one time. Even though the ring itself is quiet from 5:30 to 8:00 p.m., eating and visiting activity increases in the camp.

By 9:00 p.m., 40 dancers are in the ring, and several visiting groups are singled out for solo dances. A Deer Lake Indian makes an appreciation speech, praising a man from Canada because for many years he has brought his 3 sons and their families to the celebration. After the speech, a few names are called out to designate the recipients of several anonymous gifts. At 10:30 a qualifying dance contest is held for visitors with local men as judges. Five visitors are selected each night for a final contest on the night of the Fourth. Similarly, 5 local dancers qualify each night, in a contest judged by visitors, to compete in the final contest.

Generally a series of restricted dances are interspersed with dances open to everyone. The first may be a slow War Dance as an introductory dance. The second is the Shake Dance, which begins with a rapid drum beat to which the dancers stand and shake, rolling the upper part of their bodies, gradually bending their legs and trunks toward the ground. After half a minute, the drum is struck hard and the drummers go into a fast War Dance, with the dancers moving quickly, confining their dancing within a 10-foot-square area. Although they may do as many variations to the War Dance as they have in the repertoire, their steps must at all times keep time to the drum. Many informants have stressed that no matter how fancy a dancer may be, he is not considered a champion dancer if he does not keep time with the drum. At the end of the contest the judges choose 5 dancers, who do not compete again until the final contest on the night of the Fourth. Those not chosen may dance in later qualifying contests.

At midnight the crowd begins to disperse and the dancers filter out of the ring. The singers, however, continue, and most stands stay open. At 12:45 a.m., a drum signals the end of activity in the ring. Committeemen store the drum in a nearby tent for the night, the stands close, and the lights go out by 1 a.m.

Between 8:00 and 10:00 a.m. on the third morning of the celebration, the only activity is in the camping grounds, where people are preparing breakfast, hauling water, washing, and conversing with their neighbors. Soon after 10:00 some singers begin their activity. Committeemen announce that rations are being given out. By noon, 50 tents have been set up on the grounds; parked automobiles bear license plates from Wisconsin, Illinois, Iowa, Nebraska, North and South Dakota, Montana, Wyoming, Saskatchewan, and Manitoba.

At 1:00 p.m. the announcer appeals for singers and dancers to congregate in the ring. He is anxious for participants and spectators to be in the ring for the first Little Chief ceremonies. Soon 5 singers and several dancers are participating. The announcer interrupts only to give a gift, explain an event, or to report a lost or found object. By 4:00 there are about 400 people on the grounds.

After introducing the princess, the announcer reports the winners of the previous night's qualifying event for the dance contest. Prizes for the final 2 contests are $100, $50, and $25 for the first 3 places. After advertising several upcoming powwows in other communities, the announcer prepares for a Little Chief ceremony.

Although common in the 1940s and early 1950s, the Little Chief ceremonies were abandoned in the late 1950s. But by 1966, complaints of visiting Indians (who often receive gifts) concerning the loss of the custom led to the revival of the ceremony. During July, parents or other relatives of a 5- to 10-year-old boy pledge to sponsor him in this ceremony at the next year's celebration. As many as 5 or 6 relatives may be cosponsors. Not only will they have a dance outfit made for him but the boy's sponsors throughout the year will collect gifts of blankets, quilts, bedspreads, and yardgoods—in all, perhaps 25 gifts of material goods. In addition, donations of 2 or 3 dollars per person may total as much as 50 dollars, to be used for monetary gifts. The boy's main sponsor, usually his father or grandfather, selects gift recipients from the guest book listing visiting Indians at the celebration. Local persons usually are not given gifts.

At the ceremony, the announcer slowly calls the names on the list of gift recipients. Each visitor whose name is called comes to the center of the ring where the boy and a few of his sponsors stand. The visitors receive their gifts from the boy, shake his hand, and stand back a few feet until all the gifts have been distributed. Then the singers start a slow War Dance song during which all the recipients, holding their gifts, join the boy in a dance.

The Little Chief ceremony is variously interpreted as the boy's first initiation to the ring, his first formal recognition as a dancer, or a reinforcement of his position as a Deer Lake dancer. The sponsors say the main reason for their actions is to keep alive the memory of some recent ancestor who was deeply involved in the powwow or to be sure that the boy himself is allowed the full opportunity of becoming involved in the powwow.

Just before supper, when singers are introduced, the announcer calls forward 2 people to receive gifts of blankets. He explains that the blankets traditionally are given in appreciation of the fine qualities of the recipient. In response, one man says, "I got a blanket here, and I'm overjoyed. I don't know who it is that is giving it to me, but I'll shake the wigwam tonight and find out." This last comment evokes laughter from those who know the old ritual of divination by "tent shaking." Immediately after supper, 2 more Little Chief ceremonies are conducted, followed by the presentation of a few anonymous gifts.

The remainder of the evening is taken up with traditional war dancing, including solo and group specials, and with the qualifying contests. Several types of costumes are worn by the performers. One variation of the man's costume described above that is often worn by Canadians includes the same shirt and pants but in colors other than black. The entire outfit is decorated with cloth fringes and ribbon streamers rather than beads and feathers. Although the roach may be similar, it often lacks the wire antennae. Another type of costume elaborates on the feather decoration. The basic shirt and pants may be black, red, blue, green, or even pink; feathers are formed into circles or rings and attached to the back of the belt like a bustle. The roach is often made of feathers, and may be larger and more elaborate than others.

A third type, which seems to derive from the east, is spoken of as a Winnebago costume though several Chippewa use it. It has no pants or shirt but often includes a vest with the breechcloth, both made of black velvet and covered with woodland designs in bead outline. At the waist is a beaded belt, and the lower leg is either partially or fully covered with a leather legging. Bells are worn at the knee and/or ankle. Rings of feathers are attached to the back of the costume on the upper arm and sometimes on the knee. Some costumes include a wide cloth with rows of feathers attached to it, which hangs from the back of the belt reaching nearly to the ground. To complete the costume, a roach with no antennae or with only a single feather is worn on the head.

All the dancers wear bells, and most wear beaded moccasins. The bells vary from 1-inch-diameter round sleigh bells or 4-inch-square sheep bells and are attached to leather straps wrapped around the ankle or knee. Some dancers mix elements of several costume types to make up an outfit that is uniquely their own.

Chippewa women usually wear one of 2 basic costumes. One is called a "jingle dress." It is of one single color, usually black, brown, or green, and is decorated with 2 to 10 rows of tin cones made from snuff-can lids or beer-can bottoms, which jingle slightly as the woman dances. The other costume is a buckskin dress with fringes. It may be beaded at the shoulders and the wearer may add a beaded necklace. Dresses of both types reach to mid-calf and are usually worn with ankle-high beaded moccasins and a beaded head band. Some women also wear or carry a shawl, and all seem to carry their "store-bought" purses while they are dancing.

On the morning of the Fourth, the committeemen are especially careful about cleaning up the entire powwow area, and the announcer attempts to get the day's activities under way as early as possible. After breakfast and the distribution of rations, the preparations for the parade are begun. By 11:30 a.m., several hundred people are on the grounds, and a few trucks and cars begin forming into a line for the parade. Shortly after noon, the procession leaves the powwow grounds to drive the parade route through town. A convertible carrying the princess leads the parade, followed by another vehicle with her attendants, then a car with some costumed children, a truck with dancers and the flag, and finally a pickup truck with the drum and 6 singers. While the parade is in progress, the powwow grounds quickly begin to fill with people.

By 2:00 p.m., nearly a thousand people fill the celebration area, additional groups having arrived from California, Oregon, Arkansas, Mississippi, Ohio, Pennsylvania, and New Jersey. Shortly after 2:30, the tribal chairman welcomes the spectators and asks the singers for one more song. He then introduces visiting dignitaries ranging from local state representatives to the U.S. senator who is the featured speaker. As the senator is donning the headdress and moccasins given to him by the tribe, the tribal chairman jokes that the Great Spirit gives some people plenty of time and others very little. Consequently, as he points out, the Indian people were given "moccasin time," or extra time, with which they were able to get everything done without a lot of hustle and bustle. The chairman says this as an explanation, not an apology, for being behind schedule. The senator gives a 45-minute speech recounting the progress of the Deer Lake Band, citing government action and promising more government help. Then he dances with several young boys on each arm, followed by the old men of the tribe.

At suppertime, a fresh walleye pike dinner is served south of the ring for a dollar a plate. At 7:00 p.m, the chairman of the celebration committee gives some gifts to visiting friends in appreciation for their support of the powwow. That evening, after several special dances and the qualifying contests, the final dance contests are held. At this point the crowd numbers nearly 1,500, down only slightly from a mid-afternoon peak. Most of the white tourists have now departed, and most of the spectators are now concentrating on the traditional contests, with enthusiastic clapping after every round. There is little or no explanation of the rules of the contests, since it is assumed that everyone present is familiar with what is going on. The contests last only until 12:30 a.m.; but the grounds are not quiet until after 2:00 a.m., for the excitement of the day has stimulated participants and spectators alike.

July 5 is an anticlimax. Many of the spectators and even some of the participants have left the powwow. Throughout the day, the announcer recounts the events of the celebration to that point and thanks both visitors and local participants. As the celebration winds down, the atmosphere is more relaxed. The outside concessionaires and visitors slowly prepare for the trip home. The local people and some visitors who decide to stay another night settle down to an evening of dancing and conversation in a lower key; when this group disperses, the celebration is officially over.

Discussion and interpretation

An analysis of the similarities and differences between the powwows at Wicket and at Deer Lake should begin with a discussion of their historical derivations.

By the early 1800s the Chippewa had already borrowed many village and ceremonial organizational forms from the Dakota (Hickerson 1962:52–64). In the 1830s the Broken Reed Chippewa had a group of braves called *gigidag,* which Hickerson (1962:56) indicated means the same as *akicita* (Dakota), and he cites variants such as *okitcita* (Plains Ojibwa) and *okihtcitawak* (Plains Cree). This is, of course, the same term as *ogicidan,* encountered in the Dream Dance organization and generally applicable to the War Dance organization, for both the Broken Reed and Deer Lake groups. Though the Chippewa group of braves was not so highly structured nor so elaborate in their equipment and dress as the Dakota warrior societies, Hickerson saw the former group as a borrowed version of the Dakota institution (1962:59). Hickerson also contended that some of the extracts from Taliaferro's journals indicate "that exchanges of dances and perhaps attendant features of the ceremonial practice between Chippewa and Dakota occurred in the 1820's and 1830's" (1962:61). Thus, there is some suggestion of a long history of various exchanges between the Chippewa and Dakota before the War Dance was actually accepted. The consequent Chippewa familiarity with the dance association probably eventually facilitated their acceptance of it in the 1840s.

The continuing anthropological discussion of Chippewa atomism suggests reasons for the slow and differential acceptance and spread of the War Dance complex. Environmental factors have been cited for the individualistic and noncooperative nature of the Chippewa, particularly in their winter conditions. The arguments waver, however, between considerations of Chippewa personality and of Chippewa social organization, both of which are characterized as more or less atomistic. Exchanges between Barnouw (1963) and Hickerson (1962) can be considered representative of the ongoing argument.

Barnouw further claimed that prior to the reservation period the Chippewa lived in small hunting bands, coming together in temporary villages only during the summer when it was profitable to cooperate. Attributing this organization to a basic Chippewa personality structure, he contrasted the situation with that of the Plains environment, where a "strong sense of social solidarity was manifest in the orderly camp circle, the communal buffalo hunt, the highly developed political organization with its council of chiefs and the soldier societies which served as police force. The Chippewa lacked such institutions; they had no organized council of chiefs, no policing system, no regularly constituted military societies, and no symbols of group unity like the 'Medicine Arrows' or 'Sacred Hat' of the Cheyenne" (1963:141).

Although Hickerson admitted that overall the Chippewa political, social, and ceremonial organization can hardly compare in detail with the highly elaborated Plains organization, he held that the Chippewa did manifest on the local level some features that Barnouw claimed they lacked. It was the village rather than the tribe that served the Chippewa as the central unit within which these less elaborate, less complex organizations functioned. Hickerson cited hereditary chiefs and the *gigidag* as evidence of village political organization and recorded suggestions of their authority and ceremonial life (1962:52–61).

Even though some of the ethnohistorical materials in this study seem to be evidence for Hickerson's position, it is inconclusive evidence. The story of the Dakota peace party that went to Deer Lake about 1840 includes references to the Chippewa *ogicidan*. The informant described them as a special class of men who walked up and down policing the lines of people and keeping order by threat of force. Likewise, one function of the Plains warrior societies was to act as police. Hickerson himself was unsure about the *gigidag*'s performance of this role (1962:5), although the story itself suggests that a group of warriors did serve as agents of social control.

Perhaps an organized group of warriors among the Chippewa was associated with the War Dance as warriors were associated with the Plains War Dance. As a theme, war came to be of central importance as was true among the Plains tribes. By comparison and extrapolation from the earliest Chippewa accounts, it seems that the functions of the War Dance, even after the demise of tribal warfare, were to provide an identity-building situation for young men as braves, to integrate the community socially, and to maintain confidence in the old Indian way of life. Hickerson supported the view that the War Dance as a ceremony in a warrior society was an integral part of village life (1962:27), while one of Barnouw's proofs against village organization is that there were "no symbols of group integration" (1961:1007).

The differential acceptance of the Dream Dance by Deer Lake and

Broken Reed bands constitutes another historical problem. It is difficult to account for the differences. The early acceptance of the War Dance by Deer Lake Indians and their affinity for Dakota ceremonialism, which did not incorporate the Dream Dance, may have diminished their interest in the Dream Dance. More fruitful than seeking ethnohistorical "causes" is examining the implications of this differential acceptance.

On the Deer Lake Reservation by the late 1800s the Dream Dance had not been adopted, but the War Dance had been integrated into reservation life as an important ceremonial focus. The "closed" status of Deer Lake distinctly separated it from other Indian and white communities. Land on that reservation was never allotted to individuals; thus the Deer Lake Band continues to hold all land for the people. Difficulties suffered by the Deer Lake people in maintaining their closed reservation against local and governmental opposition suggest that they perceived themselves as a separate and special group. Their isolation has continued from the late 1800s to the present. Thus the War Dance, the central focus of the semisecular ceremonialism of the Deer Lake Band of the 19th century, easily developed directly into the powwow, the central social celebration of the contemporary Deer Lake Reservation.

On the Broken Reed Reservation conditions were quite different. The reservation was opened in the 1880s to white loggers and homesteaders, who were physically separated from the several Indian communities. Among the resident Indians there were 2 other dance organizations that may be seen as alternatives to the War Dance. As local variations of the War Dance began to decline, local communities turned to one of the other dance forms. Localization of alternative dances and fragmentation of reservation land and society precluded the development of a reservation-wide powwow celebration. When local variations phased out in the 1930s, there was no shift back to centralization and the War Dance organization. Dancing disappeared until the 1950s, when commercial and community interests sparked a revival. The community of Wicket organized a community celebration, and the contemporary powwow was initiated.

The casual observer may see little difference between the Deer Lake and Wicket powwows. Both powwow grounds have a drummers' and a speaker's stand and rings surrounded by concessions and games stands; and both powwows include mostly War dancing, with intervals of special dances and contests. Nevertheless, the powwows differ in organization and they are sponsored by their communities for different reasons.

The Wicket powwow is sponsored by the community expressly to raise funds. Their powwow committee is the community council, led by a council chairman. Work on the grounds is the responsibility of the council and of community members. The concessions and games stands are managed by volunteer council members; all proceeds revert to the council. The success or failure of the celebration is thus the success or failure of the council, and any division or strife in the council will eventually be reflected in the structure of the celebration.

The Deer Lake celebration committee is separate from the community's governing council. Work on the grounds is the responsibility of celebration committee members. Concession or game stand space is rented to local or out-of-town concessionaires. The committee's only responsibility for the stands is to ensure the supply of electricity and water and to collect rent. The committee concerns itself with the welfare of the visitors and the program, and it loses money each year in order to have a successful powwow. The Deer Lake committee functions year-round, organizing powwows and conducting bingo games in order to raise money for more powwows. In contrast, the Wicket council usually functions as a powwow committee only once a year for the big celebration.

The traditional anthropological view of ceremonialism is that it contributes to the solidarity, cohesion, and integration of a society. As Warner argued in his study of the American Memorial Day celebration, "the religious symbols, as well as the secular, must express the nature of the social structure of the group of which they are a part and which they represent" (1962:179). This interpretation of the function of ceremonies can be applied to the powwows at Wicket and Deer Lake.

On the Deer Lake Reservation the powwow developed directly from the War Dance. Until the 1880s the War Dance was a ceremony in which some themes of Chippewa culture could be expressed. Braves told many stories glorifying former days. However, with changes in way of life and the relegation of war and its associated themes to the quickly receding past, the War Dance became less useful as a mechanism for fostering social solidarity. The dance evolved into a more socially oriented and therefore more meaningful event, the powwow. The Deer Lake powwow serves as an important symbol of the separate and independent identity of Deer Lake Indians. This symbolic function is manifested in speeches and comments made over the public address system during celebrations. Speakers may extol the long tradition of dancing and singing of the Deer Lake Indians and the place these activities play in the contemporary life of the people; or they may discourse on the virtues of running on moccasin time as opposed to the way whites hurry around and worry about lost time. Beginning about 1900 the powwow was gradually integrated into the culture of Deer Lake, replacing the War Dance as an expression of social solidarity.

On Broken Reed Reservation the contemporary Wicket powwow developed indirectly from the War Dance as a response to a need for funds for community projects. The old war themes had passed without any institutional replacement. The reservation was fragmented in the early 1900s, so conditions were not favorable for the development of a reservation-wide powwow as an expression of social solidarity. When the Wicket council formed, the powwow was developed both to serve the pragmatic ends of the council and to express the solidarity that the community had achieved. The open reservation, however, and the lack of continuity with the past have resulted in a celebration not so indicative of solidarity as is the Deer Lake powwow.

An indication of the social importance of powwows is the commitment of time and money made by participants. A first-rate costume costs from $300 to $500 and a full year of labor. Usually the cooperation of one's family is needed, for several skills are involved ranging from the beadwork to making the roach. Of course, these services can be purchased, adding to total cost. In addition, it takes many years to learn to dance or sing well.

The individuals participating in powwows vary widely in their acculturation to white life-styles. At one extreme are those people who have succeeded in white cities but return to the reservation, don their costumes, and dance for 4 days. At the other, the least acculturated people on the reservation (by their own admission) will be seen in costume dancing beside the white-acculturated visitors. Indian spectators may come from as far away as the Twin Cities, a journey that requires a considerable commitment of time and money. Thus attendance at or participation in the powwow can be seen as a commitment to certain sentiments, an expression of cultural solidarity and independence.

The powwow, then, is not so much an expression of the community's integration as it is of the community's respectful attitude toward some of the old ways of life. Instilling respect for these values in children at the powwow tends to insulate the community against change, even if some members move away. When they return, it is usually for the powwow; they will again join the activities, thereby reinforcing traditional sentiments. Even though they no longer belong to the community, they are still Indian and come to express their Indian identity.

The Deer Lake powwow conforms well to this interpretation; the Wicket powwow seems to have a somewhat different function. The War, Dream and Squaw dances persisted longer on the Broken Reed Reservation; but when these dances declined, the powwow did not immediately replace the dance forms as an expression of Indian solidarity. When the Wicket residents realized that their community organization was fragmented and that they needed a coalition council, dancing was revived in the community powwow. Their expressed reason for holding a powwow was to raise money, but the celebration also served to bring a new Indian unity to Wicket.

As a money-raising event the Wicket powwow must accommodate a range of interests to appeal to the white community with which the Indian community is commingled. Therefore, the Wicket powwow is an amalgam of traditional and modern events. While the dancing and singing reflect Indian sentiments, the raffle and outside presentations, which are not Indian, emphasize other sentiments. The 2 are sometimes at cross-purposes: the Indian singers and dancers do not like having to stop their activities to let other programs go on. On the other hand, the Wicket powwow is an expression of the new Indian solidarity, which replaces at least in part the old factionalism.

Ethnic identity

Powwows have been singled out by several anthropologists as both a symbol and a vehicle of the movement known as Pan-Indianism. James Howard referred to Pan-Indianism in Oklahoma as a "supertribal culture," a situation in which a variety of tribes are losing their "distinctiveness and in its place are developing a nontribal 'Indian' culture" (1955:215). Factors which Howard isolated as contributing to the development of Pan-Indianism are ethnic discrimination, common low economic level among Indians, the use of English as the lingua franca, intertribal marriages, increased geographic mobility, and Indian school contacts (1965:161–63).

Thomas (1965:65–83) argued that Pan-Indianism is the result of 2 processes. The first is the "cultural leveling" that occurred on the Plains, leading to a great similarity among Plains tribes and to the spread of their traits as expressions of "Indianness" for all American Indians. The second process is the result of the fact that "this new identity has set up a new structure of interaction among individuals of differing tribal groups." These processes, Thomas claimed, are contrary to the conception of acculturation held by some anthropologists. The traditional conception is that of "tribal groups remaining as small societies, selecting and integrating" with "individuals leaving the tribe to become a part of the general American milieu." With Pan-Indianism the situation is actually quite different: "It is the process of Indian acculturation that is being changed by the Pan-Indian movement ... it is possible now for a very marginal acculturated Indian from a Pan-Indian area to be accepted in his community by even the more conservative Indians if he participates in the institutions and symbols of this Pan-Indian life. Even if a marginal person leaves the community he can go to an urban center and become part of a more general Pan-Indian community." (1965:81).

The situation at Deer Lake approximates Pan-Indianism inasmuch as the powwow is a central secular focus, an amalgam of Chippewa and Plains traits, and the vehicle for much interaction with the Dakota and other tribesmen. Nevertheless the powwow at Deer Lake is best explained by its history and its functional nature for the local community, not by any wider, intertribal movement. The Wicket powwow too has its own peculiar history, which makes it generically related to powwows elsewhere and also separates it into a class of its own. It has some traits and functions in common with Pan-Indianism but is not explicitly a part of that movement.

Perhaps differences in the social significance of powwows may fit into a broad typology. It appears that Pan-Indianism is most like a nativistic or revitalization movement in Oklahoma, where many tribes are pushed close together. Powwows have less in common with social movements in areas of scattered and isolated reservations, as in the north central states. A third area where powwows may or may not be connected with movements is urban centers. Where a large Indian minority in a city derives from a variety of tribes, the powwow is likely to develop as an expression of various Pan-Indian sentiments. Where Indians are a small minority, any powwow will serve primarily as a reinforcement of individual identity and group solidarity and will not be a mechanism for any larger social movement.

It may be useful to examine our powwow data in a framework of the social psychology of ethnic identity. One of Shibutani and Kwan's major premises on ethnic identity is relevant to the situation in northern Minnesota:

In well-established systems of ethnic stratification people in minority groups live in their own social world and pursue the values of their own culture. Those in the subordinate strata are just as much a part of the moral order as their rulers; most of them conduct themselves in ways that they regard as correct. They accept the classification of human beings used in the larger community, and they conceive of themselves as different, although they do not necessarily concur with the derogatory evaluation placed upon them. Customary procedures within the minority group generally discourage contacts with outsiders, hinder upward social mobility, stifle protest, and prohibit intermarriage. Attempts of ethnic minorities to maintain the integrity of their group thus tend to reinforce the already-existing system of stratification. (1965:311)

Preservation of group integrity is accomplished in part through the display of appropriate symbols of a separate culture. These identifying marks can be physical characteristics, dress, language, gestures, expressions, or any aspect of culture. The important attribute is that they be distinctive. The display of these symbols helps maintain a separate identity for the minority group, which in turn preserves the group's integrity (Shibutani and Kwan, 1965:67). This analytical framework is particularly appropriate for understanding the functions of contemporary Chippewa powwows.

For Deer Lakers the powwow as an institution serves as a system of symbols which reflects and contributes to the maintenance not only of a separate culture but also of a distinct political status. The dancing, drumming, and singing are a type of special knowledge which few if any white men are encouraged to learn. Participation in powwows is valued behavior, which is observed with respect by community members. Success as a dancer or singer is acknowledged. The best dancers are introduced over the loudspeaker, asked to dance alone, and often given a special invitation to come into the ring. Since the powwow is a phenomenon about which whites know very little, it is an important theme in Deer Lake discourse.

The Wicket Indian people are not as geographically and politically demarcated as those of Deer Lake, but they are no less distinct as an ethnic group. Their discourse and interaction is with other Indian people.

When Wicket people participate in powwows, they glorify their heritage and at the same time reinforce their identification with the wider Indian community of northern Minnesota. As Paredes has observed, "such celebrations ... may be one of the very few open and explicit statements of Indianness in more acculturated communities" (1965:1).

Finally, the powwow may be not only a system of symbols for maintaining Indian culture and identity apart from the larger white social world, but also a link to a stable position for Indian people in American society. Levine suggested that "if young Indian leaders are successful in creating a kind of generalized Indian identity, the creation of that identity in itself may, paradoxically, be a major step in the direction of assimilation" (1965:13). Similarly, in his study of Mesquakie teenagers, Polgar concluded that neither "the conception of adjustment to the dominant culture as a mask or veneer, nor the marginal man theory are adequate to fit the modern acculturating situation" (1960:233). Both Levine and Polgar suggest that the appropriate model may be found in the nature of a pluralistic society. American society has never demanded complete conformity from ethnic groups, since there is no single ideal. The only structural demand is that each group be articulated to the others, that each group have its place. Acculturation for Indian peoples may succeed through commitment to a contemporary, distinctive Indian culture which is consonant with other elements of national society. The powwow in northern Minnesota may have as one of its consequences the building of an identity for Indian people which is valued in their communities and acceptable in the dominant white society—an identity that creates a stabilized niche in a truly pluralistic United States. In this sense, then, Chippewa powwows do contribute to the development of a generalized ethnic identity as "Indian" even if they are not an expression of organized Pan-Indianism.

3

Wild Ricing: The Transformation of an Aboriginal Subsistence Pattern

Stuart Berde

James Lake is considered an "Indian town" by outsiders, but to its white residents it is a non-Indian community. A general description of James Lake, the community where most of the research reported in this chapter was conducted, is given by Pelto (Chapter 6 in this volume).

Most civic and social organizations in James Lake are dominated by middle-class, white, year-round residents—and there are a great many such organizations: the Civic and Commerce Association, Sportsman's Club, Lions, American Legion, Legion Auxiliary, League of Women Voters, Royal Neighbors, Eastern Star, Masons, and the ladies' aid societies of several churches. In strong contrast to the whites' groups and clubs, the Indians have none of their own. While a local Indian council exists, it undertakes very few projects. The white residents conceive of the Indians, who comprise a third of the James Lake population, as a fringe group. At a garden show, a woman commented to me, "Pretty soon we are going to tear down those old Indian shacks on the South Side. They are just eyesores now." Despite these attitudes, community attention focuses on the Indians during the fall of each year, for this is the time of the wild rice harvest. The money Indians obtain from ricing quickly returns to the hands of local businessmen as Indian consumption of goods and services sharply increases for a few brief weeks.

The central question of this study may be stated simply: why do contemporary James Lake Chippewa gather rice? At first the answer seems obvious. Ricing brings quick cash to Indians; and, because many local Chippewa make little money during the year, the earnings from ricing represent a significant increment to their annual incomes. Wild rice harvesting is also a traditional Chippewa activity, an important part of the heritage of Minnesota Indians. It is reasonable to hypothesize that Indians gain satisfactions from ricing in addition to financial gain. Beyond this it may be proposed that whatever other rewards Indians obtain from ricing, the activity is an important element of Indian social status and self-concept.

Contemporary wild ricing in northern Minnesota: a case study

Alvin Jackson is usually no busier than most of the other white residents of James Lake. For about 6 weeks in late summer, however, he works at a fever pitch, sleeping little more than 3 hours a night. Sleep can be sacrificed, for this is the ricing season, and Jackson is a wild rice buyer. During 3 weeks spent in the James Lake area in the 1965 ricing season, I worked closely with him, observing 5 days of ricing and helping him by driving his boat, weighing the bags of rice, and performing other jobs.

Jackson lives in a fairly expensive home on the South Side of James Lake. He earns a good living during the year by selling minnows to fishing resorts on the nearby lakes. During the ricing season, his main business is buying wild rice from Chippewa residents of James Lake and other nearby communities. With his cousin, Jackson operates an enterprise consisting of 3 trucks, 27 ricing canoes, and an army of ricers, who sell their rice to Jackson as soon as it is gathered.

It is cold in late August at 5:30 in the morning. In spite of the weather, a handful of Indians are waiting in Jackson's yard at that hour for a ride to whatever rice lake may be harvested this day, by designation of the State of Minnesota Department of Conservation. These Indians, for the most part, do not own cars to transport themselves and their boats to the lake for ricing. They are obligated to help load the ricing boats, poles, and other paraphernalia onto the trucks and to unload the trucks at the landing. They will repeat this process at the end of the day's ricing. The Indians do this happily, for their labors are quite small compared to the immediate financial gain from a day of ricing.

It is about a 40-minute drive from James Lake to the Red Point landing on Broken Reed Lake. The ride in the truck is enjoyable for the ricers. They speculate on the coming day's ricing and talk of the activities of the previous night. They comment on the condition of the rice and the price that it will bring on the market. Jackson is loquacious, and even though he has little interaction with these ricers during the rest of the year, social distance is temporarily forgotten during the ricing season. He jokes with the ricers, and they seem to enjoy the interchange. A sort of partnership akin to a patron-client relationship is formed during the ricing season between the buyer and his ricers. Their relationship leads to a mutual pride in their enterprise and places them in competition with similar buyer-ricer combinations from neighboring communities. The competitiveness of the buyers is communicated to their ricers, leading to teams of ricers pitted against each other.

Red Point is a public landing about 10 miles along a dirt road south of the town of Grand Dam. There are 2 landing docks, one better than the other. The better landing area has ample parking space for cars and trucks, and the entrance to the lake is cleared of rocks. This landing, however, is controlled by another buyer and his group of ricers. "These boys have a finger in everything, including the game warden," Jackson says of the other buyer. Jackson's landing has poor parking conditions, and the shoreline here is filled with large rocks, which are dangerous to the ricing boats. Those of his ricers who come in their own cars must park in single files along the sides of a narrow road, making it necessary for some to carry their boats a long distance between the lines of cars. These difficulties irritate Jackson, for he takes pride in his operation and would like for his ricers to have fewer difficulties.

Jackson's trucks arrive at the landing at about 6:00 a.m., and the boats are placed along the shore. A 4-hour wait ensues until 10:00, the legal starting time for ricing. The Indians who have accompanied Jackson stand around and chat or sleep in the trucks. While the Indians wait calmly for the ricing to begin, Jackson is very active; he seems to create things to do to fill his time until the starting hour. He worries while he waits, mostly about the rice crop; and he motorboats out to inspect the various rice beds on the lake to determine which can be most profitably riced on this day.

During one of these inspection periods, Jackson recalled the days when he used to "haul 9,700 pounds out of Red Point in 6 hours." Not all of the rice beds ripen at the same time on the lake; thus conservation is measured against potential profit when the buyer is choosing exactly which section of the lake he will concentrate on in a day's ricing. The factors that most affect rice growth are a matter of opinion. According to Jackson, however, rice ripens best during "cold nights and hot days with plenty of sun."

By 8:30, most of the cars have arrived for the 10:00 starting time.

The atmosphere is one of apparent disorganization, but beneath it is the nonchalant air of competence that comes from years of experience. The landing is filled with people, but there is little social interaction at this time. Ricing is an individualistic operation. While there is no overt manifestation of competition among the ricers "belonging" to Jackson, each ricer goes about his business, dealing only with the individual who will be his partner in the boat.

The buyer is clearly the man in charge, and his voice can be heard giving directions to his ricers. These ricers are "his" by virtue of their informal contract to sell their rice to the buyer in exchange for the use of a ricing boat. However, no ricer is obligated to go ricing with the buyer. If a ricer borrows a ricing boat at the buyer's home but provides his own vehicle, he may rice wherever he likes.

When all the ricing boats have been unloaded from the cars and are in the water, they are tied to each other in a long line with the lead boat connected to Jackson's motorboat. Because Jackson owns only one motorboat, he can tow only one string at a time from the landing to the rice bed. It is difficult to tow more than 20 boats at one time, and even with this number there is the possibility of tipping. Jackson's competitor at the other, superior landing owns 3 motorboats and can tow his ricers much faster; this landing, some 50 yards away from Jackson and his ricers, is a source of irritation to them. Jackson can be heard bellowing, "Get those damn boats down, and be careful, for Christ's sake!" Most of the time his aggressiveness is directed against his 2 sons and nephew and not against his Indian ricers.

A ricer dresses with three main purposes in mind: warmth, agility, and comfort. At this time of the year, it is usually cold in the early morning but much warmer when the sun comes up. Thus the ricers wear layers of clothes that can be shed easily while they are on the lake. The typical choice is long underwear, heavy pants, high rubber boots, a flannel shirt, and some type of jacket. It is important that the arms of the ricer be free to manipulate either the pole or the "knockers," depending on his specific role in the operation. Ricers seem to be willing to sacrifice warmth for agility, and many will go into the lake wearing several layers of clothes only to return peeled down to an undershirt.

Jackson tows the long string of rice boats out to the bed with care. This operation is great fun for everyone, and the sight of a long string of boats being towed by a standing driver in a larger boat is quite a spectacle. For the buyer, it represents an opportunity to display his role as leader: "I hauled 30 boats once over at Whitney; you should have had your camera then." For the ricers, it is a time of excitement but also their last chance to relax before the actual labor begins. Many of them have waited for several hours, and tension builds as the boats are towed out to their respective rice beds from every corner of the lake. When the ricers arrive at the beds, they still have to wait until the legal starting time. Whatever social interaction may have been present at the landing is now gone as each boat seeks the proper ricing area. The choice is based on the maturity of the rice. The riper the rice, the more easily it falls into the boat, and, sometimes, the better the market price. One ricer maintained that if the rice falls into the boat as you paddle through the bed, it is ready to be harvested.

There are 2 main roles in the actual operation of gathering rice from the lake: poler (or "pusher") and knocker. The poler stands in the back of the ricing boat and pushes it through the water with a long, forked pole. The ricing boat is a flat-bottomed canoe that, under Minnesota law, must be 16 feet long and no more than 36 inches wide. The ricing pole can be no more than 22 feet long. The ricers I had contact with preferred homemade wooden poles over the manufactured, duck-billed aluminum poles because the manufactured poles have a movable joint that can easily become tangled in the weeds, making the boat inoperable. The knocker sits in the middle of the boat and uses a pair of wooden devices, also called knockers, to dash the rice into the boat. State regulations require that each knocker device must weigh no more than one pound, and each must be carved to a smooth round end. These regulations, which I learned from a member of the ricing committee for Broken Reed Lake, represent an attempt to secure some degree of uniformity in the ricing operation.

Although both men and women gather rice, the division of labor is not strictly by sex; rather, it is based on the experience of the ricing pair. A knocker cannot get the rice into the boat unless the poler is adept; and an excellent poler teamed with a poor knocker is equally disadvantaged. If the knocker is a woman, she wears a shawl to keep the rice beards out of her hair. Whether the knocker is a man or a woman, sunglasses are mandatory, for a sharp-pointed rice beard in the eye can be serious.

To the casual observer ricing may appear to be relatively simple. Actually it demands difficult coordination between the poler and the knocker. (This fact was conspicuously illustrated to me when I tried ricing with one of my informants, an individual with 30 years of experience. My inability to pole the boat made our attempt ludicrous.) The poler must keep the boat in a steady pattern, while gliding toward the rice. He pushes his pole through the water in a climbing motion, constantly compensating for his last stroke. To keep the boat in a straight line, he places his pole directly in back of the boat, leaning to neither side. A good poler pushes his boat straight through the water and, if necessary, can turn the boat 180 degrees with 2 strokes. The job of the knocker is to get the rice off the stalks and into the boat with as little of the stalk as possible. To do this, he holds a knocker in each hand, using one to reach out and bring the stalks over the boat, and the other to strike the gathered stalks with a glancing blow that makes the rice fall into the bottom of the boat. Although it is important that the knocker not hit the lower stem of the stalk, the force of the blow is not the key factor. An informant commented, "If the rice doesn't come with one or two knocks, it won't come at all." A good knocker is equally adept with either hand and keeps up a steady waltz rhythm: 1, swish, swish; 2, swish, swish; 3, swish, swish. Since the Department of Conservation allows ricing for only a few hours a day, the poler and knocker rarely stop to talk, except perhaps to discuss where to aim the rice boat.

The time for chatting comes when the ricing is completed and the boats are waiting to be towed back to the landing by the buyers. The ricers are elated and satisfied at the end of the ricing. Perhaps more salient than any traditional sentiments for the Indians at this moment is the expectation of financial gain from the sale of the rice and the anticipation of the purchases they can make with their "rice money."

My field notes on the opening day of ricing season recount: "I went out with Jackson on the ride to bring the ricers back to the landing. The Indians seemed to be overjoyed with the fruits of their labor and were quite orderly. One of the older ricers yelled out, 'There'll be a great time in Bill's [the local tavern] tonight!'"

The buyer evinces a mixture of exuberance and anxiety about the possibility of making a profit from the day's harvest: "Jackson was particularly elated on this day, for he was going to surprise the other buyer by raising the price of rice to $.80 per pound. He yelled out, 'Everybody is going to get $87 today.' Then one ricer countered with 'I've got a better offer already, Alvin.'"

Jackson is worried about spilling the boats and losing the rice during the ride to shore. On a particularly blustery day on the lake: "I will have to take it easy in carrying the boats back today. Ron Fletcher's kid drowned right here." And in reference to the possibility of not making any profit from a day's harvest: "It's no good for us this year,

Stu. I don't care what we do or how hard we try—we just can't seem to come out."

Once the boats are back at the landing, the ricers begin to "clean" the rice. This process entails freeing the rice from all stalk pieces that have fallen into the boat during the knocking. A measure of the expertise of a ricing team is the cleanliness of the rice in the boat before cleaning begins. An informant explained that the rice beards sticking out of the rice in the boat should look like a porcupine.

How much effort a ricer puts into cleaning his rice before sacking it can be taken as an index of his traditional orientation. In the early days of ricing (before non-Indians were involved), an Indian took great pride in the condition of his rice. Today the cleaning process is done carelessly, and ricers sometimes place rocks in the rice bags and water the bags to increase their weight.

The problem of differentiating types of rewards for Indians in the ricing institution is illustrated by this practice of watering the rice for financial gain. It is almost as if the Indian has fulfilled his obligation to his heritage by collecting rice in a roughly aboriginal manner; but as soon as he is off the lake and enters the non-Indian world of a money economy, he becomes fully acculturated to the white man's game and plays to win. The rice is now out of the Indian's hands, and he has no further responsibility for its treatment.

When the rice has been placed in the burlap bags provided by the buyers, the ricer carries his bags to the buyer and waits in line for them to be weighed and exchanged for cash. During the 1965 ricing season, rice brought from 65 cents per pound at the start of the season to over a dollar per pound near the end of the season. Today few ricers keep any rice for home consumption.

After the buyer purchases rice from his ricers at the lakeshore, he sells it to a wholesaler, or main buyer, by one of 2 procedures. The first is referred to as buying by "ticket weight"; a subbuyer is paid by a main buyer according to the poundage designated on the ticket placed on each bag of rice as it is purchased from the individual harvesters. In the other method the wholesaler reweighs the rice several hours later before paying the original buyer; he subtracts the shrinkage from the original lakeside weight, resulting in a loss of income for the subbuyer at the shore. Alvin Jackson is a subbuyer, but he does not subtract any weight for water that he knows has been placed in the bags, even though his main buyer reweighs the rice.

The harvesters are paid in cash for their rice with money borrowed from a local bank by the subbuyer. Jackson's main buyer, unlike many main buyers, does not furnish capital for his various subbuyers, who must pay interest on the borrowed money.

After the ricer receives his money, he packs his ricing boat and equipment onto his car or helps load the buyer's truck and returns to his home, perhaps stopping off at a local tavern to exchange stories about the day's ricing. The subbuyer's day is far from over. He returns to his base of operations, usually his home, and buys rice from other ricers who went to other landings and from anyone else who wishes to sell rice. Late in the evening the subbuyer will sell his truckload of rice to a main buyer, who usually lives in a neighboring town. Some 15 hours after the day began, he will return home for a short sleep before beginning all over again the next morning.

At this purely observational level, ricing appears to be a traditional Indian subsistence activity transformed, through acculturation, into the production of a market commodity. This "observational interpretation" must be broadened, however, by examining Chippewa attitudes toward ricing.

Chippewa attitudes toward ricing

Wild ricing should not be interpreted as purely an economic venture having no traditional associations for the Indian ricer. Viewing the present ricing situation in the light of the past, one may argue that the Indian's economic attitude itself is a function of traditional orientation. In other words, what was once a subsistence item has today been transformed, through acculturation, into a type of "subsistence once removed." Wild rice used to represent a primary food source for the Chippewa; today it represents an indirect source through the cash it brings. Because wild rice was an important subsistence item in the traditional past, the attitudes of contemporary Indian ricers should be examined against the aboriginal background of ricing. The work of A. E. Jenks, *Wild Rice Gatherers of the Upper Lakes* (1900), will be used for that purpose here. Jenks's dissertation stressed the importance of the economic motive in anthropological studies.

Jenks contended that the importance of wild rice to the Indians of the Upper Great Lakes could not be overemphasized. In support of this view he collected large numbers of letters, folktales, and government documents. He commented:

It is a world wide custom of primitive people to name many months or moons of the year after that national product which by its abundance or usefulness, or by other means, emphasizes itself for the time being above all other products. *Wild rice at the time of harvest is such a product,* and it has given name to its harvest moon among many wild rice producing Indians. In the Ojibwa language the September moon is called Manominikegisiss, or Monominigisis, "the moon of the gathering of wild rice," as referring to the August moon. (1900:1089; emphasis added)

For the 3 branches of the Algonquian stock in the district of the Upper Great Lakes—Ojibwa, Ottawa, and Potawatomi—the harvest season was an important time and the wild rice harvest played a central part. Jenks reported that the Indians of the Beaver Pelt Reservation gave a feast for wild rice. "The *manomin* (wild rice) feast comes in the fall after gathering rice and before the winter hunt" (1900:1091). Tanner (1830) wrote that at the sacred feast of the Beaver Pelt Reservation, the Indians killed a dog and roasted it in rice. The Ojibwa of Canada showed some variation in the feast pattern, holding their feast before the harvest. This pattern may also have been observed at Beaver Pelt, for an informant who was born there remembered attending a feast which took place before the harvest.

Jenks used several folktales to illustrate the importance of ricing. The following *Wenibojo* tale is taken from the Ojibwa of Wisconsin:

Wenibojo, the mythic personage of the Ojibwa Indians, made his home with his grandmother, Nokomis. One day the old woman told him that he ought to prove himself a manly fellow; he ought to go without food and get accustomed to the hardships of life. So, Wenibojo told her that he was going away, that he was going to fast; and taking his bow and arrows he wandered out into the forest. Many days he wandered and finally came to a beautiful lake full of wild rice, the first ever seen. But he did not know that the grain was good to eat; he liked it for its beauty. He went into the forest and got bark from a large pine tree. From this bark he made a canoe with which to gather the rice, and sowed wild rice, and taking his bow and arrows, started away again into the forest. As he wandered along some little bushes spoke to him and said: "Sometimes they eat us!" Wenibojo at first paid no attention to the address, but finally he said: "Who are you talking to?" On being told that he

was the one addressed, he stooped down and picked up the plant.
He found a long root, as long as an arrow. It tasted very good to
him, so he dug and ate a great many roots. He ate so many that he
became sick, and lay there too ill to move. When he finally got up,
he wandered on. He became very faint and hungry; other plants
spoke to him and said: "Wenibojo, sometimes they eat us." So he
picked some of it, and ate it, and said: "Oh, but you are good! What
do they call you?" "They call us *manomin,*" the grass answered.
Wenibojo waded out into the water up to his breast and beat off the
grain, and ate and ate, which he and old Nokomis had sown; soon
he returned home to his *manomin* lake. (1900:1093–94)

Jenks did not rely only on the folktale for ascertaining the position
of rice in the hierarchy of subsistence items of the aboriginal Indian.
There are many other tales that illustrate the economic importance of
lumber, maple sugar, and berries rather than wild rice. This problem
does not arise, however, in evaluating the more objective government
reports gathered by Jenks. Head Chief Martin of the Ottawa, representing the Ottawa Lake, Chippewa River, and Lac Chetac bands, stated in
reference to use of the land: "We have no objection to the white man's
working the mines and the timber and making farms. But we reserve the
birch bark and cedar, for canoes, the rice and sugar trees and the
privilege of hunting without being disturbed by the whites" (1899:1096).

In 1843, Mr. Brunson wrote to Governor Doty of Wisconsin: "But
selecting this place to pay the Indians of the Mississippi is next to
rendering their payment a nullity: because they lose more of it than their
payments are worth to them. If taken away from their rice harvests they
lose more than the whole payment amounts to, say $7.00 per head"
(Jenks 1900:1096). This figure can be used to ascertain the economic
value of the rice in that year. Table 3.1 presents a fairly clear picture of
the relative importance of wild rice to the Indians of La Point, Wisconsin, in the year 1843. Rice made up about one-tenth of their total edible
products for that year.

Jenks's research brought together figures for wild rice production in
the years of the last half of the 19th century. Table 3.2 presents a summa-
tion of the relative values of subsistence items for the Mississippi,
Pillager, and Lake Winnebigoshish bands of Ojibwa in the year 1864.
These data are of special interest, since these bands are ancestral to most
of the present-day Chippewa of the James Lake area. With the cash value
of wild rice estimated at $25,000, rice represented about 30 percent of

Table 3.1. Annual values of subsistence items for 1843

Item	Value
Furs	$ 25,000
Sugar	30,000
Wild rice	25,000
Canoe material	10,000
Game and fish	190,000
Total	$280,000

Source: Jenks 1899.

their total production in 1864. When the relatively short harvest season for wild rice is taken into consideration, the importance of ricing becomes quite evident.

Jenks documented the dire results of occasional crop failures that yielded the Indians less than their accustomed amount of rice, mentioning failures suffered by the Sandy Lake Ojibwa in 1849 and 1850, Rainy Lake in 1857, and Ojibwa of the Mississippi in 1867. Jenks quoted McKenney, who commented on crop disasters in the years 1849 and 1850 with reference to the Pillagers: "Hunger and starvation menace them; and in order to procure means of subsistence their hunters this winter will be forced to press westward till they find the buffalo" (1900:1099). He quoted Henry Youle Hind, an Indian agent, with reference to the Mississippi failure: "This is a great calamity to the Indians as they depend largely upon it for subsistence, and I fear suffering will ensue in consequence" (1900:1100).

According to Jenks, wild rice became a market item in the last

Table 3.2. Relative values of subsistence items for the Mississippi, Pillager, and Lake Winnebigoshish bands in the year 1864

Item	Amount	Value
Furs		$40,000
Maple sugar	150,000 pounds	15,000
Wild rice	5,000 bushels	25,000
Potatoes	3,000 bushels	3,000
Maize	1,000 bushels	1,500
Total		$84,500

Source: Jenks 1899.

decade of the 19th century. He suggested that rice could have been sold commercially even earlier, since traders used rice extensively during the first half of the 19th century (1900:1104; see also Hickerson 1971:188–89). In Minnesota, rice was sold in the cities of North City, Park Rapids, Big Run, and Minneapolis. In Wisconsin, Jenks reported records of commercial sales in Rice Lake, Cheteck, Cumberland, Bloomer, Shell Lake, and Hayward. However, rice was not of great importance to the urban consumer at that time. Jenks quoted J. A. Gilfillan: "Among the whites in Minnesota it is used only by missionaries and their families, old Canadian traders and very old settlers, and by a few merchants along the line of the Saint Paul Railroad" (1900:1105).

Wild rice thus occupied an important place in the economic life of 19th-century Chippewa of northern Minnesota. The economically oriented attitudes displayed by present-day Indians reflect, at least in part, the traditional importance of wild rice as an economic good. This economic orientation, grounded in Chippewa history and joined with the present-day commercial value of rice, has generated an attitude which is focused primarily on the financial aspect of ricing.

In 1965 wild ricing was controlled by the State of Minnesota Department of Conservation under the Game and Fish Office. This department, located in St. Paul, maintained a resident administrator in northern Minnesota. This official appointed a ricing committee of Indians from local areas to aid him in the administration of the lakes in their respective areas. (*Editor's note:* In the years since completion of this study, there has been considerable change in the administration of the wild rice harvest as a result of Indian activism.)

The prevailing attitude of Indians toward the administration of wild ricing is one of antagonism. Many Indians feel that what once belonged to them has been taken from their jurisdiction and placed in the hands of individuals who know less about the rice than they do. As the distance between the administrator and the harvester increases, the ricers' antagonism grows.

The Indians' main criticism of the Department of Conservation is directed at the department's distant and impersonal nature; their resentment is exacerbated by the department's use of the State Highway Patrol to enforce regulations. Harvests in the years just prior to this study had been poor, which no doubt contributed to the Indians' antagonistic attitudes toward state regulations. The Indians generally feel, however, that a department located in St. Paul can have little understanding of rice harvesting in northern Minnesota; thus they tend to blame the occasional crop failures on departmental regulations. According to the ricers, the department, under pressure from local buyers, sometimes opens lakes for ricing so early that the lakes do not reseed themselves adequately. Because of premature harvesting, the rice is not ripe and will not receive a good price on the market; in addition, the next year's crop will be small. One ricer observed, "Now they fly over in planes and have no idea about the rice." Such mismanagement can be corrected, according to the Indians, by taking the responsibility out of the hands of the state and returning it to the Indian committee, which could check more closely before harvesting, resulting in both better conservation and more profit.

The local Game and Fish Office representative maintained in an interview that the proper reseeding of rice lakes takes place no matter how early the rice is harvested and that crop failures may be due to other factors such as birds, water level, and the particular type of lake bottom. It is of note that Jenks, too, commented on the water level as a possible problem: "In some sections of the country the rice crop fails partially or wholly as often as once in three or four years, while in other sections it has not been known to fail for long periods of time. The reason for this difference is doubtless found in the nature of the most frequent cause of failure, viz. *drowning by high water.* Where high water is never or seldom possible, failures must be less frequent. Frosts also destroy the young plant; while, when the grain is ripe, a storm of a few hours will thresh out into the bottom of the lake or river an entire crop" (1900:1100; emphasis added). As Jenk's discussion of crop failures illustrates, such failures are by no means a new event brought on by state regulations. Whatever the reasons for recent failures, the Indians blame them on the state. They are sure that if the ricing regulations were returned to the "Indian way," the rice harvest would be abundant.

The Indians' attitude toward the local administrator in northern Minnesota is related to their opinion of the local ricing committee appointed by him. The problem is somewhat circular. Because of the economic importance of ricing, the hours that a ricer can be on a lake are closely regulated; but these limitations lead in turn to more regulations because of the inevitable scramble to rice in the short time allowed. Many Indians passively refuse to obey the regulations, their resistance resulting in an increase in restrictions and in general bureaucratic red tape. This is frustrating to Indian people, who remember the days when one could rice whenever the rice was ready and for as long as one wished. What results, then, is a situation in which any regulation is met by antagonism. One informant explained the problem: "In the old days there wasn't any of this pressure that comes from the three-hour-a-day ricing. A new economic spirit has taken over the old feeling of the Indians."

Although aboriginal ricing was an important economic institution, in the past it was not associated with the myriad bureaucratic complexities that mark today's wild rice industry. The technicalities of dealing with the state government, coupled with the commercial complexities of producing a high-priced, luxury food, make ricing an overregulated industry by anyone's standards. In the face of the complications of modern ricing, an elderly Chippewa commented, "In the old days they used to pray more. They would pray for the coming year. Now all they [today's ricers] want is to get rid of the rice.... They used to thank God for the season and thank Him for letting them live the year."

The modern ricer has little time to thank God, for he is rushing out early in the morning to get his rice before the local committee arrives to close the lake for the day. Frustrations over the increasing regulation of ricing during the past 20 to 30 years are bluntly expressed: "I was born and raised on this God-damned reservation and I ain't gonna buy no [ricing] license. Do me a favor and write this down. The Indians are getting a raw deal. They got this whole thing screwed up; it should go back to the *old* committee way."

Most Indians are not against regulations that seem to be based on sound conservation principles and would lead to a better harvest. Their contention is that regulations are lax when they need to be strict— namely, in failing to keep the white ricers off the lakes that, according to many Indians, belong solely to the reservation. The Broken Reed Chippewa find it irritating to rice alongside of resident whites, to say nothing of nonresident whites. Thus, the Indian ricers feel that law enforcement should be reoriented to exclude individuals who are not members of the Broken Reed Reservation.

The Indians feel that the only feasible way to organize the wild rice activities in Minnesota is through the local ricing committee. Through control by a committee, the Indians would be able, in their opinion, to receive both local control and financial gain, which are their main concerns. The present committee is often seen as merely a pawn of the state; thus it does not have the autonomy that the Indians would like. Indians do not doubt the present committee's ability to administer ricing. They complain that the committee is ineffectual because it is empaneled by the local state representative. They would like to see rice harvesting autonomously managed by the local committee, with a return to the earlier practice of local determination of the time when the rice is ready for harvesting.

The attitudes of ricers toward the local rice buyer show little antagonism. The local buyer represents the source of cash earned by ricing, and the buyer is subject to the same rules and regulations as are the ricers. Thus ricers and buyers are united in their negative opinion of the state administration. The ricers seem more annoyed by encroachments in the name of conservation than by regulations of the buying and selling of rice per se. The rice buyers' hostility toward state regulations can be interpreted as a reflection of the Indian ricers' traditional orientation. Improper regulations, in the opinion of the ricers, ruin the rice crop, and a poor crop arouses the "traditional" sentiments of the Indians. Indians remember when ricing was free of government regulations—and crops were better. The local buyers' effect on the Indians' well-being is less drastic than the state's. While cash payments are quickly made, and by the pound, poor conservation practices can have devastating effects year after year.

Thus, we may delineate two distinct orientations toward the institution of ricing—*traditional* and *economic*. These orientations correspond to the Indians' relationship with the state and with the local buyer. Since the ricer's antagonism toward the state seems to be greater than his resentment of the local buyer, it is quite possible that his concern for the traditional aspect of ricing is greater than his concern for its economic aspect.

Statistical analysis

Interpretations of ricing based on observational and key informant data are limited by their possible nonrepresentativeness and by other kinds of biases in the investigating, even though the data were gathered in the field during ricing season (and are therefore more reliable than questionnaire responses based on recall). Quantifiable supporting evidence is needed for the qualitative generalizations already made.

An interview schedule was administered to a random sample of 21 James Lake Indian residents. Of these 21 persons, 3 refused to answer because they had not riced for several years. Four of the Indians who did respond did not take part in ricing during the 1965 season. The remainder were very receptive to the questionnaire, feeling that perhaps some positive administrative action would result from this study. Most of the respondents answered quite openly for the 25 minutes or so that it took me to conduct the interview. The following analysis is largely based on the responses of 14 individuals who actively participated in ricing in 1965.

The harvesting of wild rice by James Lake Indians has so far been examined as a traditional and an economic activity. A simple economic interpretation of ricing can be strongly supported by our questionnaire data. For example, only 4 of 14 ricers kept any rice for themselves from the 1965 harvest. Furthermore, it appears that Indians have been receptive to any organizational changes in ricing that have yielded direct financial gain.

The income from the relatively short ricing season can, in fact, be considerable. Both Indians and whites frequently made statements about the large sums that can be earned from ricing. Estimates of a day's harvest range up to several hundred dollars; and it is not uncommon to hear of persons earning $3,000 to $4,000 in one season. Although 1965 was alleged to be a poor season, the most active ricers in the James Lake sample managed to earn $1,100, and the median wild rice income for the 14 active ricers was $300 (see Table 3.4). None of these individuals worked every day during the ricing season, and, during the peak of the harvest, collecting was legally limited to 4 hours per day. These limits, combined with the brevity of the ricing season, make the $300 median income seem even larger.

The importance of traditionalism in ricing is more difficult to delineate from our questionnaire data. However, the data Jenks presented concerning feasts, tales, and the general emotional aspects of wild ricing clearly reflect the noneconomic aspects of ricing in earlier times. Some individuals close to the Indians contend that ricing remains a strongly traditional activity and interpret the economic aspect as secondary. There are in fact several wild rice celebrations in northern Minnesota today. The festive attitude of ricers observed in the field conveys the impression that ricing represents more than just an economic venture for modern Chippewa. Several individuals in the James Lake area mentioned that Indians take leave from their jobs to go ricing, risking possible financial loss. Indeed, 11 individuals in our sample of 14 answered yes to the question, "Would you rice even if no money were involved?"

Analysis of the relative importance of traditional and economic motivations in wild ricing will be approached in 5 steps. First, the dependent variable for this study—the activity of ricing—will be delineated. Second, the pragmatic economic aspect of ricing will be dealt with. Third, the subject of traditionalism will be examined and the difficulties involved in operationalizing the concept will be discussed. Fourth, socioeconomic rank and its relationship to ricing will be analyzed. Fifth, the possible relationship of "nontraditional emotionalism" to wild ricing will be presented.

Wild ricing involvement

To investigate "traditionalism" and economic "pragmatism" in ricing, it is necessary to develop some way of operationalizing these concepts. The dependent variable—extent of participation in wild ricing—was operationally specified by means of the Guttman scale shown in Table 3.3 (see Chapter 7 for the editor's brief discussion of this technique).

Table 3.3. Scalogram of wild ricing involvement

Inter-viewee	*Scale type*	*Scale item* A	*B*	*C*	*D*	*E*	*F*	*G*	*H*
5	7	x	x	x	x	x	x	x	x
13	7	x	x	x	o	x	o	x	x
2	6		x	x	x	x	x	x	x
8	6		x	x	x	x	x	x	x
6	6		x	x	x	x	x	x	x
9	5			x	x	x	x	x	x
10	5			x	x	o	x	x	x
1	5			x	x	x	o	x	x
3	4					x	x	x	x
7	3						x	x	x
4	2							x	x
11	2							x	x
14	1								
12	1								

Key to scale items

A. Riced for whole season
B. Kept same partner
C. Used own car
D. Looked at rice early
E. Went to Rice Lake
F. Owns ricing boat
G. Owns knockers
H. Owns pole

Coefficient of reproducibility = .96

This scale ranks the degree of the individuals' involvement in wild ricing by sorting them in terms of what proved to be a set of functionally related ricing behaviors. The items that scale the degree of wild ricing involvement are these:

A. Riced for the whole ricing season
B. Kept the same partner during the season
C. Used own car for ricing
D. Looked at the condition of the rice before the season

E. Went to Mahnomen Lake [tribally controlled lake on Beaver Pelt
    Reservation] during the season
F. Owns boat and uses it for ricing
G. Owns set of knockers
H. Owns ricing pole

The ricer who studies the condition of the rice bed before the season
actually begins is displaying a concern for the results of his forthcoming
labor. This ricer has adjusted to the administration of ricing by the state,
for he is aware that only a few short hours are available for ricing and has
determined to utilize these hours to their full capacity. Such an individual
is concerned with finding the best spot for rice before the brief time
allotted actually begins.

The best possible ricing pairs are members of the same family, for
these individuals can place their earnings from rice into a common fund
from which they both may derive benefits. Ricers who do not work with
members of the same family must divide their earnings. If ricing with
another member of the same family is impossible, the next best thing is
to keep the same partner for the whole season; for, as a team gains
experience, its harvest increases. Thus, item B ("Kept same partner")
may indicate an individual's concern for making the maximum profit in
ricing.

Table 3.4 ranks the 1965 wild rice incomes of respondents. If
engaging in wild rice activities is mainly an economic venture for the
Indian, then theoretically there should be a significant positive correlation between the income gained from ricing and the extent of wild ricing
involvement as revealed by the Guttman scale in Table 3.3. To test this
hypothesis, position on the Guttman scale of ricing involvement was
compared with ricing income rank by using the Kendall rank correlation
coefficient, *tau* (Siegal 1956:213–14). After correcting for tied ranks, a
significant ($p < .03$) positive correlation of .385 is found. The hypothesis is confirmed. In a loose sense, then, 38.5 percent of differences in
extent of ricing involvement can be attributed to motivations for financial gain.

Another item in the questionnaire asked, "What do you like most
about ricing?" If greater involvement in ricing derives from the hope of
financial gain, a significant positive relationship should be found between mentions of money in answer to this question and position on the
Guttman scale of ricing involvement. This hypothesis was tested by
using the Mann-Whitney U Test (Siegal 1956:116). A significant

($p<.03$) relationship was found, which can be interpreted as further evidence that simple desire for monetary gain is a determinant of extent of involvement in ricing.

The more active ricers (as revealed by the Guttman scale) are not only concerned about gaining money from ricing; they are also actually earning more money than those who are less involved. While this relationship is seemingly self-evident, it requires empirical verification, especially since contemporary Chippewa wild rice harvesting has its origins in the not-so-distant past, outside the monetary economy of the United States.

The traditional aspect of ricing

This analysis has thus far shown that the economic aspect of ricing can largely account for the ricing involvement of individuals in our sample. Traditionalism in ricing is more difficult to delineate than the practical economic aspect because the latter lends itself to more direct assessment. In defining traditionalism in wild ricing, the Guttman technique was applied to a body of data to produce a scale.

The scalogram of traditionalism is shown in Table 3.5. The items listed in this scale were chosen for their relevance to traditionalism in wild ricing based on emotional sentiment about, and participation in,

Table 3.4. Ricing incomes in rank order for 14 individuals in 1965

Interviewee	Income	Rank
5	$1,100	5
3	700	4
13	380	3
2	300	3
8	300	3
8	300	3
1	300	3
7	300	3
11	300	3
6	100	2
9	100	2
10	100	2
4	100	2
14	100	2
12	50	1

Table 3.5. Scalogram of traditionalism in wild ricing

Inter-viewee	Scale type	A	B	C	D	E	Key to scale items
7	6	x	x	x	x	x	A. Rice medicine
13	6	x	x	x	x	x	B. Ricing stories
15	5			x	x	x	x	C. Would rice anyway
8	5			x	x	x	x	D. White ricers
18	4				x	x	x	E. Rice camp
6	4				x	x	x	
14	4				x	x	x	
10	4				x	o	x	
4	4				x	x	x	
3	4				x	x	o	
16	3					x	x	
5	3					x	x	
17	3					x	x	
2	3					x	x	
1	2						x	
11	2						x	
12	1							
9	1							

Coefficient of reproducibility = .94

activities that are generally considered locally to be traditional Chippewa practices or distinctly Indian attitudes. The items for this scale are listed in fuller detail below:

A. Ricing medicine (admitted hearing of)
B. Ricing stories (admitted hearing of)
C. Would rice anyway (even without payment)
D. White ricers (perception of)
E. Wild ricing camp (past participation in)

Because none of these items is contingent on having collected rice during the 1965 season, the responses of the 4 individuals who answered the questionnaire but did not gather rice during 1965 were added to the sample, resulting in a sample of 18 respondents.

Before the introduction of rice-processing machines by whites, rice was processed by each individual ricer at home or at the rice camp. This process entailed drying the rice in the sun for several hours, parching the rice in a kettle hung over a fire, fanning the waste material out of the rice into the wind, placing this rice in a cedar-lined hole in the ground, "dancing" on the rice, and fanning it again. Only 2 individuals out of 18 in our sample still processed their own rice, unlike the early years.

In years past, rice camps, set up before ricing actually began, were a familiar sight during the fall of the year. Individuals traveled long distances to arrive at their preferred campsite. The camp was a place of great social activity, where games were played and families that had been apart for months were reunited. Participation in the activities of a rice camp can be readily seen as traditional; 13 individuals in the sample had participated at one or more of these camps earlier in their lives.

One question was designed to elicit Indian perceptions of the number of whites harvesting wild rice. Indirectly, responses to this question also indicated the hostility of Indians to ricing regulations that allow non-Indians to rice. Of the 1,900 white residents in the James Lake area, only 150 bought ricing licenses during the 1965 season. However, 13 individuals in the sample of 18 James Lake Chippewa felt that most of the white people riced. We interpret this overestimation as a display of emotional loyalty to the notion that ricing is a traditional activity properly reserved for Indians.

Perhaps the best measure of traditional sentiment in the scale of traditionalism is item C ("Would rice anyway"). Eleven individuals responded that they would rice even if no money were involved. They simply enjoyed ricing, they claimed—and while the financial reward was certainly satisfying, it was secondary to the fulfillment gained from taking part in the activity.

The final 2 items in the scale of traditionalism refer to the ricer's knowledge of wild rice folktales and ricing "medicine," that is, magical formulas. An individual who could remember ricing stories or ricing medicine in the face of present bureaucratic regulations was assumed to have been associated with a great deal of traditionalism in his youth. Five individuals remembered having heard some form of wild rice tale, usually in their youth at a ricing camp; only 2 individuals in the sample could recall any mention of ricing medicine.

The coefficient of reproducibility for this scale of traditionalism is only .94, only slightly over the usually accepted minimum level of reproducibility of .900. The subjective nature of the scale items and the difficulties in delineating traditionalism are reflected by the relatively large number of scale errors. The scale items, for the most part, are concerned with attitudes and thus are subject to errors of interpretation by the respondent and by the field-worker. The items concerned with ricing stories and ricing medicine are dependent on the respondent's recall, and it is quite possible that some individuals in the sample simply did not remember this information. Nevertheless, correlation between the Guttman scale of ricing involvement and the Guttman scale of traditionalism is necessary for testing the power of traditionalism. If wild ricing involvement is to be conceived as a traditional activity, a significant correlation should be found between the 2 Guttman scales. Employing the Kendall rank correlation coefficient, positions of the members of the sample on the 2 scales were compared. The correlation thus obtained was not statistically significant ($p > .22$). These data do not support the hypothesis that differences in traditional orientation are positively associated with degrees of ricing involvement.

Before traditionalism in ricing is dismissed completely, however, the following points should be considered. First, the fact that a scale of "traditionalism" could be constructed at all should not be taken too lightly, for it suggests that some form of traditionalism still exists as a "dimension" in terms of which ricers can be ranked. I feel that some form of traditionalism does exist in ricing today, but, because of the lack of statistical sophistication with reference to traditionalism, it is difficult to reach the level of exactness that was reached for the economic aspect of ricing. Second, the economic orientation does not (in our statistics) account for all of the variation in ricing involvement. A portion of this involvement can be attributed to traditional orientation. This interpretation is based in large part on field observation, particularly the generally festive attitude of the ricer during the ricing season. It would be a mistake, therefore, to discount completely some degree of traditional orientation.

Socioeconomic status and ricing involvement

Given the demonstrated importance of economic variables in wild ricing involvement, general levels of socioeconomic status among ricers might also be related to extent of ricing involvement. Socioeconomic status was defined in terms of 3 ranges of annual income (which might include ricing income) and 3 levels of education. This index of 6 resulting ranks is shown in Table 3.6. Since this measure involves education in white schools and earnings of cash income, it can also be regarded as a measure of nontraditionality for Indians.

At the beginning of this chapter it was suggested that wild ricing perhaps represents a means by which Indians establish a positive role for themselves in the community of James Lake, for ricing is quite important to the economy of the community. However, earlier concern was not

Table 3.6. Socioeconomic rank of James Lake ricers

	Status rank	Frequency	Interviewee
6.	High education High income	2	5, 10
5.	High education Medium income	1	8
4.	Low education High income	1	6
3.	Medium education Medium income	3	9, 12, 2
2.	Low education Medium income	4	7, 3, 1, 13
1.	Low education Low income	3	14, 11, 4
		$N = 14$	

with the Indian's socioeconomic position, but rather with the more abstract concept of his "image" in the community. Here the variable of socioeconomic status has been introduced to investigate objectively the possibility that ricing involvement may be satisfying to Indian people by reinforcing their socioeconomic position in the larger community.

Because socioeconomic status can be interpreted as a measure of nontraditional orientation, it could be hypothesized that if ricing is a traditionally motivated activity, a positive relationship should *not* be found between the Guttman scale of ricing involvement and socioeconomic rank. In fact, quite the reverse is found; there is a significant $(p < .01)$ *positive* association between ricing involvement and socioeconomic status. This correlation offers yet more evidence in support of the proposition that ricing involvement can be interpreted as a product of the pragmatic concerns of James Lake Indians. Alternatively, it could be argued on the basis of these findings that traditionalism and socioeconomic success are not mutually exclusive.

Since there is significant positive correlation between general socioeconomic status and ricing involvement, it might be expected that there would be a correlation between income from wild rice and total annual income alone. Likewise, a positive relationship between socioeconomic rank and ricing income would be expected. However, neither of these relationships reaches an acceptable level of significance: $p > .215$ and $p > .319$, respectively.

This matrix—in which ricing involvement correlates significantly with both ricing income and socioeconomic status, but ricing income does not correlate significantly with either annual income or socioeconomic status—seems to be logically incongruent. Lack of association between ricing income and socioeconomic status may result in part from the poor rice crop of 1965. It is suggested that data from other seasons could reveal a significant relationship between ricing income and general socioeconomic status. This hypothesis remains to be tested by further research.

Conclusion

In this statistical analysis, "ricing involvement" has been examined in relation to 2 main sets of variables, traditionalism and economic orientation. It has been shown that there is statistical reason to believe that economic orientation is a powerful factor in the motivation to rice. A component of traditionalism in wild rice activity is more difficult to define than the ricers' economic concern, and statistical evidence for the significance of traditionalism is inconclusive. These conclusions are diagrammed in Figure 3.1, in which a solid line represents a significant correlation and a dashed line represents a lack of statistically significant relationship.

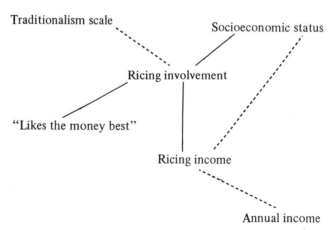

Figure 3.1. Associations among ricing variables.

Evidence for a pragmatic orientation is found in the positive correlation of ricing involvement with ricing income, with socioeconomic status, and with mentioning money as "liked best" in ricing. Absence of a significant relationship between the scale of traditionalism and the scale of ricing involvement could also be used as positive evidence for an economic orientation. The absence of correlations between ricing income, socioeconomic status, and annual income, along with the fact that traditionalism could be scaled at all, constitute the only "quantitative" evidence for an interpretation of ricing arising from traditionalism.

In James Lake there are relatively few Indian-oriented activities, so Indians are generally relegated to the fringe of the community's social organization. It has been suggested that wild ricing represents an opportunity for Indians to participate in some generally socially approved and satisfying activity. Indeed, during the ricing season wild rice is a topic of considerable concern for both Indians and whites in northern Minnesota.

Local people often say that rice gatherers seem to enjoy ricing activity for its own sake. The fact that 11 individuals in our sample stated that they would rice even if money were not involved further suggests that "going ricing" is more than just a quick way of earning cash. It is suggested, then, that in addition to the traditional and economic motivations, simply the enjoyment of active participation in rice harvesting may be a third factor for consideration.

This third factor is not intended to suggest that active participation represents another index of traditionality. The emotionalism associated with ricing participation can, rather, be seen as nontraditional emotionalism. It is possible that the Indians' somewhat alienated position in James Lake, which precludes their participation in many community organizations, leads to a situation whereby individuals of higher status participate to a greater extent in those few activities which are available to them. Wild ricing offers Indians such an opportunity. The fact that wild ricing is a traditional Chippewa institution may add to the Indians' enjoyment of the activity, but because of the difficulties in assessing traditionalism, it is not possible at this time to delineate objectively the extent to which any kind of traditionalism is involved.

In this discussion of the economic orientation of Indian ricers, it has been demonstrated that the scale of ricing involvement can be quite pragmatically interpreted, since the ricers who are the most involved, as measured by the scale, also make the most money from the rice harvest. In addition to the financial reward gained from actively participating in ricing, the individual who is high on the scale of ricing involvement may also enjoy going to Mahnomen Lake and owning a boat, pole, and knockers because of intrinsic rewards which are attached to ricing activities. Although the objective evidence for this nontraditional emotional aspect in ricing is lacking, a complete interpretation of the wild ricing institution in James Lake should include consideration of this factor. Nontraditional emotionalism is similar to traditionalism in its subjective nature and in difficulty of statistical representation. Although these heuristic difficulties have limited this analysis, I nevertheless feel that traditionalism and nontraditional emotionalism do exist to some degree in wild ricing.

It cannot be denied, of course, that this study clearly demonstrates that for James Lake Indians in 1965 the traditional Chippewa subsistence practice of gathering wild rice had become functionally transformed into an activity motivated in large part by the opportunities it provided for quickly earning relatively large sums of cash. Further, it has been shown that monetary considerations play a major part in explaining individual differences in extent of involvement in wild ricing activity. Thus, it would be a mistake to regard Chippewa ricing as merely a pastime or quaint native custom. Nonetheless, the fact that, in a random sample of James Lake Chippewa ricers, over half the respondents said that they would rice even if no money were involved suggests that many ricers are motivated by more than a desire for financial gain alone.

4

A Peyote Community in Northern Minnesota

Barbara D. Jackson

Rice Village is a tiny Chippewa Indian community in northern Minnesota. The village is unique among Minnesota Chippewa communities in that all of its members are followers of the peyote religion, or Native American Church. The principal aim of this study is to present a general ethnography of Rice Village. Emphasis is upon describing the local peyote religion in the context of other aspects of community life; general issues and comparative problems in the study of peyote phenomena are only briefly examined. A second problem addressed here is the relation of the particular geographical and sociocultural situation of Rice Village to the acculturation of its inhabitants.

Most of the data on which this study is based were gathered during a period of fieldwork from mid-June through mid-September of 1966, when I lived in a small travel trailer at a national forest campsite located approximately 2 and a quarter miles from Rice Village. Most of my time, however, was spent either in the village itself or accompanying residents of the community on their various activities outside the village. I returned to the community during the fall and early winter for short visits in order to gather supplementary data.

My initial contact with Rice Village was a brief "reconnaissance mission" one afternoon during the Memorial Day weekend of 1966. I

127

drove through the community and chatted for a few minutes with 2 individuals who happened to be standing outside their houses. My purpose on this trip was to get an idea of the physical layout and population size of the community.

My second and much more dramatic contact with Rice Village came the day I arrived to begin my summer fieldwork. The circumstances surrounding this formal introduction are perhaps the stuff that field-workers' dreams are made of. The situation could not have been better had it been planned. I walked into Rice Village and found the residents in the midst of a wake for an elderly man who had died the previous night. For me, this unhappy circumstance was quite fortunate in a number of respects. In the first place, I was introduced at once to the community as a whole and did not have to become acquainted with people one at a time; consequently, I was not associated initially with particular individuals and, thereby, reduced the possibility of negatively influencing my relations with others. Second, by attending the wake I could move rather smoothly into my role as participant observer, since one's presence at a wake or funeral does not have to be explained. In addition, I am certain that my attendance at the wake that afternoon, and at the night-long peyote ritual that followed, was of immeasurable value in establishing rapport and in reducing the barriers that exist between a white outsider and the rural Chippewa Indian villagers. It is significant that the Rice Villagers later introduced me to nonvillage Indians, not as a graduate student doing fieldwork in the community, but simply as having "stayed for the meeting [the peyote ceremony] when Paul Martin died."

Initially, traditional participant observation was my most important research technique. It was used exclusively for the first part of my fieldwork and remained an important research tool for the duration of my stay, even after more standardized forms of data collection had been initiated. I began by visiting each household daily in an attempt to acquaint myself with the pattern of life in the community and to accustom the villagers to my presence. When possible, I participated with members of each household in their daily activities, including berry picking, riding into town to pick up supplies, going to the Indian Hospital, attending powwows and other celebrations, baby-sitting, and just sitting around and chatting. The small size of the community allowed me to become quite well acquainted with all of the residents.

In addition to participant observation, I was able to collect data through informal, directed interviews and taped interviews, as well as through administration of a lengthy interview schedule to each household head and spouse.

The physical setting

Rice Village is located in north central Minnesota within the boundaries of the Broken Reed Reservation. The reservation covers 12,320 acres of tribally owned land and 13,922 acres that are held as allotments by individual Chippewa. There are 8 major communities within the Broken Reed Reservation area: Rice Village, James Lake, Acout Lake, Partridge, Wicket, Linder, Waboose Bay, and Elk River. Some of these will be described later in more detail as they relate to Rice Village.

Rice Village is an 80-acre square plot approximately three-eighths of a mile on each side (see Figure 4.1). The community lies one-eighth of a mile north of the only major thoroughfare in the area, a federal highway, to which the community is connected by a pair of winding dirt roads that pass over the property of a local resort owner.

The village can be described as physically isolated. Although only 4 miles from the nearest incorporated community, the village is 16 miles from the nearest supermarket, laundry service, commercial entertainment, high school, and medical care facility, and more than 30 miles from the population centers that provide it with legal aid, welfare, clothing, automobiles, home furnishings, and other specialized commercial items. Visits to family and friends must be made by automobile and often involve traveling considerable distances. The absence of electricity and direct mail delivery to Rice Village reinforce its physical isolation. Villagers must travel 4 miles to the nearest available phone, and the same distance to pick up their mail. In winter, access to the community from the highway is often difficult and sometimes impossible, since the community must wait for road plows from the Bureau of Indian Affairs.

Paralleling the northern east-west boundary of the village is a fairly passable logging road. It is used quite regularly by the U.S. Forest Service for access to some of their operations in the national forest lands, as well as by some of the loggers working on privately owned land to the north and west of Rice Village.

The village contains 2 distinct clusters of dwellings, to which I will refer hereafter as the southwest section and the northeast section. The first occupies the center and southwest portion of the property and consists of 5 occupied homes, an abandoned house, 4 privies, a storage shed, a woodshed, and an uncompleted garage. The community ceme-

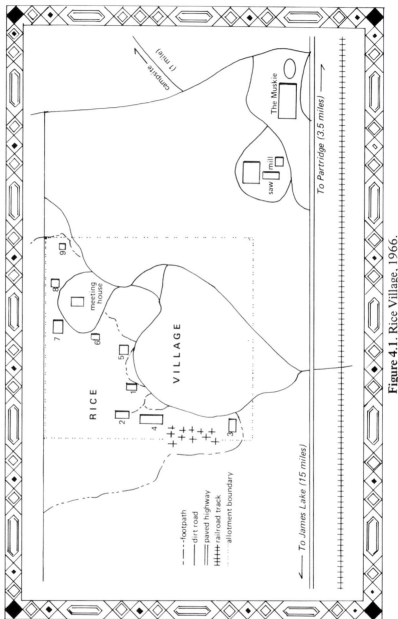

Figure 4.1. Rice Village, 1966.

tery is located directly to the south and east of the dwellings. The houses are all built on the west and north sides of a semicircle formed by a dirt road about one-quarter mile long.

The northeast cluster of the village consists of 4 occupied houses, a small, unoccupied house trailer, 4 privies, and the largest structure in the entire community, a 2-story community "meeting house," where peyote rituals and other communitywide gatherings are held. Three of the houses are located on the outside of the circle formed by the road leading into the section. The fourth house is built about 300 yards to the east of the circle and is connected to it by a narrow road. The meeting house is located inside the circle in the southwest quarter.

In the southwest section, all of the land up to and including the cemetery, the areas between buildings and directly behind them, and the large area within the semicircle are kept free of brush and neatly mown throughout the summer. In the northeast section, similarly, the areas between and directly in back of the houses around the circle, as well as the land within the circle, are maintained. Some low brush borders the short road leading to the fourth house in the section, but the area surrounding this house is also kept clear. The land is generally level, but there are slightly higher elevations in a few areas; in fact, the northeast section is located along the slope and top of a small hill.

Natural resources in the community

The land on which the community is located and the surrounding area are not particularly rich in resources. A timber survey map indicates that the northeastern quarter of the community's property is covered with jack pine saplings of medium density. Most of the southern half is open grassland, while in the extreme northwestern portion there is a stand of aspen and paper birch saplings of poor density. Immediately bordering the southern boundary of the community is a stand of jack pine of good density.

Although trees are occasionally cut for firewood, most of the wood for this purpose is provided by dead or fallen trees, and residents make little use of the limited timber resources of the community. One male informant claimed that the property has never contained any stands of trees that would be worth the effort to cut commercially. Each fall one or 2 bushels of pinecones are gathered for making Christmas wreaths. However, the woman most concerned with producing wreaths reported that cones are rather scarce on village property, and she prefers to gather them elsewhere.

Other vegetable resources located on community property are only slightly more abundant. Throughout the summer, a variety of wild fruit is gathered within the boundaries of the community. In late June and early July, juneberries (a purplish berry slightly larger than a blueberry) are gathered. During midsummer, low-bush blueberries and raspberries are fairly abundant. A few clumps of blackberry plants bear fruit in late August and early September, and some wild plums are harvested. About this time, pin cherries also ripen. Understandably, villagers do not limit their fruit gathering to community property.

There are no streams, lakes, or any other aboveground water sources in Rice Village or on the land adjacent to it. The community's water supply is drawn from two wells, one in each section.

Buildings

The houses in Rice Village are fairly uniform in both materials and construction methods, but there is some diversity in size and floor plan. Without exception, the houses are one-story, uninsulated, wooden frame and plank buildings. Six of them have been covered with a tar paper siding; the wood planking of the others is exposed, unpainted, and unprotected. All of the houses have pitched tar-papered roofs, except for Household 3, the smallest building, which has a flat tar-papered roof.

Each of the smallest houses is composed of a single room 8 feet wide and 12 feet long; the largest is a multiroom, 14-by-24-foot dwelling (see Figure 4.2). Five of the houses have been partitioned into 2 or more distinct rooms. The simplest of these has a division between the kitchen and bedroom areas; the most complex has 2 bedrooms, a kitchen, a separate living room, a storage room, and a small enclosed porch. All of the houses that have been sectioned into separate rooms have wallboard partitions from floor to ceiling.

The meeting house is the largest building in the community (14 by 28 feet) and the only one with a second story; its construction, however, is similar to that of the dwellings. In fact, the meeting house served as a private dwelling prior to being enlarged and utilized by the whole community.

The privies are small, simple, unpainted wooden structures, located in the brush behind the houses they serve.

There is one garage (utilized by Household 4), which is constructed of the same wood planking and tar paper siding as the houses. Household 4 also has a small shed directly to the northeast for storage of construction materials and tools during the summer and firewood during the winter.

The only other utilized building is an 8-by-12-foot structure in the southwest section. Villagers said that it had originally been constructed as a house but had never been used for that purpose. Today it is used for storage by all of the households in this section of the village.

There is also a vacant house in the southwest section, which in 1966 had been standing in disuse for 2 years. It had served as the dwelling for members of Household 5 before their present house in that section was built.

By local Indian standards the land and buildings of Rice Village are kept neat and in good repair. One nonvillage Indian commented that "it [Rice Village] is really kept up good for an Indian place."

The formation of Rice Village

In the short period between the 1820s and the 1880s, the southwestern Chippewa relinquished an overwhelming proportion of the lands they had captured from the Dakota. This was accomplished through various treaties of cession with the United States government whereby the Chippewa gave up all rights to occupy large tracts of land in the northern part of Minnesota.

One of these treaties, which in 1855 established the boundaries of the Broken Reed Reservation and several other reservations scattered throughout the northern part of the state, authorized the government to hold the 23,000 acres of land at Broken Reed in trust for the Indian group that occupied it. However, the possibility of Broken Reed becoming a closed, corporate entity, occupied and exploited solely by Indians, was eliminated by the Allotment Act of 1887, which specified that parcels of land could be allotted to any adult Indian who wanted land. The bill provided for the owner to receive clear title to the land, and consequently the right to sell all or part of it. Since much of the affected land contained valuable timber, there was a ready and tempting market for the new Indian landowners to consider. Many sold their land allotment to the timber interests. Today, only 19 percent of the original reservation land is still held by Indians, including both the land held by individuals and that collectively owned by the tribe (League of Women Voters of Minnesota 1962:24).

In 1887, one of these allotments was made to a Chippewa woman, *Way me tigosh e quay,* who lived on Bear Island, just off Maple Point, in Broken Reed Lake. Upon her death in 1908, this land (which she had never occupied) was inherited by her only son, *Song ah cumig.* At the time of his inheritance he was about 40, married, and the father of

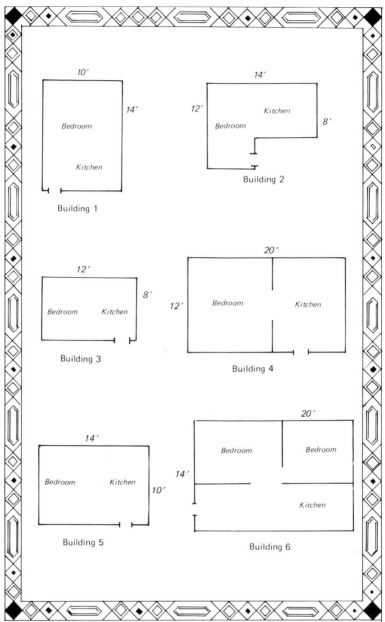

Figure 4.2. Floor plans of Rice Village buildings.

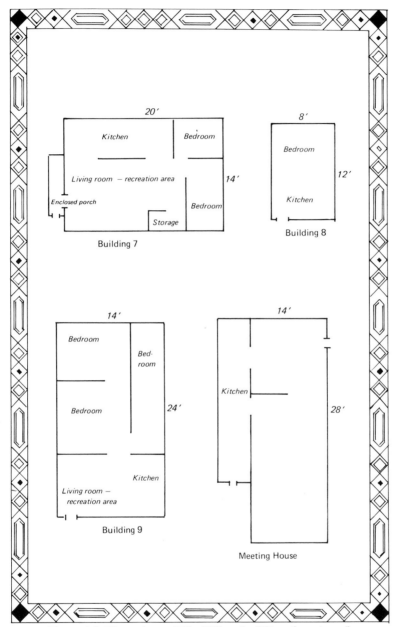

Figure 4.2. Floor plans of Rice Village buildings (*continued*).

several grown children. About 1912, he decided to move from Bear Island to his mother's allotment. His descendants who still occupy this land today claim that they have no idea what prompted his move. Some of the older people say that it was quite a daring thing to do at the time for various reasons: there were no good roads near the land, it was quite distant from the family's traditional home, and it required a good deal of clearing to make it habitable. At any rate, Song ah cumig, his wife, *Nay tah wub e quay,* all of their children, and the spouse of his oldest son moved to the allotment, founding the community that has come to be known as Rice Village.

With his sons, Song ah cumig cleared enough land on the allotment for dwellings, crops, and pasture, and made an access road to the property from the dirt highway. According to informants who remember the early days of the community, Song ah cumig and his family were relatively successful farmers. Despite the poor soil and the inhospitable climate of the area, the fields are said to have been cleared and planted with corn, and "there was no brush like there is now, so you could see clear over to where the railroad tracks are." They were also able to accumulate a small but good herd of horses, with one team for work and another for transportation.

After a few years the family had a fine 2-story log house (located near the site of Household 4), horse corrals (where the cemetery is today), a large barn for the animals, and a small shed where the women could do their weaving. A granddaughter of Song ah cumig described her grandfather's house as being quite grand. "It was like a white man's house, nicely built, with 2 stories. He didn't even build it all himself, but hired someone to come and help him."

The family prospered, with income from wages earned while working in the woods for other people and from their small, father-and-sons logging operation. Working for white timber men, Song ah cumig received an anglicized name. According to his granddaughter, "He used to have only an Indian name, but when he went to work he needed a white man's name to put on his payroll check, so they called him John Rice." She surmised that he was named after one of his coworkers. Whatever the source, the name "Rice" stuck, was passed on to his children, and provided the present-day name of the community.

This single family headed by John Rice gradually became a community as his children (3 sons, 2 daughters, and an adopted daughter) and grandchildren married and brought their spouses to live on the land, raising their families in separate household units.

The social setting

Rice Village is a tightly structured, closely knit, cooperative community. The cooperativeness of Rice Villagers is especially relevant in view of the abundance of literature describing the individualistic nature of Chippewa culture and personality.

It appears reasonable to assume that the basis for community solidarity in Rice Village has been the unique religious affiliation of its members. Undoubtedly, the peyote religion is the single most important element explaining Rice Village cohesiveness today. The history of the village stands in sharp contrast to that of most of the allotments that were made to Chippewa in this area. The typical pattern was for the land to be sold and proceeds divided among the heirs. Rice Village, on the other hand, has remained a viable, stable community for 4 generations, its lands undivided. Residence rights in the allotment on which the community is located are restricted to the lineal descendants of John Rice and their spouses. Thus, each member of this community stands in a kinship relationship, either affinal or consanguineal, to every other member.

At the time of my research, the population of Rice Village consisted of 41 individuals, organized into 9 households. Four of these households were of the nuclear family type, consisting of a married couple, with or without children. Two were composed of a female head of household and her children, 2 contained only a single individual each, and one was composed of a married couple and their grandson.

The individuals who reside in this community and the kinship relationships that exist among them are introduced in the following brief descriptions of the households in 1966. Household numbers refer to the location of households on the map in Figure 4.1 and will later be used to designate these units in the tabulation of economic data.

Household 2 consists of 33-year-old Tom Williams, his 25-year-old wife, Carrie, their son, Shanie, aged 4, and Carrie's 2 daughters by previous marriages. Tom, a Canadian Chippewa, is the first individual from outside the Broken Reed Reservation to have married into Rice Village. He met Carrie when he came to Rice Village 6 years ago, intending to take back knowledge about the peyote religion to his own reserve, where the peyote movement had just started. Tom works in the woods occasionally, but logging was not his occupation in Canada, and he dislikes it and is not very adept at it. He is sometimes employed in one of the local sawmills and likes this work much better. The Williams home is large by Rice Village standards, with a sleeping area separated

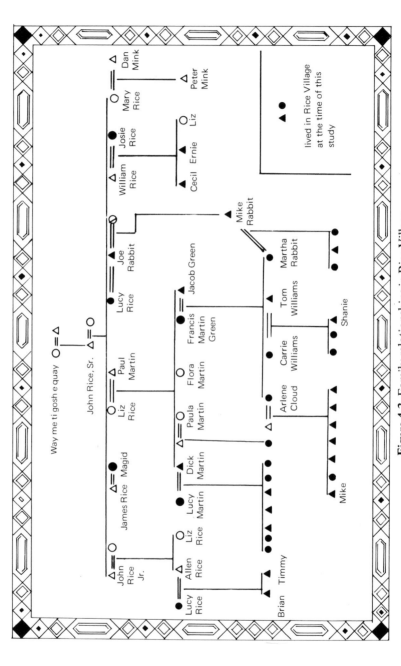

Figure 4.3. Family relationships in Rice Village.

from the kitchen and general living area. Carrie makes a special effort to keep her house in good order, decorating the walls with photographs and souvenirs of trips the family has taken.

Household 3 is headed by 25-year-old Mike Rabbit and includes his 23-year-old wife, Martha, and their 3 young children, ranging in age from 2 to 5 years. Their home is the smallest in the village, consisting of only one room. Mike works mostly in the woods, while Martha stays home with the children. Mike is very interested in automobiles and would like to become a garage mechanic. His talent in this field is apparently recognized by other members of the community, who turn to him when they are having mechanical problems with their cars. Martha is Carrie Williams's younger sister, and the 2 women are close friends.

Household 9—39-year-old Dick Martin, his wife, Lucy, and their 7 children, ranging in age from 3 to 15 years—constitutes the largest household in the community. It is also one of the most prosperous, since Dick has a permanent full-time job with a federal agency. Their house is the largest in the community, with 5 separate rooms, and they own the newest car in the village, a 4-year-old station wagon. Dick is liked and respected by other community members and often acts as a leader in an informal capacity in addition to serving as chairman of the community council. He is a large, easygoing, and friendly individual.

Household 5 consists of Joe and Lucy Rabbit, aged 45. Joe was born and raised in Waboose Bay, a fairly isolated and traditional Chippewa community on the Broken Reed Reservation. He married Lucy and came to live in Rice Village 10 years ago after the death of his first wife. Mike Rabbit is Joe's son by this first marriage. Joe and Lucy are the only members of the community who drink liquor in any quantity, which they did on 2 occasions during the course of my fieldwork. When Joe and Lucy Rabbit are drinking, other community members appear to tolerate them with good-natured reproach, because Joe is hard-working, generous, and cooperative, except for the relatively infrequent occasions when he is drunk. Joe works primarily in the woods, occasionally accompanied by Lucy, who peels the logs he has cut.

Household 4 includes Jacob Green, aged 53, his wife, Frances, who is Dick Martin's older sister, and Frances's 15-year-old grandson, Michael. Their spacious, 2-room house, with its neat and cozy atmosphere, serves as a gathering place for family and friends. Their grandchildren, their 2 daughters, Carrie and Martha, and Arlene Cloud, Frances's daughter by her first marriage, spend a good deal of time in the Green house, and visitors to the community are frequently entertained

there. Jacob is considered by other villagers to be the most knowledgeable man in the community about the peyote religion and is openly
praised for leading a proper life according to the "peyote way." Frances
and Jacob are extremely interested in the history and culture of American Indians, particularly in variations in aboriginal religious beliefs and
ceremonies. One of their most ardent hopes is to witness a Plains Indian
Sun Dance ceremony.

In Household 1, slender, 32-year-old Arlene Cloud presides over a
family group that includes 7 of her 8 children; Michael, her oldest son,
resides with her mother, Mrs. Green. The children range in age from 13
years to 6 months. Arlene supports her family with money she earns
from wild ricing and handicrafts and with her monthly welfare allowance. She has had a series of short-lived, unsuccessful marriages, the
last one terminating 6 months before the birth of her youngest child. She
is extremely fond of her large brood, though their care is a heavy burden.
Arlene says that she cannot understand women who give their children
up for adoption "as soon as the old man takes off. They may be trouble,
but they are all I have in the world." This sentiment is manifest in the
affectionate nature of her interaction with the children. Arlene gets along
well with her mother, Mrs. Green, and they spend a considerable amount
of time together; but a noticeably tense relationship exists between
Arlene and her stepfather, Jacob, and her two half-sisters, Carrie and
Martha.

Household 7 is also headed by a female—53-year-old Lucy Rice, a
widow with 2 sons, Timmy and Brian, aged 13 and 14, respectively. Lucy
is the village entrepreneur, devoting her time to a variety of economic
activities. Her business acumen and money-making abilities have made
her household one of the most prosperous in the village. Although these
capabilities are admired by other community members, Lucy is frequently criticized for being too aggressive and "bossy" and for "trying
to run everything."

Josie Rice, the 66-year-old widow of John Rice's son William,
occupies Household 6. Hers is one of the larger houses in the community,
and she lives alone now that her 3 children are grown. Despite her
arthritis and diabetes, Mary is able to supplement her federal disability
income with money she earns from the sale of intricately braided rugs.

In Household 8 is Mrs. Emma Rice, the 75-year-old widow of John
Rice's son James. She is commonly referred to by her Indian name,
Magid. She has lived in Rice Village for almost its entire history and is
the only person in the village who does not speak any English. When her

husband was alive, they lived in the large building that is now the meeting house. Never having had children, Magid lives alone in a tiny 2-room dwelling. Her strength and energy are a source of pride to the whole village: she still chops her own firewood, makes handicrafts, and baby-sits for the other women.

Community cooperative activities

Much of the cooperative activity of Rice Village revolves around the maintenance of community property—the landscape, wells, cemetery, and meeting house. When any of these properties require attention, everyone joins in. For example, when the pump in the southwest quarter broke down, members of every household, with the exception of the 2 elderly widows, participated in its repair. In the initial stages of difficulty, everyone examined the pump, trying to determine the source of the problem. Even Dick Martin and Lucy Rice (who were not affected by the crisis since they live in the northeast quarter, which has its own well) inspected the pump and added their opinions to the collective diagnosis. After lengthy discussion, the group finally agreed that the pump would have to be dug up so that the bit could be examined. Digging began the following morning around 8:30, and at one time or another during the day every adult male in the community took his turn at the shovel. When it became clear that the bit could not be repaired, Lucy Rice volunteered to purchase a replacement when she went into James Lake that day. By afternoon the new bit was installed. The next morning 3 of the men who live in the southwest quarter, aided by Arlene Cloud's 2 oldest sons, filled in the hole around the pump. This pattern of cooperation is representative of community interaction.

A community treasury, or "emergency fund," as it is called, is another example of mutual support in Rice Village. The fund is maintained through contributions from individuals in the community and through money raised from bingo games, raffles, and special sales. These sales, which feature handicrafts made in the community, are held to raise money to purchase necessary equipment or to maintain community property, such as the bit for the pump and roofing materials for the meeting house. When an individual household needs cash in a hurry, emergency loans can be obtained from the community treasury. Assistance in meeting funeral expenses is perhaps the most common use of such loans.

Another important communitywide activity is the peyote meeting, which will later be described in detail. Some peyote meetings are sponsored by the community as a whole, but even when a meeting is sponsored by an individual who accepts responsibility for organizing and financing it, the rest of the community is expected to cooperate. The village women cook and serve the food, the men donate various items of ritual paraphernalia, and the various households contribute food and lend cooking utensils. Generally, the cost and organizational responsibilities of community-sponsored meetings are met on a fairly equal basis by all of the households in the village.

Cooperation among households

In Rice Village, the more plentiful resources are shared among households. For example, the location of a particularly good berry patch will be shared with other households, and several families will go berry picking together. When berries are taken to produce stands to be sold, it is not uncommon for members of one family to act as "agents" for a neighbor.

Wild ricing season is a time of heightened economic cooperation among households. A villager with a good car and boat racks will not merely obtain a ricing boat for his neighbor from the rice buyer; he will argue with the buyer if the buyer attempts to assign one of the less desirable boats to the absentee. Individuals who inspect the rice beds or who happen to pick up a piece of news about the condition of a particular bed will share this information with others in the community. Baby-sitting is another important form of cooperation at this time. Teenagers who do not go ricing will care for the children of households in which there are no older siblings. The two elderly women, Magid and Mary Rice, baby-sit regularly during the ricing season.

Neighboring households also provide financial assistance, particularly where small amounts of money are involved. If someone needs cash very badly, he can generally find a villager, especially among those who have regular employment, from whom he can borrow money or, at least, with whom he can pawn something of value.

Foodstuffs for which no cash outlay has been made are shared quite freely. Such foods include venison, berries, and wild fruits not intended for sale and surplus commodities received from the County Welfare Department. Utensils, tools, and domestic items, such as flatirons, brooms, pots, and more personal items, circulate among different households. In the case of some of these items, the original owner is no longer even known. Safety pins, sewing notions, hairpins, combs, and some articles of clothing are commonly shared among the women.

While individual ownership of children's toys and games is more clearly established, these items, too, are freely shared. For example, the one Monopoly game in the village, owned by the Rice children, is lent without question to any adult or older child who wishes to use it.

People who can afford to purchase more costly items are usually willing to share them with neighbors, often without compensation. For example, car owners run errands for others and give rides to villagers who do not have cars. The few portable radios and 2 portable phonographs are frequently lent to other villagers by their owners. Similarly, the 2 power mowers in the community are available to all of the households, for maintaining the lawns around private homes, in the cemetery, around the wells, and around the meeting house, at no charge to the user.

The nuclear family is the basis of most households in Rice Village. In times of economic or other crises, however, resources have been pooled and extended-family households formed. In the early years of the settlement of the village, John Rice, his children, and their families formed one large household unit—but only until enough land had been cleared and materials accumulated to build separate houses for each nuclear family. More recently, when Frances Green's mother died, her father moved into Frances's home and lived there until his death. Mike and Martha Rabbit lived with Mike's family when they were first married while they saved money to build their own house. However, situations such as these are the exception and not the rule in Rice Village.

With so much interaction and interdependence between families, it is not surprising that their daily activities are closely interconnected. Every member of the community has full knowledge of the activities, problems, and plans of virtually everyone else. There is little that a person can do or say that is not soon common knowledge. Villagers are usually vocal about and at times critical of the behavior of their neighbors. Thus, the threat of gossip and, in severe cases, social ostracism and withholding of cooperation serves to curb unacceptable behavior.

The community council

As the community grew, the need for a formalized structure for decision making and planning was recognized and a community council was established. Its members are all the adult males of the village. Although women normally attend meetings of the council, they do not participate in the formal discussion and decision making. The council is presided over by an elected chairman and vice-chairman, who are aided by a secretary-treasurer.

The qualifications for holding high offices were at issue and under discussion at the time of my research. Paul Martin, who had been chairman for 12 years, had recently died. It was agreed that his son Dick, who had been vice-chairman, would succeed as council chairman. However, the vice-chairmanship then became a contested position. Some individuals felt that Jacob Green, who is widely admired and respected, would be the best choice. However, Jacob is not a lineal descendent of John Rice and thus not an heir. Some contended that this made him ineligible to be chairman even though he could still become vice-chairman; others argued that being an heir was a requirement for holding either position. Since there are currently no adult male heirs other than Dick Martin, the vice-chairmanship will ultimately go to Jacob Green or to one of the women.

Unfortunately, the council did not meet during the period of my research, perhaps due to the transition between officers. Apparently meetings are not held frequently even under normal circumstances. The consensus of informants is that meetings are called only "when there's something big that needs to be talked over and decided." In the past, decisions have involved the issues of bringing electricity into the village, appealing to the Bureau of Indian Affairs to clear snow from the roads leading into the community, making repairs on the meeting house, permitting outsiders to be buried in the village cemetery, and deciding whether bingo is an appropriate way to raise money for the community emergency fund.

Relations with the outside world

Rice Villagers tend to isolate themselves socially as a community through their attitudes, behaviors, and the infrequency of their interaction with individuals and institutions outside the village. Even among the other Indians on the Broken Reed Reservation, very little is known about Rice Village and its practice of Peyotism. Those Indians who do know something of the community express generally similar attitudes, which can best be characterized as "wary." However, there are great differences among these Indian outsiders in actual knowledge of the peyote activities. At one extreme are those who express little knowledge about Rice Village other than the belief that "something strange goes on over there"; at the other extreme are those who know a good deal about Peyotism and its associated ritual but who "never quite could get up enough nerve to go to one of their meetings."

Most villagers are aware of the cautious attitudes of the non-

Peyotists, but they tend to overemphasize the hostility of outsiders. Some of the older people tell stories of being outcasts at school. Villagers also claim that neither of the two nearest local Indian councils (in Partridge and James Lake) is willing to represent their community. This discrimination is attributed to their practice of Peyotism. Thus a barrier exists between Rice Villagers and other Chippewa on the reservation, undoubtedly maintained in part by the exaggerated conceptions of Rice Villagers about the attitudes of outsiders. In addition, Rice Villagers tend to look down on some of the habits of the non-Peyotists. Using the stereotypic descriptions one usually hears from white people, they characterize most Indians in the area as drunken, lazy, dirty, and immoral. Abstinence from alcohol is a requirement of Peyotism that Rice Villagers largely observe.

Values and attitudes in themselves do not limit social interaction but rather the behavior and structural institutions associated with these values. The boundary-maintaining mechanisms that serve as the behavioral counterparts of attitudes are revealed in the amount of time Rice Village residents spend in communities outside the village, in their patterns of friendship, social visiting, and selection of marriage partners, and in the formal and informal requirements for membership in their community. The frequency and purposes of visits to other communities illustrate the cohesiveness and separateness that villagers maintain.

The communities most frequently visited by Rice Villagers are Partridge, located 4 miles to the east, and James Lake, 15 miles to the west. Partridge is visited almost daily by most of the Rice Village adults, and Rice Village children attend school there. Gasoline and minor grocery items are purchased in Partridge, mail is received at its post office, and sawmills employing Rice Village men are located in this community. James Lake is visited at least once a week by all the adults but one. They patronize its supermarkets, laundromats, movie theater, hardware store, and other specialized commercial establishments, as well as the U.S. Public Health Service Indian Hospital. Rice Village teenagers attend high school in James Lake.

Maple Point is the community visited with the next most frequency by Rice Villagers. An isolated community on the shore of Broken Reed Lake, it is located 25 miles from the village, about half of which must be traveled on an unpaved road. The Maple Point area is considered historically significant from two perspectives. It has been a Chippewa settlement for as long as 150 years and, as the original home of John Rice, is regarded by the villagers as "the homeland of our fathers." In addition, it was the scene of a historic battle between Indians and whites during frontier times. Contacts with this community are of an entirely different nature from those with any of the others. Strong social ties are maintained with Maple Point inhabitants because many of them are kinsmen of Rice Villagers and several have become active Peyotists. Except during ricing season, when Rice Villagers harvest the excellent rice beds found off the shores of Maple Point, all visits to Maple Point are made for social reasons—to attend peyote meetings, birthday parties, and picnics and to visit friends and relatives.

North City, Big Run, and Trotter are visited somewhat less frequently, although at least several times a year and, for some individuals, as often as once a month. These three communities can be grouped together according to the functions they serve for Rice Villagers. Each is a small city or town located within 40 miles of Rice Village, and each offers specialized commercial items and services not available in James Lake, such as automobiles, "school clothes," tools, and electrical appliances. Rice Villagers rely on the funeral home in Big Run, obtain medical services in North City that are not available at James Lake Indian Hospital, and deal with officials of the county welfare system in Trotter.

Locales that are visited once or twice a year by most adult villagers include Minneapolis–St. Paul; Hayward, Wisconsin; Fort Totten, North Dakota; and the Long Plains Reserve in Canada. The Wisconsin, North Dakota, and Canadian communities are visited exclusively for the purpose of attending peyote meetings. Attendance at peyote meetings is also the main reason that Rice Villagers visit the Twin Cities, although trips are occasionally made there for medical care or for social visits to friends and relatives. The 2 largest cities in northeastern Minnesota, both located less than 200 miles from Rice Village, are almost never visited, according to informants.

Wicket and the Deer Lake Reservation may be grouped together because Rice Villagers make yearly visits to each for essentially the same purpose—attendance at large powwows held during the summer months. However, except for a young girl or 2 from the village who may don "jingle dresses" and dance shyly around the ring a couple of times, Rice Villagers are spectators at these celebrations rather than active participants. Apart from Deer Lake, other Minnesota reservations are seldom visited—or even discussed—by any of the Rice Villagers.

Thus several communities of varying size and composition located within or near the Broken Reed Reservation are visited solely to obtain commercial, educational, recreational, and medical services not available in the village. Travel to more distant communities that are visited regularly, although less frequently, is primarily for the purpose of attending ceremonies connected with the peyote religion. In more personal kinds of day-to-day relationships and activities, such as friendship, social visiting, and selection of marriage partners, the range of nonvillagers with whom members of Rice Village interact appears to be limited almost exclusively to Peyotists and relatives from Maple Point. During my fieldwork I observed that the nonvillagers visited in their homes by Rice Villagers were almost exclusively relatives and long-time family friends at Maple Point. Furthermore, only one of the persons interviewed, when asked to name his or her best friend, named someone who was not from either Maple Point or Rice Village.

Friendship patterns among the children in the village are similar to those of the adults. They play almost exclusively with each other. When the older children were questioned about friends they had in school, they all replied that they had none. The only nonvillage children who visited or were visited by Rice Village youngsters during the summer of my fieldwork were cousins from Maple Point.

The marriage patterns of those individuals who have spent most of their lives in the community are consistent with the overall pattern of interpersonal relations with persons outside the village. Of the 16 lineal descendants of John Rice who were raised in the community and have married, 10 have taken spouses from Maple Point, 2 have married members of another isolated Broken Reed Reservation community, and 2 in the most recent generation of adults have taken spouses from a peyote group in Canada. The remaining 2 descendants married non-Peyotist Chippewa from the Broken Reed Reservation; significantly, neither of these villagers was living in Rice Village at the time of marriage, and neither resided in the village for any extended length of time after marriage.

Social barriers to interaction with the outside are also reinforced by the formal and informal requirements for membership in the community. Throughout the history of Rice Village, its inhabitants have claimed that only the heirs to the original allotment and their immediate families are entitled to live there, and they appear to be fairly adamant about enforcing this rule. Informants reported that at one time the wife of one of the heirs tried to bring her sister to live in the village, but "we made things pretty hard on her [the sister], and finally she went back where she belongs."

Just prior to my fieldwork, several members of the community had been approached by a member of the Broken Reed Reservation Business Committee, who inquired about the possibility of leasing community land as the site for a low-cost federal housing project for Indians. The villagers were told that they would be given first choice of the many houses that would be built on village property, before the option to buy houses would be extended to other Indian families from the reservation. Since several of the families in the village have openly expressed a desire to improve their homes or build new ones, this would appear to be an attractive offer. For leasing their land—not selling it outright—villagers would have the opportunity to live in new, modern homes with many of the conveniences that they do not now have and have no reasonable hope of obtaining in the future. Despite this, the proposal was flatly rejected by all residents but one. Rice Villagers would simply not agree to relinquish the management of their land to outsiders, and the idea of outsiders coming to live in their community was even less appealing.

Active Peyotism appears to be an informal requirement for membership in the Rice Village community, although informants deny that anyone with legal residence rights in the village would be kept out simply because he or she was not a Peyotist. It has been the case throughout the history of the community, however, that the heirs who have emigrated have been those who either never became active peyote members or married non-Peyotists who did not convert.

From the restrictive nature of extravillage interaction it should not be inferred that social relationships within Rice Village are completely amicable and tension-free. In Rice Village, as in any human community, conflict between individuals is inevitable. Long-standing differences between villagers surface from time to time in the form of verbal and even physical battles, but these disagreements seem to occur solely at the level of one-to-one interaction. Although the physical plan of the village, with its 2 distinct residential clusters, might be conducive to the formation or indicate the existence of factions or subgroups divided over specific issues, this is apparently not the case. Patterns of interaction completely crosscut the physical divisions. Rice Village differs from other Indian communities on the reservation in its high degree of cohesiveness at the community level, which is manifest in the corporate ownership of various kinds of property, in the maintenance of a mechanism for decision making, and in the active participation of all community members in a single ritual and belief system. Despite the economic independence of nuclear families in Rice Village, relationships among the households appear to be definitely more cooperative and interdependent than those of most other Chippewa communities.

The economic setting

For families in Rice Village—indeed for many families, both Indian and white, who live on Broken Reed Reservation—employment at a single job seldom pays enough to support a family. Rather, the widespread lack of economic opportunity characteristic of the area necessitates the exploitation of a combination of environmental and monetary resources in order to eke out even the minimum required for a family's subsistence. For purposes of description, the sources of cash income can be divided into 4 categories: occupations or wage work of male household heads, wild rice harvesting, welfare, and miscellaneous sources of cash income.

Occupations or wage work

At the time that the household interview schedule was administered, 4 of the 5 male household heads were employed in the logging industry, either in cutting or mill work; the fifth was employed in an unskilled civil service job in forestry. Both mill work and logging are backbreaking, nonsteady occupations, providing relatively low remuneration. All of the men who do mill work and logging are employed by 2 small-time contractors in the nearby town of Partridge. These contractors, who bid for the opportunity to cut particular areas of secondary growth in the national forest, hire local people to cut, stack, and peel the wood on the lots, furnishing them with power saws and other logging equipment. In addition, both men operate their own small mills.

Employees of the mill and logging concerns emphasize how strenuous and hazardous woods work is and how industriously one must work to earn even a small income. "Out in the woods you can't make it sitting on a stump" is typical of the comments evoked by questions on woods work. However, all agree that there are positive aspects of this occupation, such as working outdoors and "being your own boss." The mill owners claim that a hard-working man can find full-time employment in logging 12 months a year, earning around 45 dollars a day. While this may be true under ideal circumstances, further questioning of the mill owners and workers revealed that this is not usually the case.

Climatic factors such as deep snow, muddiness at spring breakup, and excessive heat during the summer make it impossible to work for days and weeks at a time. Furthermore, due to problems in availability and accessibility of lots to be cut, there are times during the year when the contractors simply do not have work for the loggers. Finally, the 45 dollars per day earnings quoted by the contractors is regarded as unrealistic by men in Rice Village; according to them, 15 to 25 dollars more accurately represents the daily average. (The wages reported here are 1966 amounts.)

Mill work is perhaps a bit less strenuous and hazardous than is logging, but it too is subject to seasonal factors that make it nonsteady. In addition, working at the mill does not permit the same flexibility in an individual's schedule. The mill is actually in operation only 7 months of the year, from March to mid-June and from September to mid-December. Opportunity for employment is further limited within the period of operation by the closing of the mill for an occasional few days when there is not enough wood to saw or by the absence of a key member of a crew. Each of the 2 Partridge mills employs 6 people, the minimum number required to keep it in operation. Workmen include a highly experienced sawyer, who oversees the whole operation and earns $2.50 per hour; an edger, who requires about a week's training and earns $1.85 per hour; and a log turner, carriage stringer, lumber piler, and saw trimmer, who can ordinarily learn the necessary skills in a few hours and are paid $.75 to $1.50 an hour, depending on experience and performance. The men from Rice Village are normally employed in the 4 lowest skill and pay positions, with the exception of Joe Rabbit, who has been trained as an edger.

Dick Martin, the one male head of household who works for the Forest Service, is the only member of the community with steady, full-time employment. His work is usually confined to the national forest area around Partridge, where he assists in cleaning and maintaining the picnic grounds and campsites that his station operates, aids in clearing and in experimental projects conducted by the Forest Service, and works as a fire fighter during the late summer and fall.

The seasonal nature of lumbering and mill work and the lack of other economic opportunities in the area are evidenced in the job histories of the men in Rice Village. All of them show frequent and extensive periods of unemployment during their adult lives, and none of them has ever had any other type of work experience. Responses to the questionnaire item "How many weeks did you work last year?" revealed a median of 30 weeks for the 5 male household heads. However, no one except Dick Martin worked "for a full year ever."

Due to the instability of woods and mill work, income is low. In 1965, Rice Villagers employed in lumber-connected industries earned from $325 to $1,100. The average income from mill work and logging is around $700 per year—25 to 55 percent of the total family income. In contrast, Dick Martin earns more than twice as much as any of the lumbermen. His income from the Forest Service represents 80 percent of his household's total.

Wild rice harvesting

To supplement their income from employment, most households in Rice Village rely on a traditional Chippewa staple—wild rice. At one time wild rice accounted for a major portion of the Chippewa diet; today, most of the wild rice harvested is sold to whites at a substantial profit. Despite this change in their cultural pattern, the Indians of Rice Village still look forward to the wild rice season, not only for the financial rewards, but also for the enjoyment and good times associated with the harvest.

Although wild rice season does not begin until late August or early September, ricing is a frequent topic of conversation and the subject of stories and jokes throughout the summer. As the season draws near, toward the end of the summer, the anticipation heightens and preparations begin.

Due to its scarcity and the high demand for it, wild rice is under the control of state conservation authorities who determine when ricing is to begin, what lakes will be open, and for how long. In addition, they issue a $3 permit which must be purchased by anyone who rices on or off the reservation. The competence, fairness, and judgment of the authorities are widely debated before and during the ricing season. Although most informants recognize the need for a set of restrictions in the interest of maintaining the productivity of the rice beds, many question the formation and enforcement of the restrictions by officials who they feel are either incompetent or are guided by vested interests.

The more technical aspects of the actual harvesting procedure are characteristic topics of discussion during the period immediately preceding the ricing season. Debates about the most efficient techniques of poling and knocking, the merits of a wider canoe, and the advantages of lake versus river beds, for example, are frequently heard in the village. The weather, too, is a source of much concern: "When you are under that rice cover on a hot day there's just no air, especially for the one who is knocking. It's just hot. And yet, when it's a cold day, it just seems colder when you're under that rice. You don't get no sunshine." The villagers also discuss the dangers involved in ricing, retelling stories of lightweight canoes breaking loose from the towline far out on the lake on a windy day and of the tragic drownings that have occurred. Of course, the condition of the all-important rice beds is the most frequent subject of speculation: will the rice be ripe, and, if it is, will the beds be high enough?

All preparation for the ricing season is not so serious. Ricers eagerly looking forward to this time of year recount comic scenes of individuals getting their boats tangled up and having to swim back to shore and of those who "bring so much lunch along that they never get around to ricing." The villagers make plans for the good times they will have and the things they will purchase with money earned from ricing.

At least 2 weeks before the season opens, ricers begin readying their boats and testing them in nearby lakes. All of the people in Rice Village, with the exception of Lucy Rice and her sons, borrow boats (canoes or flat-bottom rice boats) from one of the local rice buyers. Although several of the other households own boats, they prefer to borrow from the buyers. Use of a buyer's boat theoretically places an individual under obligation to sell all the rice gathered in that boat to the buyer; but buyers do not make any attempt to enforce this rule.

The simple tools required for harvesting the rice are taken from storage, examined, replaced if necessary, and made ready for use. The long poles used for propelling and maneuvering the rice boats, which serve as props for clotheslines most of the year, and the wooden "knockers" used for knocking the grains into the boat are placed beside the boat in a prominent position in front of the house.

Selecting a suitable ricing outfit is another preseason preparation. During the year, each household acquires a large store of used clothing at rummage sales, purchased primarily for making quilts and rag rugs. Prior to ricing, however, almost everyone checks his supply of "rags" for warm or waterproof garments. Outfitting is often conducted in a spirit of mock elegance, with individuals choosing and modeling the worn and ill-fitting garments as though they were preparing for a fancy-dress ball.

The similarity between preparing for ricing and for a social event does not end with selecting the right clothes. One must also have a partner. All informants agreed that it is best to rice with someone in the same household, because then "all the money can be kept in the family."

The general pattern, then, is for husband and wife, siblings, or parent and child to rice together. Only 2 people in Rice Village are unable to follow this preferred pattern and must find ricing partners outside their own households.

Just before the season begins, men from the village usually go out to inspect the rice beds in the lakes and rivers where they will be ricing. Those who have not bought their ricing permits purchase them and find out which lakes will be open on the first day and for how many hours. On the night before the first day of ricing, the final preparations are completed; those without cars make arrangements to ride with neighbors, and boats and equipment are loaded to ensure an early start in the morning.

During the ricing season, a typical day is composed of a complex of activities, as illustrated by the following description of September 3, 1966, a day early in the season.

Everyone in the village is up and around by 7:00 a.m. After a hurried breakfast, people congregate sleepily in front of their houses, making last-minute checks to see that all of the equipment is loaded and the boats are fastened securely. Children are taken to the households where they will stay for the day or, if they are to stay at home with older siblings, are again warned to stay out of trouble. Those too young or too old to go ricing stand quietly in the background, watching the preparations of the ricers. Today is the first day that beds will be open just offshore at Maple Point on Broken Reed Lake. Ricing begins at 10:00 a.m. sharp; so by 8:15 the ricers leave the village in a caravan of cars, giving themselves ample time to travel the 30 miles and launch their boats.

At Maple Point the caravan disbands, each group going to the boat landing operated by the rice buyer whose boats they have borrowed. There are at least 125 cars in the parking lot, and many more are parked along the road leading to it. The landing is bustling with activity: people are unloading their boats, launching them, and making arrangements to be towed out to the beds; some are still trying to find partners. When 8 to 12 boats are in the water at the landing, they tie up to an outboard operated by the buyer and are towed out to the rice beds. These trains of canoes, slowly moving toward the rice beds offshore, make a picturesque scene in the morning light. A few pairs of ricers paddle out themselves, using their poles kayak-style.

By 9:30 most of the boats are at the rice beds, waiting for the signal to begin ricing. Activity out on the lake seems subdued in contrast to the joking, horseplay, and loud talking that goes on at the boat landing. A few people quietly sing Chippewa songs; one fellow yells out, "Come on, all you Indians, let's get together and drive the white man out," but no one responds to his call. Impatiently, someone shouts "Let's go, it's ten o'clock," but no one moves until the proper authorities give the signal. Then there is an immediate flurry of activity and ricing begins in earnest. The poler, standing at the stern of the boat, maneuvers it through the shallow waters and high stalks of rice while his partner, seated in the middle of the boat, knocks the grains of rice from the stalks and into the bow of the boat. Since this is the first day that these beds are open, ricing will be limited to 2 hours. The ricers are therefore intent on harvesting all they can and spend little time talking to their partners or to people in other boats. Later in the season, when ricing will be permitted up to 6 hours a day, the pace will slacken and chatting will be frequent.

When the signal to stop ricing is given, the boats head toward the shore side of the rice beds, where the outboards are waiting to tow the ricers and their harvests back to the landing. There the boats are pulled from the water and the rice is placed in burlap sacks. The buyer has a pickup truck and a scale, easily identified by the throng of people crowded around it, waiting to sell their rice. Each ricer gets a receipt for the number of pounds of rice he has and takes it to the front of the truck to receive his cash payment. Since the beds are fresh and the rice is high on this particular day, most pairs of ricers have gathered between 85 and 100 pounds of rice; a few loads weigh as much as 150 pounds. At $1.25 per pound, most people are realizing a considerable return for their 2 hours of work. On their way home, many of the villagers stop in Portage, a town about halfway between Rice Village and Maple Point, for lunch in the cafe. Others stop in the tavern for a few beers.

Despite the fact that wild rice harvesting is limited to a few months each year and is regulated by licensing requirements, it provides as much as 50 percent of a household's annual cash income in Rice Village. The amount of money that can be earned by ricing is affected by a variety of factors: the strength and coordination of the team; knowledge of what beds are open and which have good rice; the overall quality of the crop for the particular year; and, of course, the current selling price. In 1965, for example, household incomes from ricing ranged from $150 (for a single female head of household who had had to split her profits with someone from another household) to $725 (for a household where an extremely effective husband and wife team pooled their profits with their teenaged grandson's share). Profits from wild rice according to house-

Table 4.1. Income from wild ricing

Household	1965 total	First 4 days of 1966
1[a]	$150	$ 50
2	500	410
3	700	228
4[b]	725	462
5	300	230
7[b]	700	300
9[b]	675	503

a. Only one ricer in household.
b. More than 2 ricers in household.

hold for 1965 and the first 4 days of the 1966 ricing season are shown in Table 4.1.

With the increased market demand for wild rice as a gourmet item and the resulting high prices paid to those who harvest it, it is not surprising that the Chippewa, and Rice Villagers in particular, are willing to forego the use of wild rice as a traditional food and to sell it "almost before it's out of the boat." In 1966, nonetheless, 5 of the 7 Rice Village households that harvested rice retained a small amount of their harvest (from 5 to 10 pounds of finished rice) for use in rituals and on special occasions.

Miscellaneous sources of cash income

In addition to wild rice, which is an outstanding economic opportunity because of the high return it yields for a modest investment of time and labor, various other natural resources must be utilized to maintain the thin cushion of economic security that is characteristic of life in Rice Village. These activities, primarily seasonal in nature, require a minimum of cash investment and vary considerably in the amount of income they provide. During the course of a year, household income may be partially derived from the sale of wild berries, fruits, and smoked fish, guiding hunters during deer-hunting season, the manufacture and sale of handicrafts and Christmas wreaths, and maple sugaring.

Throughout the summer months, several varieties of wild fruits and berries are gathered by Rice Villagers. Some of these are eaten fresh as treats and a small quantity is canned, but most of the harvest is sold. For some families, the sale of fruits and berries provides the only cash income during the summer months. Beginning in late June and continuing into mid-July, juneberries are gathered. Apparently there is not a commercial market for this type of berry, even though it is juicier than the blueberry and just as sweet; so juneberries are gathered mainly for home use. During midsummer, low-bush blueberries and raspberries ripen; these, especially the former, are picked primarily for sale. Toward the end of summer, blackberries and wild plums are harvested, but they are relatively scarce and do not provide as much income as do blueberries and raspberries. Pin cherries are also harvested and sold in early fall, but most are kept by villagers and used to make a bittersweet jam. Although much of the gathering is confined to the immediate vicinity, at times villagers travel 5 to 25 miles to other berry patches.

When berries are picked for family consumption rather than for sale, women and children are the usual participants. On these afternoon outings—often occurring at the spur of the moment—a small party of women followed by several children will tie small kettles to their waists and spend an hour or 2 leisurely picking berries on community property or along the logging road just north of the village. This activity is almost recreational in nature, yielding a couple of quarts of berries; not infrequently, most of them are consumed by the pickers before they make it back to their homes.

Picking berries for sale is a different matter. Most commonly it is an all-day affair involving a husband and wife or several families and planned the night before. The destination is usually determined in advance, on the basis of either a recent visit to the site or its reputation for plentiful crops. Long-sleeved shirts and slacks are worn by both men and women as protection against brush and mosquitoes. Lunch and a jug of water are carried, as well as all the large kettles and dishpans that can be spared. Although children are frequently brought along, there is a definite no-nonsense attitude and even a 3-year-old is given a small cup for gathering berries. Everyone picks intently, with little of the small talk that is characteristic of the casual berrying sessions.

Picking stops in late afternoon, or earlier if the containers are filled. The berry pickers want to get back to the village early enough to clean the berries and sell them that same day, before the blueberries "start to look wet" or the raspberries "get dark." Fresher berries may command a slightly higher price. If the yield is less than 10 or 12 quarts, villagers will go to the nearby summer homes of whites and try to sell their berries door-to-door. With larger harvests, they travel about 30 miles east to a large produce stand that usually buys the entire amount. During the period of my research, blueberries brought 45 to 55 cents per quart;

raspberries, 35 to 45 cents; blackberries, 60 cents; and wild plums, 50 cents. The numbers of quarts of berries picked by the 6 households that engaged in this activity, the amounts they earned, and the time spent in picking are shown in Table 4.2.

Picking berries and wild fruit is a tedious and often uncomfortable chore and does not yield a very high return. In addition, the men in the community tend to view such activities as "women's work," picking berries and fruit themselves only when there is an urgent need for cash and no other means of obtaining it. For example, one male informant had been laid off from his part-time work at the sawmill for about a week

Table 4.2. Income from wild fruit and berries

Household number	Quarts of berries	Quarts of plums	Total earned in entire 1966 season	Number of days spent berrying[a]
3	70	–	$ 35.50	4
2	120	4	63.00	9
4	181	6	103.55	7.25
1[b]	41	–	22.00	4
5	53	–	27.00	3
7[b]	77	3	38.00	1.5

a. Half-days are added together. This represents only the time spent actually picking berries. It does not include the time spent finding the location.
b. Only one adult picker in household. In all other cases there are 2.

before he did any berrying. He did so then only because he needed cash to pay for a tank of cooking gas. Another said that he was berrying only until he could begin cutting timber again.

The sale of smoked whitefish provides a small amount of cash during the fall for 2 households in Rice Village. The fish are trapped in homemade nets set in one of the nearby lakes, then smoked in outdoor metal ovens. One of the households sells all of its catch to a local motel owner, who in turn sells the fish to hunters. The other sells fish directly to several hunters from the Twin Cities area who are "regular customers." Charging $1.75 per fish, each of the 2 households collected $20 to $25 a year from such sales in the mid-1960s.

Men from 2 households earn money in the fall by serving as guides to the hunters who swarm into the area during deer-hunting season. A party of 3 or 4 hunters will hire a guide to accompany them until a deer has been shot for each man in the party. In the fall of 1966 approximately 40 dollars was earned by each guide.

During the late fall and winter months, when it is more comfortable to be inside than out, most of the women in the community manufacture various handicrafts. Three of the women make colorful braided rugs from used garments purchased by the carton at rummage sales. During the fall, the garments are sorted according to color and cut into long strips. Then, in the winter, the rags are braided and wound into rugs. Apparently the rugs are popular with the local white population. One of my informants was in the process of completing an order for 8 rugs (in specific colors) for a James Lake motel owner. The women claim that during the fall and spring "lots of people come by here looking for rugs and things" and that they have no difficulty in selling their products. The rugs sell for about 8 dollars each, but the price can fluctuate depending on the intricacy of the design, the colors requested, and whether the purchaser provides the materials. The women estimate that they each make between 4 and 8 rugs a year.

Five of the women in the community earn 20 to 60 dollars a year from the sale of beadwork. They make pendants, belts, and ornaments for dance costumes and occasionally embroider leather jackets and moccasins in small, colorful beads. Although beadwork appears to be a dying art among the Chippewa at Broken Reed, Rice Village is considered to have some of the finest contemporary beadworkers in the area. Much of the beadwork is for gifts and for items to be used in peyote ceremonies, and most of the items are sold to other Indians. Beadwork for sale is done by most women only when they have an order. During the period of my research, however, one woman who needed money made a necktie pendant in a matter of a few days and then took it around to the souvenir shops in James Lake, trying to sell it.

Three of the women also manufacture woman's handbags and moccasins from leather. As with beadwork, most items are made to order. The women use only leather scraps—oddly shaped pieces of commercial buckskin—which they acquire at almost no cost from a company that manufactures leather goods. Thus, since the finished items command fairly high prices, leatherworking is a profitable activity. At the time of my fieldwork, a leather purse about one foot square, lined, fringed, and drawn with a braided string, sold for between 12 and 22 dollars, depending on the lining material and the color of the leather.

Lucy Rice capitalizes on the community's work force and natural resources each fall, supplementing her income and providing jobs through the manufacture of Christmas wreaths. These are made from cedar boughs and decorated with painted Norway pinecones. Lucy supplies the wire and pays other women in the village 2 dollars apiece for making the undecorated and untrimmed wreaths from the boughs they gather. The children are paid one cent per cone for painting the Norway pinecones that Lucy provides. She then attaches the decorated cones and trims the wreaths herself, loads them into the back seat and trunk of her car, and drives 100 miles to Duluth, where she sells the wreaths to business and professional people for their offices. Most are bought by "regular customers" who have a standing order for a wreath each Christmas. During the winter of 1965, 60 wreaths were made and sold. thus, about 30 dollars was earned by each of the 4 women who made the wreath forms and one dollar by each of the 6 children who painted cones. After deducting her expenses (wire, travel to and lodging in Duluth, and "salaries"), Lucy estimated that she cleared about 200 dollars on the wreaths that year.

Maple sugaring is another potential source of cash income in the winter but apparently seldom utilized. Although 7 of the 9 households claim that they have collected maple sap in the past, and one family even keeps a small dilapidated travel trailer especially for living in the woods while gathering syrup, no one engaged in this activity during the period of my investigation or the winter before.

Aid from government agencies

Considering the limited economic opportunities in the area and the difficulties many individuals have in earning a living (especially the old or disabled and the single parent with young children), it is little wonder that welfare payments are an important source of income in Rice Village.

Five households receive regular monthly welfare payments from the county. These payments constitute between 32 and 100 percent of a household's total cash income (see Table 4.3). Two of these recipients are elderly women, one of whom is eligible for Aid to the Disabled because she is arthritic and diabetic; the other receives Old Age Assistance. The other 3 households (1, 2, and 7) receive Aid to Families with Dependent Children. At one time or another, all of the families in Rice Village have received small amounts of emergency assistance from the community relief fund, particularly at times of seasonal unemployment.

Thus, the people of Rice Village depend on various sources of cash income, and in varying proportions, to support themselves. In 1965, total cash income for the households ranged from $768 to $3,700, with a

Table 4.3. Sources of cash income

Source	Household number	Amount	Percent of total income
Logging and	3	$1,100	55
mill work	5	1,000	70
	4	325	20
	2	400	25
Forestry	9	2,400	80
Ricing	3	700	35
	4	725	50
	2	500	30
	1	150	5.5
	5	300	24
	7	700	20
	9	675	20
Welfare	1	1,812	90
	6	1,104	100
	8	768	100
	2	684	43
	7	1,164	32
Miscellaneous	1	60	0.5
	4	450	30
	3	200	10
	5	100	6
	7	1,800	48
	2	25	2

median of $1,584. The amount of cash income and percentage of total income derived from each of the various sources for each household is shown in Table 4.3.

Noncash income

Surplus commodities distributed by the county are an important source of food for most of the families in Rice Village. Such staples as beans, cornmeal, flour, lard, tinned meat, and peanut butter can be obtained through the welfare office each month at no cost to low-income families.

Wild animals and birds are the only source of fresh meat during periods when money is low. Porcupine and other small animals are hunted throughout the summer and fall, and deer are hunted both in and out of season by Rice Villagers. When a deer is killed, each household in the community is given a portion of the meat by the hunter. During the summer of 1966, 3 deer were killed, each providing at least 2 meals for everyone in the village. Duck-hunting season is perhaps the time of the most intensive hunting, with all of the men and older boys going out at every possible opportunity and bringing back strings of ducks. There appears to be more meat consumed during this period than at any other time of the year. Since the men of Rice Village are good hunters and seem to enjoy this activity, game from the surrounding woods could provide virtually all of the community's meat. However, lack of refrigeration facilities, among other things, limits the use of this abundant food source.

As previously noted, wild berries and fruit are another source of food. Berries, fresh and canned, are eaten plain for dessert and used in pies, muffins, and jams.

The woods also provide free fuel for Rice Villagers. Fallen trees, both on community property and national forestland, are cut up and used for firewood. In addition, both sawmills have large piles of wood scraps, just the right size for firewood, that may be hauled away at no charge.

A final and significant resource is the variety of skills and services that are available within the community. Building construction, repair and maintenance of automobiles and other mechanical equipment, the manufacture of clothing and blankets, alterations of clothing, and haircuts are among the services that members of the community provide for each other, reducing the need for cash.

The peyote religion

The peyote plant (*Lophophora williamsii* Lemaire) is a small, greyish green, spineless cactus native to northern Mexico and the extreme southwestern United States. Its rounded top surface is divided into small sections that, when dried, become the peyote "buttons." Protruding from the center of each section is a small tuft of hairlike fuzz. When ingested, the plant can produce a variety of physiological effects, including visual and auditory hallucinations.

Ceremonial use of peyote in the New World dates to pre-Columbian times. As early as 1560 Spanish explorers observed its use (Stewart 1944:63). Although little is known about the early history of peyote north of the Rio Grande, it is probable that tribes there learned to use the cactus from Peyotists living within the natural habitat of the plant. Peyote was used by Lipan and Mescalero Apache as early as 1770 (Stewart 1944:64). The Lipan and Mescalero peyote ritual appears to be a transition between the Mexican ritual and the Plains Indian ceremony that later developed (La Barre 1964:40–42). Stewart noted that "All peyote rituals north of the Rio Grande are remarkably similar and appear universally to include elements of Christian ideology and ritual integrated with aboriginal ceremonial elements" (1944:64), but the stage at which the Christian elements were introduced, whether into the early Apache ceremony or into the later Plains ritual, has not been determined.

By the 1880s Peyotism had diffused from the Lipan and Mescalero to the southern Plains Indians, and a secondary diffusion center seems to have developed among the Comanche and the Kiowa (Slotkin 1952:571). It is hard to trace the development of Peyotism at this point, because there are no extended descriptions of the peyote ritual before the beginning of the twentieth century. However, Mooney's description of the Kiowa peyote ceremony, which incorporates all of the basic features of the Plains rite, indicated that this version was fully developed by 1890 (Slotkin 1952:572). From the Plains tribes the peyote religion was transmitted to many other Indian tribes in North America.

In spite of the regional and tribal differences in the practice of Peyotism, certain elements of the ritual appear to be sufficiently uniform to permit a single, generalized description. The standard ritual, commonly referred to as a meeting, is an all-night ceremony held in a tepee or meeting house "around a crescent-shaped earthen mound and a ceremonially built fire. Here a special drum, gourd rattle, and carved staff are passed around after smoking and purifying ceremonies, as each person sings four peyote songs. Various water-bringing ceremonies occur at midnight and dawn, when there may be a baptism or curing rite, followed by a special ritual breakfast" (La Barre 1964:7–8).

The primary purpose of the peyote religion is healing and protection through the worship of God by means of peyote. Among the Rice Village Chippewa and in other groups described in the literature, there seems to be no attempt to distinguish a separate peyote Supreme Being from the Christian God. Peyote is seen as the intermediary between man and the supernatural and is assigned a variety of aspects and attributes. "It is at once thought of as a medicine, a power, a protector, or a teacher"; it is prayed to "as the symbol or representative of a spirit or God"; and it is eaten "as an aid to obtaining assistance from, or offering thanks to, the Supreme Divinity" (Stewart 1944:64).

General hostility and various antipeyote legal measures that had been taken (La Barre 1964:223–24) eventually caused Peyotists to seek some sort of legal guarantee for the local practice of their religion. Prior to World War 1, various groups of Peyotists incorporated into "churches" under the laws of the particular states in which they lived. In 1918 a group of leaders from several local organizations met and formed an intertribal group, the Native American Church, incorporated in Oklahoma. The growth and success of this group seems to have impressed Peyotists in many other areas, who subsequently adopted the name and patterned their constitutions after that of the original Oklahoma group. In 1944 the articles of incorporation of the Native American Church were amended so that the association became national, known as the Native American Church of the United States. With the spread of Peyotism into Canada, the name was changed again (in 1955) to the Native American Church of North America (La Barre 1964:169).

History of Peyotism in Rice Village

At the time John Rice moved from Maple Point to the allotment that was to become Rice Village, he and his family were nominally Roman Catholics. However, according to informants, the Rices still believed and participated in the traditional Chippewa religion. Shortly after the village was established, a set of misfortunes led John Rice and his wife to have some doubts about the traditional religion. Two of John Rice's grandchildren died almost immediately after birth within the course of a single year. In both instances, John's wife had had dreams predicting the death of the infants and preventative religious measures had been taken, but to no avail. About the same time, news of a powerful "medicine" began filtering into the Broken Reed area. When used in the proper way, the medicine was reported to produce miraculous cures, bring one in direct contact with the supernatural, and reveal everything an individual needed to know in order to lead a successful life. According to an informant: "Long time before all of us here knew this Way we kept hearing about it. They said it could do miracles . . . no matter if you were very sick, even dying, it would make you well. That's what they said. They said that through this peyote the Almighty came right up to you, talked right to you, came to teach you everything, things you could never know by yourself. We didn't believe all these things we heard, said it was just talk, stories. It was too wonderful to be real."

Prior to this time Minnesota Chippewa (at least those in the Broken Reed area) had not had any contact with groups from neighboring tribes who had recently adopted Peyotism. It was through the prominent Winnebago leader John Rave and his brother that John Rice learned of the peyote religion.

In a diagram of the chronological diffusion of peyote among North American Indian tribes, La Barre (1964:122) showed Minnesota Chippewa receiving Peyotism by means of "secondary influences" from the Sioux. He gave no date for this (presumably it would be after 1910, the date he gave for the introduction of peyote to the Sioux), nor did he discuss diffusion of peyote to Minnesota Chippewa elsewhere in this monograph. Thus he either was unaware of the direct contacts between Winnebago Peyotists and Minnesota Chippewa, or he placed these later in time than Sioux contacts, wishing to show in his diagram only the earliest introduction of peyote.

John Rave had his first contact with Peyotism in the late 1880s while visiting Oklahoma. He became convinced of the power of peyote when it appeared to have effected a remarkable cure in him. He brought the plant and its accompanying ritual back to the Winnebago, and, by 1910 at the latest, the cult had a considerable following and a "definite organization" (Radin 1916:391). Albert Hensley, a Winnebago educated at Carlisle who had had considerable exposure to Christianity, was one of Peyotism's most zealous converts. It was Hensley who "revolutionized the cult by introducing the Bible, postulating the dogma that the peyote opened the understanding of the people to the Bible, and added a number of Christian practices" (Radin 1916:420). Thus, when the Winnebago version of Peyotism reached the Broken Reed Chippewa, it already had elements of Christianity incorporated into it.

After John Rice's younger daughter, Elizabeth, became pregnant, his wife again had a dream predicting the unborn child's death. Since the traditional religious practices had not saved the other two babies, they decided to try peyote. Just before Elizabeth was due to give birth, they traveled to the Winnebago, from whom they had heard of the peyote religion. The following account of that trip and the subsequent conversion of John Rice and his family was told by his granddaughter, on whose behalf the trip was made.

> Before I was born my folks didn't think I was going to live. My grandmother dreamed that I would be very sick and die. So they went to these Winnebago Indians, three, Raves and Walking Priests, and some others; today I don't know their names. I guess my folks and my mother were crying because I was dying. I was born out there in the open. They took us into that place where they have meeting and they prayed. Then they had another meeting that other night, and that's when these folks took me as their daughter and prayed for me.

They were Winnebago, their names are Walking Priest. That same morning, you know baptism usually takes place in the morning, daybreak, and that's the time I was baptized. I don't know who asked for it, they just took me. At that time, my grandmother just gave herself to peyote, she was so thankful that I didn't die. So my grandmother and I were baptized in this peyote at the same time, by a man name of Lake Rave. He's the brother of John Rave. And that's how I was baptized.

My grandfather didn't get to be baptized then. He was still hanging on in those old ways, you know, his old beliefs. I think the next time they went is when he gave up, he was baptized.

He went to that meeting and took peyote and that was it, he never went back to his old ways again. And then he came back, he knew what he was doing, all the beliefs he had and the things he had—like a drum and everything like that the Grand Medicine has — he came back, the same day or the next, got a bedspread off the bed, put it on the floor and he got everything out and put it all in there. He made a big bundle, with his drum and everything, and took them way off in the woods and made a fire and burned everything. So that was it. From there on he believed in this peyote.

After John Rice adopted Peyotism, his children and their spouses began to do so as well. All but one of his 6 children and one adopted daughter eventually converted. In addition to his immediate family, a few of his relatives and friends at Maple Point with whom he still maintained close ties also adopted the peyote religion. In the early days of their conversion, the villagers had to travel to the Winnebago in order to participate in peyote rituals, since they did not know enough about the religion to conduct their own. Peyotists perceive each meeting to be a learning experience, where personal insight into the meaning of the religion is gained by taking peyote. Furthermore, knowledge about the intricacies of the ritual is obtained by watching the performances of peyote leaders who have experience in conducting the meetings. Thus, it was not until several years after the adoption of Peyotism that a meeting was conducted in Rice Village without the aid of outsiders.

Elements of the peyote meeting

The various components of the peyote meeting as practiced in Rice Village are detailed in the following description.

Sponsorship.—Peyote meetings are commonly sponsored by an individual but occasionally by the community as a whole. The sponsor of the meeting is responsible for organizing and financing it: he sets the date, appoints a leader, makes certain that the necessary paraphernalia will be available, secures the peyote, and invites people to the meeting. The sponsor should also provide food for the ritual and social meals. However, informants say that food and sometimes cash are usually donated by the participants. The community-sponsored meetings, called "donation meetings," are financed by contribution from all of the households in the village.

Informants found it hard to estimate the cost of sponsoring a meeting: "It's hard to say. You don't pay for everything at once, and the others [other households in the village] always give some. ... You could say around 20 or 30 dollars, I suppose."

Perhaps because there are so few members, meetings in Rice Village are not conducted with the regularity and frequency reported for other peyote groups. In Rice Village, meetings are held to commemorate holidays (such as Christmas, Easter, New Year's Day, Memorial Day, Thanksgiving, and the Fourth of July), birthdays, and anniversaries of the death of a member. Meetings are also conducted for baptism of new members and at the death of a Peyotist. Peyote ceremonies in Rice Village are held in the community building maintained primarily for that purpose, known as the "meeting house.'

Officials.—Four leaders, or officials, preside at a peyote meeting: the head leader (or road chief), the drum chief, the fire chief, and the cedar chief. These are not permanent positions but are held only for the duration of a meeting. Theoretically, any male member may be appointed to any office for a particular meeting, but in reality there is a small but unofficially recognized core of older men from whom the 4 leaders are selected. It is considered an honor to be chosen to officiate at a meeting, for it is a tribute to a man's knowledge about ritual procedure and his reputation for living the peyote way.

The road chief (who "leads people down the peyote road") is always appointed by the sponsor of the meeting. In most cases the road chief then selects the other 3 leaders, but occasionally the sponsor requests that a man whom he especially respects be chosen for one of the other positions. Once appointed, the road chief is "in charge of the whole meeting; it is done his way." He determines the particular variations of ritual that occur and supplies the set of paraphernalia to be used.

The drum chief has the responsibility of caring for the water drum that is used in the ritual and of drumming for the road chief's singing.

The function of the fire chief among Rice Village Peyotists differs from that described for most other groups. Rice Villagers do not use an open fire but instead keep a small fire burning in a barrel stove in the meeting house. Thus, the only duties of the fire chief are gathering the wood and building and maintaining the fire throughout the ceremony. He does not have to clean the altar or build the ashes from the fire into a symbolic design, as ritual in other tribes dictates, nor does he act as a "combination steward and sergeant-at-arms" (Slotkin 1952:587).

The cedar chief is in charge of burning cedar incense and manipulating the smoke in purifying ceremonies. In addition, this position has evolved to include the role of the road chief's assistant, which is assigned to the fire chief in other groups.

Ritual paraphernalia.—A variety of ritual paraphernalia is necessary to conduct the peyote ceremony. Some of these items, such as the altar cloth, fans, Bible, staff, and incense, reflect the Christian influence. The more traditional Indian items used in the ceremony include water drums, rattles, and peyote fetishes.

Perhaps the Rice Village ceremony deviates most from the generalized Plains type of peyote ritual in its lack of the crescent-shaped earthen altar, or "moon." Instead, there is a rectangular piece of hemmed white cotton cloth about 2 feet wide and 1.5 feet long. On this altar cloth are embroidered the words "God Bless Our Meetings" and 2 designs: a circle at the top center, and a water bird symbol in each of the bottom corners. It is the focus for the ritual, and many of the other items of paraphernalia are placed upon it. Unlike the other ceremonial items, the altar cloth is not owned by any one individual in the community but remains in the meeting house.

A second type of paraphernalia is fetish peyote, also referred to as "peyote chiefs" or "father peyote." These especially large and symmetrical peyote buttons are cherished and highly prized possessions, especially if they are old and have seen their owner through many crises. La Barre's characterization of "some famous peyote chiefs" as "heirlooms" (1964:73) is in keeping with Rice Villagers' attitudes toward these large buttons: it is with great reverence that John Rice's grandson shows visitors his grandfather's peyote chief. The peyote chief is viewed as a "messenger between the Almighty and man"; during meetings, the peyote chiefs are placed in the embroidered circle on the altar cloth and prayers and songs are directed to them.

The staff or cane is a carved wooden stick, about 3.5 feet long and decorated with a small feathered tassel at the top. During meetings it is held by the person who is singing. Informants interpreted it variously as representing "the shepherd's staff to lead us down the right road" and "Moses' rod." Radin (1916:215) reports almost identical interpretations of the staff by the Winnebago.

Gourd rattles used in Rice Village ceremonies seem to be of the general type found among other Indian groups. They are made of brown gourds of various sizes, sometimes varnished but otherwise left undecorated. A wooden handle about 8 to 12 inches long is inserted through the gourd, so that it projects a bit at the top; to this tip is attached a small tassel. The handle is elaborately decorated in beadwork and sometimes with a buckskin tassel or a small silver cross.

The water drum is played by the drum chief to accompany the road chief's singing. The base of the drum is a small, 3-legged iron kettle containing water and 4 bits of charcoal. A piece of buckskin that has been soaked in water for about a day is stretched over the mouth of the kettle and lashed in place with clothesline. The rope is carefully wound around one of the bosses or pebbles placed around the rim and then passed under the drum and up and around another boss. When the lashing is complete, the rope forms a seven-pointed star on the bottom of the drum. The drummer can improve the tone by tipping the drum to the side to wet the head and by adjusting the head with his left thumb. Water is sometimes forced through the skin by sucking on the head. The drumstick is a slender piece of wood less than a foot long, carved with simple geometric design or left unadorned.

Fans made from a bird's tail feathers attached to a handle covered with buckskin are used to spread the incense smoke. Fans made from eagle feathers are the most desirable; since these are becoming scarce, feathers from other species are often used. Again, Rice Villagers and the Winnebago offer the same interpretation of the fans, claiming that they represent the wings of birds mentioned in the Bible. Twelve is supposed to be the appropriate number of feathers in a fan, but at least 2 of the fans in the village have fewer.

The cedar incense made from dried cedar bark is an important part of the peyote ceremony. It is burned both as an offering and to purify participants and ritual paraphernalia. Incense is kept in a small, buckskin-covered box, often decorated with beadwork, and is placed on the altar cloth during the ceremony. At appropriate times during the meeting, the cedar chief removes incense from the container and burns it in a small metal plate.

Another important piece of paraphernalia in the Rice Village ceremony is the Bible. Scriptures may be cited, discussed, or interpreted at meetings, and the Bible is used to support—or justify—certain practices of the peyote ritual. For example, meetings are said to be held at night "because it [the Bible] says that Christ prayed all night and we want to follow that as closely as possible"; the "bitter herbs" referred to in Exodus 12:8 are interpreted to be peyote. Although Bibles are common in every Rice Village household, Arlene Cloud's Bible, with its elaborate beadwork cover, is most often used in the meetings, placed on the altar cloth near the peyote chief.

The substitution of an altar cloth for the crescent-shaped altar is not the only practice which distinguishes Rice Village from other peyote groups. Another common feature of Peyotism absent in Rice Village is the elaboration of the fire and ashes complex, in which the structure of the fire and the ashes becomes symbolic of the body of Christ (La Barre 1964:77). Other elements of peyote ritual paraphernalia not observed in Rice Village include the use of sagebrush, eagle bone whistles, tobacco, and face paint. The absence of tobacco reflects the Protestant influence transmitted by the Winnebago.

Ritual activity.—Certain ritual activities are a necessary part of every peyote meeting. The particular form of some of these rituals or their exclusion for the addition of others is determined by the specific purpose for which the meeting is conducted.

Singing is always present in peyote meetings, regardless of the occasion. There are 4 sets of specific songs, sung by the road chief, that serve to mark the 3 distinct time periods into which the meeting is traditionally divided. These songs are of Esikwita or Mescalero Apache origin (La Barre 1964:82). The Opening Song "Hayatinayo" marks the beginning of the first phase of the meeting, sunset to midnight; the Midnight Song "Yahiyano" introduces the midnight to 3:00 a.m. phase; and the Morning Song "Wakaho" initiates the final, or sunrise, stage of the meeting. The fourth prescribed set of songs is the Quitting Song "Gayatina," which indicates that the meeting is at an end. Paradoxically, Rice Villagers use the Apache ritual songs even though the Winnebago, from whom they received the religion, are reported to use ritual songs in their own language (La Barre 1964:82; Radin 1916:374).

All other songs, sung by each of the participants in turn, are left completely to the discretion of the individual. Although most of the songs they know are in Indian languages other than their native Chippewa—learned through contact with other Peyotists—the people of Rice Village assert that it does not matter, because "peyote lets you understand them in your own language." Most of the songs translated by informants show Christian influences, including "You Must Know Jesus Now" (Winnebago), "This Way Is God's Way" (Winnebago), "We Will Be Saved—It Is God's Will" (Arapaho), "Jesus Lights the Way" (Apache), "Our Saviour Shows Us the Right Road to Walk On" (Arapaho), and "The Son of the Almighty Shall Show Us the Light" (Arapaho).

The single-line song is repeated over and over, and each song lasts for 3 to 5 minutes, accompanied by the beating of the water drum and rattling. Before the beginning of a song there is a very rapid beating of the drum, which gradually slows to the tempo of the singing. The conclusion of a song is frequently marked by a sudden tilting of the drum, producing a "gulping" sound, and the rapid shaking of the rattle, which stops suddenly at the last beat of the drum.

The road chief begins the singing with the Opening Song. He holds the staff and fan in one hand and his rattle in the other. The man to his right (the drum chief) plays the drum while the road chief sings the first of 4 songs. Then the paraphernalia, staff preceding drum, are passed to the left, so that each man sings to the drumming of the man on his right and drums for the man on his left.

Praying is a second activity included in all Rice Village meetings. Prayers are offered publicly by the 4 leaders of the meeting and privately by individuals throughout the meeting. Publicly led prayers precede all of the major ceremonial events: the beginning of the meeting, the passing of peyote, the water-bringing and incense-blessing ceremonies, the singing of the Midnight and Morning songs, and the ritual breakfast. The prayers offered by the leaders are usually spoken in a very soft tone of voice, barely audible to the rest of the group. I did not observe, nor did my informants mention, prayers led by the leader with the entire assembled group standing and praying together, as La Barre reported for the Winnebago (1964:81).

Some peyote groups use cedar or tobacco when offering prayers (La Barre 1964:80). The version of the peyote rite that Rice Villagers have adopted prohibits the use of tobacco, and it is completely absent from their ceremony. However, the burning of cedar in connection with prayers is still practiced, as it was in the ritual originally learned by John Rice. According to an informant, "When he [John Rice] prayed he would always burn cedar . . . it goes with that peyote. Today they still do it. Every time they're going to pray, they burn cedar."

Rice Villagers regard spontaneity as an important quality of prayer. "It has to come straight from your heart" and "you should say just what you are feeling right then," informants agreed. If an individual openly breaks down and sobs during meetings, it is taken as an indication of the sincerity of his or her desire to communicate with God and to learn the peyote way.

A third ritual practice is the eating of peyote. Rice Villagers are familiar with 4 forms in which peyote may be taken. The most common is to eat the raw, dried peyote buttons. Peyote tea can be made from soaked and boiled buttons. It is also possible to eat the green plant, but, because of their distance from the sources of peyote, few Rice Villagers have had the opportunity to eat green peyote. Those who have done so report the green plant to be more palatable than the dried buttons and more powerful in its effect. For sick or old people, buttons are pounded into powder and molded into small, moist balls. Before the dried buttons are eaten or prepared, care is taken to pick off the fuzz on top.

The amount of peyote taken by individuals at a meeting may vary considerably. Informants claim that 4 is the minimum number of dried buttons taken by a participant in a meeting. Some participants may also take the tea or powdered form of peyote at meetings, either in addition to or in place of the buttons; in these 2 forms, it is difficult to determine how much peyote has been taken. At times Peyotists abstain from taking peyote at a particular meeting, for a variety of reasons. For example, a person taking medication will usually not take peyote. When asked why she had not taken any peyote during a particular meeting, a villager replied: "I had an infection in my ear, and the doctor gave me penicillin pills to take. I didn't want to take it [peyote] on top of that. That's one thing we were told, not to mix it with anything, especially liquor or any drugs. It makes you sick or something. That's why I didn't take any."

The sponsor's wife and the women who help her also usually abstain from taking peyote at meetings. Lucy Rice explained why: "When they have a meeting over there, I don't take it because I want to do all the work—wait on people and cook. When I have to get up there, go back and forth, wait on somebody, I just can't . . . and I don't . . . take any."

Dried peyote is distributed ceremonially 3 times during the meeting. Just before the set of songs is sung to introduce the next phase of the ceremony, the road chief removes the peyote bag from the altar cloth and takes out 4 buttons. He then passes the bag to his left to the fire chief, who does likewise and then passes the bag on, until everybody has had a chance to take some. The buttons are consumed as the individual wishes. During this phase of the ceremony, anyone can call for the peyote bag or tea if he or she wants more. People offer prayers both before and during the eating of peyote.

Other objects, such as the staff, rattle, fan, and drum, are also passed around to each of the participants in a clockwise direction. Before midnight, only the road chief's paraphernalia are used. After that hour, people may take out their own rattle and fan. Water and the ritual breakfast food are also passed in a clockwise direction.

Cedar incense is burned at the beginning of every peyote meeting to bless and purify the participants and the paraphernalia. The cedar chief burns the incense in a small, shallow metal container, using the feather fan to direct the smoke toward the ritual objects and the participants. Incense is also burned at midnight and morning ceremonies and during prayers said by the leaders. People who bring their ritual paraphernalia to use after midnight take the objects to the cedar chief to have them "smoked."

Several ritual activities are incorporated in the water ceremony, which celebrates the beginning of the second phase of each peyote meeting. At midnight, the road chief announces that it is time for the "water to be passed around." The individual who at the moment holds the paraphernalia and the person who is beating the drum pass these items back to the road chief and the drum chief, respectively. After the road chief offers a prayer and sings the first Midnight Song, the fire chief goes outside to the kitchen area and returns with a bucket of water, which he places in front of the road chief. The cedar chief "smokes" the bucket while the road chief sings the second song in the midnight series. After this, the fire chief delivers a short prayer, and then the final 2 Midnight Songs are sung. A somewhat informal period follows, as the bucket and a cup are passed around to each of the participants.

Rice Village midnight ceremonies, while conforming to the general pattern reported for other peyote groups, seem to be a simplified version. Conspicuously absent are the blowing of the eagle bone whistle and the intricate manipulation and praying over the water bucket by the leaders as it is passed around.

At daybreak, essentially the same ceremony takes place, except that the water is brought in by a woman and the Morning Song is sung. Informants stated that doctoring and baptism are usually performed during the morning water ceremonies.

After the ceremony is completed, the meeting again takes on an informal tone, as participants listen to a homily delivered by the road chief or by someone whom he invites to speak. Personal experiences and advice on how to lead a proper life are the usual content of these messages.

The breakfast ceremony is another ritual component of the peyote meeting. The traditional items served at the peyote breakfast in Rice Village follow the pattern described by La Barre and others and include corn, fruit, meat, and water. Each item is served on a single plate with a single fork or spoon; these are passed around to each of the participants.

Baptisms complete the list of ritual activities that commonly constitute a peyote meeting. While I was doing research in Rice Village I did not have the opportunity to observe a baptism, but several informants described one for me. According to their descriptions, the baptism of new members follows the same ritual that Radin (1916:389) reported for the Winnebago. The road chief dips his hand into the peyote tea and sprinkles the person with the liquid. While moving his hand in the shape of a cross the road chief prays that "the person will be able to learn this Way and to follow it for the rest of his life."

Account of a peyote meeting

Only one peyote meeting was conducted in Rice Village during the course of my fieldwork, and it was held on the very first day that I entered the community. Although the timing was fortunate in some respects, it came too early in my research from other standpoints. For example, I had virtually no prior opportunity to meet most of the participants—let alone talk with them about their religion or acquire a basic understanding of the significance and meaning of the parts of the ritual. Although Frances Green very graciously sat next to me during the meeting, explaining and interpreting the ritual for me, I was hesitant about asking too many questions lest I disrupt the proceedings or offend Frances by my curiosity. Thus my observations of this meeting are not as detailed as they might be. However, I reviewed my notes carefully with 2 informants on separate occasions, making additions and corrections where needed. My description is taken from the revised version of these field notes (see also Figure 4.4).

The meeting I attended was a "wake meeting" for Paul Martin, a highly respected, elderly member of the Rice Village community, who had died the day before. A wake had been in progress all afternoon and into the early evening. Several non-Peyotists, Indians as well as whites who had known the deceased, had come to the meeting house to view the

Figure 4.4. Diagram of meetinghouse and positions of participants at the peyote meeting that concluded the wake for Paul Martin.

body and pay their final respects. By 9:00 p.m., most of the "outsiders" had left, and preparation for the meeting began. The following account begins at 9:30.

Wayne Perkins, from Wicket, has been asked by the family to be the leader (road chief) for this meeting. He has been a peyote member for many years and was a close friend of the deceased. His black case (like a large doctor's bag) has been placed near the coffin. Out of his bag he takes a fan of eagle feathers, a rattle, a striped bag containing peyote buttons, a small buckskin bag containing his peyote chiefs, and a silver cross. One of the women brings him an embroidered cloth (the altar cloth); a second gives him a Bible with an elaborate beadwork cover. Perkins takes down a decorated staff that is hanging on the wall above the coffin. While he is unpacking the paraphernalia, Danny Green, Jacob Green, and Tom Williams are preparing the drum.

At 9:45 Dick Martin brings in a small bundle of kindling, places some in the stove, and stacks the rest next to it. Perkins spreads the altar cloth on the floor about 4 feet from the coffin, in front of several cushions and blankets, and arranges the equipment from his case on the cloth.

At 10:05 there are about 25 adults and 10 or 12 children of all ages in the meeting house; most of the women are in the kitchen area, talking. Dick Martin makes a small fire in the stove.

By 10:15 Perkins has apparently given a signal to start, because people are beginning to file into the main area of the meeting house. Most of the men and a couple of women (their wives) seat themselves along the east and west walls of the building. Frances Green, the deceased's daughter, sits in the southeast corner near the coffin, diagonally across from her husband. Two of the women sitting in this area have small children with them, who fall asleep almost immediately on the blankets provided for them. All of the people nearest the coffin are sitting on blankets they have brought, except for the 4 men seated in front of the altar cloth. They are sitting on a set of cushions with a blanket tacked like a backrest to the wall behind them.

Within 5 minutes all but one or 2 of the women have come in from the kitchen and seated themselves in the back half of the room. People here are also more or less lined up along the walls, sitting on chairs or the couch. The older children have taken the younger ones home to bed, leaving only the adults and the 4 very young children who are asleep next to their mothers. Everyone is now seated and silent. Wayne Perkins, the road chief, is seated in front of the altar cloth. To his right sits Leland Green, the drum chief, a lame, elderly man who is a long-time friend of the deceased and the father-in-law of the deceased's daughter. To his left sits Dick Martin (son of the dead man and sponsor of the meeting); he is going to be fire chief for this meeting. To his left sits Tom Williams, the cedar chief.

At 10:35 Perkins raises both his arms briefly to signal that he is ready to begin. He then folds his hands together in front of him, bows his head, and begins to pray. He is speaking in Chippewa but so softly that I can't imagine that the people in the back hear what he is saying. I am told that he is asking the Lord for guidance in running this meeting, that he is only human and does not have the knowledge or power to do it alone. He asks everyone there to pray for him and help him through. He prays for about 5 minutes, then turns to the drum chief on his right and asks him to speak. The drum chief tells the group that the purpose of the meeting is to ask the Lord to deliver and protect this "fine man who has led a long and honorable life." He also asks for help in getting through all they must do tonight. He explains that he has witnessed many of these wake meetings and has learned much from each one. He urges the young people to pay close attention to everything that goes on so that they can learn Indian ways. He thanks the road chief for the honor of being drum chief, explaining that this meeting is very special for him because Paul Martin was his closest friend, and, since he too is getting old and doesn't know how many more meetings he will be able to attend, this may be his last.

At 10:55 the cedar chief takes some incense from the small rectangular container, places it in the iron plate, and lights it, using a twig from the fire in the stove. While doing this, he is supposed to be praying. When the incense begins to burn, with his hand he fans the smoke toward the objects on the altar cloth. Then the road chief picks up the fan and hands it to him, and he proceeds to fan the smoke in the direction of the participants. The ones sitting along the east wall lean forward as if to meet the smoke. I was told that this is a blessing and makes the objects and people "clean." The drum chief hands him the water drum and drumstick, and the cedar chief holds them over the smoke for a while and then returns them.

About 11:05 the road chief picks up the striped bag containing the peyote buttons, holds it in front of him, bows his head, and prays that the purpose of the meeting be fulfilled. After taking 4 peyote buttons out of the bag, he passes it to the fire chief, who is sitting on his left. The fire chief also takes 4 buttons, then passes the bag to the cedar chief. The peyote bag is circulated in a clockwise direction around the room until it finally reaches the drum chief. He takes 4 buttons and hands the bag back to the road chief, who places it back on the altar cloth and announces that if anybody wants more they can "call for it."

Next, the road chief picks up the staff and the fan in his left hand and the gourd rattle in his right. The drum chief turns to face him and begins to drum. The road chief sings the Opening Song, then 3 other songs. While he is singing, most of the people are chewing on the peyote that they took from the pouch. A few are simply sitting quietly with their heads bowed. Three of the women did not take any peyote.

The road chief finishes his set of 4 songs at about 11:25. He passes the paraphernalia to the fire chief and asks the drum chief to take his place and drum for the fire chief. The drum chief sits in front of the fire chief, drumming while he sings. This rotation—each man singing while the man on his right plays the drum and then drumming for the man on his left—continues around the room. However, not everyone participates. Only the 8 men sitting in the front part of the room take part in the singing and drumming.

It takes more than an hour for the drum and paraphernalia to make the full circuit, ending with the drum chief. He hands the staff, rattle, and fan back to the road chief, who places them on the altar cloth. At 12:40, the fire chief rises and tends the fire. When he returns to his place, the cedar chief gets up and goes out to the kitchen, returning with a covered pail (filled with water) and a cup, which he places in front of the road chief. He then burns incense, while saying a short prayer, to purify the cup and pail. Almost immediately, the Midnight Song begins. At the end of the first song in the set, the road chief uncovers the pail and dips the cup into it. He drinks from the cup, then puts a few drops of water into the palm of his hand and goes through the motions of washing his hands. When the road chief is finished, the cedar chief rises, picks up the bucket, and takes it around to everyone in the room, starting with the fire chief. By 1:10 a.m., everyone has had water and performed the ceremonial cleansing. The cedar chief brings the cup back to the road chief so he can place it on the altar cloth and then takes the pail outside. The road chief sings the final 3 songs of the midnight series. When he finishes, he announces a recess so that people can refresh themselves. They will need strength "for what still lies ahead of them." Some people file out to the kitchen area, others go outside.

Most of the people are back in their places after a 20-minute break, including the 4 leaders. The fire chief adds more wood to the fire in the stove; the cedar chief burns more incense and performs the ritual smoking of objects and participants again. The leader announces that people may now use their own outfits (ritual items) if they wish. Several of the men take rattles out of rectangular lacquered boxes; 2 have their own fans. Everyone who has brought articles of paraphernalia takes them up to the cedar chief so he can purify them.

By 1:35 the bag of peyote is circulating again. This time the road chief instructs people to "take as much medicine as you want." He leans over and whispers something to the cedar chief, who rises and goes into the kitchen area. He comes back carrying a pail (not the same one that was used for the water ceremony) and a cup and places them in front of the drum chief. The pail contains peyote tea. The drum chief takes a cupful and sips it slowly. The cedar chief waits until he is finished, then presents the cup to the road chief. After the road chief has finished his tea, the cedar chief moves on to the fire chief, then continues around the room offering the tea to everyone. While this is going on, the peyote bag has completed its circuit and is placed on the altar cloth.

The fire chief finishes his tea about 1:50. The road chief makes some laudatory remarks about both the deceased and the fire chief, asking the fire chief to lead the second round of songs. The cedar chief is still bringing the tea around. One of the women who had refused peyote when the bag was passed has left ("to look after her kids"), and the other 2 women who did not take the dried buttons also decline the tea when it is offered. The second round of songs proceeds like the first, with the same individuals participating, except that all but 2 of the men are using their own rattles and 2 are using their own fans. Even though they have their own equipment, the men still accept the road chief's paraphernalia when it is passed to them, holding his rattle in their left hand with the staff and fan and using their own rattle to accompany their singing. The road chief's fan is held along with their own fan in their left hand. It is considered an insult to the road chief to lay down his equipment and use only one's own.

At 2:45 everyone who wants peyote tea has had it. The cedar chief places the pail on the left side of the altar cloth and resumes his position next to the fire chief. Meanwhile the singing continues. Most people have their heads bowed and appear to be sleeping. I was told that this was not the case, however, because "you can't sleep when you take peyote . . . the medicine is working, and they're concentrating all they can to learn this Way."

By 3:25 the paraphernalia has made the full circuit, and it is the road chief's turn to sing. He sings 4 songs, 3 of which are in Winnebago and the other in Kiowa.

Next, it is the cedar chief's turn to sing (since this round began with the fire chief), but the road chief asks the cedar chief to deliver a prayer instead. After burning some incense, the cedar chief begins aloud: "Great Spirit, Our Savior, and Your Son, thank you for permitting us to carry on with this meeting. We still have a long piece of the road to go, so please give us the strength to continue. We thank you for letting our guests be here tonight; we pray that they may return in safety to their homes. You know that we are gathered here tonight to pray for your child who has died. You know that he lived a good and faithful life and followed your Way as best he could. Now we ask you to bless and comfort these people who are mourning him. We ask you especially for his daughter and for his son who offers this meeting to honor his father. They ask you for the power to continue in the footsteps of their father. We all ask you for that gift. We pray to you to let us learn the mysteries of this Way, that we might lead our lives as you might wish. We are not strong, do not know very much about things, and so we ask for your guidance, your light, to teach us what we need to know" [translation].

The road chief thanks the cedar chief for delivering the prayer and says that they must "move ahead toward morning." It is now about 3:40. The cedar chief burns more incense and again fans smoke toward each of the participants. This time, however, instead of simply fanning the smoke in the direction of the objects on the altar cloth, he picks up each article and holds it for a few seconds over the smoke. At 3:55 the road chief picks up the peyote bag and passes it to his left again, without taking any peyote for himself. Then he begins the third round of songs with the Morning Song; he finishes this series of songs at about 4:10. Instead of drumming for the fire chief (as he did in the last round) he signals to Danny Green, who is seated diagonally across from him along the east wall. Danny rises, takes the drum from the drum chief, and sits down facing the fire chief. (This practice, I later learned, is known as "calling across.") When the fire chief finishes his series of songs, Danny Green returns to his place and the third round of songs proceeds without further variation.

As the singing continues, people begin to pray quite audibly, and many weep intermittently. At daylight (about 5:15), while the drum chief is singing, the road chief signals to Frances Green to "bring the morning water." She rises and leaves the room.

When the drum chief finishes the last of his Morning Songs, he passes the paraphernalia back to the road chief, who places it on the altar cloth. The cedar chief burns incense and repeats the purification of the items. Then the road chief picks up his rattle, fan, and staff and sings the final Morning Songs. At 5:45 (the road chief is on the third song), Frances Green enters, carrying the same water pail that was brought in at midnight. She places the bucket between the road chief and the altar cloth and then kneels on the other side of the cloth, facing the road chief. She begins to pray. The cedar chief burns incense and smokes the water pail, and the road chief picks up the cup from the altar cloth and repeats the drinking and washing ritual that he did at midnight. He then hands the cup to Frances, who goes through the same motions. She takes the pail around (again in a clockwise direction) until everyone in the room has participated in the morning water ceremony.

At 6:15, after everyone has taken some of the water, Frances takes the pail outside. She returns with it refilled and places it in front of the road chief. She leaves again, this time returning with 3 plates, each with a spoon, and places these in front of the road chief. The plates contain canned corn, canned peaches, and boiled beef, respectively. The road chief bows his head and prays in a very low voice. Sitting back beside me, Frances explains that he is thanking the Almighty and praying that the kinds of food that are represented—vegetable, fruit, and meat—will always be plentiful. At the end of the prayer, the road chief takes a cupful of the water from the pail and drinks it. The fire chief does likewise, then rises and places the pail in front of the cedar chief, offering him a drink. The fire chief then proceeds around the room, bringing the water to each person.

After drinking the water, the cedar chief burns some more incense and fans the smoke toward the 3 plates of food. The road chief picks up the dish of corn, bows his head and prays briefly, takes a spoonful, and passes the dish clockwise to the cedar chief. The same is done with the other 2 dishes of food until all 3 dishes are in circulation, with everyone sampling each type of food. At 7:10 the water pail and food have made the complete circuit, and the road chief begins to pray: "Great Spirit, Almighty God, I give you thanks. Thanks for seeing us through this long night. Amen." Then he announces that he will now sing the final songs and close the meeting. He sings 4 songs, the last of which is called the Quitting Song. When he has finished the last one, at 7:23, people slowly stand up. Some remain in the meeting house, milling around, while others leave immediately.

Singing parties

Another type of gathering of Peyotists, less formal and less complex than a peyote meeting, is the singing party. The arrival of an unexpected visitor, the return of a man from a trip to another peyote group who has learned new songs to teach to his neighbors, or just the desire to "sing and pray together" are characteristic reasons for holding a singing party. This type of gathering has the 3 major elements of a regular meeting—singing and drumming, the taking of peyote, and praying—but takes less time to organize and costs less to sponsor. Singing parties are conducted in the sponsor's home with as few as 2 or 3 participants. There is no fixed order of ritual activities.

Use of peyote for curing and protection

The residents of Rice Village can cite many examples of miraculous cures that have been effected by peyote. As a curative agent it is administered in meetings, but it is also used outside of the ritual context, more or less as any other medication would be taken. Informants all reported that at one time or another they had taken peyote at home, not only when they were very sick but also on occasions when they "just didn't feel right." During the period of research, peyote was used only once (to my knowledge) for curing. This was when a one-year-old child was running an extremely high fever. Instead of taking her child to the Indian hospital where, she felt, they would just tell her "to put him to bed and give him aspirin," the mother brewed some peyote tea. While the grandmother held the screaming child, the mother tried to coax him to drink some tea from his bottle. They managed to force a small quantity down his throat before giving up.

Peyote is also used as a good-luck talisman. Buttons kept for this purpose are usually large peyote chiefs, which are carried when the individual is embarking on a dangerous trip or on an activity of which the outcome is extremely important. It was reported that the one young man from the community who was in the army at the time of my fieldwork carried with him at all times an especially large peyote chief that had belonged to his father. Informants also mentioned that they sometimes carried a peyote chief along on wild ricing expeditions.

Reported effects of peyote

A detailed account of the physiological and psychological effects of peyote has been compiled by La Barre (1964:93–104, 139–50, 197–98, 219–23, 227–36)). Here I have recorded only the responses of Rice Village informants who were asked to describe their personal experiences with peyote. All agreed that there were certain unpleasant aspects of eating peyote, such as its bitter taste and the nausea that often follows. Fatigue, but not sleepiness, was reported to be another sensation experienced. Distortions of sound, color, and spatial relationships and a heightened sensitivity to stimuli were also noted: "Sometimes funny things happen. You think something is right up close to you, so you may reach out to grab it and it won't be there. You'll find that it's really way on the other side of the room." "You feel everything around you just strong. The drum—you know that drum they use—you'll feel like it's right inside you, beating right inside your head."

Feeling the "power of the Almighty" or the "power of that peyote" was another sensation reported. "It comes up inside you, and you feel like you can understand everything or can do just about whatever you want. You feel that nothing can touch you, that this power will protect you and show you the right way. It's just a wonderful feeling."

Belief system

In the field I was not able to investigate systematically the villagers' conceptions of the supernatural, eschatological beliefs, the nature of the power of peyote, and other ideological or theological considerations; however, I did examine in detail legends about the origin of Peyotism and its relationship to other religions. For a thorough ethnographic treatment of the ideology of the peyote religion, the reader is directed to Slotkin's account of Menomini Peyotism (1952:578) and Chapters 11 and 12 of Aberle's Navajo materials (1966).

The Rice Village account of the origin of the religion is similar to that reported for other tribes (La Barre 1964). Villagers say that peyote was first revealed to a tribe in the south, perhaps Apaches, but they are not certain.

> One of their women was out looking for berries or something, and she lost her way. Wandered around out there for quite some time. In the desert and all, you know, it gets pretty hot. Couldn't find her way back home, and had nothing to eat or drink. They say she found a place to lie down—maybe she wanted to go to sleep, maybe she thought she was going to die. Well, she felt something cool touch her hand. Of course she didn't know what it was. Well, it sort of spoke to her, started singing, you might say. That's how guys who are out in the peyote field find it. You look and look, but you won't find nothing until it calls out to you. Well, anyway, she ate some of it. After that she didn't feel tired anymore, or thirsty either. And it taught her all about the Way, told her how to live right, how to run meetings, just everything. So she began to search again for

the way back home, she was just anxious to get there and tell them all she had found out. That's how the Indian got this religion. At least that is the way I've heard it told.

Rice Village Peyotists believe that this took place quite a long time ago, "way before any white man set foot in this country."

Peyotists see their religion as the Indian counterpart to the white man's Christianity. "It's the same God for both Indians and whites." "This peyote Way is just the Indian way of worshipping God. You might say that it is purer than the white man's way, because he needed to have Christ reveal it to him. But God revealed himself directly to the Indian through peyote." This view implies a relativistic attitude toward all Christian denominations, which seems to be extended to the religious beliefs of all people. "As long as you are worshipping the Almighty it doesn't really matter how you go about it." "We don't criticize, say things, about the way others believe. They should respect our rights too." "We don't go around saying that our way is the only way, we don't try to force people to change their minds."

Visiting other peyote groups

Individuals in the community regularly receive invitations to attend meetings in Wisconsin, the Twin Cities, North and South Dakota, Nebraska, and Canada. These meetings are eagerly anticipated for both social and religious reasons. Rice Villagers enjoy visiting with old acquaintances and making new friends among "our own boys." Gossip is exchanged, marital matches may be made (2 Rice Village women have married men from a group of Canadian Peyotists), and items of ritual paraphernalia and peyote jewelry are traded. These visits also provide the opportunity to learn new peyote songs and details of ritual.

With the exception of the 2 elderly women, individuals from all of the households had made at least one trip to another peyote group during the year prior to my research; several people reported that they make at least 3 or 4 such trips a year.

Factors influencing rates of acculturation

One concern of the student of cultural change is differential acculturation, that is, variation in the ways groups respond to pressures for social and cultural change. Social scientists have focused on 4 main types of variables responsible for rapid change or, conversely, marked resistance to change.

One of the more common factors used to explain differential rates of acculturation is the philosophy or ethos of a group. For example, in the Tewa resistance to the acculturative and assimilative influences of the Hopi, Dozier cited the traditional role of the Tewa as "defenders" of the Hopi as an important device that "bolsters group pride and prestige" and helps to maintain the cultural integrity of the group (1951:60).

A second variable that may facilitate or retard change is the physical and social setting of the group. Proximity to other groups, towns, and cities, the degree of economic self-sufficiency, and the position of the group or community in a regional or national social hierarchy may be important determinants of the type and degree of acculturation.

The nature of the contact situation is a third factor often considered significant in the acculturation process. Wallerstein (1966), Service (1955), and Spicer (1961), among others, have emphasized the importance of this variable with regard to the types and amounts of change that will occur.

A fourth factor frequently emphasized in studies of acculturation rates is the social structure of the group undergoing acculturation. Wolf (1957), for example, discussed boundary-maintaining mechanisms such as endogamy and the fiesta system as effectively inhibiting change in Latin American peasant groups. Adair and Vogt (1949) contrasted the "loose" structure of Navajo social organization with the "tighter" structure of Zuni society in order to explain the differences in the responses of these 2 groups to returning war veterans. The role of these 4 sets of variables in the cultural isolation of Rice Village is most clearly illustrated by means of a brief comparison with the Indian population of the nearby reservation community, James Lake.

Rice Village and James Lake compared

James Lake, which is described in greater detail in Pelto's chapter in this volume, is a town of approximately 1,500 people, about half of them white and the other half Chippewa. Although economically, politically, and geographically, James Lake is a single community, a strong case can be made for the existence of 2 culturally distinct communities within its boundaries—the Indian community and the white community. Even though it is technically part of the Broken Reed Reservation, most of the land in James Lake is owned by whites. Historically, the town was settled first by Chippewa in the mid-18th century. However, at the turn of the 20th century its character changed drastically as it burgeoned from a small Indian village into a lumber boom town, which continued to grow rapidly for the next 20 years. The establishment of a national forest in 1908 foreshadowed the inevitable decline of the lumbering industry by closing off huge tracts of land to the lumber companies. By the 1920s, the mills had finished sawing the remaining timber. This drastic reduction in the town's source of employment was offset by the establishment of various government agencies in the community (including the Forest Service, Public Health Service Indian Hospital, and, for a time, the Minnesota office of the Bureau of Indian Affairs) and the emergence of a tourist industry, which capitalized on the attractive lakeshores and forests.

Today James Lake is still a commercial and administrative center and the largest town on the Broken Reed Reservation. Two government agencies are still maintained there, as well as a high school (which many children from outlying areas, including Rice Village, attend) and a grade school. It also has its own police force and jail. Commercial buses traveling north and south (to and from the Twin Cities) stop in James Lake. In addition, there are many resorts and summer homes located on or near the lake itself, and vacationers swell the population of the community each summer.

People from smaller towns on the reservation come to James Lake to use its commercial, educational, recreational, and medical facilities. James Lakers travel to and from North City and Trotter quite regularly.

Most male household heads in James Lake, as in Rice Village, are employed in the timber industry. In the mid-1960s, at the time of this study, annual household income ranged from under $1,000 to over $7,000, but the median for Indian households was a modest $2,000. As in Rice Village, cash income is supplemented by fishing, hunting, berrying, and surplus commodities.

The Indian community in James Lake is subdivided into several distinct neighborhoods. Two of these neighborhoods, one to the south of town and the other to the north, are almost exclusively Indian. The other 2 are mixed Indian and white. A good deal of social interaction occurs among these neighborhoods since they are within easy walking distance of each other. In fact, James Lake is so compact that owning a car is a convenience, not a necessity. James Lake Indians seem to spend much of their time in town—shopping, visiting, and sitting around in the taverns.

When patterns of social interaction with individuals outside the community are examined, James Lake Indians do not exhibit the social isolation that is characteristic of Rice Villagers. Since there are no physical barriers or ideological forces prohibiting interaction, James

Lakers take marriage partners from, have friends in, and visit a much broader range of communities than do Rice Villagers. Further, there are no restrictions on membership in the James Lake community, as there are in Rice Village, so Chippewa from all over Minnesota have come to live in James Lake.

Compared to Rice Village, James Lake has a much looser structure, evidenced by considerably less cooperation and interdependence at both the community and interhousehold levels. Formal organization of Indians is weak, and various community projects have met with little success. For example, in the 1930s a cooperative association was formed to market Indian crafts. In spite of apparent economic success, the organization was disbanded after a couple of years, supposedly because Co-op members could not agree on division of profits. The prevailing sentiment for a complete per capita distribution of Indian land claims money rather than the appropriation of funds for community projects, as well as the widespread lack of support for the Community Action Project financed by the Office of Economic Opportunity, may be taken as more recent evidence of the relatively individualistic nature of the James Lake Indians.

The same individualistic and largely noncooperative pattern is apparent in historic relationships among households. In striking contrast to Rice Village, most James Lake Indian land allotments were sold, and those not sold were frequently subdivided among the heirs rather than maintained as larger holdings of extended families.

Not unexpectedly, nuclear families in James Lake appear to be more independent economically than those in Rice Village. In response to an interview schedule item, "Is there anyone outside the household who contributes to family income?" 27 of the 30 James Lake Indian respondents reported no outside support. In 2 of the 3 affirmative cases only small sums (money for laundry, candy, etc.) were involved. It also appears that economic pressure is rarely met by pooling resources and extending the household unit. Unmarried mothers seldom share a house with relatives or friends.

In summary, Rice Village, compared to James Lake, is more isolated physically and geographically from commercial and population centers. Rice Village is also socially isolated, its members interacting with a very restricted group of people outside the community. James Lake Indians, on the other hand, have much wider social contact outside their own community.

Structurally, Rice Village is a small, intimate, and cooperative community. Members depend on one another in religious and economic activities and other aspects of daily life. The Indian community in James Lake has little cohesion at the community level, and its households are much less interdependent economically. Furthermore, social sanctions against deviant behavior can be felt much more immediately and strongly in Rice Village.

The value orientations of the 2 communities differ considerably. The people of Rice Village have a highly visible value system centered on the peyote religion, whereas no such homogeneity of beliefs and values exists in James Lake.

Because of the differences between the 2 communities, one might expect to find differences in their patterns of acculturation. Specifically, it is hypothesized that the James Lake Indians exhibit a greater degree of acculturation than do the people of Rice Village, as measured by the extent of articulation to elements of "white American" culture and the degree to which traditional Chippewa behaviors have been maintained.

A number of indicators of articulation are available in data collected through interview schedules used in James Lake and Rice Village:

1. Attended school events (athletic programs, etc.)
2. Voted in 1960 or 1964 national election or both
3. Subscribed to or read at least one magazine
4. Read a local newspaper
5. Read a metropolitan daily newspaper
6. Read a metropolitan Sunday newspaper
7. Regularly listened to or watched a specific radio or television program, or mentioned one as a favorite program
8. Belonged to a community or church organization
9. Rated nationality (being an American) as the most or next most important item in a hierarchy of "life aspects"

Each of the interviewees (31 in James Lake and 9 in Rice Village) was given a score from zero to 9 based on the presence or absence of each of these 9 indicators of articulation. As Table 4.4 shows, the highest Rice Village score is 5, the median for both sets of scores combined. Indeed, most of the villagers scored well below the median of the combined scores.

To test the statistical significance of these data the Mann-Whitney U Test was applied to the ranked individual scores. The difference between the distribution of Rice Village and James Lake articulation scores was

found to be significant at $p > .0003$. Thus James Lake Chippewa show a
significantly higher degree of articulation to white institutions than do
Rice Village Chippewa.

One of the cultural patterns that is most widely used as an index of

Table 4.4. Articulation scores and ranks

Rice Village			James Lake		
Interviewee	Articulation score	Rank	Interviewee[a]	Articulation score	Rank
			27	9	40
			9	8	36.5
			10	8	36.5
			12	8	36.5
			19	8	36.5
			24	8	36.5
			26	8	36.5
			18	7	31.5
			22	7	31.5
			23	7	31.5
			59	7	31.5
			5	6	27
			6	6	27
			16	6	27
			21	6	27
			28	6	27
4	5	18.5	1	5	18.5
7	5	18.5	4	5	18.5
			8	5	18.5
			15	5	18.5
			20	5	18.5
			80	5	18.5
9	4	14	11	4	14
			13	4	14
			19	4	14
			25	4	14
			7	3	10.5
			14	3	10.5
3	2	8.5	17	2	8.5
1	1	6	3	1	6
2	1	6			
5	0	2.5	2	0	2.5
6	0	2.5			
8	0	2.5			

a. See Chapter 6 of this volume for an explanation of the seemingly
nonsensical numbering of the James Lake interviewees.

traditionality is the persistence of aboriginal language use. Other possible indicators of traditionality (ricing, for example) may persist in modern Chippewa tribes for purely economic reasons; similarly, to the observer it may not be clear whether attendance at powwows indicates adherence to traditional Chippewa beliefs or to the modern Pan-Indian movement. For this reason, use of the Ojibwa language has been selected in this study as the most significant indicator of maintenance of traditional patterns of behavior.

Data on the use of the Chippewa language in James Lake are taken from a subsample of 15 of the households that participated in the interview schedule. Actually, reported data include 17 individuals, because 2 of the responses contain data for both the main interviewee and spouse. In addition, 7 of the respondents gave information regarding use of Chippewa by their children. Ten of the James Lake adult respondents said that they could speak Chippewa; 7 said they could not. In the small sample of James Lake children, 2 could speak Chippewa and 7 could not.

For Rice Village there are more complete data: information is reported for all of the adults as well as for all of the children in the community 5 years of age and older. All of the Rice Village adults speak Chippewa. Seventeen of them said that they could speak it fluently; one responded that she could speak it, "but not too well." In contrast, only a little over half of the adults in the James Lake sample speak Chippewa.

The case for the greater traditionality of Rice Village is made much stronger when the variable of age is introduced. For the James Lake sample, ability to speak Chippewa appears to be strongly correlated with age (see Table 4.5). Although the older adults who reside in James Lake tend to speak Chippewa, it appears that the Chippewa language is not being learned or spoken by the younger generations.

In Rice Village, on the other hand, ability to speak Chippewa among the adults is not correlated with age. All of the adults, ranging in age from 23 to 75, use the Chippewa language. Further evidence of the

Table 4.5. Use of Chippewa language by
James Lake interviewees

	40 years old or younger	*41 years old or older*
Speaks Chippewa	3	9
Does not speak Chippewa	13	1

continuity of their language tradition can be found by examining the data concerning the use of Chippewa and the amount understood by the children. The degree of fluency of all the children in the community between the ages of 5 and 15 is shown in Table 4.6.

At the time of this study, the children in Rice Village learned English as their first language. However, they were able to comprehend some Chippewa at an early age, and by the time they were nearing adulthood they were able to speak it. Use of the traditional language by these children is the result of a conscious effort by the adults in Rice Village. Parents who normally converse with each other in English make a special point of occasionally speaking Chippewa to each other and to their children—issuing commands and questions that require the child to respond in Chippewa. These language training sessions are generally conducted in a spirit of fun when one or both parents are playing with the child. Correct responses to commands and correct use of Chippewa are usually rewarded with praise and good-natured joking. With older children, parents and other adults in the community occasionally engage in short conversations in Chippewa. The teenagers are motivated to learn Chippewa so that the adults "can't say things in front of us that we don't understand." The several older people in the community who use Chippewa as their preferred language provide the youth with another stimulus for speaking Chippewa and an opportunity to use the language.

Table 4.6. Use of Chippewa language by Rice Village children

Interviewee	Age (years)	Speaks	Understands all	Understands some
1	15	x		
2	15	x		
3	13	x		
4	13	x		
5	12	x		
6	12		x	
7	10		x	
8	10		x	
9	8			x
10	8			x
11	7		x	
12	5			x

In summary, in the maintenance of this important element of Chippewa culture, the Rice Villagers appear to be much more traditional than the people of James Lake. All of the adults in Rice Village can and do speak Chippewa, and there is evidence that this is being continued in the younger generations. Quite the opposite appears to be true in James Lake. Most James Lakers who do speak Chippewa are 41 years old or older. The younger adults and their children generally do not speak Chippewa.

Conclusion

In this study acculturation has been regarded as "those phenomena which result when groups of individuals having different cultures come into continuous first hand contact, with subsequent changes in the original cultural patterns of either or both groups" (Redfield, Linton, Herskovits 1936). On the Broken Reed Reservation, acculturation has been largely uni-directional. That is, the Indian people have been modifying their traditional patterns of behavior and adopting elements of white culture to a greater extent than the whites have adopted elements of Chippewa culture.

Two factors that are crucial in determining the rate at which a group adopts new or alternative patterns of behavior are access to information about the contacting culture and the degree to which the social situation permits experimentation with and adoption of new patterns of behavior. It is within this framework that the physical, geographical, and social differences between James Lake and Rice Village converge to produce different rates of acculturation.

The differences in location, in community size and composition, and in patterns of social interaction have affected significantly the amount of information about white culture to which these communities are exposed. James Lake Indians, who reside in the midst of a large and active white population, continually observe and interact with whites and thus have access to much information about white culture. The physical isolation of Rice Village from white commercial, administrative, and population centers, coupled with limited patterns of social interaction outside the community, result in little observation of and interaction with whites. Therefore, Rice Villagers have less access to new cultural information.

The factors that influence whether group members can experiment with alternative patterns of behavior appear to be even more important than exposure to new cultural information. In this regard both community structure and the attitudes of the local white population must be considered. The greater economic and social interdependence of Rice Village households and the community interest in maintaining a common religious affiliation and communal property have resulted in a relatively intimate and "tight" social situation. The detailed knowledge that people have about the activities of their fellow villagers and the intensity of interaction with them make possible effective social sanctions against deviant behavior, which includes experimentation with and adoption of white culture.

In James Lake, the larger population, greater individualism of households, and lack of organization at the community level produce more anonymity, thus permitting individuals more freedom in experimenting with new behavioral and cultural patterns.

When the direct influences of whites on Indian acculturation patterns in these communities are examined, important differences between Rice Village and James Lake are found. The James Lake Indians hold a minority status in a town that has a substantial and dominant white population. This white majority controls the economic, religious, educational, and other social institutions of the community. Thus the Indians are continually exposed to the "superiority" of white culture and to the whites' negative evaluation of behavior judged to be "Indian." This stratification results in social pressure to accept white culture, and the sanctions operating to combat nonconformity to white standards are clearly visible.

Rice Villagers are not subject to the same kind and amount of pressure to adopt white behavioral patterns. They are well aware of the minority status that Indians as an ethnic group hold within the context of American society. In terms of their everyday activities, however, villagers are not exposed to the negative evaluation of their cultural heritage, nor do they experience the indignities of subordination to the same degree as James Lakers. In addition, the tenets of the peyote religion ascribe positive values to their traditional "Indian" behavior.

In summary, data indicate that Rice Villagers have been slower than James Lakers in accepting elements of white culture while maintaining greater adherence to certain traditional behaviors. Factors accounting for these differences appear to be the result of the interaction of a number of variables, none of which should be considered in isolation. Had it not been for the particular circumstances of physical setting and family history, the peyote religion would probably not have been as effective an organizing and solidifying force. Conversely, geographical location alone could not have produced the present level of community solidarity. All of these factors must be considered together in the analysis of social and cultural change in Rice Village.

5

Social Structure and Community Development in a Chippewa Village

Timothy Roufs

While I was doing fieldwork in James Lake, Minnesota, during the summer of 1965, a friend suggested that I go to Wicket, a small Chippewa settlement some 35 miles to the east, for additional information. The Wicket Indians, she explained, were more "progressive" that those of James Lake, trying to help themselves and yet remaining conscious of their traditions. They were at that time planning their annual powwow, which she thought was the best in the area.

I first visited Wicket on July 14, late in the afternoon. A dozen people were busily preparing the grounds for the powwow. In the absence of the local council chairman, another man assumed the role of spokesperson and quickly extended to me the community's hospitality. They had been busy, he said; among their recent accomplishments were a completely furnished community hall, which provided a recreation center for children and teenagers, a baseball diamond, a sodded powwow ring. Wicket also had an active, independent Teen Council—at that time the largest in the state. In the works, I was told, were an arts and crafts center, a camping area, new housing and sanitation facilities, and a community library.

Later that evening I talked with the chairman of the local council, who carefully explained that the local people had spent considerable

194

time and money to use high-quality building materials and equipment in the new community hall. He made sure I noticed the new jukebox and soft-drink machine that the Teen Council had purchased, and he showed me a pile of books that was the beginning of the community library. Outside, the chairman pointed to the sodded powwow ring and baseball diamond and told how the men had sweated to prepare them. He was especially proud of the powwow singers' pavilion, shaded by leafy branches, which lent a traditional touch to their celebration.

He talked of Indian lands and of the values of both present and past Indian ways of life. It would be desirable and possible, he thought, to adopt ways of the white man without losing valuable elements of the Indian tradition. I warmed to the community spirit and to the pride in their Indian heritage held by these people, who were, nevertheless, eager to obtain for their children what they considered the best of the white man's life. The residents of Wicket, it was obvious, felt themselves to be a "successful" community.

During this summer field session of 1965, I learned that the Wicket community had received much local recognition. Members of the local Bureau of Indian Affairs (BIA), the Community Action Program (CAP), the Reservation Business Committee (RBC), and Indian and white residents of the area had all come to recognize Wicket as a dynamic Indian community able to initiate and complete significant programs and activities.

What were the elements in the background and social situation of Wicket that made the community's concerted efforts successful, in the view of both its own members and its neighbors? This study will attempt to identify the elements that are significant for successful community action. Such information may be useful to others concerned with the development of American Indian communities.

Research setting and research design

Although my research began in the summer of 1965 and continued for several years, the research for this study was conducted mainly between June and September, 1966. During this time I lived in the home of the local council chairman and slept in a tent in his backyard. There I could work freely on my field notes and on analyzing data.

The present discussion is concerned with the 3-and-a-half-year period beginning with the formation of the Wicket Local Indian Council in May of 1963. Although approximately 15 percent of the people of Wicket are non-Indian, the history, current composition, and characteristics of the Wicket Indian population are the subjects of this inquiry into Wicket's experience of successful collective action.

There are 3 reasons for excluding whites from the discussion. First—although existing relationships between Indians and whites tend to be very amicable—the white households located in the surrounding area participate minimally in the activities of the community center and of the council. Members of these white households tend instead to identify and interact with the neighboring and predominantly white community of Buck Lake, where they commonly receive their mail, attend school and church, shop, and visit friends.

Second, because few whites live within the Wicket village itself and many of those who do are married to persons of Indian descent, the only active organization during this 3-and-a-half-year interval was the Indian local council, which was acknowledged to be primarily responsible for the community's development. The white residents of Wicket (in both the village and the surrounding area) do not have any exclusively white formal organization that unites them politically or socially. While the whites have not formally participated in the activities of the council, they have supported it financially.

Third, although the business establishments located in Wicket are owned by whites, 3 are primarily dependent on markets outside of town, one depends heavily on the tourist trade, and 2 are open only part-time. Of the remaining 3 businesses, 2 are owned by men married to Indian women, who assist them in running the businesses. Thus, the merchants who depend on local customers have kinship ties with the Indian community. This condition tends to accentuate the image of Wicket as an Indian community.

Field techniques used in this study included participant observation as well as informal and formal interviewing, the latter incorporating the systematic administration of a schedule of interview questions in a random sample of households. A table of random numbers was used to select the households from an alphabetical list of all Indian households in the research area.

In this study an Indian household is defined as a household having one or more adult members of Indian descent. The Minnesota Chippewa Tribe includes in this category all persons on the "basic membership roll," which consists of all persons of Minnesota Chippewa Indian "blood" whose names appear on the annuity roll of April 14, 1941. In addition, all children of Minnesota Chippewa Indian blood born between this date and July 3, 1961, are included in this category, as are all children of at least one-quarter degree Minnesota Chippewa Indian blood born after July 3, 1961 (Minnesota Chippewa Tribe, Constitution and Bylaws, Article 2, Section 1, March 3, 1964).

Of the total of 89 Indian households in the research area, 39, or 43.8 percent, were selected for formal interviewing. During the period of fieldwork for this study, 2 of the 39 moved permanently from the area while 2 others left temporarily and were not available for interviews. Of the remaining 35 households, only 32 responded to the schedule of interview questions. The first direct refusal was by the 39th household randomly selected. Then another head of household, after postponing our meeting, eventually refused to be interviewed. Another randomly selected respondent agreed to the interview but never kept our appointments. These contacts were considered as refusals. Lack of responses by these informants does not technically affect the randomness of the sample. All percentages cited in the study, unless otherwise indicated, are percentages of those responding to the household interview schedule.

In order to check the representativeness of the sample, 4 Wicket residents were asked to name the occupation of each of the household heads in the research area. Table 5.1 compares the occupations named by the 4 informants with the self-responses of the heads of households in the sample. The high correspondence between the sample data and the 4 informants' statements about the total list suggests that, in terms of occupations, sampling error is minimal.

Although complete data were not available to test reliability, a check on some of the respondents' information suggests that reliability is relatively high. Birth and death rates were obtained from headstones in 2 of the 3 local cemeteries and compared with the dates given by the respondents for their parents. (Answers of respondents who explicitly stated that they were not certain were omitted in the following comparisons.) Data were available to check 9 responses, about 20 percent of the total. In those 9 cases only one error was found. One individual indicated a year of death 3 years earlier than that on the marker, but stated correctly the deceased's age at death. None of these respondents referred to written materials in answering the questions. Furthermore, for any question the interview schedules permitted respondents to respond "Prefer not to answer." Although this response was chosen only 5 times for the entire set of interviews, this procedure seemed to minimize or eliminate deliberate distortion or falsification of responses.

The research instrument used in these structured interviews was a

Table 5.1. Occupations or income sources in random sample
compared to informants' assessments of
total population

Occupation or income source	Informants' assessment of total list		Sampled interviewees' ratings		Difference
	%	No.	%	No.	%
Mining (all types of jobs)	21.7	18	18.8	6	−2.9
Woods work; common labor	26.6	22	28.2	9	+1.6
Auto repair, carpentry, etc.	6.0	5	6.2	2	+0.2
Odd jobs, general repair (skilled)	1.2	1	3.1	1	+1.9
Farming	2.4	2	6.2	2	+3.8
Guiding; minnow selling	1.2	1	0.0	0	−1.2
CAP, Civil Service work	4.8	4	3.1	1	−1.7
Sales	1.2	1	0.0	0	−1.2
Small business	2.4	2	0.0	0	−2.4
Hurt, ill, disabled	3.6	3	6.2	2	+2.6
Retirement pension	19.2	16	21.8	7	+2.6
Public welfare	8.4	7	6.2	2	−2.1
Unemployed	1.2	1	0.0	0	−1.2
	N=83		*N*=32		

modified version of the Upper Mississippi Research Project (UMRP) interview schedule. I had used the UMRP instrument in James Lake during the previous summer with both white and Indian respondents. Modifications of the schedule based on this prior experience were made for the Wicket study.

The 28-page schedule took from one to 2 hours to complete; so it was usually administered by appointment. The UMRP and Wicket instruments covered the topics of economics, kinship, religion, politics, social relationships, life story, and general attitudes on specific subjects. The Wicket schedule, in addition, included questions pertaining to ricing, the Chippewa language, the Indian religion, band membership, the *dodaim* ("totem"), powwows, and local council activities. Only a small part of the data collected is analyzed in this chapter.

The chairman of Wicket's council read a draft of this study at my request to ensure its accuracy. The description of the Wicket Local Indian Council is liberally drawn from written records of the council as well as from the interview materials. But because all of the early records of the community were destroyed by fire, the account of community leadership prior to the establishment of the Wicket Local Indian Council is based on the recollections of some of the older residents of Wicket.

Historical and descriptive overview

Wicket is a relatively small, unincorporated Chippewa Indian village located on the Broken Reed Reservation in northern Minnesota. It is one of 9 major Indian communities on the reservation and has about 80 Indian families living in an approximately 5-by-10-mile area surrounding the village center (see Figure 5.1). The boundaries of the larger community are designated by the local council; persons living within those boundaries are eligible for membership in the council. People in the few Indian households located immediately north, south, or east of the boundaries consider themselves members of other communities. Excluding the Indian families living in the village of Buck Lake, Indians comprise approximately 50 percent of the population in the research area.

The village itself extends approximately one-half mile from the intersection of the east-west state highway and the paved county road running north on the west side of Wicket Lake. A detailed sketch of this area appears in Figure 5.2.

To travelers along the main highway, Wicket is little more than another "wide spot in the road." Traveling from east to west along the highway, one first encounters on the outskirts of the village 2 rather old and outdated resort motels. A mile or so down the road is a yard with a dozen or more wrecked cars in it, a small machine shop, a cafe that was remodeled from an old service garage, a grocery store, a gas station and bar, and a few small houses and abandoned buildings. On the east side of Wicket is a barely noticeable old dance hall, which has been converted into a residence, and a one-pump gas station, which appears to be inoperative. Turning north at the intersection in the middle of town, within the distance of a city block are the local post office (connected to a residence), a "3.2" beer tavern, the community hall and its adjoining

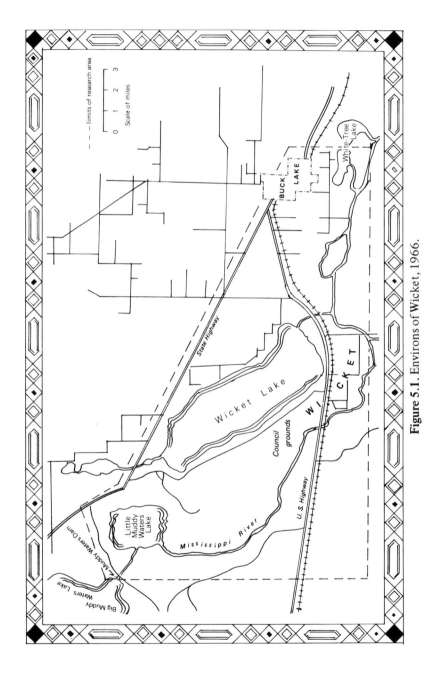

Figure 5.1. Environs of Wicket, 1966.

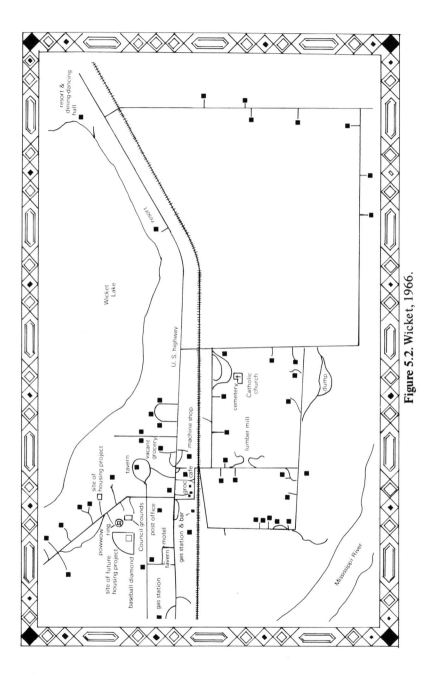

Figure 5.2. Wicket, 1966.

grounds, and the site of the new community housing project. Continuing north out of Wicket, for the next 40 miles the motorist passes little but lakes, trees, a few small houses, wood-framed and paper-sided, and a couple of resort motels. Spread out in the wooded areas just off of the main highways, however, are the homes of most of the residents of Wicket. These small groupings of households are known by the residents as units and referred to by their geographic place names. These units generally tend to coincide with family and friendship groups.

The present site of Wicket is at the approximate center of the territorial range of the ancestors of the modern Wicket Chippewa. The ancestors of the present-day citizens probably occupied the research area beginning around 1748. They began to migrate west from the area of Sault Ste. Marie in the latter part of the 17th century, generally in response to population pressures and the lure of the fur trade. This migration has been well described in the literature (Hickerson 1962, 1966; cf. James 1954, Dunning 1959, Roufs 1976). Hickerson summarized these movements and their effects:

> The Chippewa, who had been living in their fishing settlements in the northern Great Lakes region where the furred game supply was quickly exhausted after the first real impact of the fur trade in the mid-17th century, were located at various places on the north slope of Lake Superior and going a short distance inland to trap and hunt. This was the first stage in a movement which saw them permanently occupy lakes and streams to the north of the lake as they gradually came to remain in very small groups in the interior. To abet this process, traders began accompanying them inland or seeking them out in their trapping grounds. The last stage in the migration, the permanent location of small bands in the interior, probably took place during the last third of the 18th century as the Chippewa settled virtually the entire region south of the Hudson's Bay muskeg.

> ...The northern migrations began at about the same time as the southern Chippewa migrations, in the early 1630s. The Northern Chippewa, however, never achieved a village organization based on the subordination of the clans to a superordinating tribal authority. The reorganization of their communities followed lines dictated by needs arising from the fur trade in a poor ecological region. (1966:19)

Hickerson's work suggests that among the southern Chippewa the idea and practice of acknowledging a village or tribal authority dates from early times. This tradition is interesting and important to note, especially in light of the current political situation on the reservations. Thus, around the middle of the 18th century the Chippewa peoples settled here, and their descendants have continued to occupy the same general area.

The east-west axis of the research area is formed by the largest east-west highway in northern Minnesota. As late as 1890, however, maps of the area show neither trail nor road corresponding to the present highway. By about 1915 maps show a "fair road," in contrast to a "better road." By 1925 the road had been taken over by the state, and in the 1930s it was changed to its present location. A northwest-southeast path around the west side of Wicket Lake appears on the 1915 version of state highway maps. The town of Wicket is at the intersection of these 2 paths.

At the turn of the century, logging camps and the railroad promoted rapid development of the village center. Logging in the area began around 1868 and continues to be important in the local economy, although far less important than in earlier days. In 1896 the True Head Lumber Company moved its logging railroad from Sagoquas to Buck Lake and built a line north from there. This change shifted the trading center of the western part of the county from Sagoquas to Buck Lake, thus placing it within the research area. The Buck Lake mill closed in 1921; the big logging camps in the area had closed by 1916, most of the area's timber having already been cut. The railroads had come to the area in the late 1890s as a direct result of the logging boom. They arrived in Wicket in 1904, making the town a relatively important junction where people coming from both north and south could board trains bound east or west. It is reported that the rail line originally turned north and ran through the Big Cloudy Waters Dam area because the Indians would not grant the railroad company an easement. In earlier days train departures would frequently be delayed in Wicket while the conductor and passengers paused to watch the spontaneous powwows that took place when the local Indians came to meet the train.

Although the nearby Sleeping Giant Iron Range was discovered in 1865, the mines were not commercially opened until the 1890s. From 1891 to 1900 some 43 million tons of iron ore were extracted from the range. Iron ore mining so increased that 643.5 million tons were taken from Minnesota between 1941 and 1950 (Rottsolk 1960:34). The first mining camps were similar to those of the lumber industry. Unlike logging, however, iron mining was to become a more permanent and important part of the regional economy, playing a significant role in the economic development of Wicket.

In addition to those entering the area for the trapping, logging, and mining industries, white settlers came to Wicket to "homestead." Most of these settlers originated from a town 65 miles to the south, which around 1900 was a great lumbering center as well as a major terminal for the river traffic coming from Wicket by way of Big Run. In addition to bringing in settlers, river transport played a major part in the early commercial development of Wicket. The White Tree Point Band, to which the majority of Wicket Chippewa belong, takes its name from the point in a small lake near the junction of the Mississippi and Broken Reed rivers. Every old-timer in the community remembers the days of local riverboat travel. At the beginning of the present century, Wicket thus served as a convenient terminal for both the riverboat and railroad systems, then the area's 2 major modes of transportation.

Wicket's central location in the transportation network of the white settlers and lumberjacks promoted the development of the town center. A hotel built prior to 1900 housed the first post office in the Wicket area, but it burned down during the 1930s. A combined tavern and dance hall was built in 1936; later it was converted into a residence and gas station. Also in the mid-1930s, a barroom opened in the old hotel and there was an old saloon across the street from the present grocery store. In the early 1900s a schoolhouse, a general store, and a jailhouse were erected; but after the decline of the logging industry the log jail fell into disuse, and the general store burned down around 1915. Of the old buildings, only the school remains, serving now as one of the local taverns.

Rural Electrical Association services became available in 1935 and provided a new source of energy to the community. However, the effects were not great. With the passing of the lumber camps and the riverboats, Wicket became another small, often unnoticed widening along a state road.

Demography

Demographic factors alone cannot determine community development, but they may be important elements in such change. Table 5.2 illustrates the demographic profile of Wicket and compares it with that of the United States, Rice Village, and the Indian population of James Lake. The profile reveals all of the characteristics typical of a rural nonfarm population: a high ratio of females to males, a low median age, a high fertility ratio, and a demographically immobile population. Wicket's percentage of dependent children is much higher than that of the United States in general, but lower than that of Minnesota, Rice Village, and James Lake.

Migration from the area is an important factor in the population structure of the community. In Wicket 61.7 percent of the children aged 16 and older have moved out of the research area; in the nearby white community of Lakewood, the figure is 64.1 percent (Schensul 1965:21).

Table 5.2. Demographic profile of Wicket compared with profiles of James Lake Indian population, Rice Village, and the United States

	Wicket	James Lake Indian population	Rice Village	United States
Median age (in years)	17.0	13.0	13.0	26.1
Dependent children under 15 years of age (% of total population)	43.5	53.9	50.0	26.9
Active population aged 15 to 64 years (% of total population)	31.0	38.9	42.0	61.8[a]
Dependent elderly, aged 65 years or older (% of total population)	5.5	7.2	8.0	8.5
Index of aging[b]	12.7	13.4	10.5	28.7
Average household size	4.8	n.a.	n.a.	n.a.
Nonmobile population[c] (% of total households)	81.3	66.7	100.0	76.5
Sex ratio[d]	1,130	667	1,111	1,057
Fertility ratio[e]	1,265	1,333	2,660	717

n.a.: not available

a. For Minnesota, 55.6%.
b. = 100 × [(no. persons 65 or over)/(no. persons under 15)].
c. Households living in same house previous 2 or more years.
d. Females × 1,000 males.
e. Children under 5 per 1,000 women aged 22–24.

Sources: Peterson 1961, Chapter 4 and passim; Minnesota Department of Conservation 1963:72; Upper Mississippi Research Project field interviews.

In Wicket 70 percent of the males in this category and 53.5 percent of the females have emigrated from the research area, which accounts in part for the slightly higher ratio of females to males.

Almost all of the adults now in Wicket—especially those between 45 and 69 years of age—have left the area at some time in their lives and lived elsewhere for a year or more. Well over half of these have lived in 2 or more communities before moving back to Wicket. Informants' statements indicate that such migration patterns are not new. In checking the present location of respondents' and their spouses' siblings, it was found that the general outmigration pattern has not changed significantly in recent years and has been relatively constant for the past 2 generations. In the white community of Lakewood, Schensul similarly found that 63.8 percent of the respondents' siblings had left the area (1965:21). The outmigrations for children and siblings of Wicket Indians are presented in Table 5.3; the number of years a family has lived in the same house in Wicket is given in Table 5.4.

The differences between percentages of outmigration for female children and female siblings suggests that there was a greater tendency for the older generation of females to marry and reside outside of the research area. Supporting this interpretation are statements made by older members of the community about a prohibition against marrying someone of "any known degree" of kinship, including that of the *dodaim*. Although 20 years ago nearly a third of all marriages were with persons from a more traditional Indian community to the north, only one such marriage has occurred in recent years, showing a tendency to move away from this aspect of the traditional way of life.

Although the older adults in the community who have previously lived elsewhere for a year or more have returned, most of those now leaving—about 70 percent—do not come back to settle permanently.

Three items are particularly important in the relationship between

Table 5.3. Outmigration of children and siblings of interviewees

	Total %	Male %	Female %	Deceased %
Interviewees' children aged 16 years and over, not in research area	61.7	70.0	53.5	—
Interviewees' siblings not in research area	66.7	69.8	64.1	23.8

Table 5.4. Years lived in house by Indian interviewees
of Wicket and James Lake

Years	Percentages	
	Wicket	James Lake
Less than 1	3.1	6.7
1	15.6	16.7
2	15.6	16.7
3 to 5	15.6	23.3
6 to 10	9.4	16.7
11 to 20	21.9	13.3
21 to 30	18.8	10.0
Don't know	0.0	10.0
	N=32	*N*=30

the demographic profile and the current development in the community.
First, with the relatively low median age (especially of males) and the
low percentage of active population, economic conditions are sufficient
to provide a high percentage of the population with jobs.

Second, the leadership of the community has been stratified by age.
Table 5.5 lists the Wicket leaders (by pseudonyms) with their ages and
occupations. Lone Bird, Mike Fox, and Tom Blackbear are involved in
reservation-wide affairs. At the time of this study, Leo Feather had
unsuccessfully attempted to take over the chairmanship of the local
council. The current chairman, William Drummaker, who wanted to

Table 5.5. Age and occupation of Wicket leaders

Name	Age	Occupation
1. Lone Bird	1886-1960	Logging
2. Mike Fox	80	Farming, retired
3. Tom Blackbear	61	Mining, retired
4. Jim Hunter (son-in-law of no. 2)	67	Mining, retired
5. William Drummaker (son-in-law of no. 2)	51	Mining
6. Bill Allen (son of no. 1)	38	Construction work
7. Leo Feather	31	Construction work; mining

resign, was unsure of Feather's capability; Feather himself claimed that he was no longer interested. Bill Allen became chairman of the Reservation Business Committee and subsequently was not interested in running for local office. The problem of finding a successor to Drummaker has caused the people of the community to be concerned about the need for dynamic leadership, although their concern is most often projected into the next decade. Some have asked Drummaker to remain in office until they can train a person to take his place, and he has so far maintained his leadership position. [*Editor's note:* He remained in this position until his death in 1979.]

Finally, most of the recent community activities and programs were undertaken by individuals over 45 years of age. Members of the community are concerned that their youth are not interested in maintaining the projects started by the older generation.

Economy

Wicket is located between the mining and logging regions of the state and can thus utilize the economic advantages of both. In addition, the region supports a relatively large game and wildlife population, which allows the members of the community to supplement their salaries with locally available noncash income.

A major state recreation area around Wicket supports popular camping, hunting, fishing, boating, sight-seeing, picnicking, and winter sports activities, which contribute indirectly to the economy of Wicket. Of similar importance are the national and state forests, which frequently provide part- or full-time jobs. Persons who depend on the cutting of pulpwood for a living are inconvenienced by an average annual snowfall of 70 inches. The Wicket area has a total average annual rainfall of about 24 inches and only 115 frost-free days per year.

Tourism is potentially important in the economy of Wicket. The average daily traffic flow through the community is 1,780 vehicles, of which only 450 are commercial (Minnesota Department of Conservation 1965:85). Members of the community want to attract tourists. Early in the development of the local council, its members considered putting up a large sign on Wicket's major highway reading "Home of Wicket, an Authentic Indian Village." A merchant in a large nearby community consented to donate the sign, but it had not yet been erected at the time of this study. Community members had also talked about establishing an Indian handicrafts factory to produce souvenirs. This plan led to the establishment of industrial crafts centers by the Community Action

Program in six reservation communities and ultimately to a reservation-wide crafts cooperative. The original intent was to make high-quality traditional Indian articles, not items that would compete with those "made in Japan."

The community's annual celebration, "an authentic Indian pow-wow," also aims to attract tourists in order to raise funds. Shortly before and during this celebration, large signs are erected on the main highway to advertise the powwow. Local Indian council intentions, however, are to run as noncommercial and authentic a powwow as possible.

Finally, the new owner of a small, attractive cafe formerly called the Ranch Kitchen has changed the name of the cafe to the Totem Inn. He also has considered remodeling the outside of the building to resemble a tepee.

Noncash income

Hunting and fishing are important in the overall economy of Wicket (see Tables 5.6 and 5.7). Deer is a major source of meat. Other animals valued as delicacies are partridge, moose, porcupine, cottontail rabbit, duck, and to some extent, bear and turtle. Most of the fish consumed are whitefish taken with nets, but other kinds of fish are also plentiful.

Free heating and cooking fuel is another source of noncash income. Of the 65.5 percent of the Wicket sample population heating their homes

Table 5.6. Household participation in
noncash income activities

Activity	Percentage[a]
Deer hunting	84.4
Small-game hunting	53.2
Fishing	59.4
Berrying (% of those berrying and not selling = 50%)	37.5
Truck gardening	28.1
Ricing (% of those ricing and selling all rice = 53.8%)	81.5

a. Households in which oldest male participated in activity.

Source: Minnesota Department of Conservation 1965:102.

Table 5.7. Consumption of fish and meat not purchased

Minimum percentage of total fish and meat supplied by fishing and hunting	Percentage of households	
	Fish	Meat
100	35.4	3.1
90	44.8	9.4
50	59.5	25.0
25	68.8	40.6
	N=32	N=32

with a wood stove, 91 percent cut the wood themselves. In a climate having an average of 250 days of frost a year, this results in a considerable cash savings.

Finally, gardening provides a small amount of noncash income for Wicket residents. The relatively low percentage of people having a garden may be accounted for mainly by the poor condition of the soil. Most of the produce grown was either consumed by members of the household or given away.

Berrying is a source of both cash and noncash income. In a fairly good year berrying can provide a family with up to a hundred or more jars of sauce, jam, and jelly made from wild blueberries, low-bush cranberries, choke cherries, strawberries, and pin cherries. Wild berries can also be sold to local retailers.

Although some Wicket people still consider wild rice harvesting as a traditional opportunity to get together with friends and relatives, many now regard it as a means of making a relatively large amount of money in a short period of time. Of the 81.5 percent of the Wicket people who go ricing, 44 percent said they would not go if they could not make money at it. In addition, 46 percent of those who riced in 1965 failed to keep any "green" (unprocessed) rice at all. Those Indians who keep rice for home use keep only a small portion of their harvest. As one ricer said, "I can buy a tremendous amount of macaroni and cheese with a pound of rice!" In 1965, a year considered by the ricers to be a very poor one, slightly over half of the people in Wicket made only $50 to $100 from the sale of wild rice. In 1966, my ricing partner and I were each able to make $100 in 2 hours.

Two additional sources of cash income are available, namely, pinecone picking and fur trapping. Pinecones are picked up from the ground in the fall and sold to buyers, who extract their seeds. In 1966 these cones brought from 7 to 8 dollars per bushel, but few Wicket residents gathered them.

Although the respondents were not systematically asked about trapping, this activity is an important source of added income for a number of individuals. A local trapper estimated that in a moderately good year one can make from $400 to $500. Mink and muskrat are the animals most frequently trapped. There are still beaver in the locale, but their importance has declined since the turn of the century. Although fur trapping was one of the major factors in the early development of this area, it has now become a relatively unimportant endeavor, and many Indians consider it to be a lot of hard work for only a little money.

Earned wages and benefits

Among the people of Wicket the principal sources of cash income are mining, logging, and pensions. Table 5.8 compares the income groups of the Chippewa in Wicket, James Lake, and Rice Village.

In all 3 communities more people are actively employed in logging than in any other occupation. Logging jobs are generally of 2 types: "cutting" and "skidding," both performed on a piecework basis for small contractors, who make the arrangements to cut timber in the state or national forest areas. Cutting includes felling, trimming, cutting, and peeling the timber, and then piling the resulting 8-foot "sticks." A worker in 1966 received from 8 to 16 cents per stick, depending on the type of timber being cut and on the local market situation. A good cutter can average about 200 sticks per day. Skidding involves transporting the small piles of sticks scattered throughout the woods to a central loading area at a piecework rate of 4 dollars per double cord. Truckers (usually the contractors themselves) then load the timber onto their trucks with a log jammer and transport it to boxcars standing on railroad sidings in the communities. The entire logging operation ceases during "mud vacation," which occurs with the spring thaw and may last as long as a month.

The second most common occupation in Wicket is mining. Many of the miners are employed by the same mining company, although some work for other small companies in the same mining area. The people employed in the mines commute from 60 to 90 miles each day, and most of them change shifts from time to time. Work in the mines involves many types of jobs, including ore truck drivers, brakemen, construction workers, heavy equipment operators, maintenance workers, and laborers. Most of the miners have been employed by the mining companies for 15 to 20 years. In addition to the currently active mine workers, 5 of

Table 5.8. Income groups of Wicket, James Lake,
and Rice Village Chippewa

Occupation or income source	Wicket %	Wicket No.	James Lake %	James Lake No.	Rice Village %	Rice Village No.
Woods work; common labor	26.6	22	33.3	10	22.2	2
Mining	21.7	18	–	–	–	–
Retirement pension	19.2	16	13.3	4	11.1	1
ADC benefits (only income source)	8.4	7	–	–	11.1	1
Auto repair	6.0	5	–	–	–	–
CAP, Civil Service work	4.8	4	6.7	2	11.1	1
Hurt, ill, disabled	3.6	3	3.3	1	11.1	1
Farming	2.4	2	3.3	1	–	–
Small business	2.4	2	–	–	–	–
Odd jobs, general repair (skilled)	1.2	1	–	–	–	–
Guiding; minnow selling	1.2	1	–	–	–	–
Sales	1.2	1	–	–	–	–
Unemployed	1.2	1	13.3	4	–	–
Forest Service and other low-echelon government work	–	–	13.3	7	11.1	1
Military service	–	–	–	–	–	–
Custodial work (housemaid, janitor)	–	–	–	–	11.1	1
Mill work (all types)	–	–	–	–	11.1	1
Reformatory or prison (inmates)	–	–	–	–	–	–
Other or don't know	–	–	3.3	1	–	–
		N=83		N=30		N=9

those retired or injured were formerly employed in the mines. Thus, a total of 37.3 percent of the households in Wicket have normally depended or still depend on mining as their major source of income.

At the time of my study, 67.7 percent of the household heads in Wicket were employed. The Wicket unemployment rate was only 1.2 percent, a fraction of the Indian unemployment rate in the region at the time, and lower than the national rate. However, for persons not retired or employed in the mines, income is subject to seasonal and other fluctuations. Seventy-five percent of the respondents reported that they had received unemployment compensation at least once during their lives.

Compared to the general area, Wicket is about average with regard to its dependence on logging, but above average in its reliance on mining occupations. The effect of the mining industry on the miners' material life-style in Wicket is clear from their position on the scalogram shown in Table 5.9. (See Chapter 7 in this volume for a brief discussion of the Guttman scaling technique.) Two-thirds of the miners occupy the top positions on the scale, with only one mining household falling below the midpoint. As the scale shows, even those having a laboring job in the mines are materially better off than those employed in similar jobs elsewhere.

The reservation's Community Action Program (CAP) has also contributed economically to the community—a contribution not fully indicated in the above data, which pertain only to household heads. Also, a beautification program administered under the Nelson Amendment has had a short-term impact on the community, employing its senior members and persons physically unable to secure other types of employment. Since the program was relatively recent when this information was being compiled, its permanent economic effect on the community could not be ascertained.

The 1966 median income of Wicket, $3,500, was slightly above the $3,000 poverty level for a family of 4 set by the U.S. government (1966). It was also above the median income of other Indian communities in northern Minnesota: Rice Village, $1,584, and James Lake, $1,950. The Wicket figure was even higher than the median incomes of whites in James Lake ($2,856) and in Lakewood ($2,900), a white community to the west (Schensul 1965:56). In addition, 25 percent of Wicket households had an annual cash income of $5,000 or more, compared with only 6.9 percent in James Lake and none in Rice Village.

The higher incomes of Wicket families cannot be accounted for on the basis of formal education. In Table 5.10 the amount of formal education of Wicket residents is compared with that of James Lake residents, showing only a slight difference in the educational levels of the 2 communities. The 6 Wicket miners listed in the scalogram (Table 5.9), who have the highest incomes as an occupational group, completed 14, 12, 9, 8, 5, and 8 years of formal education (respectively, reading from the top of the list), a range and distribution approximating those of the community in general.

Table 5.9. Material style of life in Wicket

Inter-viewee	Occupation	Scale type	A	B	C	D	E	F	G	H	I	J	K	L	M	N	O	P	Q	R	T	U	V
15	Mining	17	x	x	x	x	x	x	x	x	x	x	x	o	o	o	x	x	x	x	x	x	x
23	Mining	16	x*	x	x	x	x	x	x	x	x	x	x	o	x	x	x	x	x	x	x	35	x
12	Mining	16	x*	x	x	x	x	x	x	x	x	x	o	x	x	x	x	x	x	x	x	35	x
18	Mining	16	x*	x	x	x	x	o	x	x	x	o	x	o	o	o	x	x	x	x	x	20	x
6	ADC	15			x	x	x	x	x	x	o	x	x	o	x	x	x	x	x	x	x	x	x
30	Common labor	15			x	x	x	x	x	o	o	x	x	o	x	x	x	x	x	x	x	35	x
22	Farming	15			x	o	x	o	o	o	x	x	x	o	o	o	x	x	x	x	x	x	x
13	Farming	14				x	x	x	x	x	o	o	x	o	o	x	x	x	x	x	x	x	o
2	ADC	13	(x)	(x)		x	x	x	x	x	o	o	x	o	o	o	x	x	x	x	x	30	x
19	Logging	12				x	x	x	x	x	x	o	x	x	x	x	x	x	x	x	x	x	x
8	Mining	11	(x)*					x	x	x	x	x	x	x	x	x	x	x	x	x	x	x	x
27	Construction	11						x*	x	x	x	x	x	x	x	x	x	x	x	x	x	x	x
3	Retired	10						x	x	x	x	x	x	x	x	x	x	x	x	x	x	x	x
31	Logging	10						x	x	x	o	o	o	x	x	x	x	x	x	o	x	x	x
21	CAP	9		(x)				x	o	x	o	x	o	x	x	x	o	x	o	x	40	x

Scale items

Key to scale items

A. Owns house valued at $10,000 or more
B. Life insurance (*=included as part of wages)
C. Hot and cold running water
D. Bathtub or shower
E. Indoor bathroom
F. Telephone
G. Gas, coal, electric, or oil heat
H. Cold running water (*=pump inside house)
I. Food freezer
J. House has 4 or more rooms
K. Camera

Inter-viewee	Occupation	Scale type	A	B	C	D	E	F	G	H	I	J	K	L	M	N	O	P	Q	R	S	T	U	V
11	Retired	8		(x)			(x)							x	x	x	x	x	x	x	x	x	x	x
14	Retired	8												x	x	x	x	x	x	x	x	x	x	x
10	Mining	8			(x)*									x	x	x	x	x	x	x	o	x	x	x
17	Common labor	7													x	x	x	x	x	x	x	x	10	x
1	Common labor	6				(x)	(x)		(x)	(x)					x	x	x	x	x	x	x	x	30	x
25	Injured	6									(x)				x	x	x	x	x	x	x	x	x	x
20	Retired	5														x	x	x	x	x	x	x	x	x
4	Retired	5						(x)								x	x	o	x	x	x	x	x	x
7	Retired	5									(x)								x	x	x	x	13	x
9	Odd jobs	4							(x)				(x)	(x)						x	x	x	x	x
29	Retired	3			(x)				(x)											x	x	x	x	x
26	Logging	3											(x)	(x)						x	x	x	x	x
32	Injured	3																		x	x	x	x	x
16	Common labor	3																		x	o	x	x	x
28	Construction	2			(x)								(x)	(x)								x	x	o
24	Logging	1			(x)*		(x)									(x)			(x)				x	x
5	Common labor	1			(x)*								(x)	(x)									x	x

Key to scale items

L. Subscribes to at least one magazine
M. Clothes washer
N. Toaster
O. Electricity
P. Iron
Q. Refrigerator
R. Television
S. Radio
T. House has 2 or more rooms
U. Owns house valued at $100 or more; pays $45/mo. rent or amount listed
V. Range

Note: Unlike the quantitatively analytical scalograms in Chapters 3, 6, and 7 of this volume, this table is intended to display as much in-formation as possible about the levels of living of Wicket Indians. For comparative purposes, all the items from Pelto's material-style-of-life scalogram (Chapter 6) have been included in this table, leading to redundant scale items. A coefficient of reproducibility would there-fore not be meaningful.

Table 5.10. Years of school completed by interviewees
of Wicket and James Lake

Number of years completed	Male		Female	
	Wicket	James Lake	Wicket	James Lake
14 or more	1	0	0	0
13	1	0	0	0
12	2	2	3	0
11	1	2	1	0
10	2	6	6	2
9	4	1	3	5
8	12	6	7	7
7	0	3	2	2
4 – 6	3	7	4	6
1 – 3	2	2	1	0
0	0	0	0	1
Don't know	0	0	0	2

Community integration and orientation

Religion

Religion is one of the most important and paradoxical aspects of Wicket
community life. Most residents of Wicket consider themselves Catholics
(see Table 5.11). Non-Catholic households tend to be geographically and
socially peripheral to the community and the council. Of the 8 non-
Catholic households in the sample, 5 are on the extreme boundaries of
the research area and 4 are mixed Indian-white households. Only one
non-Catholic individual reported ever attending a local council meeting.
These households form an informal grouping in that they are closely
related by blood or marriage.

Even though most Wicket residents are nominally Catholic, their

Table 5.11. Religion of household heads
and spouses

Catholic	81.8%
Methodist	10.9
Episcopalian	3.6
Christian and Missionary Alliance	1.8
Indian (traditional)	1.8
	$N=35$

actual religious observances range from traditional Chippewa practices and beliefs to faithful participation in Catholic rites. Between these 2 extremes lies a wide range of variation encompassing the majority of the community. Although many people talk about "past" Indian beliefs, some current non-Christian beliefs and practices are not generally openly discussed, even though most community members are likely to be aware of their continuing presence.

During a discussion of religion, an older Catholic man explained to me that in his opinion there was really not much difference between most of the beliefs of the Catholic church and those of the traditional Indian religion. The only major difference, he maintained, was that the Indian religion emphasized the appreciation of nature and was not limited to worshiping inside a building.

Almost all of the people that I talked with, however, espoused at least a few practices and beliefs considered by more strict Catholics as "superstitious Indian beliefs." They told stories of cures that took place in their immediate families, extraordinary phenomena such as the occurrence of "fireballs," and tent-shaking ceremonies. In telling about the treatment of a close relative by an Indian medicine doctor, 3 different individuals began with the statement, "When your loved ones are involved and everything else fails, you'll do anything you can to help them." Two of the 3 noted that the treatment was successful.

People also told about incidents involving "fireballs." Rather common in earlier years, these balls of fire were said to have perched on trees, waiting to chase travelers down the road. Several people reported that they or members of their immediate families had been chased by fireballs and that they had often sought protection through the use of holy water, thus indicating a belief in both the Indian and Catholic religions. Some people who said they had seen fireballs as children maintained at the same time that stories about fireballs are used to scare children. Others suggested that the accounts of fireballs are comparable to reports of flying saucers or contemporary bogeyman stories.

A frequent story told about tent shaking involved a shaman who misused his tent-shaking powers by publicly showing off. One of his tricks was being put into the tent bound in a fishnet and emerging untied. During one performance, an assistant inserted a crucifix in the fishnet and he was unable to escape. The shaman did not know that the crucifix was there, but felt something acting against his power that he could not overcome. An old man came by and pulled an object out of the back of the shaker's neck. Some of the people asked the old man what it was, and he said it was the shaker's power, a power that once removed could not be given back.

Contemporary practices vary in their degree of association with traditional Indian beliefs. One nominal Catholic, for example, has recently become a medicine doctor and has returned to many traditional Indian beliefs. In a short period of time he has gained among "believers" a reputation of having much power and has been visited by Indians from Minneapolis, St. Paul, and Duluth-Superior and by local people as well. Another Wicket resident is a member of one of the larger Christian denominations and a leader in the Native American Church. He led the services of the only peyote meeting held in the area during the summer of 1966 (see Chapter 4 of this volume). A third religious practitioner is an ordained minister of the American Indian Evangelical Church. Traveling from house to house preaching a "hard gospel" and delivering sermons as a guest speaker in neighboring parishes, he identifies himself primarily as an "Indian preacher," and his views are similar to those of the more fundamentalist Christian denominations.

In addition to these individuals, there are at least 6 persons who are considered to have specific powers for healing certain ailments, for controlling the weather, and for providing good luck in hunting. Methods of effecting a cure or controlling the weather include the administration of roots, the use of incantations, and the carrying and possession of powerful medicines.

Minor syncretic religious elements are present in the everyday life of Wicket Indians. Many of the middle-aged or older people, for example, refer to "the Great Spirit" as being the same as the Christian God. Mourners at Catholic wakes remain with the corpse all night, singing Christian hymns translated into Chippewa. Christian objects such as the rosary have been given a traditional meaning. A Wicket friend noted a rosary hung on an outside door for protection and observed, "See here, this guy believes in God." At a philosophical level some individuals compare their inability to understand the more complex theological concepts of Christianity with their inability to understand certain phenomena connected with the Grand Medicine Society. The implication is frequently made that in reality it is personal preference that determines belief in one or the other of the alternatives.

In sum, although nearly 82 percent of the residents of Wicket profess Catholicism, their attitudes and practices range from a belief solely in the Indian religion to a strict, exclusive belief in Catholic doctrines. Although many of the clergy and the more devout Catholics interpret the inclusion of Indian religious practices simply as deviations from an expected ideal, these practices seem better interpreted as a form of religious syncretism. The failure of outsiders to understand some of the elements underlying these middle-range practices has had important consequences in the development of Wicket.

Religion is thus a critical element in the personal lives of the community members and in the community as a whole. In a structured interview item, over 40 percent of the interviewees selected religion as the most or next most important aspect of their lives. The fact that most of the people of Wicket in one way or another think of themselves as Catholic serves as a strong focus for community integration. Additionally, the church is the only community institution in which the Indian and non-Indian members alike identify themselves as a single group. Common religious identity serves to facilitate an amicable relationship between these 2 racial-ethnic components of the community. Finally, although the local council clearly sees itself as a secular institution, the church has played an essential role in its development.

Political behavior

The voting behavior of Wicket residents indicates political homogeneity and community involvement. In 1960, 87.8 percent of those eligible voted in the national presidential election; in 1964, 82 percent voted. Only one respondent indicated that in these years he had voted for a Republican candidate. In 1966, 120 Wicket residents cast votes for governor of Minnesota, 68 percent for the Democratic candidate (*Herald-Review* [Big Run, Minn.] 1966:8–9). Considering that these 1966 figures include local whites and that Truehead County as a whole conformed to the statewide Republican trend, the number of Democratic votes in Wicket is significant. In James Lake only 65.2 percent of the eligible Indian voters cast their ballots in 1960, and 64.4 percent in 1964; in these 2 elections only 3 respondents voted Republican. While the voting pattern in Wicket reflects the Democratic party preference among Indians in the region, the voting participation rate is significantly higher than in James Lake and many of the surrounding Indian settlements.

These data, which support field observation, reveal the relatively high importance that Wicket Indians place on political participation. Much political discussion took place during the summer of 1966, especially during the district commissioner and county sheriff races. Wicket was one of the first communities in the county, as well as the first Indian settlement on the Broken Reed Reservation, to schedule a meeting at which the people could meet the county candidates. Discussion at this meeting centered on discrimination in county government against Indians and the absence of local law enforcement in Wicket. Nevertheless, when Wicket respondents were asked in a structured interview item to rank according to importance a list of "life aspects," politics fared poorly. No one in either Wicket or James Lake chose politics as the most important aspect of his or her life, even though local council officers and Reservation Business Committee members were among those sampled in each community. Only 2 interviewees in Wicket indicated that politics was the second most important aspect of their lives. Conflict generated by non-Indian politics is generally not intense and usually revolves around personal preferences for particular Democratic candidates; differences usually disappear after primary elections. Since Wicket citizens are politically involved and are loyal to the same political party, politics serves as a unifying force and thus promotes community solidarity.

Friendship patterns and personal values

Intrafamilial relationships in Wicket also foster community integration. Individuals in the structured interview sample, when asked who they considered their 3 best friends, replied simply that they had no "best friends," or that "all of the people are my friends." Even when the question was modified after such a response to read, "Who would you consider 3 of your *good* friends?" 3 individuals still refused to name anyone in particular. Respondents having at least one friend in common with another individual in the survey sample are included in the sociogram of Figure 5.3 along with general family groups. In this figure a double arrow indicates sampled respondents who selected each other as a good or best friend. However, the *absence* of a double arrow often means that only one of the 2 individuals was included in the sample.

Although only 4 main family groups are indicated in Figure 5.3, other relationships can be traced through genealogical connections. The sociogram indicates that most of the primary friendships occur among relatives. The choice of a relative as best friend by most Wicket respondents is similar to the social pattern within peer groups at Deer Lake (Copeland 1949). Copeland concluded that the clique structure of Deer Lake is based on kinship. She also notes that "friendship choices are not based on the necessity of having no nonrelatives from whom to select, but are based on their own expressed preferences for relatives" (1949:56). In Wicket, the network of friendships serves to integrate the

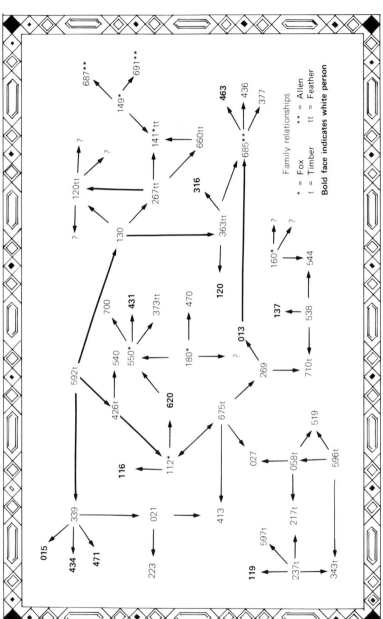

Figure 5.3. Intrafamilial relationships among 4 family groups in Wicket, 1966.

community, since even in a random sample of 32 persons, over 70 percent of the respondents have at least one good or best friend in common with one or more of the other respondents. As has been indicated earlier, the 4 groups in Figure 5.3, sometimes referred to in Wicket as "bunches" or "factions," are those defined by the people themselves.

Value preferences that Wicket respondents imputed to their friends suggest a situation conducive to a high degree of community integration. Respondents were presented with a list of characteristics and were asked, "Generally, which of the following would you say your friends think are most important in their lives?" Table 5.12 shows the responses to this question. These data suggest that friends are thought to value most highly friendliness (most or next most important for 53.7 percent); second, trustworthiness (35 percent); and third, generosity (27.3 percent). Negative support of these characteristics appears in the relative devaluation of ability to get ahead (least important for 25.6 percent) and cleverness (least important for 20.5 percent). The remaining items support the general descriptions of the Indians of this area given by Indians, whites, and outsiders. Being smart, thrifty, and brave are all given both a low positive and a low negative rating, suggesting an ambiguous attitude toward these values; the apparent disinterest in thrift and educational advancement coincides with similar observations made of other American Indian groups. The fact that 19.5 percent of the respondents chose "being able to get ahead of others" as the most or next

Table 5.12. Assessment of friends' value hierarchy
(percent of those responding)

	Most important	Next most important	Least important
1. Being generous	9.8%	17.5%	10.0%
2. Being educated	2.4	9.8	7.7
3. Being able to get ahead of others	14.6	4.9	25.6
4. Being brave	0.0	2.4	7.7
5. Being friendly	31.8	21.9	5.1
6. Being clever	0.0	2.4	20.5
7. Being a hard worker	7.3	12.2	5.1
8. Being religious	0.0	17.5	2.6
9. Being thrifty	2.4	4.9	2.6
10. Being one who can be trusted	27.5	7.5	12.8
	N=41	N=41	N=39

most important characteristic of their friends suggests that, while the general picture is that of a homogeneous and integrated community, there are potential threats to total community integration and cooperation.

Table 5.13 summarizes the responses to a similar question regarding the most important aspect in life and compares these responses with James Lake Indian responses. Wicket and James Lake are similar in their deemphasis on cultural activities, pastimes, and politics, and in their only mild emphasis on social group and race. While both groups generally emphasized the importance of relatives, work, religion, and nationality, the Wicket respondents exhibited a stronger tendency to select work and religion. These data reflect the major role of economics and

Table 5.13. Hierarchy of life aspects of Wicket and
James Lake interviewees

	Most important		Next most important		Least important		Row total		
Item	*M*	*F*	*M*	*F*	*M*	*F*	*Important*	*Least important*	
Cultural	0	2	0	0	1	1	2	2	Wicket
activities	0	1	0	1	1	1	2	2	James Lake
Pastimes	0	0	1	0	3	10	1	13	Wicket
	2	1	0	1	4	7	4	11	James Lake
Relatives	2	3	4	3	3	1	12	4	Wicket
(other than	2	5	5	2	0	0	14	0	James Lake
immediate									
family)									
Work	14	5	2	2	0	2	23	2	Wicket
	4	3	1	3	1	0	11	1	James Lake
Religion	5	5	4	4	1	1	18	22	Wicket
	1	4	2	6	0	3	13	3	James Lake
Social group	0	0	2	1	0	0	3	0	Wicket
(the people	0	4	1	3	2	0	8	2	James Lake
associated									
with most)									
Politics	0	0	0	2	7	3	2	10	Wicket
	0	0	0	0	5	7	0	12	James Lake
Race (being	0	0	2	2	3	0	4	3	Wicket
Chippewa)	0	2	0	4	1	0	6	1	James Lake
Nationality	1	3	6	5	1	1	15	2	Wicket
(being	4	4	3	4	0	3	15	3	James Lake
American)									
Don't know or	1	2	2	0	2	1	5	3	Wicket
no response	2	1	3	1	1	4	7	5	James Lake

religion in the development of Wicket. It is interesting to note that although 50 percent of the respondents indicated that religion was the most important aspect of their own life, no one indicated that religion was the most important thing in the lives of their friends (Table 5.12). This difference in perception indicates a significant deviation from the community's perception of itself as a whole, a deviation which seems best understood in terms of the syncretic or folk nature of local Catholicism.

Intercommunity contacts

In order to determine relative community isolation, respondents were asked how often they went to each of 18 Minnesota locations within the past 12 months. (Responses excluded locations on main roads unless that location was the respondent's specific destination, since one must pass through these communities when traveling to other locations.) The data from the responses to these questions appear in Table 5.14.

Interaction with communities on other reservations is quite restricted, limited to once a year in all cases but 4. This finding supports the popular belief that inhabitants of the various reservations in Minnesota keep to themselves, and it is consistent with the tendency of reservation residents to identify themselves as a "Reed Laker," "Deer Laker," "Hook Laker," and so forth. Of the 4 people who travel to other reservations, 2 respondents, who go to Deer Lake once a month, are brothers who have a third brother living there; this is one of the few instances of a relationship between a Wicket resident and a person at another reservation. The other 2 individuals go to Deep Lake. One is the local council chairman, who conducts business with the Minnesota tribal chairman, who lives at Deep Lake. The second was born at Deep Lake and most probably returns to see his relatives and friends. Thus, except for attendance at powwows, the Wicket community is relatively isolated from other Chippewa reservation communities in Minnesota.

As one might expect, interaction with other communities is independent of community size, but negatively correlated with distance; interaction more than once per year decreases as one moves away from Wicket. However, daily interaction takes place with the neighboring communities of Big Run (22 miles away) and Buck Lake (6½ miles away). For example, 56.3 percent of the respondents go to Big Run at least once a week, while 65.7 percent go to Buck Lake at least that often. Wicket residents do most of their shopping in either Buck Lake or Big Run. Most recreational activities, with the exception of drinking, also

Table 5.14. Intercommunity interactions

Frequency:	2–3 per week	1 per week	2–3 per month	1 per month	2–3 per year	1 per year	Almost never
White communities							
Big Run	6	13	4	5	3	0	1
Buck Lake	13	8	1	2	1	0	1
Runner	0	1	1	1	8	0	21
Minetown	0	0	1	3	6	8	14
North City	0	0	2	3	4	9	1
Twin Cities	0	0	0	1	8	3	20
Duluth-Superior	0	0	1	1	4	7	19
Canada	0	0	0	0	0	4	28
Indian reservations							
Deep Lake	0	0	0	0	2	2	28
Deer Lake	0	0	0	2	0	11	19
Hook Lake	0	0	0	0	0	7	25
Beaver Pelt	0	0	0	0	0	3	29
Twenty Mile Lake	0	0	0	0	0	2	30
Indian communities							
Partridge[a]	1	4	3	4	4	5	11
Wife Lake	0	1	2	3	3	6	17
Mide	0	1	2	3	4	3	20
Portage	0	0	1	0	0	1	30
James Lake[a]	1	2	6	10	4	4	5
High Water[a]	1	0	1	4	3	7	16

a. Mixed Indian and white community.

take place in these 2 communities. Buck Lake is so important to the residents of Wicket that it has come to be known as "town." In everyday conversation, people always distinguish between being in "town," and being in Wicket. Big Run is simply "the Run." With the exception of "The Cities" (Minneapolis-St. Paul), no other community in the general area is called anything but its official name.

In sum, Wicket is relatively dependent on 2 larger neighboring communities for its goods and services. While theoretically one could live in Wicket without visiting either of these communities, in practice this is rarely, if ever, done. Although many people do not have automobiles, transportation is seldom a problem since one can get a ride to Buck Lake either with friends or relatives or by hitchhiking. It is quite common to see a car filled with Wicket people in Buck Lake or 2 or 3 hitchhikers on the road. With the exception of Buck Lake and Big Run, contact with other communities is relatively infrequent, occurring mainly during the ricing season or occurring out of necessity (for instance, most visits to James Lake are to the Indian hospital).

The local council: history, organization, and activity

In accordance with the constitutional changes of March 3, 1964, the Minnesota Chippewa Tribe is governed by the Tribal Executive Committee (TEC), which is composed of the chairmen and secretary-treasurers of the 6 reservation business committees. The members of the Tribal Executive Committee elect a president, vice-president, secretary, and treasurer, who serve 2-year terms. Any resolution or ordinance enacted by the TEC is subject to review by the U. S. secretary of the interior, who technically has final authority in matters of reservation governance.

Each of the 6 reservation business committees (RBC) in the Minnesota Chippewa Tribe consists of 3 to 5 members, including a chairman, a secretary-treasurer, and one to 3 committee members. On the Broken Reed Reservation, the chairman and secretary-treasurer are elected in a reservation-wide election, while each of the 3 reservation districts elects one committee member. All RBC members serve 4-year terms that are staggered to provide continuity.

In April, 1964, the Broken Reed Reservation was divided into 3 districts; however, the 9 voting precincts, centered around the 9 larger reservation communities, remained. Six of the Broken Reed communities have active local councils, namely, Wicket, Mide, Partridge, James Lake, Portage, and Highwater. The new tribal constitution does not specifically provide for these local councils, but recognizes "any community organizations, associations, or committees open to members of the several reservations...subject to the provisions that no such organization, association, or committee may assume any authority granted to the Tribal Executive Committee or to the Reservation Business Committee" (Minnesota Chippewa Tribe, Constitution and Bylaws, Article 5, Section 1, Paragraph b, 1964). Prior to the redistricting of 1964, each community on the reservation generally sent a representative to serve on the "reservation council."

Each of the 6 active local councils is headed by a chairman, vice-chairman, secretary, and treasurer who are elected each spring. Wicket's local council, which has been actively functioning since May, 1963, was the first council to appoint both male and female sergeants to serve as minor officials. Before the recent organization and activation of the

Wicket council, Wicket Indian political activity was limited almost exclusively to the yearly election of the reservation council representative from the Wicket area. This election frequently did not take place, and a local member, usually the same individual for many years, was appointed by other members of the reservation council.

History of the Wicket Local Indian Council

Most Wicket people, when asked what occurred politically before the recent official establishment of the Wicket Local Indian Council, stated simply, "Nothing," or "Not much." Except for the initial phase of the current local council, the political history of Wicket has been characterized by factionalism and individual participation. As indicated earlier, Wicket has always sent a representative to the governing body of the Broken Reed Reservation. This effort, however, was primarily individual and usually did not involve community activity or cooperation. Wicket people frequently tell stories of how Lone Bird, the major representative during the 20 years preceding reorganization, "looked out mainly for himself" and did little for the community. The other individuals who held the post prior to Lone Bird apparently served in a similar manner. In speaking of former tribal politics, one of the current Reservation Business Committee members from a neighboring community noted that "up until just recently, tribal politics was a laugh." He said that in the past, the prevalent pattern was for a person to get into office for a couple of years and then "bring in all of his relatives," whereupon they would "pretty much do things for themselves, and to heck with the others."

The following account helps illustrate the political pattern prevalent in Wicket in the past. The brother-in-law of the present chairman recounted that "before we got organized" he had served as chairman of a more informal Indian organization for 5 years, beginning around 1931 and continuing through the initial days of the New Deal programs of Franklin Roosevelt. "Before the New Deal, things were going fairly well," he said, "insofar as they were going at all." During his term of office, however, "Roosevelt came in here [i.e., initiated programs] and was going to do something for the Indians, but succeeded only in splitting the community into 2 groups, mine and his [another leader's]. It was just like what's going on now with William's bunch and the Feather bunch . . . just like this we had a split-up." He went to Duluth for 2 weeks and returned to find out not only that the other faction had taken over control of the organization, but that it had "notified" him that he had been "written out" of the entire Chippewa Tribe and was "off the rolls." In his words, the opposing faction had "come and taken over power, and I felt myself out of power." Although in the past the power was officially in the hands of one faction or another, other individuals not in power exerted much indirect influence over the local activities.

In the early 1960s, the various factions in the community combined efforts to attain a common goal. This effort—the first in the history of Wicket—resulted in the establishment and maintenance of the present council and accounts for much of the relatively rapid development of the local community. To understand one of the primary reasons for this united action, it is necessary to consider certain events at that time that involved the local Catholic church.

As noted earlier, the majority of the people in Wicket are at least nominally Catholic, and in the past the church has helped promote community identity. For much of the recent history of the community, the resident priest was an exceptionally well-liked man. Every adult member of the community interviewed for purposes of this study mentioned Father David and talked of his personality and his warm relations with the local people. A visit by Father David was anticipated as the highlight of the first annual church dinner in the fall of 1966, and everyone waited eagerly to see and talk with him. Many people mentioned that he danced at the local powwows, that he established particularly active St. Mary's and St. Joseph's societies, and that he permitted the Wicket Indian people to meet and even to conduct traditional Indian wakes in the basement of the local church. The minutes of the council record the names of only 2 people accorded special invitations to the new council hall dedication: Father David and the lieutenant governor of the state.

A few years before the formation of the Wicket Local Council, Father David was replaced with a man who created much antagonism in the community. One of the first actions reportedly taken by the new priest was to remove the sign reading "Indian Mission" from the church. The chairman of the local council, apparently still quite irritated by this action, asked me on my second visit to Wicket if mission status was reserved "for the Pope alone to change." Dissatisfaction with this new priest was so intense that one of the local white residents wrote a letter to the bishop of the diocese in the name of the Indian community, formally stating the complaints of the people. The letter created a disturbance among some of the clergy in the region, because they felt that "the Indians were trying to dictate theology" to them. As a result of the actions of the new pastor, the Indians in Wicket no longer participated in the activities of the St. Joseph's and St. Mary's societies. The relationship between the Indians and these societies became such that the Indians sent a delegate "to clarify to the ladies of the Rosary Society . . . that there is no segregation among the whites and Indians of the community; anybody is welcome to our Indians' community hall and grounds; if they want to send a delegation to one of our meetings they are welcome to do so." This message of January, 1964, which indicates both perceived social segregation as well as a verbal denunciation of it, is especially significant since just a few years earlier some of the most active members and officers of the religious societies had been Indians.

Reportedly, the most significant action taken by the new priest was to refuse the sacraments and a Christian burial to anyone not practicing the Catholic religion strictly. The minutes of the 1965 council indicate that the new pastor refused, by letter, to give a talk at the annual celebration, evidently for the same reasons he withheld the sacraments. It seems that from a relativistic point of view the position taken by the pastor was unrealistic since he failed to take into consideration the local religious traditions.

In addition to his other actions, the new priest no longer permitted Indian wakes to be held in the basement of the church. As might be expected, reaction against the new priest was a very important factor in increasing cooperation among Wicket Indians. One influential community member stated bluntly, "The reason that the new community hall up there was built was so we could hold these wakes and meetings if we wanted to." Although some community members explain the sudden impetus for cooperating to build a community hall only in terms of the need for a meeting place, others note that the community began to feel this need acutely when they no longer had access to the church building and had to conduct their wakes in homes that were too small.

When one of the older, more active council members was asked why Wicket was so successful compared to other communities in the area, he said that a successful community has to have a "leader who will organize things and who is willing to stick out his neck." He named several people who were particularly influential in the early development of the council.

Although council development occurred through the efforts of several individuals, one took more initiative than the others, becoming the council's leader. In the first election, William Drummaker was elected council chairman by an 85 percent majority vote, and he has served in that position for most of the time since. Significantly, he was the first Indian from the community to obtain permanent employment with one of the mining companies, and he was instrumental in getting mining jobs for community members. When he was quite young, Drummaker headed the St. Joseph's Society. One older community member said that he had been very surprised to hear of Drummaker's election as president of the society since he was so young, but added that he had known that Drummaker would be a successful leader despite his youth. The extent of Drummaker's effect on the council is shown in the minutes of a 1964 preelection council meeting, where a statement indicates that a certain matter would be taken care of "if William got back into office," and therefore "it [his reelection] was a sure thing."

The council's first meetings took place in 1963 in members' homes and places of business. The first action recorded in the council's minutes was the election of delegates to the general sessions in James Lake and to the Broken Reed Reservation Council. In this election Drummaker was elected chairman; Leo Feather, vice-chairman; Rita Blackbear, secretary; and Mike Fox, treasurer. It was important that members of 3 of the 4 local factions were thus elected to office (a member of the fourth faction had already been elected a delegate to the reservation council), indicating a lack of factional domination at that time.

The council's early efforts were directed toward building a community hall, constructing a baseball diamond and skating rink, developing a housing program, and establishing an arts-and-crafts center. To raise funds for these activities, potluck dinners, donations, raffles, bingo games, and powwows were organized. Council records indicate that, during the first year, members of all the major Wicket factions contributed both goods and services. These early fund-raising activities were so successful that by November 21, 1963, only 6 months after their first formal meeting, the local council passed the following resolution:

Whereas the Wicket Community is in need of a community hall, and

Whereas the community has shown its initiative and willingness to help itself by sponsoring activities to raise money for such a building and has raised $1,000,

It is resolved that the Wicket Community Council requests the support of the Reservation Council in this endeavor and asks that the Tribal Executive Council of the Minnesota Chippewa Tribe make an application to the [Housing and Home Finance Agency]

on behalf of the Wicket Community for a grant of $7,500 for construction of a community hall, to be needed at Wicket.

On the same date the council requested use of tribal lands for building a hall, a ball field, and "fair grounds," and requested that the Tribal Executive Committee cosign a note for additional funds to cover building costs.

For more than 2 years following the council's first formal meeting, its members and others worked hard to get a community hall. The tenacity of the council is documented in the minutes of early 1964: "Mr. [Richard Truefellow] has read a letter from the Housing and Home Finance Agency in Chicago, Illinois, concerning our community building, and we were given a number to refer to. Our number is APW-MINN, 1750, but our plans have been filed away; we Indians of the Wicket Local Community cannot have this matter set aside. We must take action now, and keep this project going; we must speak up for our natural rights as citizens, NOW! or forever be still!" The persistence of the council members is seen in this resolution of January 10, 1964:

> Whereas, the Indian people of the Wicket, Minnesota, Council have long needed a community meeting facility for civic, youth, tribal, and other activities; and
> Whereas the members of the Wicket Local Indian Council, despite unemployment, layoffs, and economic depression, have earned $994.45 by putting on basket-socials, Indian dances, and other events towards the construction of a community building; and
> Whereas an application for aid in financing the community building at Wicket is on file with the Housing and Home Finance Agency, 360 N. Michigan Ave., Chicago, Ill., Project No. APW-MINN, 1750; and
> Whereas the need for this project is urgent:
> Now therefore be it resolved that the Broken Reed Reservation Council, which encompasses the Wicket Community, urges HHFA to give every possible and prompt consideration to this worthwhile application and examine the application carefully on the basis of the need of the applicant.

As it turned out, the plans were not set aside, and action was taken that resulted in the construction of the community center in 1965.

One individual particularly responsible for the completion of the community hall project was Richard Truefellow, an adult education specialist of the Bureau of Indian Affairs. From October 12, 1963, he served as community motivator and director, guiding and channeling community energies and efforts to help the residents help themselves. Various council members have repeatedly acknowledged Truefellow's contributions to the development of the Wicket community. In recognition of his work, the local council adopted him into the Chippewa Tribe at Wicket's 1964 powwow, presenting him with an Indian dance costume valued at $250. Although the local council chairman and other council members give Truefellow credit for much of the community's success, Truefellow himself insists that Wicket's success was due to the community's efforts.

Like the community hall, a ball field and powwow complex were constructed relatively early in the council's history. More recently an arts-and-crafts center, an ice-skating rink, and 12 housing units have been constructed. Since the council's inception a major goal has been attaining adequate housing for Wicket residents. The housing units, erected in Wicket during the summer and fall of 1966, were the result of efforts made by the Housing Division of the Bureau of Indian Affairs and the Housing Commission of the Broken Reed Reservation. In January, 1964, Wicket's council chairman accepted a position as housing commissioner for the whole reservation, and his efforts helped to secure housing for other reservation residents.

In the council's short history, it has taken action on many other matters. Early in 1963 it established a health committee to work with the Bureau of Indian Affairs regarding "medical curative," "preventative," and dental public health programs as well as sanitation. Partly because of the council's efforts to improve public health, Wicket received a $47,092 federal grant to provide proper sanitation facilities for the community.

In the fall of 1963, the council campaigned to obtain free hot lunches for local Indian children, one of its earlier and more successful attempts to acquire goods and services for the community. In April, 1965, the council officially supported the requests of 4 Indians for telephone service. Their earlier petitions had been refused because they could not afford the advance service charge for 18 months' service. Council members argued that a businessman from Buck Lake had had a telephone installed at his summer home without being required to pay any service charge in advance, a claim of discrimination that prompted the Minnesota Railroad and Warehouse Commission to investigate the case. The council's action also disturbed the relationship between the residents of Wicket and the people of Buck Lake. Events were further complicated upon the arrival of the commission's investigator, who happened to be black, and a few weeks later of a black VISTA [Volunteers in Service to America] worker, who planned to stay in Wicket a year. Some of the townspeople began interpreting the entire incident as a test case of racial discrimination. At this point the people who had originally requested telephone service refused to write a request, not wanting to be liable for payment in advance. Since legal action could not be taken without a written request, the council dropped the matter.

In August, 1966 (the time of this study), the council was trying to obtain local police protection for Wicket residents. Police had to be called in from Big Run, taking 30 minutes to 4 hours to arrive. At the August meeting of the county's political candidates, Wicket residents forcefully asked each candidate three questions: Why didn't Wicket have police protection? Why had only one Indian in the past 20 years been called for jury duty? Why were no Indians employed in any department of the county courthouse or maintenance shops? As a result of the meeting, action was taken to secure a part-time deputy sheriff for Wicket.

Early in 1964 the teenagers of Wicket established a Teen Council, which quickly became the largest Indian teen council in Minnesota. The young people themselves conducted meetings and activities, keeping their own minutes, collecting their own funds, and keeping their own financial records. Two sponsors supervised in an advisory capacity. To raise money to purchase a jukebox and pop machine for the community hall basement, the Teen Council sponsored dances and concession stands at the annual powwow. Although most members of the local council encouraged Teen Council members by giving them responsibilities and privileges, some adults made complaints about the young people's emphasis on dances. A change of membership has since led to a decline in the Teen Council's activities.

In January, 1965, after a regional leader of the Girl Scouts spoke at a council meeting, Wicket residents immediately decided to develop a Girl Scout program, which materialized shortly thereafter with the aid of VISTA volunteers.

The first announcement that VISTA volunteers were to arrive on the reservation was made in February, 1965, by the newly appointed reservation VISTA supervisor in James Lake. Four VISTA workers arrived in Wicket on September 30, 1965, and remained there until late summer in 1966, concentrating their efforts on the community's youth. These

VISTA workers were well liked and graciously accepted by the community. Almost everyone I interviewed during the winter of 1965 and summer of 1966 made a special point of discussing the good job that the VISTAs were doing. (Several times I was complimented as being "almost like one of the VISTAs.") Some went into detail about various characteristics of the volunteers, invariably noting that 2 of the VISTA workers were members of minority groups and, like some of the local people, had language and cultural differences to overcome.

A few months before the arrival of the VISTA volunteers in Wicket, the reservation Community Action Program (CAP) was introduced to the community. As with the VISTA program, 10 percent of CAP funds were supplied by the Reservation Business Committee. One of the largest reservation CAP programs in the United States, Broken Reed's CAP directed its efforts toward relieving hard-core poverty in the reservation. Besides staff working out of James Lake, the program operated with local "directors" and "aides." Originally, Wicket had 5 locally paid program positions: a recreation counselor with 2 aides and a home economics counselor with one aide. Later CAP components included a Head Start program (for preschool children), a Nelson Amendment program of environment beautification employing the elderly and persons chronically unemployed, a Neighborhood Youth Corps program (a work-study program employing high school students), and a janitor for the community hall.

On October 13, 1964, in a special meeting, members of the Wicket Local Indian Council discussed the entire antipoverty program and expressed their expectations regarding the program to the directors. The minutes of this meeting outlined their suggestions:

1. Preschoolers' classes half-day for a full year
2. Health education, eye and dental clinic
3. Having an after-class study hall period for grade and high school students
4. Cabinet making, carpentry, masonry classes
5. Shorthand and typing classes for high school students and adults
6. Leadership training classes for youth and adults
7. Nursery facilities (for ricers and loggers, etc.); training in caring for a large group of children in a day nursery
8. Physical education director
9. Library facilities—open to all, for references, since most don't have the proper references as a library would have

10. Adult education classes in homemaking, business (such as book-keeping), upholstery
11. Handicrafts, art, silk screening
12. Mechanics
13. Transportation for facilities
14. Home economics (budgets and buying)
15. Teen-age Indian council, with tutoring service, that functions properly
16. Coordination of Indian councils in consulting with county and state officials (such as social workers, etc.)
17. Self-preservation (for the youth), hygiene, health, and education in job employment

It should be emphasized that all the major programs of Wicket's new council were well under way or completed before the arrival of CAP. As a result Wicket was CAP's exemplary community early in the history of the program.

The council's primary continuing activity is an annual powwow, formally called the *Mi-Gwitch Mah-Nomen* celebration—the Wild Rice Thanksgiving Days. (See Rynkiewich, Chapter 2 in this volume, for a full description of the Wicket powwow.) During this well-organized celebration, raffle tickets are sold for locally made Indian products such as deerskin jackets, moccasins, rugs, quilts, and canoes. No admission is charged since residents feel that a fee is not compatible with the traditional spirit of the powwow; also, an admission fee would make the council legally liable for accidents occurring on council property. The celebration has netted about $500 annually. Considering that up to $150 is given as prize money in the powwow's dance contest, its gross income is probably more than that of comparable celebrations in the area.

Although the council continues to function in its original form, several significant changes have occurred in recent years. The 3 most important of these have been the arrival of the Community Action Program, new disagreements among members of the 4 factions, and the replacement of the unpopular pastor of the Catholic parish with a dynamic and well-liked priest.

Conclusion

The purpose of this study has been to describe and discuss a small, "successful" Chippewa village and to isolate the elements that contributed to its relatively rapid development. Wicket has attracted considerable regional attention because of its success in achieving its goals. Additionally, it has served as a model for other communities on the Broken Reed Reservation.

Some general characteristics of the community's structure and activities may now be reviewed. Most older members of the demographically young population have lived elsewhere for a year or more before returning permanently to Wicket. Mobility remains high for younger people. Although the community is located in an area with a history of depressed economic conditions, Wicket residents are fortunate in having access to both the mining and logging industries of the state and in having opportunities to supplement their cash income with a variety of nonmonetary resources. Wicket residents have approximately as much formal education as most Indians in northern Minnesota. Religion, political behavior, family structure, patterns of social interaction, settlement patterns, and preferred personal values all suggest a situation that fosters community solidarity. Although the community has a long history of nominal involvement in Indian politics, no significant actions were taken until the founding of the Wicket Local Indian Council in 1963.

Eight major elements have been of particular importance in the council's development:

(1) A relatively stable economy coupled with a high positive valuation on work has provided a steady income for a large portion of the population. Over the past 20 or more years, the mining and logging industries have played an important part in the economy of the community, currently providing Wicket with both a relatively high median income and a comparatively low unemployment rate. This stable economy made it possible for minimal personal needs to be met, thus making community activity possible. It is almost a truism to say that if people are living on the margin of poverty, as are many of the people in northern Minnesota, it is very difficult for them to find the time, money, or energy to devote to community cooperation and development.

(2) The members of the community and their leaders took the initiative in establishing and sustaining community improvement projects. In a sense the efforts of the Wicket residents can be considered a type of revitalization movement, that is, "a deliberate, organized, conscious effort of members of a society to construct a more satisfying culture," occurring through the initiative of a major local leader who had the assistance of a "small inner circle of disciples or lieutenants who were already influential men" (Wallace 1956:265). As has been shown, community leadership has been concentrated in one segment of the

village. However, the total enthusiastic support of the active council members was necessary to make the primary leader successful.

(3) There was intracommunity cooperation among the 4 locally defined factions, in addition to general community cooperation with outside individuals and organizations. All of the locally defined groups or factions took an active part in the early development of the community. This fact is especially significant since the Ojibwa are ethnographically characterized as "atomistic" or "individualistic." In this reservation situation, Wicket Chippewa were able to cooperate intensively long enough to meet commonly perceived community needs. The members of the community supported their leaders and even added new positions to accommodate other locally influential individuals, maximizing coordination of community efforts.

(4) The community was able to define a common need or want that took precedence over the separately existing needs and wants of the various smaller groups in the community. Ward Goodenough has noted that a serious problem in community development can occur when factional differences include the area of "public value" (1963a:101 and passim). Since people resent outside interference in their internal affairs, Wicket's ability to define a common goal has made community development possible. The definition of a common need prevented the problem of intracommunity nonrecognition occurring when one individual or small group of individuals might have tried to make a change incompatible with the desires of the rest of the community.

(5) Outside assistance was given to the community by specialists representing governmental bureaus and by interested private individuals. This assistance was important in Wicket's case because, although the local members demonstrated initiative and had well-defined needs, they lacked the necessary bureaucratic information to obtain funds, materials, and services. Representatives of the Bureau of Indian Affairs, the Minnesota Consolidated Chippewa Agency, and the Minnesota state government were especially helpful in the development program. Local whites also provided necessary guidance and assistance in promoting community projects.

(6) Recognition was received at points along the way from private individuals outside the community, including attention from prominent political figures. As Ward Goodenough pointed out: "To regard community development as a process of collective identity change, in which the community's members come to look upon themselves as a different kind of people and on their community as a different kind of place, calls attention to the importance of recognition by others—in this case by

outsiders, especially those outsiders who have been their severest critics. Such comment reassures them that their efforts are being recognized by others and that they are on the way to a collective identity of which they can be proud within the larger world community" (1963a:241).

The people of Wicket have come to look upon themselves as a different kind of people living in a different kind of place; thus, positive recognition from the usual critics of Indians—the white population—has been important to them. Indeed, the community has received much outside recognition. Among those who have shown interest in and support for Wicket are white business people in neighboring towns, distinguished political figures who twice visited the community, and a feature writer from a large metropolitan newspaper. Another person who read of Wicket's early activities in a newspaper was so impressed that he had his company anonymously donate $1,500 to Wicket. Similarly, a lawyer from out of state, hearing about the council's activities, donated an expensive gas range for the community hall kitchen. The council has also received many small donations from interested outsiders and carefully recorded all of the details in its minutes, signifying that outside recognition has been both gratifying and encouraging.

(7) The actions of the Indian residents of Wicket were initiated in response to a changing social-institutional situation. In answering the question why this development took place when it did, one must consider the events connected with the local Catholic church. Prior to the recent organization of the council, the local church had served as the major integrating institution of the community. It ceased to serve this function, however, shortly after a successful, well-liked pastor was replaced with one whose views were incompatible with those of many of the community's Indian members. Some council members have stated that the conditions resulting from the change in pastors were the primary reason for building the local community hall. Recently, a factional split that occurred in the council was offset by the appointment of a new, better-liked pastor; members of the dissenting faction began redirecting their energies to church activities. Thus available evidence indicates that the policy changes made by the unpopular Catholic priest caused Indian community members to perceive a common goal and cooperate to establish the Wicket Local Indian Council.

(8) Underlying all of the above elements is an attitude of valuing the traditional Indian way of life, yet wanting the younger generation to have what older members of Wicket feel are the benefits of the white man's way of life. This attitude is evidenced by the community's preoccupation

with having a traditional and authentic powwow, and with their tendency to identify Wicket as an "authentic" Indian community. One can sense each community member's pride in being an Indian citizen as well as his or her desire to have some benefits of the white man's life-style. Wicket's pride in its Indian heritage has promoted a community *esprit de corps*, which has been an important element in the development of the community. As Goodenough suggests, it is difficult to overrate this spirit as an element in social change (1963a:90–92, 312–18).

The changing situation: areas for further research

Since the formative days of the local council, the major changes that have occurred in Wicket are these: the arrival of the Community Action Program; a revival of local factionalism; and the replacement of the unpopular local pastor with a dynamic, well-liked priest.

The Community Action Program has had an important effect on the local people, although the Wicket community program was already well established by the time CAP arrived. Local positions in CAP were initially difficult to fill because they were unfamiliar, but soon residents eagerly sought such jobs. Although assessing the permanent effects of CAP is difficult at present (1967), apparently CAP has begun to establish a new social class in Wicket. Local criticism of CAP includes statements indicating that the CAP workers—all local Indians—think that they are "a bit better than the rest of the community." The CAP workers are also accused of having larger automobiles than the rest of the community, inadequately doing their jobs, and lacking the necessary training for their jobs.

One community leader stated that the Community Action Program has created a "split" within the local community. He said, "If the government in Washington sat down and tried to figure out a way to split up the Indians on the reservation, it couldn't have done a better job." Another leader commented that the current split is strikingly similar to the one that occurred in the 1930s as a result of Roosevelt's New Deal programs.

Soon after the arrival of CAP, some of its employees who had formerly been active in the council reportedly stated that they were now working for CAP instead of for the council. Other council members not employed by CAP refused to help with several council activities, stating, "Why should we do it for nothing when the CAP people are getting paid to do similar jobs?" A local CAP critic asserted that CAP has divorced itself from the community and has reified itself as "the

CAP program." He maintained that the program's major value has been to bring funds into the area. Although VISTA volunteers have recently been working very closely with the program, the original VISTA volunteers in Wicket frequently complained about the program's operation, especially with regard to its method of "dumping only money into the community."

An incident that occurred early in 1967 dramatically illustrates the divisiveness CAP has fostered in Wicket. At that time several CAP workers took the proceeds from a fund-raising event sponsored by the local Indian council and started a separate bank account under the names of the CAP workers in Wicket. Although this action was severely criticized by the director of the CAP program, the fact that it occurred at all illustrates the conflict between these 2 groups. Wicket's reaction to CAP has not been unique; similar criticisms have been leveled at the Community Action Program in James Lake.

More community conflict, resulting in a recurrence of factionalism, arose over a series of minor disagreements among council members. The conflict began over a dispute about the price of a council-sponsored fund-raising dinner, escalating into a debate about who should be responsible for the skating rink and baseball teams. A series of personality clashes between members of the 2 major factions increased the conflict. At its height, the members of the Feather faction withdrew their support from the council and refused to attend further meetings. The governing body of the local council now structurally expresses this factionalism, consisting of the chairman, his brother-in-law, his father-in-law, and his sister-in-law. Members of factions not directly involved in this series of disputes and not employed by CAP have generally continued to support the council's activities. Those not currently active in the council have become very active in the local Catholic parish. Wicket's wave of factionalism could be interpreted as a "normal" reaction to rapid social change. As Nicholas observed, "In situations of rapid social change, factions frequently arise—or become more clearly defined—because factional organization is better adapted to competition in changing situations than are the political groups that are characteristic of stable societies" (1966:55).

A third change in the community, the replacement of the unpopular pastor of the Catholic church by a man enthusiastically accepted by Wicket's Indians and whites, has reawakened many residents' interest in church activities. As a result the community once again has an alternative institution in which people can participate and with which they can identify. The church also contributes to integration of the white and Indian segments of the community, although probably to a lesser extent than was true before the formation of the council.

Faced with the effect of these changes on the Wicket Local Indian Council and with the current inability of the council to raise enough money to cover its operating costs, the local chairman suggested 3 alternative courses of action: (1) Since the Community Action Program is currently the major occupant of the community hall, the local council could transfer its authority for administration of its property to CAP; (2) further action could be taken to reunite the 4 local factions in order to achieve the cooperation and participation that was characteristic of the earlier council; (3) the council could continue along its present course and hope that something happens to promote greater participation in council activities.

The first suggestion has since been tabled. In pursuing his second suggestion, the chairman of the local council submitted his resignation in April, 1967, so that someone else could assume the position. The community members rallied behind him at this point and, in what was reported to have been one of the best attended meetings in the council's history, refused to accept his resignation. Late in May of 1967, the chairman had decided to accept another term in office if elected and seemed confident that the period of factionalism and discontent was gradually coming to an end.

6
Chippewa People and Politics in a Reservation Town

Gretel H. Pelto

In April, 1965, the Minneapolis newspapers reported a civil rights case in the northern Minnesota town of James Lake, a mixed Chippewa-white community of 1,500 people. The Indians were suing the mayor and the chief of police, charging police brutality and asking for damages of $120,000. Earlier in the year, the newspapers had reported a James Lake municipal judgeship election in which a write-in campaign for an Indian had nearly succeeded.

Against the background of intense civil rights activism throughout the country, the situation in James Lake was intriguing and raised a number of questions. Was the lawsuit the result of an organized effort by the Indian community? Was the black civil rights movement the model for this effort? If so, where did that put the James Lake Chippewa in comparison to Indians and blacks elsewhere?

In view of prevailing anthropological theories about the Chippewa, these reports of activism were startling. The Chippewa have been described as an atomistic, introverted people. Their apparent lack of social cohesiveness has been the subject of much debate. In the ethnographic literature they are, perhaps, the type case for the "individualistic" society. Their civil rights activism, therefore, appeared incongruous and inexplicable. Did it indicate the development of new organizational forms, or were there other, idiosyncratic explanations for these events?

This study examines the James Lake civil rights activism of the mid-1960s in its local context. The aim of the study was not to describe in detail the social and political organization of the Indian community but to focus on political behavior relevant to the question of Chippewa "individualism."

The geographical boundaries of James Lake as an incorporated village are readily specified; they may be seen on any detailed political map. But political boundaries do not isolate cultures or communities. In fact, the James Lake village boundaries cut through two of the town's major residential neighborhoods. So, for our study, the village limits were enlarged to include the two outlying school districts served by the town.

Specifying James Lake as a geopolitical unit of the State of Minnesota was simple compared to defining the James Lake Indian community. It might have been easiest to regard the community as including all persons who were served by or were eligible to be members of the local Indian council. While that definition had a measure of formal validity, it often did not identify persons who considered themselves part of the community. The local Indian council did not have a list of community members. Eligibility for office-holding was based on the Broken Reed Reservation tribal rolls. Because of confusion over eligibility for tribal enrollment, this list by itself did not identify all James Lake Indians. And geographic boundaries did not define the Indian community, since residences were intermingled with those of non-Indians.

Specifying the entire Indian community also involved consideration of the question of "Indianness," that is, who exactly is an Indian. There are blue-eyed, light-haired people in James Lake who, despite those physical characteristics, are unequivocally recognized as Indians.

A twofold approach to the problem of specifying the community was used. For sampling purposes, the James Lake community was stratified into Indian and white subpopulations. To make this separation, a number of informants in each residential neighborhood were asked to name their neighbors and identify them as either white or Indian. When informant reports were cross-checked, interinformant reliability proved to be high. In only one or two cases did informants' judgments of ethnic identity differ. One measure, then, of "Indianness" in this study population was social consensus.

We also attempted to identify the Indian community descriptively. First, James Lake is here described as a whole; then several sociocultural characteristics of Indians are listed. Structured interview data from the Indian respondents are compared with responses of whites. These data suggest that two relatively independent communities can be distinguished in James Lake—one white, the other Chippewa.

Whether in popular usage or in academic discussion, the terms "political behavior," "political action," and the like have a wide range of connotations. Many theorists find it useful to distinguish between governmental structures and processes of influence. In this regard, M. G. Smith's definitional scheme is illustrative. Smith conceives of the study of government as a broad domain of inquiry. He defines government as "the management, direction, and control of the public affairs of a given social group or unit" (1960:15). Within government he distinguishes between two "essential components": political actions and administrative activities. The latter have to do with conducting the public's business. Political action involves the processes whereby "decisions are taken about the ways in which public business shall be regulated and carried on and about the modes, functions and aims of government" (1960:15). It is "that aspect or form of social action which seeks to influence decisions of policy by competition in power" (1956:48).

These distinctions—useful, perhaps essential, for the analysis of complex, autonomous social units—are difficult to apply to the situation of the Indians in James Lake. Here the administrative structure was rudimentary and virtually without power, and there was little expression of public policy or evidence of effective authority.

Attempting to specify the meaning of the term "political" in this study is problematical because of the nature of the material examined. "Political action" is used here to refer sometimes to "social action which seeks to influence decisions" (Smith 1956) and sometimes to events that fall under Smith's category of "administrative activities." For, in this community, the lines separating actions addressed to forms of decision making from actions aimed at specific collective goals were blurred. The Indians themselves referred to their political activities as "Indian politics." A person who became involved in political activity, particularly an officeholder, was an "Indian politician." These terms frequently were applied pejoratively.

The fieldwork for this study was conducted during the summer of 1965 while I was employed as a field-worker in the Upper Mississippi Research Project (UMRP). In each community studied by the UMRP, field-workers administered a comprehensive interview schedule to members of randomly selected households. In the James Lake area, the sample consisted of 30 white and 30 Indian households. The sampling area covered the two townships that were served by the James Lake schools. It was larger than the village limits and included a small proportion of rural residents. The population of the town itself numbered 1,587 persons (1965), of whom approximately 800 were Chippewa Indians. In James Lake I worked with only Indian informants. In addition to those in the interview sample, major informants were the chairman and the secretary of the local Indian council, the wife of an officer of the Broken Reed Reservation Business Committee, a key informal leader and his wife, and the Indian minister of the Episcopal church. Another source of extremely valuable information was the Indian family that cared for my 4-year-old son. Daily contact with the members of this family gave me a chance to see another side of the community and its day-to-day activities. Because they were part of a large network of kin, as a matter of course I met a number of persons who might have been difficult to reach otherwise. Thus, having a small child was a tremendous help in building rapport with at least part of the Indian community.

Although most of the research was completed during the 3 summer months, I later returned to James Lake several times to complete the interviewing. In addition to my own data, I had available to me all of the information gathered by my co-workers in the UMRP and—probably more important—the benefit of their insights and ideas. The cooperativeness and frankness of my informants made my task of discovering "what was going on" much easier than it might have been, and increases my confidence in the validity of the description that follows.

An overview of the community

Since in many respects James Lake is sharply divided along ethnic or cultural lines into 2 distinct subcommunities, an overview of the town is perhaps most informative if it is presented from an "integrated" perspective.

James Lake is located in north central Minnesota in the heart of the lake country. Going north from the Twin Cities, the highway toward the North Woods passes through 100 miles of rich, flat farmland, then into the hilly pine woods. Through the next 100 or so miles of pine forest there are small towns every 15 or 20 miles, preceded by billboards advertising each town's resort accommodations and tourist attractions.

An automobile junkyard on the left of the highway and the piles of lumber at Frank's Mill on the right are the first indications of James Lake. A large weatherbeaten billboard announces, "Welcome to James Lake Resort Area. 100 Resorts—500 Lakes." The highway then passes a paved street and two parallel dirt roads which lead to a residential neighborhood known variously as "South of the Tracks," "the South Side," or "Mexican Town." (Considerable numbers of Mexicans and Mexican-Americans work as agricultural laborers in the farming region 50 to 100 miles northwest of James Lake. A few Chippewa women have, at one time or another, married men with Spanish surnames.) Continuing north, the road crosses the railroad tracks and passes a gas station and a drive-in restaurant. A small sign points to the right, indicating the location of the business district. Unless the traveler turns up the street indicated by the sign, all he sees of James Lake are some frame houses and the Jehovah's Witnesses' Kingdom Hall.

Most of the business establishments of James Lake (see Figure 6.1) line two east-west streets. On Main Street, the stores begin 3 blocks from the north-south highway. On the left side of the street, there is a supermarket, a clothing store, a pool hall, the American Legion Hall, a tourist shop, and a gas station. The next block includes a 2-story brick hotel (now closed), a few houses, and a laundromat. On the right side of the street are a small grocery store, a clothing store, the affluent-appearing municipal liquor store and bar, a hamburger shop (a teenage hangout), a restaurant (which doubles as the bus station), a drugstore, and the only bank. In the next block one finds a five-and-dime, another drugstore, the post office, a tackle shop, and a general store.

The principal north-south street, once part of the main highway, also has a number of businesses. The businesses include 3 taverns, an ice cream stand, a gas station, a laundromat, and, at the south end of the street, the old movie house and hotel.

On the second east-west business street, parallel to Main Street and one block south, is the brick office building of the James Lake *Gazette,* a supermarket, a bait shop, a hardware store, a beauty shop, a small restaurant, and a tavern.

On a side street just east of Main Street stands the town hall, a small one-story building. It has, in front, the office of the town clerk; in the center, the courtroom, complete with judge's dais and jury box; to the rear, the police offices and a jail (no longer in use). The garage attached to the town hall houses the fire engine and a police car.

The next block to the north is a park and playground; the land belongs to the Minnesota Chippewa Tribe, although the town maintains the playground. At one end of the park is a small log building owned by the tribe. It is called the Co-op, because in earlier days it was used by an

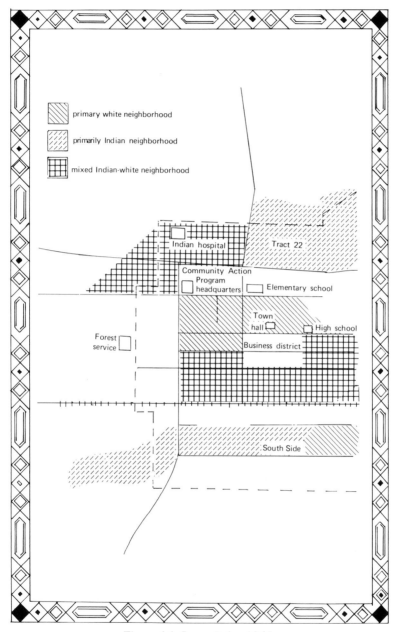

Figure 6.1. James Lake, 1965.

Indian cooperative association. In 1965 it was the headquarters for the Broken Reed Reservation Community Action Program.

East of the playground is the pink stucco elementary school, and, a block beyond that, the high school with its new addition. Across from the high school is a strikingly modern building, the Roman Catholic church. Several other churches, including the Episcopal church and two Lutheran churches, are scattered throughout this neighborhood. Most of the other buildings in the northern section of town are private homes. The majority of these are frame houses, 50 to 60 years old, and are owned or occupied by non-Indians.

The neighborhoods just east and south of the business district have mixed Indian and white populations (see Figure 6.1). The style, size, age, and condition of the homes in this area vary more than in the northern section. Trailer houses and tar-papered shacks are interspersed among frame or shingle-covered log dwellings. Many of the homes lack indoor plumbing; most lack central heating. The Christian Missionary and Alliance church and the Church of Jesus Christ of Latter-Day Saints are in this part of town. A sign proclaiming "All Indians Welcome" is prominently displayed on the front of the Mormon church.

The range in values and styles of houses in these neighborhoods is also typical of the two outlying neighborhoods, the areas south of the tracks (the South Side) and the tribally owned land north of town (Tract 22). These districts are isolated from the main part of town by physical barriers: the South Side by both railroad tracks and the extensive pole yards of the White Lumber Company, and Tract 22 by the 4-lane east-west highway. The north-south highway provides the only automobile access to these neighborhoods.

In the western half of the South Side, the great majority of the residents are Indians. To the east, the South Side becomes an almost exclusively white neighborhood. While many of the white-occupied homes are relatively modern, most of the Indian homes are small 2- and 3-room buildings, some in very poor condition. With but one exception, there is no indoor plumbing, and a few dwellings are at least half a block from a water pump. Although the houses are close together and roughly arranged in blocks, the area appears more rural than the districts nearer the town's center. One resident raises ponies in her front yard; another family keeps a few cows. Few homes have grass lawns, and in some of the yards the weeds are knee-high by mid-July.

Residence on Tract 22, the tribally owned land, is limited exclusively to Indians. Enrollment in the Minnesota Chippewa Tribe is a requirement for occupying a tax-exempt lot. The Tract is crosscut with dirt roads and footpaths, and the houses are scattered over the land in an irregular fashion. The few houses that front on the highway are well constructed and carefully maintained. Farther from the paved road, tar-papered houses like those on the South Side are the most common kind of dwellings. Still farther back in the woods, there are some dilapidated houses where it is not unusual to find families with 6 and more children occupying a one-room shack. Unlike the South Side, however, many more of the houses in this area have indoor plumbing, the result of a recent federal project.

Across the road from Tract 22 are the James Lake Indian Hospital, operated by the Public Health Service, and several houses for the resident staff and their families. With its white buildings and well-kept green lawns, the hospital complex is an impressive contrast to James Lake's many run-down dwellings. The town's only other imposing structure is the National Forest Service headquarters located west of town off the main highway. Like the Co-op, it has the characteristic log-cabin style of many buildings in northern Minnesota constructed by the Works Progress Administration in the 1930s.

The official northern limit of the town crosses through the middle of the tribal tract. North of the boundary line, beyond the tribal land, is another white neighborhood of permanent homes and resorts; many front on James Lake. A similar area is located on a bay east of town; this is the town's fashionable neighborhood, and houses on the bay are comparatively large and costly.

A casual visitor, driving through town on a summer day, would be likely to see a great deal of activity. He might even have trouble parking on Main Street, particularly at times when buses are arriving from the north and south. The bus service is the only commercial transportation available to James Lake residents, and when a bus arrives there is usually a small crowd of people standing around waiting to board or to greet visitors.

In summer there are people on the street at all times of day. The lively movement of town residents going in and out of stores, checking for mail at the post office, and carrying on business contrasts with the more leisurely pace of the tourists. The purposeful activity on Main Street contrasts too with the behavior of groups that gather about several favored spots. On the corner by the movie house, Indian men and boys congregate, leaning against the building or standing in small groups; the participants in these gatherings change during the day, but the corner is seldom unoccupied. The ice cream stand is a favorite spot for children, of course, and for the older Indian women, who sit in its shade. At the laundromat across the street, the younger Indian women chat while they wait for their washing. The white women prefer the laundromat on Main Street and are rarely seen at the one across from the ice cream stand. On cool days the taverns may open early, but during the summer they frequently remain closed until 4:00 p.m.

At night the scene changes. The young mothers walking their babies disappear from the street. In the early evening, there are still children around the ice cream stand, but by 10:00 p.m. most of them have gone home. At dusk the police car parks at the main intersection; usually 2 policemen patrol the area. Evening activity centers on the bars and taverns. The American Legion Hall and the municipal liquor store and bar are frequented by whites. The Indians are more likely to make the rounds of the smaller taverns. The restaurant on Main Street remains open all night, and when the taverns close at 1:00 a.m., people go there for food and coffee.

In winter Main Street looks very different. By mid-January the buildings are usually half-hidden behind piles of snow. All business and socializing take place indoors and the streets are deserted. Snow blankets the junk in the barren yards, but the general air of poverty remains. Even in summer, when there are many people around, the town is somewhat shabby in appearance. Summer or winter, nothing about the town suggests that it was once a boom town with a hopeful future.

History

The first residents of James Lake in modern times were Chippewa Indians, who entered the area in the mid-18th century. Beginning early in the century, bands of Chippewa from the Lake Superior region pushed west and south into north central Minnesota (Hickerson 1962). One of their major settlements was a series of villages along the western shore of Broken Reed Lake. The village at James Lake, 20 miles to the north, may have been established coincidentally with the Broken Reed villages, or later, as Hickerson argues (1962:40), by a group from the main settlement at Broken Reed.

The early ties between the people of James Lake and the groups at Broken Reed Lake have continued to the present day. Schoolcraft noted in 1832 an instance of cooperation: a group of Broken Reed warriors who "in company with warriors from nearby [James Lake] had just returned from a war excursion against the Dakota" (Hickerson 1962:55). When the Broken Reed Reservation was established, James Lake was included within its boundaries.

James Lake village may have been established as early as 1760. The *Citizen's Manual,* a booklet on the town's history, government, taxes, and the like (prepared by the local League of Women Voters), reports the existence of a French trading post prior to 1760. The village was clearly in existence in 1797, for a historic record of that year indicates that there was a partition of sugar groves among several families in James Lake. According to Hickerson, this agreement was reached by the people "acting in council" (1962:34). The fact that use-rights in an annual crop were allocated to families suggests a degree of permanency of residence in the village.

During the 18th and early 19th centuries, the Minnesota Chippewa villages had a diversified economy. Hunting and trapping were, of course, the major subsistence activities. Fishing supplied important food. Maple sugar, berries, and wild rice were gathered in season, and some villages raised pumpkins, beans, and squash.

The boundaries around the Broken Reed Reservation, which includes the James Lake area, were established by treaty in 1855 (U. S. Bureau of Indian Affairs 1965a:3). Originally the 23,726 acres of reservation land were held in trust by the government for the group. With the Allotment Act of 1887, over 11,000 acres were assigned to individuals. The act provided for an individual to receive clear title, and consequently, the right to sell his land. The result was rapid sale of much of the land. In 1966 only 19 percent of the original reservation land was Indian-owned, either by individuals or collectively by the tribe (League of Women Voters of Minnesota 1962:24).

Large sections of northern Minnesota have poor soil for farming; the land on the Broken Reed Reservation is particularly poor. Before the lumber boom in the late 1890s, few whites moved into the area, and the land around James Lake was probably not sold to any great extent. Aside from a few hardy settlers, the only whites were government agents, itinerant traders, and missionaries. The Congregationalists established a mission in 1854; the Episcopal church followed around 1881.

At the turn of the century, James Lake village began to produce lumber and changed radically, acquiring all the characteristics of a boom town. It was chosen as the site for an important railroad depot and switchyard. Hotels, restaurants, and stores were opened. In 1899, 48 residents voted unanimously for incorporation of the town.

The 20 years following incorporation were a time of growth and prosperity. By 1910 there were 2,109 people in James Lake, some of them transient lumberjacks and railroad men. But the presence of a box factory and sawmills, the availability of land, and the demand for various consumer goods and services attracted a more stable population as well. By 1920 the town had a bank, school, churches, newspaper, movie theater, and 3 clubs—the Commercial Club, the Choral Club, and, after World War I, the American Legion Post. Seven churches in so small a community were evidence of the heterogeneity of the population.

Despite the churches, not all of the citizens were respectable. One older informant recalled in 1966 that, as a young girl, she used to watch the "painted ladies" going past her house on their way to town, and had considered them "very elegant." Today the marble dining hall of the hotel is gone, and the painted ladies are far from elegant.

The first hint of decline came just 9 years after the village's incorporation and during the height of its prosperity. In 1908 the government established the Ojibway National Forest, closing off to the lumbering companies tremendous tracts of the land around James Lake. The mills, however, did not finish sawing the remaining virgin timber until after World War I. While woods work continues to the present day, big-time lumbering operations ended in 1921.

The loss of revenue from lumbering was offset in part by the establishment of 2 government agencies in James Lake. The Forest Service opened a branch in the community in 1918. During the WPA era a new headquarters building was constructed, along with several campgrounds in the forest itself. In addition to providing jobs for local men, the Forest Service was important to James Lake because it brought in government workers and their families. According to several informants, these families always took an active role in community affairs and social life.

In 1920 the main office of the newly organized Consolidated Chippewa Agency was established in James Lake. Because the administration of 6 of the 7 Minnesota Chippewa reservations was delegated to this office, it became the center of a great deal of activity. The Chippewa agency office brought a core of professional workers into town; it also brought Indians.

After the early 1920s there was a small but steady in-migration of Indians into the vicinity of James Lake, continuing to recent times. Since many of the incoming Indians settled in the countryside and "in the woods" rather than within the village limits, their arrival was not officially recorded. However, the in-migration is apparent both from verbal reports of informants and from our sample of Indian family histories.

During the days of heavy government subsidy, the Indians were attracted to the Indian office. For some, whose parents had earlier chosen to live on the Beaver Pelt Reservation, moving to the area was a return to their ancestral homeland. The Public Health Service Hospital built in 1937 provided another incentive for in-migration. The new arrivals may have contributed to the growth of Indian organizations and the flush of activity in the 1930s and 1940s. Between 1925 and 1940, there were 3 Indian women's groups and an Indian cooperative association. One of the women's clubs continued past that period, but with a much reduced membership.

Otherwise, for the community as a whole the period between 1920 and 1940 was inactive, in sharp contrast to the boom years and to the war years that followed. The local *Citizen's Manual* lists only 4 events for the entire 20-year history: the construction of the high school, the disbanding of the Congregational church and its purchase by the Trinity Lutheran church, the construction of the hospital, and WPA activity. These years seem to have been a period of readjustment. Gone were the optimistic days of "easy money"; the town had not yet developed the extensive voluntary associations that characterize it today.

A number of organizations were begun in the 1940s: the League of Women Voters, the Civic and Commerce Association, the Lions Club, and the VFW (Veterans of Foreign Wars) Post. Of these social clubs, the League and the Civic and Commerce Association were oriented toward community improvement; the League, for example, started the community library in 1947. The clubs sponsored town improvement programs as part of an effort to attract more tourists to the growing resort business. The need to attract visitors became especially pressing after 3 events that further weakened the town's already uncertain economy: within 6 years, the box factory burned down, a new east-west highway bypassed the business district, and the Indian office was moved to North City, 15 miles away.

When the box factory was destroyed by fire in 1947, scores of men were suddenly out of work. The company decided not to rebuild, and many residents were forced to leave the community to seek work. One informant, a man of considerable prestige, told us that there was a "major exodus" during which most of the "good citizens" left. In an emotional tone, he said, "Those were a couple of hundred or so damned good citizens."

Until 1952 the main highway connecting North City with the metropolitan centers of southern Minnesota passed directly through the James Lake business district. The new highway was built to skirt the center of town by several blocks, but it still passes through the outskirts. In theory, the town's location at the junction of 2 major highways is a favorable one. Few efforts were made, however, to develop or to landscape the land that fronts on the highway. In 1963, the Village Council appointed a committee to study the problem; the committee applied for and received an Area Redevelopment Administration Grant. Most of the grant money was used to develop the marina (not visible from the highway); some was spent to clear brush and plant trees on highway frontage.

In 1954 the Bureau of Indian Affairs reorganized the Minnesota office, changing its name from Consolidated Chippewa Agency to Minnesota Agency. Headquarters were moved to the Federal Building in North City. Although a few people continued with the bureau and commuted to work daily, James Lake lost another source of employment.

James Lake in 1965

The James Lake economy was heavily dependent on the surrounding woods and lakes, which were exploited in a number of ways by the town's two major industries, lumbering and tourism. The railroad operated solely for the lumbering interests and was therefore directly dependent on the area's timber resources. At the time of the study, the railroad employed 30 men locally.

Three sawmills were in operation in 1965. The largest employed from 16 to 22 men, about half of them Indians. A second mill, which normally hired 16 men, sharply reduced the number of its employees in the summer of 1965. The owner reported that usually three-fourths of his workers were Indians. The third mill was a family operation in which relatives (non-Indians) were employed.

The White Lumber Company, a subdivision of a large Michigan firm, was the town's largest employer. In James Lake, the company manufactured poles and at full capacity employed 50 men, a fourth to a third of them Indians.

Small contractors—local men who bid for the opportunity to cut secondary growth in the national forest—hired some loggers. The loggers cut, peeled, and stacked logs, then cleared a path to the logging road, for 12 cents per "finished" foot of logs. Other men were hired as truck drivers and "skidders," who loaded the logs onto the trucks. Compared with lumbering techniques in other areas, these methods were quite primitive. Although cutting was done with power saws, peeling was usually done by hand and even loading was sometimes unmechanized.

As is often the case when a single occupation predominates in a community, a special ambience pervaded it. Accidents in the woods, the quality of a tract of timber, the merits of particular employers, and the skill of various workers were frequent conversation topics. Some men expressed great hatred for the backbreaking, and sometimes dangerous, woods work. A former woodman who had become a mechanic said that he wouldn't go back to cutting timber even if he were starving. Others, while they complained about low pay and hard work, claimed to like their jobs. The opportunity to be outdoors and "to work at your own pace" were frequently cited as important aspects of woods work.

Although the major attractions of the area for vacationers were the lakes, the forest was also important for the tourist business. The forest campgrounds were becoming more and more popular; on weekends families arriving late in the day sometimes found all of the campsites taken. The intensive use of the campgrounds provided work for a number of local people hired by the Forest Service as maintenance persons.

The campers, resort vacationers, and summer residents brought income to the town through their trade with local businesses. The stores counted most of their profits during the summer, some closing altogether in winter, when there were few tourists or vacationers.

The 2 government agencies that remained in James Lake—the hospital and the Forest Service—provided jobs for Indians and for whites. Although the Bureau of Indian Affairs office had been moved to North City, several of its employees continued to live in James Lake.

In the interview sample, the distribution of the occupations of males reflected the town's basic economy. The majority of the men in the sample were employed by the government or by lumbering or tourist-related industries. Table 6.1, representing a time span of approximately 15 years, includes the deceased husbands of female respondents.

The schools were a source of employment for both men and women. Teachers were usually recruited from the outside, but other staff members were residents. The grade school had a total staff of 19; the high school, a staff of 26. Women were also employed by the restaurants, resorts, laundries, and stores.

Table 6.1. Occupations of male interviewees

Occupation	Indian	White	Total
Logging or mill work	13	5	18
Government work (hospital, Bureau of Indian Affairs, Forest Service)	7	4	11
Business	0	6	6
Labor (other than woods work)	1	5	6
Farming	1	3	4
Railroad work	0	3	3
Other	1	2	3

Note: This distribution includes the then-current jobs of male household heads, former occupations of retired male household heads, and occupations of deceased or divorced spouses of female household heads. For the total sample of 60 families, there was no information (or no male head of household, past or present) for 7 Indian and 2 white respondents.

The distribution of respondents' income provides further information on the general economic situation in James Lake. The data (see Table 6.2) suggest the economic problems that James Lake residents faced. It should be recalled that at the time of this study the U. S. government regarded a family of 4 with an annual income of less than $3,000 as living in poverty. Equally striking was the disparity between Indian and white incomes. (For an overview of economic adjustment in this area of northern Minnesota, see Schensul, Paredes, and Pelto 1968.)

These figures, sorted into age groups, show that younger men had higher incomes than older men (see Table 6.3). However, the economic advantages of youth were far more significant for whites than for Indians. The gap between incomes of older groups of Indians and whites narrowed considerably.

The financial base for the village government was the municipal liquor store and bar. Revenues from various kinds of permits and the village's share of state property and cigarette taxes were minor compared with the liquor store profits. Heavy drinking was a cultural pattern in James Lake, alcoholism was a problem, and law enforcement was an explosive issue. The town's citizens did not readily discuss the ironic fact that policemen's salaries were paid out of liquor store profits.

Village governance was the responsibility of 5 elected officials: the mayor, the village clerk, and 3 trustees; together they made up the Village Council. The mayor and the trustees acted primarily in a decision-making capacity, while the clerk, the only full-time employee,

Table 6.2. Income distribution of sample households

Yearly income	Indian	White	Total
Under $1,000	3	6	9
$1,000 – $1,999	11	4	15
$2,000 – $2,999	4	5	9
$3,000 – $3,999	5	5	10
$4,000 – $4,999	3	0	3
$5,000 – $5,999	2	4	6
$6,000 – $6,999	1	2	3
$7,000 or over	0	4	4
No information	1	0	1
Total	30	30	60
Median income	$2,000	$2,856	

Note: The difference between the distribution of Indian and white incomes is significant at $p<.035$ using a Mann-Whitney U test.

was responsible for carrying out the day-to-day operations of government. The mayor and the trustees were paid a token sum for their services, and they all had other full-time jobs.

The village clerk was Margaret Blake, wife of the Episcopal minister, himself a Chippewa Indian. She was reputed to know more about the town than any other resident and was invariably suggested as the first person to see "if you want to know what's going on." Her knowledge of community affairs and the range of her official duties gave her considerable power. She was described as the "village's conscience." One informant claimed that "She keeps the men [village officials] in line."

Mrs. Blake's position in the village social structure appeared ambiguous. Her role in the council differentiated her from the other women, whose influence had to be exerted less directly. Her obligations as the minister's wife in a church that had a 90 percent Indian congrega-

Table 6.3. Median income of sample households by age

Age range of household heads	Indian	No.	White	No.	Difference
21 – 40 years old	$3,120	13	$5,495	6	$2,375
41 – 60	$1,900	9	$3,493	11	$1,593
61 plus	$1,896	7	$2,148	13	$ 252

tion also set her apart. Furthermore, she was the only white woman in the community married to an Indian.

Her husband, Rev. John Blake, was also an important figure in village affairs. He was active in community organizations, including the Improvement Committee and the Lions Club. His social responsibilities extended far beyond the boundaries of the community; he was a member of the James County Nursing Board and served on the Governor's Human Rights Committee. The latter position afforded him opportunities to participate in government activity at the national level: he attended several organizational meetings of the federal antipoverty program and participated in President Lyndon Johnson's civil rights conferences. As a minister he had a wide variety of contacts. Reverend Blake was probably the most experienced man in James Lake in the social and political world outside the community. Though Blake was highly respected and frequently mentioned as an important figure in community life, white informants never failed to mention that he was an Indian.

The members of the Village Council were not members of the financial "elite." In contrast to the $10,000-plus annual incomes of several of the town's business and professional men, the Village Council members had middle-range incomes. The mayor was a foreman on the railroad; one of the trustees was a foreman at the mill, and another was a general handyman. However, there did not appear to be any important division between the businessmen and the wage earners. Social ties that were developed as a result of the town's numerous clubs provided a basis for a rather diffuse organization of white families. The councilmen met the businessmen and other town residents in the social clubs, and it was probably in these settings that most decisions regarding town affairs were actually made.

The Village Council seemed to be primarily a maintenance operation, and relatively unimportant to the citizens of the community. Other than the appointment of a committee to develop plans for improving the town's appearance, the council had not taken an active part in initiating new programs. By contrast, the police and judicial divisions played much more significant roles. At the time of this study, in addition to James Lake's problems of maintaining public order, an Indian-initiated lawsuit against the police and a write-in campaign to elect an Indian municipal judge had thrust the police and the judge into the public spotlight.

The legal personnel of the local government included a judge, a village attorney, and a constable. The constable, referred to as the chief of police, was assisted by 2 full-time policemen. A state highway patrol officer was also assigned to duty in James Lake, giving the town of 1,500 persons a 4-man police force. Between the spring and fall of 1965, 2 white police officers "retired" and were replaced by 2 brothers, who were Indian.

The chief of police was Chuck Burrows. Large, ruddy-faced, and grey-haired, he was a conspicuous figure as he drove around town in the police station wagon, which had been converted to a paddy wagon by the addition of a grate separating the front from the back seat. An Indian informant explained the grate: "He [Burrows] is scared someone will hit him over the head some night."

Municipal Judge Krammer, a man well past the age of retirement, had a propensity for speaking harshly. He was disliked by the Indian residents, who claimed that he was very prejudiced. For "drunk and disorderly conduct" he often sentenced an offender to 72 hours in jail. Even though the James Lake jail was condemned by state examiners in 1963, it was used until April, 1965, when it was finally closed by a court injunction. Subsequently, persons sentenced by Judge Krammer were sent to jail in Trotter, the county seat, 20 miles to the south.

The village attorney conducted routine legal business for the village and also served as a county juvenile judge in the court in Trotter. Although he spent most of his working day in Trotter, he was an active member of the James Lake community, holding membership in the Lions Club, the Sportsman's Club, the Athletic Club, and the American Legion. His attitude toward Indians was noteworthy. In an interview with one of our field-workers, he said, "The Indians are like kids; they fight among themselves and are polite to whites." After commenting on their inability to hold either jobs or liquor, he concluded, "They're Indians and there's nothing you can do with them."

This brief sketch of James Lake is based on materials from the village newspaper and the *Citizens Manual*, and on interviews with local residents. However, it is incomplete and one-sided, having no place in it for nearly half of the town's residents; a description emphasizing the structural elements of administrative and social organizations fails to account for the Indian population. Indeed, many white James Lakers did not seem to think of the Indians as full-fledged members of the community. Except for Reverend Blake, there were no Indian participants in the town's social clubs. The absence of Indians from the town's formal organizations was one way, then, of distinguishing the Indian community as a separate entity within James Lake. The white residents seemed generally disposed to think of the Indians as people to be ignored, although undoubtedly there was also an element of fear and hostility in their attitude.

Although most of the land is white-owned, James Lake is technically a part of the Broken Reed Reservation. However, conversations with white residents revealed that they did not think of themselves as living on a reservation, and that they conceived of James Lake as a white community, not essentially different from other small Minnesota towns. In contrast to this view, the impression of James Lake held by residents of neighboring towns was quite different. Interviews revealed that people in communities without Indian residents, or with only a small Indian population, tended to think of James Lake as an "Indian town." One standard question asked by field-workers in the larger UMRP project—"Are there any towns here that you would avoid going to?"— was originally included to elicit information on intervillage antagonism and to get comments on the large, "closed" Deer Lake Reservation; a surprising number of respondents replied that they would avoid going to James Lake. Further probing revealed that James Lake was thought to be a "rough" town, a setting for a great deal of drinking and fighting.

On two separate encounters in which my identity as a field-worker was not immediately apparent, people from other towns voiced concern about my safety in living in James Lake. They advised against speaking with "certain people" and suggested that I stay off the street at night. As these conversations progressed, it became obvious that they too thought of James Lake as an "Indian town" and as a place to avoid whenever possible.

Sociocultural characteristics of the Indian community

The Indian community as a separate entity within James Lake may be approached from at least two different perspectives. In terms of its sociocultural characteristics, the group existed only in the behavior of individuals, so that the adequacy of a sociocultural definition depends on how well the generalizations about the economic, religious, and kinship patterns of James Lake Indians fit individual cases. The generalizations made in this study have a higher probability of accurately characterizing the situation of any randomly selected Indian individual in 1965 than of being applicable to any randomly selected white resident.

The James Lake Indian community can also be described as a quasi-formal unit of the Minnesota Chippewa Tribe. All Indians enrolled in the tribe living in the town or its immediate surrounding area were, by definition, members of the unit.

The conceptualization of these 2 perspectives, as a heuristic device, helps to clarify certain features of the community; but it is an artificial separation. Explaining the sociocultural characteristics of the community requires occasional reference to the tribal government, and the operation of the government can be understood only against the background of general features of the Indian community.

The social segregation that characterized Indian-white relations in James Lake was not altogether reflected in the residence patterns of the town, which was composed of mixed as well as Indian and white neighborhoods. Except for the "better" residential neighborhood north of the business district, the central parts of the village were nonsegregated; Indian and white families lived intermingled with one another. Of all the areas (apart from Tract 22, north of town), the term "segregation" perhaps most appropriately describes the east end of the South Side. There were no Indian residents for several blocks in the east end. A white woman from this neighborhood, who had lived in James Lake for only two years, felt that the absence of Indian families was the result of a consciously pursued segregation policy. She claimed that before she bought her house, an Indian family who wanted to buy it was told that the house had already been sold.

In contrast, the west end of the area was primarily (though not exclusively) an Indian neighborhood. One informant who assisted in mapping the neighborhood remarked, "We're all Indian around here." However, when asked to sort the actual list of households, he distinguished between Indian and white families, pointing out what he considered to be questionable cases. For example, he hesitated in the instance of a white woman who had once been married to an Indian, but who was now divorced. When asked to categorize her, he replied, "Well, she *is* white." Verbal distinctions between "Indian" and "white" were encountered frequently. This practice extended even to relatives; an Indian woman, speaking of her mother, said, "Grandma Mary is white." Undoubtedly, the frequency with which the labels were applied reflected and helped to maintain the "we-they" distinction that appeared to characterize Indian-white relations, regardless of proximity.

The other Indian neighborhood was Tract 22, the tribal land north of town. The Bureau of Indian Affairs listed 39 households on the tract. According to our Upper Mississippi Research Project census, the Indian population outside of the Tract included 48 Indian households in the South Side and 53 in the central part of town. (The totals of white households in the two latter areas were 69 and 268, respectively.)

No significant pattern was found in informants' reasons for choosing between the Tract and "in town" as a place of residence. The usual reply was that the choice was dictated by the availability of housing at the time of need. One South Side resident wanted to move to a wooded corner of the Tract, but his teenage daughter objected to being so far from the center of town.

It did not appear that social distinctions were drawn among Indians on the basis of residence, nor that the people on the tract were more "Indian" in their outlook or life-style than those who lived on nontribal land. The rate of social interaction within the two Indian neighborhoods was probably greater than between them, but the short distances involved and a general willingness to walk prevented any meaningful separation between the two residential groups.

Indians in James Lake did a great deal of walking, even in the coldest weather. Within town, owning a car was a convenience but not a necessity, since distances (to stores, the post office, etc.) were short. But for the men who worked in the woods or traveled to jobs outside of town, a car was practically an economic necessity. Fifty percent of the Indians in the sample owned cars, as compared with 83 percent of the non-Indians. Those who did not own cars usually paid for transportation. The village taxi was readily available but expensive, and people seemed to prefer asking relatives and friends for rides. Much of the time, these rides were paid for; one woman charged her sister-in-law 25 cents per trip to drive her to and from work, a distance of about a mile and a half. This arrangement was probably typical, and, in our experience, rides which were given without charge were always gratefully acknowledged.

In the past, many Indian families preferred to live in the outlying areas of the reservation, but in recent years there has been a movement into town. At the time of the study Mission Village, located 6 miles from James Lake at the site of the old Episcopal mission, was no longer a community of 30-plus families; only a few people still lived there. In the rural areas of the two townships in the James Lake school district there were 179 white households and 18 Indian households. Several small Indian villages "back in the woods" remained, but they did not appear to be closely articulated to the Indian community in James Lake.

Economic differentiation

Despite general economic depression in the region, James Lake Indians could be differentiated from the local whites in economic terms. It is apparent from Table 6.1 and Table 6.2 that the limited economic resources of the region, resulting in restrictions on both job opportunity and income, had a more serious effect on Indians than on whites. There were fewer *kinds* of jobs open to Indians; the better-paying jobs in business and the professions were the least accessible.

A lower cash income was only one aspect of the economic problems that confronted Indian families. The majority of Indian men were employed as lumberjacks, construction workers, and Forest Service workers. Most of this work was seasonal, with periods of unemployment in the winter and spring. The extent of seasonal unemployment is reflected in the job histories of the men in the household sample. In contrast to the men in the white sample, many Indians reported extensive and frequent periods of unemployment. One indication of unemployment is the number of weeks worked during the year (1964–65). The figures reported by Indian respondents ranged from 12 to 50, with a median of 40 weeks' employment; for white respondents the range was from 32 to 52, with a median of 50 weeks' employment.

Most men who worked seasonally had to rely on unemployment compensation or welfare for a part of their income. Of the 14 working Indian household heads interviewed in the sample, 8 received unemployment compensation during 1964 and 1965. Two men did not receive it, although they were unemployed for part of the year. Of the 14, 4 received additional welfare and 12 received surplus food commodities.

For the comparable white sample, 3 men (all of whom were unemployed at the time of their interviews) received unemployment compensation. Two men received veteran's compensation. None of the 17 white households headed by an employed male used surplus food commodities. The distribution of surplus food was under the control of the James County Welfare Department, which, in contrast to those in many other counties, appeared to have a liberal policy about requirements for eligibility. In the total sample of 30 white and 30 Indian households, 27 Indian families and 4 white families received surplus food.

A comparison of the income sources of nonworking respondents shows that the Indian families were more dependent on welfare than the whites; 8 of the Indians in the nonworking sample were supported

Table 6.4. Income sources of nonworking interviewees

Male head of household	Indian	White
Social security and/or pension	3	7
Welfare	2	0
Female head of household		
Social security and/or pension	1	5
Welfare	6	1

entirely by welfare, compared to only 1 white respondent (see Table 6.4).

The foregoing data provide clear evidence of economic differences between Indian and white families. They indicate the nature of economic problems and the general level of living standards in the area. Living standards may also be described in terms of a material-style-of-life scalogram, using the Guttman scaling technique (see Paredes, Chapter 7 in this volume).

The items on the scale are material goods or devices, all of which require some monetary expenditure. The scale provides not only a graphic illustration of the material conveniences that these families had obtained, but reveals the range of difference in material life-styles within the community. For James Lake, the scalogram was constructed from the data on the 60 families in the total James Lake household sample (see Table 6.5). In the scale, Indian respondents are indicated by an I in parentheses. In these data, as in other comparisons, there is a striking difference between Indian and white families. The figures on actual income suggest serious poverty among a portion of the sample population. An examination of the families in the lower end of the scale reveals some of the effects of these low incomes. Nine Indian families did not have a refrigerator; 5 did not have a stove; and 5 did not have electricity.

Significant differences existed between Indian and white males in occupational choice and amount of unemployment, and between Indian and white families in income and reliance on welfare; yet there was little overall difference (in this sample) in the proportion of families with employed *versus* unemployed household heads (see Table 6.6). To an extent, this similarity was the result of the skewed age distribution of the white sample. As can be seen in Table 6.3, there was a disproportionate number of older people in the white sample, which reflected the high rate of out-migration of white young people in the general area. However, the difference in the proportion of older people did not account for the similarity that is seen in Table 6.6. The stereotype of the "lazy Indian" living on welfare was certainly contradicted by these data from James Lake. Many Indians as well as whites worked long hours for minimal wages, often needing additional help to survive more difficult times of the year.

The economic adjustments of Indians in James Lake included sources of income and food other than regular employment and various forms of welfare and subsidy. Harvesting wild rice, fishing, hunting, and gathering wild berries were for the Indians (and some of the whites) important subsistence activities. Of these, harvesting wild rice was the most important in terms of its potential contribution to family income. Hunting, fishing, and gathering berries often provided little or no cash income, but they were additional, though seasonal, sources of food. The role of wild rice in the economic, social, and political life of the Indian community was a complex issue (see Berde, Chapter 3 in this volume). Yields in bumper years may be many times the amount of rice harvested during lean years. Accordingly, wild rice prices fluctuate from year to year.

Because of the value and scarcity of wild rice, the harvest was carefully controlled by state conservation authorities. The complexity of the ricing regulations, together with the considerable emotional involvement that characterized the Indian people's attitudes about ricing, generated serious political issues. These involved questions of: (1) the right of non-Indians to gather rice, since this activity was regarded by many as a distinctively Indian pursuit, (2) the right of Indians to rice on one another's reservations, (3) the complex regulation of hours and locations, (4) the adequacy of enforcement of regulations, and (5) the competence of the officials to whom both the rule making and the enforcement powers were assigned.

Indians in James Lake and on the Broken Reed Reservation generally thought the laws too liberal in certain respects and too restrictive in others. On lakes outside reservation boundaries, any individual who purchased a 3-dollar permit could harvest rice. Within the reservation, ricing was limited to local residents, but was not limited to Indians. At Mahnomen Lake on the Beaver Pelt Reservation, 75 miles west of James Lake, rice harvesting was limited to members of the Minnesota Chippewa Tribe, not just to residents of that particular reservation. The Indian people of James Lake wanted laws placing greater limitations on the ricing privileges of non-Indians. They also wanted to exclude the Deer Lake Indians from any of the lakes in the Broken Reed Reservation area,

Table 6.5. Scalogram of material style of life in James Lake

Household	Scale type	A	B	C	D	E	F	G	H	I	J	K	L	M	N	O
White	15	x	x	x	x	x	x	x	x	x	x	x	x	x	x	x
White	15	x	x	x	x	x	x	x	x	x	x	x	x	x	x	x
White	15	x	x	x	x	x	x	x	x	x	x	x	x	x	x	x
White	15	x	x	x	x	x	x	x	x	x	x	x	x	x	x	x
White	15	x	x	x	x	o	x	x	x	x	x	x	x	x	x	x
Indian	15	x	x	x	x	o	x	x	x	o	x	x	x	x	x	x
White	15	x	x	x	x	x	x	x	o	x	x	x	x	x	x	x
White	14	x	x	x	x	x	x	x	x	x	x	x	x	x	x	x
White	14	x	x	x	x	x	x	x	x	x	x	x	x	x	x	x
White	14	x	x	x	x	x	x	x	x	x	x	x	x	x	x	x
White	14	x	x	x	x	x	x	x	x	x	x	x	x	x	x	x
White	14	x	x	x	x	x	x	x	x	x	x	x	o	x	x	x
Indian	14	x	x	x	o	x	x	x	x	x	x	x	x	x	x	x
White	14	x	x	x	x	x	x	x	x	x	x	x	x	x	x	x
White	14	x	x	x	x	x	x	x	x	x	x	x	x	x	x	x
White	14	x	x	x	o	x	x	x	x	x	x	x	x	x	x	x
White	14	x	x	x	x	x	x	x	x	x	o	x	x	x	x	x
White	14	x	x	x	x	x	x	x	o	x	x	x	x	x	x	x
White	13	x	x	x	x	x	x	x	x	x	x	x	x	x	x	x
White	13	x	x	x	x	x	x	x	x	x	x	x	x	x	x	x
Indian	13	x	x	x	o	x	x	x	x	x	x	x	x	x	x	x
Indian	13	x	x	x	x	x	x	x	x	x	x	x	x	x	x	x
White	13	x	x	x	x	x	o	x	x	x	x	x	o	x	x	x
White	13	x	x	x	x	x	x	x	x	x	x	o	x	x	x	x
Indian	13	x	x	x	o	x	o	x	x	o	x	o	x	x	x	x
White	12			x	—[a]	x	x	o	x	x	x	x	x	x	x	x
White	12	x	x	x	o	x	o	o	x	x	x	x	x	x	x	x
White	12	x	x	x	x	o	o	o	x	x	x	x	x	x	x	x
Indian	12	x	x	x	x	x	x	o	x	x	x	x	x	x	x	x
Indian	12	x	x	x	x	x	x	o	x	x	x	x	x	x	x	x
Indian	12	x	o	x	x	x	x	o	x	o	x	o	x	x	x	x

Key to scale items

A. Owns house valued at $10,000 or more
B. Life insurance
C. Hot and cold running water
D. Subscription to at least one magazine
E. Telephone
F. Owns house valued at $100 or more; pays rent of $45 / month or more
G. Indoor bathroom
H. Cold running water
I. House has 4 or more rooms
J. Refrigerator
K. Television
L. Gas, coal, electric, or oil heat
M. Range
N. House has 2 or more rooms
O. Electricity

Guttman scalogram (rows read left to right across columns A–O):

	Score	A	B	C	D	E	F	G	H	I	J	K	L	M	N	O
Indian	11				x	o	x	x	x	x	x	x	x	x	x	x
White	11				x	x	x	x	x	o	x	x	x	x	x	x
White	11				x	x	x^a	x	x	x	o	x	x	x	x	x
Indian	11				x	x	o	x	x	x	o	o	o	x	x	x
Indian	10			(x)		x	x	x	o	x	x	x	x	x	x	x
White	9			(x)			x	x	x	x	x	x	x	x	x	x
White	8							x	x	o	x	x	x	x	x	x
Indian	8							x	o	x	x	x	x	x	x	x
Indian	8							x	x	x	o	x	x	x	x	x
Indian	7				(x)				x	x	x	x	x	x	x	x
Indian	7				(x)	(x)			x	x	x	x	x	x	x	x
Indian	7								x	x	x	x	x	x	x	x
Indian	7								x	x	x	x	x	x	x	x
Indian	7								x	x	x	x	x	x	x	x
Indian	6				(x)					x	x	o	x	x	x	x
Indian	6				(x)					x	x	x	x	x	x	x
White	6									x	x	x	x	x	o	x
White	6									o	x	x	x	x	x	x
Indian	5										x	x	x	x	x	x
Indian	4								(x)			x	x	x	x	o
Indian	3												x	x	x	x
Indian	3												x	x	x	o
Indian	2													x	x	x
Indian	2													x	x	x
Indian	2							(x)	(x)						x	o
Indian	1								(x)							x
Indian	1															x

Coefficient of reproducibility = .94

a. Missing information

Source: Prepared by T. Roufs.

Table 6.6. Distribution of interviewees by economic status
of household head

Economic status	Indian	White
Employed male head-of-family	12	16
Employed widower	2	1
Employed female head-of-family	2	0
Employed widow	1	0
Total – employed interviewees	17	17
Retired male head-of-family	4	7
Widow – pension and/or welfare	4	6
Female head-of-family – welfare	4	0
Disabled, single male	1	0
Total – unemployed interviewees	13	13
Total sample	30	30

yet retain access to Mahnomen Lake. They preferred that restrictions on hours and locations for ricing be abolished or at least drastically liberalized.

Conservation officials determined the locations for ricing on a given day. The ricing regulations put considerable pressure on the ricers. They had to know ahead of time which beds were open in order to be at the correct landing, ready to begin at the starting hour. Furthermore, they had to work rapidly, particularly during the early part of the season when the harvest was most abundant and the hours most restricted.

The regulations generated feelings of resentment and hostility against those people whom the Indians believed responsible for their enactment. The Indians had always felt that the rice belonged to them, viewing the laws as attempts to deny them their rights. This feeling was both deep-seated and widespread and occasioned much political discussion and many exhortations for Indian political action.

The element of recreation associated with ricing was secondary to its value as an economic enterprise. But in hunting and fishing, also subsistence-related activities, the recreational aspect was more important. The fishing in the area was excellent, and there was also a wide variety of game animals and birds. Deer were the most highly prized game. In Minnesota the deer-hunting season was limited to 10 days, but treaty rights allowed Indians to hunt on tribal land at any time. The problem, however, was that the meat could not be taken off tribal land. On the Broken Reed Reservation, which had small sections of tribal land interspersed between nontribal sections, deer hunting was virtually limited to the hunting season unless the hunter was willing to risk transporting game illegally.

The extent to which Indians and whites engaged in illegal hunting was difficult to gauge. During structured interviewing, we noticed that the item asking for the number of pounds of venison brought into the house during the year sometimes made respondents uncomfortable. One family with several teenage sons admitted, "We go out and get a deer any time we want to." Illegal hunting may have been a source of cash as well as food. There was a market for venison, and it is probable that a few people supplemented their income by selling illegal deer meat.

Judging from the sample interview responses, many families depended to some extent on "free food" from hunting and fishing. For the 14 Indian families with an employed male head, the percentage of meat and fish "gotten on your own" as compared with "bought in the store" ranged from 0 percent to 90 percent, with a median of 25 percent. These figures contrast with the comparable group of white families who apparently engaged in hunting and fishing primarily for sport. In 15 families, excluding 2 white families who were farmers and butchered their own animals, the range was 0 percent to 30 percent, with a median of 2 percent.

Of the 4 activities that may be categorized as both economic and social or recreational activities, berry gathering provided the least economic gain. Wild berries could be sold in stores or roadside stands, but the price that dealers were willing to pay was small compared with the time and energy required for berrying. Occasionally women would go to other areas where berries were plentiful, often selling just enough of their harvest to pay for transportation expenses.

Wild blueberries, strawberries, raspberries, and blackberries were gathered throughout the summer as they matured. One frequently saw small groups of women or girls walking along the road carrying pails filled with berries. Berries in cream for dessert or in muffins and turnovers were considered a special treat, and many women made an effort to gather them for their families; some preserved or froze a few pints, saving them for special occasions such as Thanksgiving and Christmas dinners. Judging from frequent discussions about berrying, which often included comments about the fun of gathering them, it seemed to be an important recreational activity that provided an opportunity for socializing and also contributed, in a small measure, to the family's economic well-being.

In summary, the general economic pattern of Indian families was characterized by seasonal wage work, considerable reliance on welfare, and income supplementation through ricing, hunting, and fishing. The relative importance of these subsistence sources varied from one family to another. Within the Indian community the range of income and material life-style varied from bare subsistence in run-down shacks to income and housing that was above the average for this area of northern Minnesota.

The economic differentiation existing *within* the Indian community provided a potential basis for social stratification, but this had not developed to any marked degree. Occasionally we encountered some indication that social stratification was present. Negative comments were sometimes made about people who "drink up all their money." Such people were criticized particularly for depriving their children of adequate food and clothing. Differentiation was also suggested in the use of the term "good family." An anthropologist who had visited another Indian community reported that after a dance a teenage boy brought home two girls from James Lake. His mother, discovering the girls' presence, insisted that they be taken home immediately because "They're from good families," and she did not want any hint of scandal.

Kinship was probably the most important of the mechanisms that prevented the development of social stratification. Within a large family of siblings and cousins there were likely to be some members who were financially somewhat better off than others, but a high rate of interaction among kinsmen helped to counterbalance any tendency toward exclusiveness on the part of the more well-to-do. Sharing a minority status and the identity of being Indian also may have tended to reduce social stratification. Speaking of the one family that was consciously exclusive, an informant said, with a hint of sarcasm, "They try to pretend they're not Indian."

Criticism of heavy drinking was expressed by two different segments of the Indian community. One group, which consisted of hardworking men who wanted to improve their families' standard of living, were critical of drinkers because of the expense and lowered working capacity involved. As one man put it, "By the time I get my paycheck, I haven't got enough left to buy a beer." A second group, more adamant than the first, condemned drinking on moral grounds. The members of the Mormon church and the Christian and Missionary Alliance church, who believed that drinking is a sin, were very disturbed by the fact that many Indians were heavy drinkers.

Religious affiliations and religiosity

Due to historical circumstances, many of the Indians in James Lake were Episcopalian. The Episcopal church sent missionaries into the area in the mid-1800s and has maintained an active mission in the village since that time. Catholic missionaries were also very active in Minnesota. Of the smaller denominations, the recently established Church of Jesus Christ of Latter-Day Saints was the most active in seeking Indian converts. In fact, membership in the James Lake mission was open only to Indians; non-Indian Mormons in James Lake had to attend church in North City. The Christian Missionary and Alliance church had a few Indian members and operated an Indian Bible school a few miles from town. However, most of the pupils in the school were from other parts of Minnesota and the Midwest; few local residents showed interest in their activities. The religious affiliation of the families in the James Lake sample are presented in Table 6.7.

Table 6.7. Religious affiliation of interviewees

Religious affiliation	Indian	White
Lutheran	0	12
Catholic	10	8
Episcopalian	12	1
Methodist	0	3
Presbyterian	0	1
Jehovah's Witness	1	1
Christian and Missionary Alliance	1	1
Seventh Day Adventist	0	1
Church of Christ	1	0
Church of Jesus Christ of Latter-Day Saints	2	0
No religious affiliation	3	2

The data on reported frequency of church attendance and other measures of participation in religious activities suggest that Indians tended to be less involved in church activity than did whites. In the religiosity scalogram (see Table 6.8), two-thirds of the Indian respondents fall below the median.

Eight Indian respondents attended church at least once a week. Of this group, the 4 who attended more than once a week were all members of the smaller denominations. Seventeen Indian respondents said that they attended church "rarely" or "never." These figures compare with

Table 6.8. Scalogram of religiosity in James Lake

Interviewee	Scale type	A	B	C	D	E	F	G	H	I	J	K	L	M
White	14	x	x	x	x	x	x	x	x	x	x	x	x	x
Indian	14	x	o	x	x	x	x	x	x	x	x	x	x	x
White	14	x	x	x	x	x	o	x	x	x	x	x	x	x
White	14	x	x	x	x	x	o	x	x	x	x	x	x	x
Indian	14	x	o	x	x	x	x	x	x	x	x	x	x	x
White	14	x	o	x	x	x	x	x	o	x	x	x	x	x
Indian	14	x	x	o	x	x	x	x	x	_a	o	x	x	x
White	13		x	o	x	o	x	x	x	o	x	x	x	x
Indian	13		x	o	x	o	o	x	x	x	x	x	x	x
Indian	13		x	x	o	o	x	x	x	x	x	x	x	x
White	13		x	x	o	x	x	o	o	x	x	x	x	x
White	12			x	x	x	x	x	x	x	x	x	x	x
White	12			x	x	x	x	x	x	x	x	x	x	x
Indian	12			x	x	x	x	x	x	x	x	x	x	x
White	12			x	o	x	x	x	x	x	x	x	x	x
White	12			x	o	o	x	x	o	x	x	x	x	x
White	12			x	x	x	o	x	o	x	x	x	x	x
White	12			x	x	x	o _a	_a x	_a x	x	x	x _a	_a x	o
White	12			x	o	x	_a _a	_a x	x	x	x	x	x	x
White	11				x	x	x	x	x	x	x	x	x	x
White	11				x	x	o	x	x	x	x	x	x	x
Indian	11				x	x	o	x	x	x	x	x	x	x
White	10					x	x	x	x	x	x	x	x	x
Indian	10					x	o	o	x	x	x	x	x	x
Indian	10					x	o	x	x	x _a	x	x	x	x
White	10					x	x	o	x	x	_a x	_a x	_a x	x
White	10		(x)											

Key to scale items

A. Five entries on questions related to practice of various aspects of religion
B. Change to "more" church attendance in last 5 years
C. Belongs to church organization
D. Attends church weekly
E. Three or more entries (as in A)
F. Response of "religion most important" or "next most important" in life
G. Attends church "more than once a week," "weekly," "about once a month," or "every few months"
H. Prays privately daily or weekly
I. Some entries (as in A)
J. Has knowledge of church organization(s)
K. Sometimes attends church
L. Belongs to a denomination
M. Religion not least important in life (as in F)

		A	B	C	D	E	F	G	H	I	J	K	L	M
White	9						x	o	x	x	x	x	x	x
Indian	9						x	o	x	x	x	x	x	x
Indian	9			(x)			x	x	o	x	x	x	x	x
Indian	9						x	x	o	x	x	o	x	x
White	9						x	o	x	x	x	x	o	x
White	8			(x)		(x)		x	x	x	x	x	x	x
Indian	8							x	o	x	x	x	x	x
Indian	8				(x)	(x)		x	x	x	x	x	x	x
White	8				(x)	(x)		x	o	x	x	x	x	x
Indian	8							x	x	x	o	x	x	o
Indian	7			(x)				x	x	x	x	x	x	x
White	7							x	x	x	x	x	x	x
Indian	7							x	x	x	x	x	x	x
Indian	7							x	x	x	x	x	x	x
Indian	7							x	o	x	x	x	x	x
White	7							x	x	x	x	x	x	x
Indian	6			(x)					x	x	x	x	x	x
White	6								x	x	x	x	x	x
White	6								x	o	x	x	x	x
White	5									x	x	x	x	x
Indian	4							(x)			x	x	x	x
Indian	4										x	x	x	x
Indian	3						(x)						x	x
White	3											x	x	x
Indian	3											x	x	x
Indian	3											x	x	x
White	3												x	o
Indian	2								(x)				x	x
Indian	2													x
White	2													x
Indian	1													

Coefficient of reproducibility = .93   a. Missing information frequent attendance for 14 white respondents and "rarely" or "never" for 11 white respondents. The difference between the Indian and white groups on this measure of religious involvement is not significant in a statistical test. However, taken together with the other scalogram items, it suggests differences in attitudes toward church and church-sponsored activities.

The lesser involvement of Indian families in religious and church-related activities may have been due in part to differences in the orientation of the churches that Indians attended. Reverend Blake, the Indian minister of the Episcopal church and the most influential religious figure in the Indian community, considered his role as a counselor and social worker more important than his role as a spiritual leader. At times he almost appeared to be underplaying the importance of religion. In describing his work, he said, "I believe in ministering to the whole man." Basing his opinion on his many years of observing and working with Indians, he felt that Indians' problems could not be solved through group-oriented programs such as those begun under the antipoverty program. Although he made some contradictory statements on the subject, his general attitude was that social problems (that is, poverty, lack of economic opportunities, and prejudice against Indians) were less important than the psychological confusion that they produce. For him, the most serious obstacles preventing "progress" were lack of motivation, poor self-image, and defeatist attitudes. Consequently, the only way to proceed was on an individualistic basis, establishing close friendships that promoted identification and learning by example.

Reverend Blake spent much of his time and energy helping his parishioners in various ways. He counseled them, supplied them with clothing and toys for their children, raised money for scholarships, and used his contacts to help them find jobs off the reservation. He devoted a considerable amount of time to children and young people, hoping that he could influence some of them to get an education and set higher goals for themselves. His activities, however, were not particularly designed to build the church as an institution in the community. It was the personality of the man, rather than his church per se, that was the influential factor in the lives of some members of the Indian community.

The priest of the Catholic church was described as a resentful and embittered man who made derogatory statements about Indians from the pulpit. None of the 10 Indian Catholic families in the sample belonged to organizations in the church, and according to several reports, they were actively discouraged from joining. White Catholic respondents participated in church clubs and programs as frequently as did white families in the other town churches. For the majority of the Indian respondents, the Catholic church was apparently viewed as a place where one went on occasional Sunday mornings; 6 of the 10 Catholics reported attending "rarely" or "never."

A Mormon missionary and his wife, assisted by 4 elders, began proselytizing in James Lake in 1961. A small church, financed and built with labor supplied by the national headquarters in Salt Lake City, was constructed in the spring of 1965. Like Reverend Blake, the Mormons devoted much of their time to children. They developed an attractive recreational program that included such activities as dances for teenagers, picnics, excursions, and fishing trips. A number of parents allowed their children to attend these events, although they themselves had no intention of joining the church. The missionary reported that 30 of the 45 "members" of his congregation were teenagers or young children. However, the few adults who had converted were staunch followers and active participants in the church.

The Church of Jesus Christ of Latter-Day Saints included among its converts some of the politically involved members of the Indian community. Peter Benhild, one of the 2 effective Indian community leaders, was president of the congregation, and his wife was president of the women's club. Another convert was Susan Marshall, the wife of a member of the Reservation Business Committee. Her husband, however, did not share her enthusiasm for the church and was, perhaps, somewhat antagonistic toward it. Both the Benhilds and the Marshalls participated in the church's educational program, sending their children to foster homes in Utah to live with Mormon families and attend public school.

Yvonne Bear, who claimed to be the first Mormon convert in James Lake, was a striking figure in the Indian community. She was knowledgeable in village affairs, both past and present. At the time of the study, she held a minor office in the local Indian council; earlier she had played an important role in a number of Indian organizations. Her husband, a construction worker, was not interested in the Mormon church or in village and reservation politics.

The relationship between the converts' interest in the church and their political behavior would seem to be correlational rather than causative, with the possible exception of Peter Benhild. Both Mrs. Bear and Mrs. Marshall were active in community affairs before their conversion to the Mormon church. They were intelligent, thoughtful women, and it is likely that their conversion was motivated, in part, by their dissatisfaction with the status quo. Mrs. Bear, who saw herself (probably quite accurately) as a woman of superior intellect, had been deeply interested in religion for many years, and had had a number of mystical experiences. She was also deeply concerned about the welfare of Indians, whom she referred to frequently as "my people."

Mrs. Marshall was less religious than Mrs. Bear. In interviews she stressed the church's work with children. She wanted her own children to be well educated and to be able to leave James Lake—a factor that may have influenced her conversion.

Benhild suggested that his conversion was partially motivated by a need for answers to questions about his identity. He said, "Before I read the Book of Mormon I sometimes wondered about being Indian; why, if God is supposed to love every man, did he make some of them Indians?" After he read the book, "All of these things became clear to me, and I didn't have any more questions about being Indian."

An old woman named Lucy Michaels was a noteworthy figure. She had not actually converted to Mormonism, but she attended the women's club meetings and other church events. Although she did not hold any formal position in the local council, she attended council meetings regularly and occasionally expressed herself publicly on issues. Such unusual characteristics might well accord her the status of a minor political personality.

Also active in church life was the leading Indian member of the Episcopal congregation. This man, who was chairman of a highly successful fund drive for the church, was a would-be "Indian politician." He followed the civil rights activity with great interest, although he did not take an active role in it. He claimed that the reason for his reticence was that his employer, one of the government agencies, discouraged any participation in "Indian politics."

For the majority of the Indian community, religion did not appear to be important. Furthermore, we would suggest that conversion to Mormonism was not related, in a causal fashion, to the civil rights activity; this activity should not be regarded as part of a religiously inspired revitalization movement. However, for some of the Indian leaders, there did seem to be some relationship between their interest in religion, or church-related activities, and their concern about political affairs. This relationship was particularly important in the case of Peter Benhild, but it does not appear to have been of any consequence for most of the others.

There was also some relationship between greater concern with religion, as measured by the religiosity scalogram, and higher standard of living, as indicated by the material-style-of-life scalogram. For the Indian sample the correlation of the two scales is statistically significant ($p<.05$), although fairly low ($r=.21$). Thus, the Indian families that had a higher socioeconomic status tended to be more involved with church activities than their neighbors. In contrast, religiosity among whites in James Lake was unrelated to material life-style.

Social organization and kinship

The paucity of formal social organizations and clubs in the Indian community was one of its most striking contrasts with the white community. In the white community, participation (by whites only) was actively encouraged; most of the respondents in the white sample claimed membership in at least 2 organizations. In the Indian sample, 28 of 30 respondents did not belong to any formal social club. The lack of such organizations among Indians is a very significant factor in analyzing their political behavior and in understanding the nature of the Indian community.

A distinguishing feature of Indian social life was that much of it involved kinsmen. Although no data are available on the ratio of visiting, kin to nonkin, it seems likely that there was more kin interaction for Indians than for whites. In part, this is explained by the fact that Indians had more relatives living in town or in the immediate area; some of the information from household interviews makes it possible to assess the extent to which this generalization held true. By combining the data on location of respondents' children with the data on location of "other close relatives" (an open-ended question), we can estimate the percentage of listed relatives living within a 25-mile radius. The average (mean) for the Indian sample was 48 percent; for the white sample, the average percentage of relatives who resided within 20 miles of the respondent was 19 percent of listed relatives. The average number of total relatives was 9.9 for the Indian sample and 11.9 for the white sample.

The data on frequency of visiting with local relatives support our hypothesis directly:

Percent of locally resident relatives seen:	Indian	White
Daily	50%	24%
More than once a week to weekly	36%	61%
Less than once a week	14%	15%

The Indians in this sample not only had more relatives living near them than did the non-Indians; they also saw them more frequently. A general hypothesis suggested by these data and field observations is that kinship was one of the primary integrating mechanisms in the Indian community.

In summary, the sociocultural features by which the James Lake Indian population differs from the white population include: (1) lower cash income, (2) narrower range of occupational choices, (3) greater reliance on welfare, (4) less involvement in religious activities, (5) greater reliance on noncash income, (6) higher rate of interaction with kin, and (7) near absence of formal organizations and clubs.

"Indian politics" and tribal government

In the revised Constitution and By-Laws of the Minnesota Chippewa Tribe, the Tribal Executive Committee (TEC) was given the authority to: (1) "employ legal counsel," (2) "prevent the sale or lease of tribal lands," (3) "manage, lease, permit and otherwise deal with tribal lands, interests in tribal lands and other tribal assets." (4) "administer funds within the control of the tribe," (5) "contract agreements on behalf of the tribe with federal, state, and local governments or private individuals and corporations," and (6) "engage in any business that will further the well-being of members of the tribe."

Each reservation had a Reservation Business Committee; its powers paralleled those of the TEC when the lands or funds involved belonged wholly to the individual reservations. In addition to administering reservation resources, the business committees were responsible for "requesting advancements to the control of the Reservation of tribal funds under the control of the Tribal Executive Committee."

The constitution included provisions making most of the executive committee's decisions "subject to the approval of the Secretary of the Interior or his authorized representative." Using these clauses, the Bureau of Indian Affairs could, if it desired, maintain considerable control over tribal affairs. Although local councils formed an integral part of the government, the constitution did not include specifications for them, at least not on the Broken Reed Reservation. However, the TEC and the business committees were authorized to recognize "any community organizations, associations or committees open to members of the (several) reservations. . . ."

The activities of the TEC were not directly pertinent to political life in James Lake. Most of the Indians in James Lake, including some of those who were active in the local council, knew little about the TEC's role. Indifference and isolation were important factors in explaining this ignorance, but there were other reasons as well. Some local people expressed suspicion and hostility toward "those politicians in the TEC," and some dismissed the committee as a "bunch of crooks."

The Broken Reed Reservation Business Committee

The chairman of the Broken Reed Reservation Business Committee, who also happened to be the chairman of the TEC during the time of this study, was a man in his mid-30s. He was ambitious for himself, but also for the reservation, and he had a serious interest in Indian problems. He was a resident of Wicket, a small but very active Indian community 30 miles from James Lake. The secretary of the TEC, the other Broken Reed representative on the committee, lived in James Lake. A man of about 60, he was experienced in "Indian politics." It was widely reported, with derisive comments, that he went on periodic drinking binges. In public meetings he was soft-spoken and deferred to the chairman.

Since Broken Reed is a large reservation, it had 3 business committeemen; one of them was from Wicket, another from Bigoshi. The third was Bob Marshall, from James Lake. Marshall had also had previous experience in Indian organizations. He had served as secretary-treasurer of the Broken Reed Reservation. Before the 1963 reorganization of the tribal government, he had been a delegate to the General Council, a council of 64 delegates that, under the old constitution, elected the Tribal Executive Committee.

The new constitution granted the Reservation Business Committee greater authority than it had had under the old system, and it also strengthened the power of individual leaders by giving them dual roles at the reservation and tribal levels. In theory, the business committeemen were elected at large and represented everyone on the reservation. However, there was evidently competition among communities within the reservation, and some felt that the committeemen supported and defended the interests of their local groups. In a discussion with Marshall and his wife, this point was made quite clearly. Marshall was a quiet, rather shy man who was not politically ambitious. When his term as secretary expired, and the reservation governmental structure was revised, he wanted to retire from political office. But his wife had other ideas; while he was out of town working on a construction job, she put his name on the ballot. She justified this action by saying, "If I hadn't put

your name down, there wouldn't be anybody to represent James Lake."
The remainder of the discussion between Marshall and his wife was
interesting not only as an indicator of Marshall's attitudes, but also for
what it revealed about community attitudes toward tribal officials.
Marshall countered his wife's statement, pointing out that another James
Lake resident was already on the ballot. His wife replied, "Well, he [the
other candidate] would be worse than nobody. He would just sit around
and wait for his check and wouldn't go to meetings. Besides, he's always
drunk." Marshall answered, "To hear them tell it, I'm as good as no one
too." He went on to say that if he "ever got out of this," he would never
do it again.

The constitution specified that the Reservation Business Committee had to hold at least 4 meetings per year. During 1965 and 1966 the
Broken Reed committee met very frequently, sometimes as often as 3
times a week, because the committee had planned and put into operation
a government-financed Community Action Program (CAP). Since
Reverend Blake had participated in the president's antipoverty program
conferences, the James Lake people were among the first groups to learn
about the availability of the new community action funds. With the
assistance of Blake and a Bureau of Indian Affairs (BIA) consultant, the
committee drafted a proposal for a community development project and
submitted it to the Office of Economic Opportunity in the fall of 1964.

Before the proposal was submitted, the committee held a series of
meetings in reservation communities to win support for the program and
gather suggestions for desired project activities. Each local council was
asked to write a proposal for its own community. The final plan, based on
the community proposals with suggestions added by BIA, was very
ambitious. It included plans for home improvement courses; teenage,
Golden Age, and Junior Achievement clubs; recreation programs; study
halls and remedial reading courses; guide training; guidance and referral
services; and day care centers. The committee asked for $357,000 to put
the plan into effect.

The government approved the plan but did not award the full
amount. After receiving the grant, the committee subleased the Co-op
building in James Lake as headquarters for CAP. The building was
owned by the tribe and leased to the James Lake Local Council. During
the late 1930s, it had been occupied by an Indian cooperative association
that sold handicrafts to tourists, an enterprise that failed after a few
years. Afterward the building was used as a meeting hall for the local
council during summer only. The expense of heating the building was

greater than the council could afford, so they held winter meetings in the Village Hall. The council sublet the building to the business committee with the understanding that it would be available to them, on a year-round basis, for meetings.

James Lake was a logical choice for the CAP headquarters. It was the largest Indian community on the reservation and had a number of facilities, including two large playgrounds and an excellent beach, that other reservation towns lacked.

The business committee hired a former casework supervisor from the James County Welfare Department as the project director. Working in collaboration with the director, they then hired a staff of 33 people, including 3 professional workers—a social worker, a recreation director, and a home economist. In each of the 6 main communities on the reservation, 5 local residents were hired as aides, with the objective of bringing in "poor people" and training them to be effective community workers.

Once the hiring had been completed and the building occupied, the program began in earnest in May, 1965. It had been operating less than a month when we began our fieldwork in James Lake. However, in this short period, serious antagonisms toward the CAP director and his staff had already arisen. The first meeting of the local council that we attended was a special meeting which had been called ostensibly to further plan the CAP program, but which rapidly turned into a session devoted to grievances and antagonisms. We later discovered that this was typical of most council meetings.

The James Lake Local Council

The local council consisted of an executive body—chairman, vice-chairman, and secretary—and various subcommittees appointed by the officers. The meetings, which were supposed to be held once a month, could be attended by anyone, but eligibility for office-holding was limited to enrolled Broken Reed Reservation members who resided in or near James Lake. The local council operated on a small budget allocated by the Reservation Business Committee.

The relationship between the local council and the business committee was, in theory, a cooperative one; in practice, cooperation was severely strained by local hostilities. As described by the vice-chairman of the local council, the relationship between the two bodies was seen as one in which "We pass resolutions at the local council and these are taken to the Reservation Business Committee and then, sometimes, to the

Tribal Executive Committee." When asked if resolutions were also passed from the committees to the local council, he replied, "Yes, sometimes, but the main channel is from the local to the business committee."

The officers of the local council in the mid-1960s shared several characteristics. They were all unusually light-skinned, rather Caucasian in appearance, all native residents of James Lake, and all older people. The youngest was the 60-year-old chairman, Mrs. Andrews, a talkative and outgoing person who had been active in community affairs for many years. She was the president of one of the Indian women's clubs, and was instrumental in establishing a hot lunch program for Indian children. Until her election to the chairmanship in 1964, she had not held any office in the local council.

In view of previous descriptions of people active in the political life of the community, it is interesting to note that Mrs. Andrews lived in one of the finest Indian homes in James Lake. She was the widow of a white carpenter and, although her income was not high (just below the median in our household sample), her home was unusual in a number of respects. It was one of the few on the South Side with indoor plumbing, and the kitchen was equipped with an expensive array of electrical appliances.

The vice-chairman, George Letendre, was a retired construction worker. He was very different from Mrs. Andrews in both life-style and personality. He also lived on the South Side, but in one of the several shacks that were shared by the members of his large extended household, which was composed of several nuclear families. Compared with Mrs. Andrews, they had a low standard of living, although their income was comparable to hers. When interviewed, Letendre was taciturn and supplied only "proper" answers, making it difficult to know very much about his views on important matters. He was widely described as knowledgeable, if "peculiar," and informants frequently noted that his wife was "very nice."

Of the 3 council officers, the secretary, Mrs. Vaille, had had the most experience in Indian organizational life. She was the granddaughter of a chief and told vivid stories about the old days when the men "sat and counseled together." Like Mrs. Andrews, Mrs. Vaille was active in the Indian women's clubs. She had been a delegate under the old system of electing the Tribal Executive Committee, and, during the WPA period, was the director of a sewing project designed to provide Indian women with jobs. She spoke infrequently in meetings, but her soft-spoken, deliberate style was often effective in bringing an argument to an end.

The council officers were elected for one-year terms. The secret ballot election took place in a regular council meeting and was not usually announced beforehand. The chairman accepted nominations from the floor, after which slips of paper were handed to everyone present, and the new officers were elected. Usually there was a white "outsider" present to count the ballots.

The council meetings, regularly scheduled for the first Thursday of each month, were never announced, although the newspaper carried notices for most club and church group meetings. On the evening of the July meeting, there was a heavy rainstorm and no one, not even the officers, appeared. This "cancellation" was never discussed, but was apparently accepted as a matter of course. Further indication of such irregularity came from Mrs. Andrews, who commented that during the previous winter there had been no meetings for several months while she was in the hospital.

Casual scheduling was apparent also in the calling of elections. An election of new officers designated for June had not taken place when we left James Lake in September, 1965. However, this particular instance of neglect seemed deliberate rather than careless. When asked about the election, Mrs. Andrews said that they should be held soon, but added that she felt the present officers ought to be reelected since they were involved in several important activities.

The suggestion of motivations other than carelessness was confirmed in a conversation with Susan Marshall. We were discussing the fact that all of the council officers were older people and that few young people in the community attended meetings. She said, "They [the current officers] want to have everything their way, and they're old-fashioned. As long as they're controlling things, nothing will change." When questioned as to why the middle-aged members of the community didn't elect officers of their own choosing, she replied, "It would take a lot of organizing to get them [the present officers] out."

In addition to the executive officers, the local council included several subcommittees—the Hospital Committee, the Planning Committee, the Loan Committee, a liaison officer to the James Lake Village Council, and the Defense Committee. These committees did not add many more people to the list of active participants, since they were composed mainly of executive officers. For example, the Hospital Committee members, who were expected to attend bimonthly meetings of the Indian Hospital Board and report back to the council, were Mrs. Vaille, Letendre, and Letendre's son-in-law.

Had the local council and its subcommittees been studied a few years earlier, the research would have been very different, since there would have been little to report about the activities of the council or other related groups. The council was an organization without obvious function, other than formally representing the James Lake Indian community. They held meetings, which few people attended and in which there was little to discuss because there were no ongoing programs or projects. Beginning in 1963, there was a series of events involving the council in new activity and leading to political action, or projected action, in a number of spheres.

The events that led to the formation of the Defense Committee, the unit primarily responsible for the increase in council activity, originated outside of the Indian community. The Indian population in James Lake had greatly increased in the period after World War II. Along with the increase in numbers, there had also been an increase in heavy drinking accompanied by fighting and rowdyism. Several years before, the whites on the Village Council had decided that James Lake needed a strong police force to meet these new problems, and 2 additional officers were hired, expanding the force to 3 men. In 1963 there was a shift in personnel, for reasons not discovered. According to our Indian informants, the new officers were vicious, prejudiced men who were hostile toward the Indians. The officers were accused of making unnecessary arrests and of being excessively rough. More serious were the accusations that they beat and robbed the drunks whom they jailed, and that they sexually attacked Indian women. Though these accusations were not proven, their effect was quite important.

Complaints about police brutality were made to the local council and the office of the Bureau of Indian Affairs, which, in response to the complaints, asked the FBI to investigate. The FBI agents conducted their investigation early in the spring of 1964, concluding, "The charges are without provable substance" (*Minneapolis Tribune,* August 18, 1964). In "The Indian and the Law," a special series in the *Tribune*, S. Newland stated: "The FBI found either no witnesses to specific events or supposed witnesses who were willing to testify; or allegations proved to be untrue; or... the line between police beating and reasonable force in subduing drunken belligerent people is too hard to define." The FBI report was submitted to the Justice Department's Civil Rights Division and to the state attorney general.

Meanwhile, incidents continued to be reported, and the local council decided to act. They appointed a 3-man Defense Committee, which was shortly reduced to 2 men, Peter Benhild and Ed Thomas, when the third member resigned. Working through the Reservation Business Committee, the Defense Committee asked the tribe for $2,000 to finance legal action. In May, 1964, the money was granted. The title of the committee referred not so much to the legal defense of Indian offenders but to the defense of Indian civil rights. In the lawsuits that resulted from the Defense Committee's work and were financed with the $2,000, the Indians were the plaintiffs.

During the summer of 1964, following the formation of the committee, several incidents involving Indians and the white police aroused anger in the Indian community. In one case a teenage boy was shot in the leg by a policeman. According to Indian informants, 2 boys were fighting one night behind a tavern. Policemen arrived on the scene, the boys started to run away, and an officer called to them to stop. When one of the boys ignored his order, the officer fired, hitting the boy in the leg. Later, the officer claimed that he hit the boy accidentally and had intended only to scare him.

The Defense Committee did not attempt to do anything about this incident, perhaps because of the officer's statement. But they did act in another case in which a man suffered a permanent injury. Jim Ranger was arrested for drunkenness; according to witnesses, he was not "doing anything" at the time he was arrested, other than sitting, very drunk, on the curbstone. But when the police tried to put him into their car, he became angry and began attacking them. Finally, they succeeded in getting Ranger into the car, and, from the time they left the street until Ranger was taken to the hospital with parts of 2 fingers severed, there were no witnesses. Ranger claimed that the police kicked and beat him, then slammed the jail cell door on his hand.

The Defense Committee hired a St. Paul lawyer who filed a suit on Ranger's behalf. The lawyer was not one of the attorneys regularly hired by the Bureau of Indian Affairs for Indians who need legal service, nor was he a lawyer for the Minnesota Chippewa Tribe. He had done some legal work for the Twin Cities Indian Council, a private organization of Twin Cities Indians. According to Benhild, it was through personal contact with the Twin Cities group that the Defense Committee learned about the lawyer. However, it seemed probable to us that the lawyer, after learning of the existence of the Defense Committee, contacted the James Lake group. In addition to the two lawsuits, for which he was legal counsel, he continued to play an active role in other Indian political affairs.

In the suit, filed under Minnesota's new Civil Rights Act, several white officials were named as defendants. One of the police officers was accused of slamming the door on Ranger's hand. The chief of police, Chuck Burrows, was accused of "beating and kicking" Ranger and also of having for many years "engaged in acts of brutality, beating and cruel treatment and unauthorized conduct involving citizens arrested and imprisoned in James Lake" (*Minneapolis Tribune,* April 29, 1965). The mayor and the police commissioner (one of the 3 village trustees) were also named because "They knew, or should have known, about [Burrows's] practice in attacking prisoners, especially members of the Indian race." In addition to a sum of $120,000 in damages, the suit also asked for a court injunction against the continued use of the jail.

The injunction was granted immediately since the jail had been condemned by state examiners 3 years earlier. At the time of our fieldwork, the summer of 1965, the case was still pending. In December, 1965, the case came to an end with Ranger's death. The circumstances surrounding his death seem to epitomize the nature of the problems that the Indian community faced in their attempts to deal with what they regarded as intolerable situations. A week before the first scheduled hearing on the case, Ranger was arrested by the James Lake police on suspicion of robbery and taken to the jail in Trotter, where he was held for several days before the Defense Committee could contact their lawyer. When the lawyer arrived, Ranger was released without being charged. That same day he received $200 from his mother's estate. He used part of the money to buy presents and liquor, then went to the "Indian" hotel to join his friends for a party. He became very drunk and "passed out." Because of the imminent arrival of a social worker, expected by the girl who lived in the apartment where the party was being held, one of the men at the party took Ranger into an empty room in the hotel. There he died, supposedly from choking on his own vomit.

Although Ranger's death was adjudged accidental, it was surrounded by a cloud of uncertainty. During the following summer another project field-worker was told that one way to kill a man is to pour liquor down his throat, after he has passed out, until he chokes to death. The informant claimed that he knew of cases in which this bizarre method had been employed. It is difficult to understand why any of the Indians present at the party would have been motivated to kill Ranger. However, one of the men was charged with stealing what remained of Ranger's

$200. He was released on bond and, before he could be brought to trial, died of exposure on a night when it was 30 degrees below 0.

Ranger's death was a bitter disappointment for the Defense Committee. They had hoped that the case would bring about major changes in the town's political structure. However, there were some changes. In the spring of 1965, after the suit was filed, the Village Council fired the police officer accused of slamming the jail door on Ranger's hand. He was replaced by an Indian. Later in the year, the second white officer resigned, and another Indian policeman was hired. The chief of police remained in his job. The suit was thus effective in forcing a change in personnel. The members of the local council and the Defense Committee felt that, while the situation was far from ideal, things had "improved." Other individuals in the Indian community were less positive; some of them said they hoped it would get better. It was difficult to discover "typical" sentiments on this issue because many people were reluctant to discuss it. Sometimes it appeared that confusion and lack of knowledge were responsible for reticence, but much of it was obviously due to fear or antagonism toward us because we were white outsiders.

It is difficult to predict the long-range effects of the lawsuit. Such an assessment would have to be based on a thorough study of the white community as well as the Indian group—something we were not in a position to do. White residents however, appeared to react with resentment and confusion. In contrast to their overt, positive reaction of hiring Indian police officers, the white power structure initiated another change which was viewed negatively by the Indians. The Village Council planned a voter's registration program for the fall of 1965 in response to a protest tactic the Indian Defense Committee had employed in the fall election of 1964. The mayor, village trustees, and municipal judge were to be elected to 4-year terms in this election. The incumbent judge had held office for many years in spite of his alleged prejudiced and patronizing attitude toward Indians. The Defense Committee, who had no way of implicating Judge Krammer in the Ranger suit, decided to express their disapproval of him through a protest vote. Originally they planned to ask Indian voters to write in Mickey Mouse as an opposition candidate to Krammer. A sympathetic outside observer suggested that their protest would be more effective if they wrote in the name of a real person; the committee then persuaded one of the town drunks to be a candidate. Stickers with the write-in candidate's name were mimeographed and distributed widely in the Indian community the night before the election. The operation was kept secret for fear that, should the

Village Council learn of the plan, the candidate would be justifiably disqualified.

To the surprise of everyone, including the members of the Committee, the write-in candidate received a considerable number of votes; he came in a close second behind Krammer. The outcome of the election could not be directly contested, since Judge Krammer did receive the most votes, but the committee, or their lawyer, found a way to bring suit against him. The judge had been at the polling place throughout Election Day, greeting people in a friendly manner. His justification was that the polling place, the central room of the Village Hall, was his office. Nevertheless, the lawyer felt that he could make a strong case against this illegal election practice.

The near success of the write-in campaign was important because it demonstrated that the committee was able to mobilize a great deal of support, even though they had to work quickly and in secrecy. Perhaps the humor of the situation appealed to people who otherwise would not have voted. Benhild said that after the election several whites came to him expressing approval of the committee's action. They too disliked Krammer and claimed they would have voted for the write-in candidate had they known about the plan. It seems likely, however, that the majority of whites reacted unfavorably and approved of the Village Council's counteraction the following year: the decision to require voters to register for local elections.

Outwardly there was nothing particularly significant about the Village Council's decision. However, the state law does not require towns the size of James Lake to make voters register. State legislators have occasionally suggested that registration should be universal at every level of government, and the Village Council and the League of Women Voters cited such statements in justifying the new requirement. The League was active in supporting voter registration, posting notices around the town and setting up a registration booth at the annual fall fair. A League member admitted that one reason for requiring registration was to prevent people who lived near but not in the legal village limits from voting. The northern boundary of the village runs through the middle of Tract 22, and on the eastern side of the town it cuts through a primarily Indian neighborhood.

According to Benhild, the Village Council claimed that many Indians had voted illegally in the 1964 election. He contended that the charge was untrue, that care had been taken to prevent ineligible voters from coming to the polls. However, the size of the protest vote and our personal knowledge of ineligible voters who did cast ballots suggests that the committee was not as careful as they claimed. When the voter registration plan was announced in the summer of 1965, the Defense Committee and the local Indian council reacted with anger, but they decided to run their own campaign to see that every adult James Lake Indian registered.

The Defense Committee originally included 3 men—Bill White, Ed Thomas, and Peter Benhild. White, who was Letendre's son-in-law and the youngest of the 3, resigned from the committee shortly after his appointment and played no significant role in the committee's affairs. His reasons for resigning were not clear, but there were rumors that he was "scared out" by harassments and threats from the police. During the period of our fieldwork in James Lake, he attended almost every meeting of the local council and sometimes assisted officers by opening the hall, arranging the chairs, and doing other chores, but he never voiced an opinion publicly. In private conversation he was a severe critic of the local council's executive officers, complaining about their ages and old-fashioned attitudes.

Ed Thomas, a man in his mid-50s, lived with his wife and small children in a dilapidated house on Tract 22. Like many of his fellow townsmen, he made his living in the woods cutting timber. In 1954, Thomas had held an office in the tribal government. Although the facts concerning his term in office were difficult to determine, stories then in circulation accused him of malfeasance. One rumor was that he had embezzled tribal funds; another, that he had taken a tribally owned car without authorization and wrecked it when he was drunk. The general hostility toward anyone, even a local resident, occupying a formal office and the common tendency to accuse such a person of thievery made it difficult to assess the truth of these stories. Thomas's social position in the community, which may have been affected by his former political maneuvering, was further complicated by his heritage. He was half Chippewa, half Sioux. His public image was that of an angry, embittered man. In his speeches he expressed great hostility toward whites, the BIA, and other government officials, and he was strongly oriented toward political action. In meetings he was very emotional, and, on several occasions when he was angered by the turn of events, he left the meeting, yelling and slamming the door behind him.

Benhild was 39, a vigorous man who was known throughout the community as an exceptional worker. Like his friend Thomas, he worked in the woods, but because of his stamina, dedication, and pursuit of secondary occupations, he earned an unusually good income. Compared with our random sample of 30 Indian households, his annual income of $7,300 was very high, second only to that of a family in which both the husband and wife were employed by government agencies. The Benhilds lived on the South Side in a small, unpretentious house. Although they possessed some material items that most Indian families lacked (such as a new car, a television set, and a washing machine), in some ways their standard of living was little different from that of their poorer neighbors (for example, no running water or telephone).

In conversation Benhild appeared to be self-assured, speaking fluently and easily. In public he was more self-conscious and his speech was often halting, with only occasional expressions of the ready humor and good-natured smile that were characteristic of his style in more private settings. When Benhild and Thomas held the floor together in meetings, as they frequently did, Thomas had a tendency to interrupt Benhild and make statements for him.

According to both Mrs. Andrews, the chairman of the local council, and Benhild, the council decided to appoint the Defense Committee when it became clear that no outside authorities were prepared to act. Benhild claimed that he did not initiate his involvement in the committee, and that he was not even present at the council meeting in which the committee was established and appointments made. However, he was present at the meeting a month earlier, even though he did not usually attend council meetings. His evasion on this point is understandable; it is likely that being appointed to a position rather than seeking it would have made him seem less self-serving in the eyes of the community, always suspicious of its officials. When asked why they selected him, Benhild replied, "Well, there was a job to be done and I suppose they thought I was the man to do it." He added wryly that the fact that his 16-year-old stepson was frequently in trouble with the police and therefore in some danger may have been an additional reason; the council may have thought that he would be willing to work hard because a problem of police brutality could affect his own family. It seems clear that the evolution of Benhild's political consciousness was influenced to some degree by at least 2 specific factors: his friendship with the militant Thomas and his conversion to the Mormon church, shortly before his appointment to the Defense Committee.

General influences which may have affected the formation of the Defense Committee included other factors in addition to the personalities and personal experiences of the committeemen. One important influence was a staff member in the Bureau of Indian Affairs, a former labor organizer who was deeply concerned about the economic and social problems of Indians on the reservation. He was also action-oriented and apparently had the skills to develop organizational activity. He had formed friendships with several informal leaders, both in James Lake and in other reservation communities, and his influence on these men undoubtedly contributed to the formation of the committee.

Since the members of the council and the committee discussed their activities in the language of civil rights, to what extent might the James Lake Chippewa have been influenced by the black civil rights movement? They did not live in isolation from the national scene; many of them had television sets and radios, and a few read the newspaper regularly. (It is important to note that the events discussed took place several years before the idea of "Red Power" was developed and before the establishment of militant Indian organizations.) The influence of black activism was probably an underlying factor, although it would not be directly acknowledged as such by James Lake Indians—mainly because Indians did not identify with blacks as fellow holders of a minority group status. In general, their attitudes toward blacks were quite negative and prejudiced. We frequently heard antiblack comments, including the opinion that blacks were "too pushy."

The combinations of motivations and influences that brought about the civil rights action in James Lake were obviously very complicated. Consideration of only the Defense Committee's actions from the spring of 1964 to the spring of 1965 leads to quite different conclusions than if data from the summer of 1965 are also taken into account. In contrast to the image of well-directed, generally effective organization presented by the early Defense Committee activities, a series of Indian meetings held during the summer of 1965 created another impression.

Most of these meetings included participants from several areas of the reservation and were concerned with issues of reservation-wide interest. Some of the meetings were in James Lake, others in neighboring communities, but in all of them James Lake residents were actively involved. The 3 major topics discussed in these meetings were the Community Action Program, wild rice harvesting, and land claims against the federal government. Although most of the meetings were called with the objective of discussing only one of these topics, usually all of them came up for debate during the course of an evening.

The Community Action Program

The Reservation Business Committee and the CAP director had sole responsibility for the administration of the Community Action Program. However, it was intended to be a program "by the people, for the people." Individuals in the community were expected to take part in planning and executing the programs as well as to participate in the activities themselves. Clearly, to have this kind of involvement members of the community had to conceive of the program as somehow "belonging to them" and they also needed to understand their role in it. Unfortunately, these essential conditions were not realized.

Many people in the community thought of the program as another government agency with the main function of providing jobs for local people. The aide jobs that were open to unskilled workers were extremely attractive; the salaries ranged from $2,000 to $4,000 per year, and a year-round income was guaranteed. Consequently, people were very annoyed that only 5 of these jobs were available to James Lake residents, and much resentment was directed toward the business committee and the director for their choices in hiring workers for these positions. The fact that 2 jobs were given to a mother and her daughter was considered particularly unfair, even though the women maintained separate homes and the daughter had 6 children to support.

At a special meeting of the local council, attended by the CAP director and Reverend Blake, much of the resentment against the program was expressed. In addition to his hiring practices, the director was also criticized for his lack of accomplishments. The program had been operating for only a month and, at that stage, the newly hired aides were still being trained. However, there were several challenges about why the workers were not out in communities "doing something." Some of the critics were private citizens in the community, but members of the local Indian council also expressed their general agreement with the criticism. The director and Blake argued at length, trying to explain the purpose of the program and appealing to the people to set aside their animosity and begin to work actively for the projects. They asked for volunteers and suggestions, but no one responded.

From this meeting and from minor discussions in other meetings, it was clear that local residents thought of CAP as another outside program for which they had no responsibility. None of the critics demonstrated that they understood the basic ideas behind the program. Even CAP supporters expressed approval in terms of noninvolvement: "I think that *they* are doing a good thing for us, and we ought to stop complaining."

Ricing regulations

During the summer of 1965, state wild rice regulations were discussed in a series of public meetings. The stated purpose of the meetings was to review the problems and to devise means of changing the regulations. However, the meetings were used primarily as a forum to express grievances and, as in the CAP meetings, little was accomplished in the way of effective planning for future action.

At the first "ricing meeting," a joint meeting of the James Lake Local Council and the Bigoshi Local Council, the chairman of the Twin Cities Indian Council was present. He described how the Twin Cities group, with the assistance of their lawyer, had drafted a new wild rice bill to be presented to the state legislature. They first approached the Tribal Executive Committee for support in their endeavor, but the members of the committee were not enthusiastic about the bill and did not lobby for it. When the group was unable to find a legislator willing to sponsor the bill, the campaign was dropped temporarily.

The audience of Broken Reed residents reacted to this account with strong criticism of the TEC (ignoring the equally disturbing behavior of their legislative representatives, who had apparently first agreed and then suddenly refused to sponsor the bill). Anger against the TEC was compounded because of a recent action concerning ricing permits that was rumored to have been taken by the committee. For many years it had been a TEC policy to sell permits for ricing at Mahnomen Lake to any Indian who had the requisite 10 dollars. Members of the Beaver Pelt Reservation, where the lake was located, were required to purchase permits, along with Broken Reed residents and Indians from other parts of the state. Members of the "closed" Deer Lake Reservation could also purchase permits, a privilege which members of the other reservations thought to be unjust. Hostility against Deer Lakers was strong, and most people felt that they should not be allowed to rice on Mahnomen Lake.

At Broken Reed we encountered some evidence of in-group feeling at both the community and reservation level, but it did not seem to generate strong hostility against members of the other five "open" reservations. The attitude toward the Deer Lakers stood in sharp contrast. The quality of feeling against them was revealed in comments such as "Deer Lake—that's no man's land!" and "I wouldn't live there if you paid me." Some of the hostility may have been a reaction to the Deer Lakers' exclusiveness. They were very protective of their hunting, fishing, and ricing resources and were said to protect their boundaries by throwing out intruders. Allowing Deer Lakers to rice on Mahnomen

Lake was particularly offensive because the privilege was not reciprocated by them in ricing or other economic activities.

The rumor which caused so much antagonism was that the TEC had
arranged to establish a station to sell permits directly to Deer Lakers on
their own reservation, whereas in the past they had had to purchase them
at stations on either the Broken Reed or the Beaver Pelt reservations.
Later it was learned that the TEC had only agreed to allow an individual
from Deer Lake to take a number of permits to sell for the committee. In
any case, the action was viewed with great resentment.

The most vocal participants in this particular meeting were
Benhild, Thomas, and the chairman of the Bigoshi Local Council.
Finally, after a great deal of discussion, Thomas introduced a motion
requesting the TEC to reconsider the permit situation and close Mahnomen Lake to Deer Lakers. The motion passed unanimously with a vote
of 42 in favor. Two weeks later the TEC responded to the motion with a
minor concession; they removed the permits from Deer Lake. However,
they did not actively prevent Deer Lakers from purchasing permits at
other locations.

The resentment against the TEC was not merely a secondary effect
stemming from the hostility against Deer Lake. Money from the sale of
permits went directly into the treasury of the Minnesota Chippewa Tribe,
yet most people seemed to regard the tribal treasury as a private benefit
enjoyed by the executive committeemen. In their view, income for the
tribe did not result in any benefit to them.

Two other resolutions, introduced at another joint meeting of the
local councils, also reflected distrustful and antagonistic attitudes
toward the TEC. The first resolution proposed that tribal lands no longer
be leased to "outsiders" for resorts; the second stated that the chairman
of the TEC should not be allowed to make trips to Washington "unless
we send him."

When Thomas proposed the first resolution, the Minnesota Chippewa Tribe business manager, who was a tribal enrollee from the Beaver
Pelt Reservation, objected strongly, explaining that the tribe received a
substantial income from land rental and that the Bureau of Indian Affairs
had worked for many years to convince resort owners that land-lease
contracts would be honored. Thomas argued that the money was of no
benefit to the people and that they were being deprived of lakeshore land
for their own use. This resolution was passed unanimously.

When the second resolution was introduced, the discussion that
followed was a recital of complaints about tribal officers and business

fiascos of tribal enterprises, past and present. Of all the complaints, the most concrete were those which accused the TEC of failing to communicate with the constituency. The people at Broken Reed reasoned that, since the chairman did not tell them why he was going to Washington, there must have been something devious in his motives; many were convinced that he intended to "sell out to the politicians." Someone suggested that the resolution be amended to prevent the chairman from making any trips without announcing the purpose beforehand. However, the amendment was rejected and the resolution was passed unanimously.

The claims

The Chippewa had several land claim cases pending in the federal courts. In the mid-1960s a large claim was settled; when all of the procedural and political problems were worked out, the Indians at Broken Reed, Beaver Pelt, and a third, smaller reservation were to receive a substantial portion of the $3 million involved in the claim. But the problems were nearly as great as the sum itself.

(1) Who were the people who had a legal right to the money?

Since the original land-ceding treaties were made by representatives of aboriginal bands, the money had to go to the descendants of those same bands. In this particular claim, $2 million would be awarded to descendants of the P__ Band, a group located aboriginally on the shores of Broken Reed Lake. The other million was to be divided among the descendants of 2 bands which were scattered over a large territory that included portions of Broken Reed, Beaver Pelt, and the third reservation. Historical records of these bands were not complete enough for proper descendants to be easily and accurately identified; some argued that it would be virtually impossible to identify them. An alternative method for distributing the claims money would apparently have to be found.

(2) What formal unit (or units) of the tribal government should be responsible for distributing the money?

Since the aboriginal bands were no longer formally in existence, the responsibility for the funds had to be delegated to some unit of the tribal government, either the Minnesota Chippewa Tribe or the business committees of the 3 reservations. However, these units did not appear to have the administrative capabilities to deal with such large sums of money. Furthermore, some of the people who were eventually to receive funds strenuously objected to the MCT because the Tribal Executive Committee included representatives of reservations other than the three directly involved; given the general hostility toward the TEC, it seemed unlikely that there would ever be a decision allowing the money to go the Minnesota Chippewa Tribe. The Indians on the Broken Reed Reservation objected to the second choice—dividing the money among the 3 reservations—because they had descendants of all 3 bands represented in their membership and felt that they should get the largest portion of the grant. However, unless the descendants could all be identified, it would be impossible to determine exactly what portion of it was to be theirs.

(3) What plan for the distribution of the award would be acceptable to Congress?

The U.S. Congress had the final authority for granting a claim once it had been approved by the court. In the past, with claims of other tribes, Congress had insisted that the groups have a plan for the use of the funds which included reservation development programs. They had never agreed to per capita payments of all the money, unless the reservation was being terminated. The Chippewa on the northern Minnesota reservations were very much afraid of termination, but nearly all the Broken Reed members wanted a 100 percent per capita distribution; many appeared not to understand that it was highly unlikely that Congress would approve the award unless an alternative plan was proposed.

These problems and related ones were of primary concern in the 1965 summer meetings. In order to understand the discussions in these meetings, we must examine other local developments concerning the claim. At the time of the reservation reorganization in 1963, there had been a referendum on the claims, in which the majority of the voters had asked for a 100 percent per capita distribution. The referendum stood on record without further comment or action until the spring of 1965. Then, when it appeared that the claim would be awarded in the near future, the Bureau of Indian Affairs urged the reservation leadership to devise a reasonable plan for expenditure of the award that included some reservation development provisions.

Along with several Indian BIA staff members, the chairman of the Broken Reed Reservation Business Committee held a number of meetings in outlying reservation towns. (None of the meetings was conducted at James Lake.) The purpose of the meetings was: (1) to outline the situation to the reservation membership, (2) to get a vote of current opinion on the issue, and (3) to urge the communities to submit plans for development programs. The meetings were informal, and the vote was understood to be unofficial. Although the record of the voting was preserved, there were no public records or minutes—an unfortunate circumstance, because the rumors about the meetings that spread in James Lake and Bigoshi caused a great deal of trouble. The rumors accused the BIA staff and the business committee chairman of threatening people with termination or the loss of the Public Health Service Hospital if they did not vote for a 50-50 split of the money (half for community development and half for individuals).

In late July, Thomas and Benhild convinced the James Lake Local Council to call a special meeting, invite the BIA staff and the Reservation Business Committee, confront them with the rumors, and ask them to clarify their position. Several staff members from the Minnesota Agency office of the BIA (located in North City) attended the meeting, although the director did not; the area office was unable to send a representative but did send an official apology. The chairman of the business committee failed to appear, and the 2 business committee members who came did not offer any explanation for the chairman's absence. Three BIA staff members spoke in defense of the bureau and the business committee, denying the rumors and insisting that people had misunderstood. The audience was not satisfied with these answers, and they were annoyed because the business committee chairman had not attended. The meeting ended with a resolution, put forward by Benhild, that a second meeting be called and that measures be taken to ensure the attendance of the entire business committee.

The chairman of the business committee was present at the next meeting, a month later, and he too denied the rumors. He took the position that he wanted a full per capita distribution of claims money as much as anyone else did, but that it would be impossible to get a so-called "family plan" (100 percent distribution of the money) approved. Led by Thomas and the chairman of the Bigoshi council, the members of the audience verbally attacked the business committee chairman. They were against a 50-50 split because they did not believe that the business committee or the TEC would handle the communal share of the money properly. In a series of pointed questions implying that the chairman had been dishonest in accounting for expenditures, the audience asked him for detailed information on the tribal budget.

This meeting was essentially a repetition of the earlier one. The same themes—ricing permits and regulations, land-lease contracts, the Community Action Program, and the chairman's trips to Washington—were all reintroduced and debated. The meeting concluded with the TEC chairman's promise that he would present all of the complaints and the resolutions to the TEC.

Meetings dealing with reservation political affairs were usually scheduled to begin early in the evening, but 7:00 p.m. "Indian time" meant that they actually began around 8:00. Local council meetings often drew 15 to 20 people; joint meetings attracted 50 to 60, which was still only a very small proportion of the James Lake Indian population.

Business was conducted in a slow, informal fashion and was rarely completed before 11:00. During the course of a meeting many people wandered in and out of the hall; some parents brought their children, who occasionally had to be admonished for being too noisy. Although some effort was made to follow Robert's Rules of Order, there was often uncertainty about what the correct order ought to be. Questions were raised and answered, then raised again by someone else. Sometimes a meeting dissolved temporarily while the problem was discussed by small groups of people.

Most of the meetings were characterized by confusion and by antagonistic, hostile interaction. The Community Action Program meeting and the joint meetings of the local councils were scenes of direct confrontation between local people and the officials whom they so disliked and distrusted. Even at the local meetings, when no officials were present, the atmosphere seemed charged with tension and discussion of almost any issue aroused anger.

Interpreting Indian politics in James Lake

The structure of political organization and the nature of politically relevant behavior, as it existed in James Lake during the mid-1960s, clearly presented several serious problems for effective action. The corporate-controlled assets and annual budget of the local council were, for practical purposes, trivial, and the council had scant means for influencing the behavior of higher-level officials or of its constituency. With very few exceptions, neither the local leaders nor the public seemed to be motivated to strengthen the corporate holdings of the council or to develop firmer political organization for the purpose of advancing the general welfare.

There are several theoretical frameworks that may be used in interpreting the political behavior of the Indian people of James Lake: on the one hand, the cultural values, attitudes, and psychological traits which presumably have deep-seated historical roots; on the other, the ongoing structure of political and economic power as it operated at the time of the study. To some extent our choice of analytic modes depends on our basic assumptions about the nature of cultural behavior. If our theory places major emphasis on long-term patterns, on the importance of traditional and relatively fixed belief systems, or on deeply rooted personality configurations, then we might well seek to explain political patterns in James Lake as arising from long-standing cultural syndromes that continue to affect behavior; such a view has, in fact, commonly been invoked by anthropologists and others in explaining the behavioral patterns of various groups. An alternative theoretical approach is to focus on individuals as actively adapting to their environments through conscious decision-making processes (cf. Graves 1970). Emphasis in this approach is on the *present* context and on elements of the socioeconomic and political environment, the factors which constrain and influence the day-to-day decisions of James Lake people.

Before exploring further the implications of the latter approach, we shall review some of the anthropological description, analysis, and debate concerning what has long been called Chippewa, or Ojibwa, "individualism" and "social atomism."

Chippewa "individualism"

Beginning with Landes's and Hallowell's studies of Canadian and U.S. Ojibwa, students of Chippewa culture have tended to emphasize the interplay of culture and personality patterns in explaining individual behavior and life-styles (though the 2 concepts are not always clearly distinguished in their writing). Consequently, much of the literature on the Chippewa is psychologically oriented and does not always include systematic examination of social organization. The personality theory (as well as the cultural theory) of several earlier analysts differs considerably from the theoretical position taken in this study, and these theoretical differences have inevitably affected not only our interpretations but also our presentation of data about the Chippewa.

Ruth Landes did fieldwork among the Ojibwa on the reserve at Emo, Ontario, in 1932–33. At that time the residents were dependent primarily on trapping and hunting for their livelihood. Although tied into the white man's market economy (through sale of furs and purchase of goods), and feeling the effects of the laws of the dominant society, these Ojibwa nevertheless lived in rather isolated circumstances and maintained a distinctive and traditional way of life.

The characteristic of Ojibwa life which most impressed Landes was the extreme emphasis on the individual. The idea of personal property was highly developed; concepts of individual ownership covered a range of possessions, from trapping territories to songs, dances, and cures. So great was the importance of individual ownership that a man's secret knowledge could be lost with his death, should his son lack the necessary funds to purchase it from him. Landes documented what might be called the structural elements of individualism; with regard to property, she wrote, "The scale of property right is graduated thus: the absolute owner of property is the individual, regardless of sex or age. He lives most intimately with his domestic family but does not yield his ownership rights. He shares goods with his spouse and immature children. He has sentimental ties with his lateral family, to whom he extends courtesies respecting his property. Beyond this he personally extends ties in any direction he will. Throughout, the rights of the individual are stressed" (1937:144).

Landes also explored some of the social-psychological correlates of Ojibwa individualism. She found a "striking lack of generosity," which she attributed to the emphasis on personal property. She described the brittleness of the nuclear family, the child's socialization aimed at developing independence, and the fear of sorcery (curers can practice "bad medicine" as well as good), and suggested that all of these elements contributed to the development of a personality which was isolated, individualistic, hostile, and anxious. Landes's interpretation was based on observed individual behavior and the verbal reports of her informants, rather than on psychological tests.

Hallowell's original work among Ojibwa groups was carried out in Canada in the late 1930s. With a few exceptions, his description of the group in the Lake Winnipeg area was very similar to Landes's description. He found his subjects to be more generous than the people at Emo, but he attributed their generosity to fear of offending someone who might work sorcery in retaliation for a slight. In contrast to Landes, he stressed the fact that hostility was repressed and aggression never expressed in face-to-face contact; however, he agreed that the level of aggression among Ojibwa was very high. Perhaps the most important of Hallowell's studies, in terms of its effect on the development of theories about Chippewa culture and personality, was his analysis of personality in acculturation.

Hallowell administered the Rorschach test to 2 groups of Ojibwa in the Berens River area of Manitoba and later collected protocols from a group on the Lac du Flambeau Reservation in Wisconsin. He assumed that the composite profile of one of the Manitoba groups—a group which was extremely isolated and had relatively little contact with white society—could be considered representative of the aboriginal "personality structure." The test results of this group were used as a baseline against which the other, less isolated groups could be compared. Hallowell felt that this procedure was justified because the test results of the first group were in close agreement with the picture of aboriginal personality which he had constructed on the basis of missionary and trader accounts from the 18th century. He described the native Ojibwa personality in the following terms: "The type of personality structure that we find was highly introverted. It functioned in terms of internalized controls; the individual felt the full brunt of responsibility for his own acts. Sickness and misfortune were thought to be the penalty for wrongdoing and experiences of this sort provided the occasion for deep feelings of guilt.... Psychological security was never absolute since besides sickness and misfortune even the strongest man might be menaced by sorcery. Therefore it was necessary to be extremely cautious in interpersonal relations lest aggression be aroused and covert hostility released. So a surface amiability and emotional restraint, tinged with latent suspicion and anxiety, were characteristic" (1955:349).

The Rorschach data of the most isolated group were interpreted as approximating this description very closely. Hallowell concluded that he had demonstrated "psychological continuity" as an "empirically established fact." Equally interesting was the finding that the composite (mean) profiles of the more acculturated groups showed the "same basic psychological pattern" regardless of the number of white behavioral traits characteristic of the group in question. Hallowell wrote: "There is a persistent core of generic traits which can be identified as Ojibwa. Thus even the highly acculturated Indians at Flambeau are still Ojibwa in a psychological sense whatever their clothes, their houses, or their occupations, whether they speak English or not and regardless of race mixture. While culturally speaking they appear like 'Whites' in many respects, there is no evidence at all of a psychological transformation" (1955:351).

However, Hallowell noted that while there was psychological continuity, there were also important differences, particularly between the Canadian and American groups. The Flambeau (American) group exhibited in the protocols less control and more apathy, and in general appeared to be "less well adjusted." Hallowell felt the Flambeau Rorschach data showed "an introspective personality structure being pushed to the limits of its functional adequacy . . . . Those people are being thrown back on their psychological heels as it were. They are compelled to function with a great paucity of inner resources" (1955:352).

Hallowell's description of Ojibwa culture and personality was, then, substantially in agreement with Landes's and added the weight of a second source of data—Rorschach protocols. Furthermore, he raised the intriguing problem of the persistence of personality characteristics in the face of many years of acculturation. The specific questions about persistence of Chippewa personality traits and the sources of both the traits themselves and their persistence have been subjects of continuing interest since Landes and Hallowell set forth their findings (cf. James 1970 and Paredes, Roufs, and Pelto 1973).

In 1949 Caudill published a detailed analysis of Thematic Apperception Tests collected from children on the Flambeau Reservation. He found that the personality characteristics of the children, as they were reflected in this projective test, were "nearly identical" to the results that Hallowell obtained with the Rorschach. Like Hallowell, he turned to the general sociocultural environment for an explanation. In Caudill's view, "The Ojibwa of Lac du Flambeau live in an environment that is socially, economically and psychologically depriving. Social cohesiveness is almost nil, the individual is isolated from his fellows and each person pursues his own particular ends. At most, people are brought together because of a common task, but they remain a 'collection of individuals' and never form themselves into a 'group' " (1949:421). In agreement with Hallowell's hypothesis of personality persistence, Caudill believed that this extreme characterization was not due to the impact of Western civilization alone. However, he emphasized the role of Western contact and the ill effects of this experience. To his generally negative portrait he added the suggestion that a "detailed, practical, noncreative approach to problems" and "a wary and practical approach to life" may be adaptive under the social conditions in which the Flambeau group exists today, just as such an approach may have been adaptive in the "natural environment of the Ojibwa."

In 1950 Barnouw published a systematic and detailed argument in which he built the case for Chippewa atomism. He described the role of the individual in Wisconsin Chippewa society, traced the sources of fear and isolation which, he believed, help to produce the typical personality traits, and, on the basis of their acculturation history, offered a hypothesis to explain the persistence of these traits. In the "atomistic constitution of Chippewa society" Barnouw included the following elements: (1) little or no economic cooperation outside the nuclear family, (2) the dispersal of families during much of the year, (3) a lack of organizations comparable to the Plains military societies (which functioned as integrating mechanisms in groups that were also dispersed for much of the year), and (4) a lack of religious ceremonies to promote the general welfare of the group. Of the modern reservation, he wrote: "Even today the average Chippewa household is a world to itself. There is little visiting back and forth, no groups of women working together, no spontaneously formed work groups, cattle associations, no system of return help ... the only social unit is the working team of husband and wife" (1950:17). He noted that group efforts—as when the tribal council attempted to organize a powwow—were exceptional and were marked by dissension and bickering. The organizers were critized for being too bossy and accused of pocketing the money; there was rivalry over jobs and disapproval of public speeches. But "little of this criticism is of the face-to-face variety. It circulates in the form of gossip and bickering."

In examining the role of the individual in Chippewa society, Barnouw considered a number of "sources of fear and isolation." He included the following items: (1) fear of sorcery, (2) use of "scaring techniques" by parents to discipline their children, (3) undemonstrativeness, (4) suspicion of outsiders, (5) "supernatural power as a private resource," and (6) uncertainty about supernatural resources. In his view, these elements contributed to the development of an isolated, anxious personality, and established expectations that made group cooperation difficult, creating a situation in which no one would accept leadership.

In sum, Barnouw sought the origins of Chippewa personality traits in aspects of *aboriginal* social organization and belief, hypothesizing that the continuation of these traits might be explained by the continuation of a basically atomistic social organization throughout the period of white contact and into the present day. He pointed out that prior to 1870 the Chippewa did not actually have a great deal of contact with white society even in Minnesota and Wisconsin, where their areas of settlement were not penetrated by permanent white residents until late in the 19th century. Most of their early contact was with traders, missionaries, and loggers. Barnouw suggested that the Chippewa's relationship to the trader, whom he singled out as the most important source of contact, was one of dependency, in which the trader made decisions and guided actions—a relationship which formed the prototype for the Indians' attitudes toward the American government and the Indian agent. Barnouw suggested that, within the structure of this dependency relationship, the atomistic elements of Chippewa culture continued unchanged.

One of the first criticisms of the Hallowell-Barnouw formulation came from James, who suggested that not all the Chippewa were as individualistic as they had been portrayed. He felt that the ethnographic description of the northern (Canadian) Ojibwa had been uncritically applied to the southern Chippewa, citing a number of facts gathered from historical sources which indicated that the southern groups had achieved a considerable degree of organization, at least by the early contact period.

James argued that the personality characteristics of the modern Chippewa were to be understood in relation to current conditions of reservation life, and that the apparent continuity was fortuitous, maintaining that "Contemporary personality is an isomorphic psychological version of the contemporary social situation in which it develops" (1961:735). In what he termed a "situational" analysis, James made use of constructs such as role, conflict, status differential, and self-image to explain contemporary personality; he placed particular emphasis on the role of the negative stereotype of Indians held by whites. He felt that "These stereotypes are crucial to Ojibwa acculturation because they are projected into the vacuum produced by the destruction of aboriginal institutions and they now dominate the reservation's accommodation to its environment" (1961:732).

A concept critical to James's thesis was "deculturation," defined as the "loss of Ojibwa culture traits" and the "minimal appropriation of new traits" which produced a "poor white" type of subculture. The negative stereotype, then, functioned as the "only viable system of values." In summary, he believed that modern Chippewa personality is the result of deculturation, poverty, and racial prejudice.

Friedl has also offered a hypothesis to explain the persistence of certain aspects of the Chippewa personality configuration, suggesting that there might be an "underlying sociocultural characteristic" which persisted "throughout Chippewa history . . . in spite of obvious acculturation . . . ." Her hypothesis was aimed specifically at the characteristic described by Caudill as the tendency toward "a detailed, practical, noncreative approach to problems." In her view, this trait and other aspects of Chippewa behavior could be understood in terms of the expectations engendered by both aboriginal and contemporary Chippewa culture, namely, that each event is unique and short-lived in consequences. These expectations arise from the conditions of "incessant change" which are characteristic of Chippewa life and have been "maintained throughout Chippewa acculturation history, thus making it possible for the same expectations to continue and for the same approach to problems to continue to have some adaptive value" (1956:823).

Hickerson also challenged the "atomistic" and "individualistic" label placed on Chippewa social organization and behavior. As James had done earlier, he stressed the importance of distinguishing between the northern Ojibwa and the southwestern Chippewa groups. He granted that the northern Ojibwa were "particularistic" both economically and socially, but felt that it was a serious error to generalize from them to the southwestern groups, who lived in settled villages. The 2 main purposes of his monograph (1962) were to delineate factors which led to the development of the village pattern and to describe features of village organization. His sources of data were historical records (missionary, trader, and traveler accounts, and government records) and the histories of the Minnesota-Wisconsin area written in the late 19th century.

According to Hickerson, the shift from a "kin-centered to a village-centered political organism" could be traced to the ecological and historical conditions that the southwestern groups faced. He proposed that the first villages were founded shortly after the beginning of the fur trade, when the Chippewa served as intermediaries between the French traders and other Indian tribes. In the early 18th century alliances between tribes were disrupted, and the Chippewa moved south and west into territories claimed by the Dakota. As a result, they were in a state of constant warfare with the Dakota and had to readjust their economic operations to meet this new condition. The northern system of land tenure, in which families claimed permanent use-rights to particular tracts, was no longer feasible; it was more effective for groups of men to travel together to a hunting territory, which was then "allocated" to individuals for temporary use during a single season. Hickerson suggested that "The exploitation of the hunting areas was by bands consisting each of several households organized within the villages, at times armed for war, at times centered in fortified camps" (1962:87). Conditions of warfare also made it dangerous for small families to live scattered across the land at great distances from one another. It was safer to leave the women and children at home in villages, removed from the "battlefront." Other factors which made village life possible were the rich sources of wild rice, maple sugar, and fish.

Hickerson characterized the hunting band as the primary economic unit and viewed the village as a political unit. He outlined the major elements of village political organization and suggested how they may have been related:

The political solidarity of the village exemplified itself in intertribal relations, in relations with the government and to some degree with traders and missionaries, in ceremonies, in councils of war and peace, and, more subtly perhaps, in relations with neighboring congenitive villages through the need of a common defense of territories. Civil chiefs whose offices were often ascribed through heredity, and whose influence may have in part stemmed from their gens memberships, were the instruments of policy as spokesmen, as men of influence but without overt coercive authority. But an extensive and integral village political life led also to the emergence of societies of younger men, the warriors, who could place themselves as a group in opposition to the reigning policies of the chiefs, or could attempt to enforce their will on the civil polity, and thus help determine policy. (1962:63)

The collapse of the fur trade destroyed the economic base of the southwestern villages. The Chippewa had little choice but to cede their land to the U. S. government. With the establishment of the reservations, they also lost their political autonomy. In Hickerson's view, then, the "modern particularism of the reservation Chippewa" is the result of the "decay of collective institutions" and thus cannot be attributed to anything inherent in Chippewa culture or personality.

In the works we have briefly reviewed, the writers' emphasis on their differences may have obscured one major point on which they all seem to have agreed: their characterizations of *contemporary* Chippewa society were consistently similar. They used a term like "atomism," "particularism," or "individualism" in describing the distinctive features of modern Chippewa communities in both the United States and Canada. They would also probably agree that *precontact* Ojibwa organization tended to be "individualistic."

There has been little disagreement, then, among various researchers about the behavioral picture at the present time or in the distant past; the arguments have centered around the question of whether this is a continuous or a discontinuous phenomenon. James and Hickerson took the position that the southwestern communities in the 19th century were relatively well organized and not individualistic, and that the present situation is thus a discontinuous one. On the other hand, Hallowell and Barnouw traced a continuity of personality characteristics and found nothing in the sociological structure of the communities which would prevent such continuity.

In addition to individualistic behavior, many of the studies were concerned with another element of Chippewa culture and personality: the pervasiveness of interpersonal hostility. This concern was especially dominant in the earlier works; in Landes's analysis the 2 elements were linked theoretically. Hallowell claimed to find the sources of aggression in traditional Chippewa culture (1940), but did not develop a causal link between hostility and individualism since he did not keep these factors conceptually distinct. Other writers also treated hostility as if it were an integral part of Chippewa individualism. With the exception of Landes, none of the other Chippewa analysts discussed the relationship directly, but dealt with the 2 elements as aspects of a single phenomenon.

We suggest here that individualism and hostility must be kept conceptually distinct and that their equation can be very misleading; our arguments on this issue will be presented later in greater detail. For the moment, we propose the separation as a pragmatic device; individualism, uncomplicated by the addition of hostility, is a complex construct.

James and Hickerson were undoubtedly correct in criticizing the looseness of definition which is typical in the use of the term "individualistic." Whenever a common understanding of the definition of a concept is assumed, rather than carefully delimited, confusion and argument are likely to arise. In this case, the confusion is probably compounded by the fact that the concept is a cultural postulate of the anthropologists' own culture. We may be especially wary of applying the term "individualistic" to Chippewa culture, because of the value loadings that the word carries as a result of its multiple, and frequently emotionally tied, meanings in our own culture.

In spite of the problem in defining it, anthropologists have found "individualistic" to be a useful adjective for describing certain cultural patterns, and its use has not been limited to the Chippewa; examples include Gardner (1966), who applied it to the Paliyan; Embree (1950), to the Thai; Oliver (1965), to the Kamba; Honigmann (1949), to the Kaska; and P. J. Pelto (1962), to the Skolt Lapps, as well as P. J. Pelto (1968), in a cross-cultural study. From its several applications we may abstract a core of attributes which will serve as the defining characteristics of an "individualistic" society.

The main attributes may be grouped into two sets, one of which is structural, having to do with economic and social organization, and another which can be termed "social expectations" and their behavioral consequences. Within the first set, the criteria for individualism include:

(1) individual property ownership, (2) economic independence of the nuclear family, and (3) a lack of significant social groups larger than the nuclear family. With the second set, diagnostic criteria include: (1) individual responsibility for decision making, (2) individual responsibility for meeting needs, crises, and problems, and (3) a self-interest orientation. This last factor produces a situation in which any appeal to action is frequently couched in terms of the individual's self-interest, rather than an appeal to duty or obligation to the group. In practice, each of these criteria has numerous ramifications; for example, their character is modified by the nature of the economy and by the level of technology. For our purposes, the criteria, unmodified by the elaborations that would be necessary in a more complete explication of individualism, are probably sufficient. We may use them as a checklist by which to gauge the presence of individualism in James Lake Chippewa society.

Let us determine how many of the components of our definition existed in James Lake, in order to discover whether individualism is a useful concept for the study of this community. The following analysis is, admittedly, post hoc. As a result, the evidence which we present is anecdotal rather than systematically gathered to support an argument; it is suggestive rather than definitive. More rigorous, quantified, and comparative measures would be necessary to prove the case for Chippewa individualism.

"Individualism" in James Lake

The economic organization of the Indian community in James Lake, like that of the white community, was individualistic according to the first 2 structural criteria. Individual property ownership was perhaps not a particularly significant element because few of the Indians in the community owned large amounts of property. A large proportion of the land allotments had been sold, and the few remaining holdings were small, as they had been subdivided among the heirs of the original owners; the fact that many families preferred to divide the land into small lots, rather than maintaining a larger section as an extended family holding, is indicative of an individualistic attitude.

Data on James Lake Chippewa family organization and economy from the household interviews provide other indicators of individualism. As would be expected, nuclear family households predominated in the white sample (see Table 6.9). Nuclear or subnuclear (single men, single women, or mothers with their children) households were also the rule in the Indian sample. Apparently, the response to economic pressure was not to pool resources by extending the household unit. Unmarried mothers rarely remained with their parents; widowed or single adults did not often share a dwelling with relatives or friends.

Further evidence of nuclear-family economic independence is supplied by the answers to the question "Is there anyone outside the household who contributes to the family income?" Twenty-seven of the 30 Indian respondents and 25 of the 30 white respondents reported no outside support. In 2 of the 3 affirmative answers by Indians, the sum involved was very small (e.g., money for laundry, candy, and cigarettes).

Table 6.9. Household composition of James Lake random sample

Household composition	Indian	White
Nuclear (husband–wife; children)	13	20
Subnuclear (single adult; mother with children)	13	5
Other (e.g., adults – two generations, adult siblings)	4	3

The organization of work may also be labeled individualistic. Each man was hired independently, whether by a larger institution, such as the Forest Service, or by a small contractor. In the woods, the men frequently worked alone rather than in teams. There were few cooperative work groups, and plans for a community-owned sawmill never materialized.

In the late 1930s, a cooperative association was formed to market Indian crafts. The association flourished, largely due to the efforts of its Indian manager, who toured the state establishing outlets. In spite of its success, the Co-op was disbanded after a couple of years, reportedly because of dissension among the members over profit sharing. (Anyone could become a member by contributing a single item for sale; the membership grew rapidly, and some of the more active members apparently felt that they were not receiving a just share of the profits.)

The failure of the Co-op, as well as the other items discussed, are all evidence of individualism in the economic sphere. Investigation of the third criterion on the list (a minimum number of social groups outside the nuclear family) reveals a striking contrast between the white community, which had numerous social clubs in the James Lake white community, and the Indian community, which had only the local council and the Ladies' Aid club.

Except for political data, there is a scarcity of evidence for documenting the presence of social expectation criteria. Social expectations can perhaps be inferred from some of the economic data; of particular note is the pattern of payment for services between relatives. In the household sample there is a case of a widow who cared for her son's children in return for a salary, which was her sole source of income and with which she maintained a separate residence. Another woman paid her sister-in-law for automobile transportation. The fact that unmarried mothers and old people usually maintained separate residences may also be indicative of individualistic social expectations, as well as economic individualism. These instances are clearly not adequate to support a judgment of individualism in everyday life by the second set of criteria. However, examination of the political data discloses a number of events or features of political action which could be interpreted in terms of individualism: (1) the position taken on the distribution of the claims money, (2) the ricing permits resolution, (3) the land-leasing resolution, and (4) the lack of support for the Community Action Program.

The prevailing attitude toward the distribution of claims money is the most dramatic evidence of individualism. Each person wanted his or her full share of the money and was unwilling or unable to give up a portion for a project that would benefit the group as a whole. There seemed to be little awareness of the possibility that such a project might ultimately benefit individuals by providing employment, or new resources that individuals could use, or even a large loan fund. The group (meaning any communal organization) was not perceived as a source of individual reward and was not viewed as a mediator through which one might achieve desired goals. The demand for a 100 percent per capita distribution can be characterized as an individualistic position, and another factor contributed to the strength of the position: people not only wanted the money for themselves; they explicitly did not want any of it managed or controlled by the Reservation Business Committee or the Tribal Executive Committee.

The dual motivations of individual gain and of undermining the financial base of the tribal organization seemed to be operating in the ricing and land-leasing resolutions as well. The purpose of the resolutions was to return privileges to members of the local community. Every pound of rice gathered by an outsider was a pound less for local Indians to sell; every yard of lakeshore leased to a resort was a yard less for local

Indian residents. While it is true that the situation regarding land-leasing and ricing permits may in fact have affected individuals in James Lake negatively, the extent of deprivation from these arrangements was not great; furthermore, the tribe as a whole benefited from them because of the income they provided for the tribal organization. In view of these considerations, it seems likely that the resolutions were motivated by a desire to weaken the financial base of the tribal organization as well as to gain greater privileges for local people.

The Community Action Program is a more ambiguous item. Viewed from the perspective of the Reservation Business Committee, the initiation of the program was not particularly congruent with an individualistic outlook. Our concern, however, is not with the higher levels of tribal leadership. In the local community the aims of the program were poorly understood, and public criticism of the projects and the staff made it still more difficult to establish the program as a viable organization. People were not being asked to give up anything for CAP (as they were with the claims money), yet they remained suspicious or uninterested.

In each of these situations, the favored position was one which brought immediate rewards to individuals. A second common element was distrust and disapproval of the higher-level formal organizations. We would suggest that the reluctance to work within the structure of the tribal organization was determined by a complex set of factors. Hostility toward tribal leaders, which had historical and structural sources, interacted with individualistic values to produce certain kinds of political action in the Indian community. The most dramatic political events were the lawsuit against the police and the write-in campaign for municipal judge.

The lawsuit was a collective effort to ensure the civil rights of Indians, but it did not require the organization of the community for a group purpose, nor was there any attempt to establish a long-term association. In the sense that its goals benefited individuals (without the mediation of the group), and that it did not require individuals to give up something for a group purpose, the lawsuit had an individualistic orientation. Nevertheless, it did require the continued cooperation of a number of people (the plaintiff and witnesses, as well as the members of the Defense Committee) and the support of the local council. Moreover, the success of the write-in campaign depended on the cooperation of much of the Indian community. The contradictory nature of these events raises a question: are cooperation and relatively intense political activity congruent with an individualistic interpretation of the Indian community, or do they contradict such an interpretation?

In the earlier literature, the Chippewa were described as noncooperative, and this description was given considerable emphasis in the theory of the formulation of Chippewa individualism. It is likely that Hickerson was following this reasoning when he used the presence of cooperative action (in hunting and war making) to refute the characterization of Chippewa society as atomistic. We may, however, question the necessity of including noncooperativeness within the social construct of individualism, although an extreme "ideal-typical" concept of individualism might do so. An alternative to such a rigid definition is to view social organizations in terms of a continuum in which various features receive relatively more or less emphasis. If individualistic societies (as defined by the six criteria listed above) occupy one end of a hypothetical continuum, the other end may be defined by "communalistic" or "corporate" societies, for which the diagnostic criteria are the converse of those given for individualistic societies. In corporate societies, significant production property is communally held, and the economy of the nuclear family is tied to a larger group. (We would add the additional hypothesis that household units would tend to be larger than the nuclear family.) There are social groups that extend beyond the family and may have considerable control over the individual's actions. The responsibility for meeting individual needs, solving individual problems, and making decisions is assumed by the group. A group-interest orientation prevails, and appeals to action are therefore couched in terms of duty or obligation to the group, rather than self-interest.

The two ends of the continuum have been described abstractly, as ideal types. Empirically, we would not expect to find pure individualistic or corporate societies. But we can hypothesize that societies vary in the extent to which individualistic or corporate features predominate. Most human groups occupy the middle range of the continuum, and we would expect that societies which tend toward either extreme have a low frequency of occurrence.

How does cooperation fit within the framework of this hypothetical continuum? Clearly, cooperation is a generic human trait that occurs in every society. The economic organization in a corporate society usually requires a considerable amount of cooperation among its members, resulting in more occasions for cooperative action as well as strong social sanctions associated with failure to cooperate. In a more individualistic society there are fewer occasions for cooperative action, and therefore fewer rewards for cooperating and fewer sanctions or punishments for not doing so. This does not mean, however, that instances of cooperative action are nonexistent; theoretically, there is no reason to assume that cooperation is incongruent with either the structural features or the social expectations of individualistic societies.

But how can we fit the several different characterizations of Chippewa social organization, particularly those of James and Hickerson, into this characterization of "individualism-with-cooperation"? As noted previously, Hickerson considered the present-day situation to be the result of the decay of "collective institutions." We would argue that the 19th-century Chippewa villages were not communally organized; rather, they maintained many individualistic as well as cooperative features. To the extent that cooperative activity was regularly patterned and rewarded, we may say that the 19th-century Minnesota villages were somewhat less individualistic than other Chippewa groups have been at other periods of time, but that they nevertheless tended toward the individualistic end of our theoretical continuum. The following arguments are presented in some detail because of the implications of this conclusion. If the 19th-century villages were essentially individualistic, then we may view James Lake today in the light of a long history of a pervasive, individualistic mode of organization.

Some of the elements that Hickerson used to support his position are: (1) communal hunts, (2) the organization of war parties headed by chiefs, and (3) the existence of civil chiefs who acted as representatives for the village.

The practice of collective hunting is well documented; however, communal hunts do not appear to be, by themselves, strong evidence of permanent, communalistic organization. Periodic communal hunts have been reported among the Shoshone of the Great Basin, the Eskimos, the Lapps, and many other peoples whose social organization can only be characterized as individualistic. Communal hunting frequently requires only a single day, or at most a few days, of intensive cooperation. Temporary leaders may be selected, and temporary discipline exercised over individual participants. The proceeds of the hunt, however, are distributed among individuals, and nothing remains in the way of communally held assets or permanent social organization.

The groups which participated in such cooperative ventures among the Shoshone varied markedly in membership from one hunt to the next; among the Chippewa there may have been greater permanence of membership in communal hunting groups, but it is unlikely that membership was fixed and unchangeable. Modern Chippewa communities have communal hunting groups, but membership is flexible. Lack of corporacy of such groups is further expressed in the fact that individuals not participating directly in the hunt characteristically do not have rights to the spoils unless a share is allotted to them by particular *individuals* who did participate.

John Tanner's journal contains some interesting information on hunting groups and the sharing of the proceeds of hunting. Tanner was a kidnapped white man who lived much of his adult life "as an Indian" among the "Ojibbways" of the southwestern area in the late 18th century. His journal is a rich source of information, and Hickerson cited it a number of times.

Although Tanner cannot be taken as completely typical of Chippewa peoples of the Minnesota area early in the 19th century, he was a member of an extended kin network and hunted cooperatively with a number of different groups. The extreme flexibility of membership in hunting groups (shifting with the availability of food) is evident in Tanner's accounts, and persons outside the hunting groups appeared to have had little claim to shares in food. Tanner mentioned several instances when requests for food for his starving family were refused. Once he was refused at an encampment of his wife's relatives, although ample meat was available.

The successful completion of a war expedition depended upon the cooperation of many men, evidenced in the Chippewa's success in fighting the Dakota. There were planned raids that failed because the members of the party decided to go their separate ways; the leader of an expedition had no sanctions that he could use to hold a group together.

Tanner vividly described an instance in which a large war party disintegrated. After many days of travel, one of the men made a speech expressing dissatisfaction with the expedition. In a matter of hours the party disbanded. Tanner commented: "For the greater part of the day did A-gus-ko-gaut (the war chief) and the few that remained firm to him, continue sitting upon the ground, in the same spot where he had listened to the speech of Ta-bush-shah: and when at last he saw his band diminished from sixty to five, the old man could not refrain from tears" (1830:114).

The historical data on the system of hereditary chiefs among the Chippewa are scanty, ambiguous, and open to a variety of interpretations. Hickerson suggested that, through the role of the civil chiefs, the villages achieved "political integration." Nonetheless, the fact that village fragmentation occurred may indicate that the political authority of the chiefs was extremely limited; when people disagreed with his policies, they apparently experienced little difficulty in moving to a new location.

An anecdote related by the secretary of the James Lake Local Council provides interesting conjecture about the former role of the civil chief. This woman—who claimed to be the granddaughter of Chief ___, one of the treaty signers—said that before the appointment of chiefs by a delegation of officials from Washington, "there were no chiefs." Her grandfather was made a chief because he was one of 3 men in the village who could count to 10. These statements certainly cannot be taken as proof of the absence of hereditary chiefs in the late 19th century in a Broken Reed village, but it is notable that one of the more sophisticated women in the community viewed this feature of Indian political authority as having somewhat ambiguous origins.

Although Hickerson presented many instances of cooperative action, they fall far short of documenting any strong communalistic orientation. The village as a collectivity seemed to lack forceful sanctions; bonds of loyalty toward a chief appear to have been tenuous. While families were economically interdependent to some extent, the concept of self-sufficiency was well established. A closer examination of the "collective institutions" suggests that the villages were not, after all, highly corporate entities.

To the extent that our indicators tap a relevant dimension and that they coincide with other investigators' conceptions of atomism, we are basically in agreement with the anthropologists who characterized Chippewa culture as reflecting and continuing a long history of individualistic organization. However, Hallowell can be criticized for not attempting to specify the factors that support continuity, thus creating the impression that continuity of personality is the result of some mysterious force, a kind of Chippewa zeitgeist. Barnouw attempted to correct this weakness in Hallowell's analysis, but did so in historical rather than theoretical terms. Friedl supplied the foundation for a theoretical explanation, although she limited its application to a single characteristic. Friedl's and James's argument—that personality is controlled by factors operative at a specified time—can be translated into the language of learning theory, allowing us to develop an explanation of continuity which is not only historical but also theoretical.

The statement "Personality is isomorphic with culture" can be rephrased in learning-theory terms: "Behavior is shaped and controlled by the operations of reinforcers." In psychology, a reinforcer is defined empirically. A positive reinforcer is "anything which, if made contingent upon a response, will lead to an increase in the probability of occurrence . . . of the response." Conversely, the pairing of a response with a negative reinforcer will lead to a decrease in response occurrence. Therefore, behavior that occurs frequently is being or has been highly reinforced. To a considerable extent, adaptive behavior is reinforced behavior. If we assume that well-established patterns are, for the most part, adaptive, we may then ask, what are the environmental and social factors that reinforce them?

An examination of Chippewa history suggests that the types of reinforcers that were important in prereservation times are different from those that have been influential in the postreservation period. In preservation days the primary reinforcers were ecologically and environmentally determined and consisted mainly of the variable sources of rice, maple sugar, and (especially) game. In the later period, the reinforcers were bound up with the social environment, and negative reinforcers seemed to assume a more important role in the explanation of individualism.

For prereservation Chippewa groups, whose economy was based on hunting and trapping, mobility and flexibility were primary requirements. Before trapping was part of their economy, obtaining sufficient food for a family must often have been a difficult task. Game animals were scattered over a wide area and rarely occurred together in large numbers. Families had to be free to range over wide territories and had to be small enough that the game, once found, would feed everyone. When trapping became important, the traders established business relationships with individual Indian trappers. The one-to-one relationships with the trader continued to reinforce individual (rather than collective) effort. Much later, when Indians looked for employment in white businesses, the same pattern continued.

Collective behavior was not a frequent response in prereservation days. It was reinforced mainly in situations where it was temporary and not based on permanent corporate assets. During the harsh winters, such behavior was negatively reinforced, if it occurred, because people experienced the frustrations of having too many mouths to feed from restricted local food sources. On the other hand, during the period of war with the Dakota, cooperation was rewarding because it was important in defeating the enemy. Our only argument with Hickerson on this point is that cooperation did not increase to such an extent that it pervaded all forms of activity and changed the Chippewa system of values and expectations.

One could hypothesize that continued rewarding of cooperation would eventually have affected social organization, particularly since the ecologically determined demand for individualism declined after the formation of the reservation. A number of factors help to explain why this did not happen to the extent that it might have.

One factor is that the dominant white economy is also individualistic, so that Indian involvement in the new economic patterns did not produce any basic changes in this respect. Other features of the acculturation situation also helped to reinforce individualism. For example, rations were distributed by the Indian agent to individuals rather than through the tribal chief. In addition, the allotment of land rewarded people in terms of individual property ownership.

In the following discussion some of the factors that have operated as negative reinforcers of communal organization during the reservation period will be described, and hostility toward tribal leaders will be shown to be the product of specific situational variables. In the past, investigators have equated hostility toward tribal leaders with the supposed Chippewa personality trait of generalized hostility. Considered from a different theoretical perspective, the James Lake data suggest a quite different conclusion.

The many elements involved in negative associations with organizational activities are so highly interrelated that it may be misleading to separate them; however, for purposes of clarity of analysis, we may isolate at least 2 major factors. First, there is a long history of negative experience with governmental agencies, which is closely related to hatred and resentment of whites. Second, the structure of the reservation and the nature of Indian-white power relations have created a situation in which there are few rewards for Indians who attempt to assume leadership. Participation in tribal government tends to be a punishing experience; consequently, a strong and effective Indian leadership failed to develop. Furthermore, negative expectations with regard to tribal activity have assumed the character of a self-fulfilling prophecy, so that it is very difficult, even for determined leaders, to break the cycle of failure.

There were few models of organizational structure (such as corporate kin groups or extended kinship networks) in aboriginal Chippewa culture that could serve as the foundation for developing a reservation organization. Consequently, the only models the Indians had available were white models. In James Lake their participation in white social organizations was extremely limited. Until recently the major source of experience with organizations was the U. S. government and its agencies.

The Indians' first extended contact with the government was through the Indian agent. Later, when the Bureau of Indian Affairs established an office in James Lake, Indians had an opportunity to observe a larger unit at first hand. However, as a model of organizational functioning, the BIA falls considerably short of ideal standards. The history of erratic government policy in Indian affairs has been characterized by disappointment, betrayal, and inefficiency; in short, it is a history of negative experience.

Friedl felt that the experience of the Chippewa with consistently erratic government policy has played a major role in shaping their expectations (for example, that life is unpredictable and that plans should be formulated on a short-range basis). From numerous conversations with informants and statements made in public meetings, it appeared that James Lake residents had well-established expectations concerning the government which were similar to those postulated by Friedl. Their attitudes toward the BIA involved the assumption that no promise would be fulfilled and no project would be completed. A minor incident was reported to us by 2 informants, apparently because it was regarded as typical of the bureau's operation. The James Lake League of Women Voters sponsored a clean-up campaign in the fall of 1964. The local council agreed to help and requested the bureau office in North City to send a truck to pick up the trash in Tract 22. Reportedly, the bureau promised to comply and the council convinced many families to clean up their yards and put the junk in a pile for the truck. But the bureau never sent a truck, in spite of several reminders from the council, and during the winter the trash was scattered over the yards once again.

The bureau does not function in a social and political vacuum, and the Indians do not regard their problems with the government as an isolated phenomenon. Indians' attitudes toward whites and their perception of whites' attitudes toward them are an integral part of their negative feelings about the bureau. Some of the major sources of hostility toward whites are (1) the feeling that "the white man took away our land and never gave us anything in return"; (2) recognition of white prejudice against Indians and its manifestations (such as discrimination in housing, employment, and education); and (3) gross inequalities in economic and political power.

Over the years, resentment toward whites and erratic government policies (accompanied by repeated failures of government-sponsored projects) have combined to establish a set of negative expectations among the Chippewa. Indians tend to feel that "If it's white, it's bad; if it comes from the government, it's bad." The most prominent models for building an organization have been contaminated by negative experiences and expectations.

It is unlikely, however, that these factors alone could produce the antiorganizational bias that seemed to exist among the majority of Indians in James Lake. The fate of Indian-organized projects, the structure of the reservation, and the experience of Indians who attempted to assume leadership were also highly relevant.

We noted earlier that Indians in positions of formal leadership become targets for hostility and suspicion; in particular, they are susceptible to charges of dishonesty. There are several complementary explanations for this attitude, one being that it may be founded in reality. If tribal officers in the past have stolen funds, the expectation that all officials will steal, given the opportunity, results from the generalization of past experience. Today it is probably not easy to steal funds outright, but tribal officials may be in a position to exploit various kinds of situations. For example, on the Beaver Pelt Reservation one of the tribal officers was a rice buyer and used his political position to further his business activities. It seems likely that there are opportunities for officials to arrange affairs to their own advantage, and it is not unreasonable to expect them to do so, particularly since the nonmonetary rewards (such as prestige and respect) are minimal. One project frequently mentioned as an example of official malfeasance was the tribally owned ranch. During the Second World War, the tribe purchased a ranch, but it was operated for less than a year. The cattle had to be sold because of an unexpected shortage of feed. An informant commented wryly, "They [the tribal officials] told us the wolves ate the fodder."

Of course, mismanagement of funds or other administrative errors are not necessarily the result of deliberate planning. An equally likely alternative is that inexperience and inefficiency have been primary causes for the failure of tribal projects. Nonetheless, whether failure is the result of inefficiency or dishonesty, the effect is the same: the money vanishes or the enterprise collapses, and negative expectations are reinforced.

Another element to consider is the lack of resources available to the leadership. Tribal officers have never been able to meet the wants and needs of their constituents because they generally have neither the financial resources nor the necessary authority to do so. Leaders may have been both honest and efficient, but the reservation situation itself precluded the possibility of success. The frustrated population perceives only the failure, and they vent their hostility on the highly visible leadership.

Another factor contributing to the maintenance of hostility is the lack of adequate communication between tribal officers and the public. Many people in James Lake expressed the feeling that they were not given information on important issues. Neither the Reservation Business Committee nor the Tribal Executive Committee issued regular reports of their meetings; most information was passed only through informal channels. While these channels appeared to be very efficient in the communication of gossip, they apparently did not function well for the dissemination of official information. The causes of the problem are multiple: inexperience, uncertainty about what kinds of information can legitimately remain confidential, inadequacy of communication at higher levels of government, and the hostility of the public itself may all be contributing factors.

Finally, we may include the effects of our hypothesized "individualistic expectations." In a society in which many people have been convinced of the necessity for self-interest and self-responsibility, it is logical to assume that a tribal leader would be similarly self-serving in motive and action. In summary, there is a combination of factors which create negative expectations among community members toward tribal officers and produce few rewards and many punishments for those who assume positions of leadership.

In the preceding discussion, we have argued that both hostility toward leaders and lack of support for the tribal organization have been the result of an interaction of historical and structural factors. These factors have produced cognitive expectations reflected in antiorganizational behavior, ranging from disinterest to active efforts to undermine the tribal organization.

The alternative explanation—that James Lake Chippewa behavior reflected long-standing cultural patterns of individualism plus a modal personality characterized by antisocial hostility and suspicion—does not seem supported by the data. The "modal personality" interpretation may also be questioned on the grounds that other individualistic societies do not seem invariably to produce hostile personalities (cf. Pelto 1962). While other investigators have commented on the unfriendliness of the

Chippewa, we did not find them unfriendly in James Lake. On the contrary, there appeared to be a great deal of informal socializing. During fieldwork we came to expect that most interviews would be interrupted by the arrival of unplanned visitors. The high rate of interaction among kinsmen has already been described. Interaction with nonkin was also high and, although the Indian community lacked the formal social clubs of the white group, they appeared to be equally "sociable."

Data from the household interviews provide strong support for our impressions of Indian sociability. The responses to a sociometric question are tabulated in Table 6.10. Each respondent was asked to name the people with whom he spent time. Additional information on frequency of visiting, usual activities, and the like was also requested. In this analysis all individuals named were summed for each group (the number of persons listed varied from one respondent to another), and a simple frequency distribution was tabulated. The results clearly indicate a high rate of social interaction. Thus, we believe that generalized hostility and uncooperativeness (as cultural traits) do not account for the political behavior we have described; rather, such behavior results from a series of behavioral responses and expectations that have their roots in contemporary social structures and specific historical conditions.

Conclusions

We began research in James Lake with the intention of finding out the meaning of the civil rights actions that were occurring in the community in the mid-1960s. We particularly wanted to discover the extent to which the lawsuit represented an awakening of political consciousness among Chippewa members of the community. As the research progressed and our understanding of the situation grew, we began to feel that the actions of the Defense Committee did not reflect a growth of political activism in

Table 6.10. Frequency of interaction with "people you spend your time with" except for members of the household

Frequency	Indian	White
Daily	20	14
Once a week or more	40	22
Less than once a week	4	10
Number of people listed	64	46
Number of respondents	30	28

the population as a whole. The manner in which other sociopolitical problems (such as the land claims issue, ricing regulations, and the Community Action Program) were handled suggested that most community members and some leaders were operating primarily in terms of an individualistic orientation to the solution of problems. In contrast to the issue of the claims money and CAP, the lawsuit and the last-minute write-in campaign for the municipal judgeship did not require any long-term commitments from people nor any significant involvement in collective action. In fact, the Defense Committee had great difficulty in getting witnesses for their case and did not receive wide community support.

If the foregoing description of political behavior of Indian people in James Lake is correct, then why do they behave in these ways? The question has practical as well as theoretical importance, for different theoretical explanations suggest different courses of action. We have argued that the political behavior and individualistic orientation of Indian people in James Lake can be seen as a rational strategy based on a long history of disappointments and negative reinforcements. Much of the recent reinforcement of their individualism derives from the shifting and untrustworthy policies of the BIA and from the particular conditions of their minority group status, as we have tried to demonstrate.

In addition, Indian people have to cope with many problems that they share with their poor white neighbors. For the majority of the population in north central Minnesota, making ends meet is a considerable struggle. Yet all of the institutions of the society—schools, welfare agencies, religious groups, mass media—continue to assure the populace that "success" is possible if one will only exert enough effort. The structure of rewards is such that individualistic expectations are engendered. Whether one assumes that there is a deliberate policy of "divide and rule" on the part of the establishment or simply notes the combined effects of existing social and economic organizations, there is little reason for the people of James Lake, Indian or white, to expect any favorable outcomes from collective activity.

We do not intend to imply that these people are incapable of cooperative, affiliative behavior, nor that collective action will never occur in individualistic communities. In some areas of the world where individualistic orientations have predominated, people have been able to develop intensively cooperative modes of dealing with socioeconomic problems. But we feel that those who make efforts to bring about truly significant changes in the life situations of Indian people in this area must confront the fact that the social institutions that shape the expectations and experiences of most community members have convinced them of the advisability of an individualistic and cautious approach to decision making. To expect them to do otherwise is to ask them to behave irrationally in the light of their earlier experiences. More programs based on the model of community development that led previous efforts to falter can only reinforce the attitudes and expectations that play an important part in preventing effective political action in the James Lake Indian community.

7
Chippewa Townspeople

J. Anthony Paredes

In North America the study of urban migration and adaptation has been left largely to sociologists. Since the late 1950s, however, studies of American Indian urbanization have begun to appear in the anthropological literature. The authors of these studies have often viewed the city as an alien environment, and have consequently emphasized the disconformities and discontinuities between the city and the reservations from which the Indians originate.

Hodge (1969), however, in his study of Albuquerque Navajos, describes the reservation and the city as parts of a system consisting of 2 overlapping "orbits": an urban orbit and a reservation orbit. Each orbit has its own centripetal and centrifugal forces ("pushes" and "pulls"); thus, an individual moves between the 2 orbits of the "urban-reservation system" according to the relative strength with which the forces in the 2 orbits impinge upon him or her at any given moment. Hodge's study is a step toward recognizing the functional relations between the city and the reservation as parts of a larger, encompassing national system. Going a step further, one recognizes that the overall adaptation of Indians living in a city cannot be judged solely from the perspective of the city, that is, by whether they "accommodate" (Ritzenthaler and Sellers 1955:160) to the city or exhibit "adaptive-like" behavior (Martin 1964:294) in the city context. In other words, the total sociocultural environment to which urban Indians must adapt consists of more than their immediate urban surroundings.

The Indians studied by Ablon (1964) in the San Francisco Bay area

324

are separated from their home reservations by great distances. Ablon has therefore concerned herself little with the relation between reservation and city (although she notes that many of the Indians would return to their reservations under certain circumstances). Ablon has shown that these Indians seek a substitute for reservation society by participating in formal Indian organizations and by confining their informal social interaction largely to other Indians. Although she mentions some tribal differences, Ablon makes general statements that apply to all Bay area Indians regardless of tribe. For example, "few have aspirations of social mobility," "those looking for formal social activity turn to Indian organizations," or "if one cannot be surrounded by members of his home community, at the least, it is more comfortable to associate with Indians of other tribes than with whites." Ablon describes the city Indian as a "neo-Indian type" (1964:301–4).

Other researchers have constructed typologies of urban American Indians. Hodge (1969) and Hurt (1961–62) begin with the observation that not all Indian migrants to cities intend to stay and that reservation life remains a viable alternative for Indians living in Albuquerque, New Mexico, and Yankton, South Dakota. They then proceed to categorize urban Indians into a small number of distinct types. Hodge's scheme consists of "permanent residents" and "nonpermanent residents," and is further subdivided into "traditional" and "anglo-modified." Hurt constructs a typology of "adjustment" based on two dimensions: "logical" possibilities for reactions to the environment, including "selecting," "rejecting," or "accepting"; and Indians' orientations to their surroundings, including "urban-oriented," "migratory-oriented," or "reservation-oriented."

Because these typologies do not deal with the interrelations of city and reservation as parts of the same larger social system, they ignore the issue of urban Indians' adaptation to their total sociocultural environment—the city and its many subsystems, other cities and states, the nation, the reservation, and traditional culture. In addition, these typologies require the imputation of motives and psychological orientations that appear difficult to identify empirically. But more important, individual differences within types are ignored; and a method for discriminating *between* types is not clearly specified. These typologies reduce to 1, 3, or 5 discrete types what is in all likelihood a gradient of individual differences along a multitude of cultural and social dimensions.

This study concerns Chippewa Indians living in North City, Minnesota, a small urban center located near the state's 3 largest reservations. As in previous American Indian urbanization studies, the adaptation of individuals is the primary subject of the research, which focuses on 2 closely related problems. The first problem is to determine why Chippewa Indians are in North City. Instead of assuming motives or "intentions" of individuals to explain their relocation to North City, this analysis will posit that movement to a particular city is, in and of itself, a strategy by which Indian individuals attempt to adapt to their total environment over time. The objective here will be to show that the character of relationships of North City Indians to major elements of their *total* environment are such that North City becomes for them an advantageous habitat.

The second problem is to describe patterns among North City Indians in adapting to elements of their environment. This involves a threefold procedure: identifying dimensions of adaptation, specifying individual variations within these dimensions, and examining the relationships among these variables. Solving the second problem will contribute to our understanding of the first, since determining the nature of the Indians' adaptations to various components of the North City environment is essential for specifying the adaptive advantages of North City residence.

This study concentrates on quantifiable behaviors and reports of past experiences. Attitudes, orientations, and beliefs receive less consideration, not because they are less important but because such data are more difficult to deal with in the context of the aims of this study. This methodological approach facilitates operationalizing the notion of adaptation.

The method and organization of this study may be contrasted with those of Hodge and Hurt. These researchers first posit a set of logically conceived *nominal* categories. The characteristics of each category are then described by a number of variables such as education, occupation, and family history. That process is reversed in this study. Using primarily the Guttman scaling technique, several *ordinal* typologies of North City Indians will be operationally derived, each representing a single dimension. These unidimensional typologies, along with other rankings of individuals, will then be compared statistically to determine the direction and the degree to which adaptation to one element of the overall environment is associated with adaptation to other elements.

In this study, the individual—the primary unit for analysis—is seen as adapting to a complex of sociocultural influences by integrating several systems of behavior. Specifically, Goodenough's formulations of "private culture," "operating culture," and "public culture" (1963a: 257–81) have been used in the conceptualization of this research.

North City provides an ideal laboratory for studying urban Indian adaptation to a number of environmental elements besides the city itself. The city is small and is close to home reservations; although relatively remote from metropolitan areas, it has numerous direct links to state and national systems.

I conducted the fieldwork for this study between November, 1965, and June, 1968. Quantitative data were collected in interviews with Indian household heads and Indian spouses of white household heads in 26 North City Indian households. "Indian household" is defined as any independent domicile occupied by one or more adults (over 18) of 25 percent or more Chippewa ancestry or recognized by oneself or the community as "an Indian." In conjugal households I interviewed the husband unless he was non-Indian; in those cases I interviewed the Indian wife. In consanguineal households the eldest female was ordinarily the one interviewed.

These interviews constitute a random sample that includes approximately 36 percent of the Indian households known to exist in North City in early 1966. To compile a random list of households, I used lists of Indian families and individuals (obtained through local schools, churches, the Department of Public Welfare, and informants), arranging them according to a table of random numbers. I conducted the interviews in the order of this randomized list, which included approximately 70 households. I encountered 5 refusals, 4 cases of families or individuals who moved out of town before they could be interviewed, and one death before obtaining the final (26th) interview. All but 2 of the interviews were conducted during the spring and summer of 1966. An additional set of 23 nonrandom "other responses" to the interview schedule was also obtained during later phases of the research.

I also obtained tape-recorded life history materials from 3 female and 7 male informants. Although these materials have not been incorporated in the statistical analysis, they have contributed to my thinking and have been drawn upon for illustrations.

In addition to structured interviews and formal life history interviews, data were collected through informal interviews or casual conversations and through direct observation. Occasionally, some informants were observed in settings outside the city, such as reservation celebrations.

Although the research documented here took place in the period 1965–68, the city is often referred to in the present tense for purposes of presentation.

North City: an overview

North City lies between Lake Izzy and the southwestern shore of Lake Gamog (see Figure 7.1). The city extends northward along the west shore of Lake Gamog and southward, across a major river, around the lake's southern end to its eastern shore.

In the 18th century Canadian and American fur companies had outposts on Lake Gamog, but little is known of them (Vandersluis 1963:2). In 1888 a trading post was established by a private businessman on the south shore of Lake Gamog, and a small settlement soon developed around it. North City quickly became the hub of local activity in the heyday of the timber industry. In 1896 the first hotel was built, and in 1897 Cramton County was organized with North City as the county seat. In 1904 another community, Melby, was established across the river from North City; it was later incorporated into the municipality of North City. In 1906 the city's 10-year-old newspaper began daily publication, and a high school was established. In 1918 a state normal school was built, which later became North City State College. Eventually the big timber was depleted, and the large sawmill at North City closed in 1926 (Vandersluis:16). The city nevertheless continued to grow and hold its place as the center of commerce and transportation for Cramton County and the surrounding counties.

In 1966 North City had a population of approximately 10,000 persons and covered 15 square miles. Population density was slightly more than 650 persons per square mile, in contrast to 9.3 per square mile for the county as a whole. The city is primarily a trade and administrative center for the surrounding area. The largest percentage of workers is employed in retail trades and less than 20 percent in manufacturing (Rand McNally 1965). The largest of the few small factories is a plywood plant employing about 60 workers.

Weekends and the Christmas season find North City crowded with farmers, loggers, small-town residents, and reservation Indians, who come from the countryside to shop. A movie theater, 2 drive-in theaters which are open in the summer, and several taverns provide recreation. City retailers included 13 grocery stores, 9 hardware stores, several clothing stores specializing in men's or women's clothing, and 6 department stores representing national chains. The city has automobile

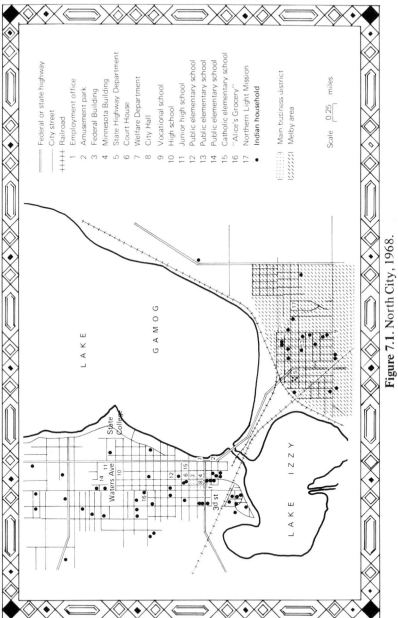

Figure 7.1. North City, 1968.

Federal or state highway
City street
Railroad
1 Employment office
2 Amusement park
3 Federal Building
4 Minnesota Building
5 State Highway Department
6 Court House
7 Welfare Department
8 City Hall
9 Vocational school
10 High school
11 Junior high school
12 Public elementary school
13 Public elementary school
14 Public elementary school
15 Catholic elementary school
16 "Alice's Grocery"
17 Northern Light Mission
● Indian household

Main business district
Melby area

Scale 0.25 miles

LAKE GAMOG

LAKE IZZY

State College

Waters Ave

3d st

dealerships representing all the major U. S. manufacturers. It is situated at the crossroads of several rail, trucking, and bus routes and is the only place in the region with daily commercial airline service. Area offices provide electrical, gas, and telephone utilities. Additionally, 14 physicians, 11 dentists, an 82-bed hospital, and 4 pharmacies serve the community.

Vacationers and tourists are important sources of income for North City. In summer the streets are lively with tourists drawn by shops, cafes, and service stations. A private entrepreneur operates, under a city franchise, a small amusement park on the shore of Lake Gamog adjacent to large concrete statues of Paul Bunyan and his blue ox—hallmarks of the city. The local Jaycees sponsor a midsummer carnival and a beauty contest, and the Chamber of Commerce pays a few Indians from Deer Lake to dance by the lake shore several evenings during the summer. A summer stock theater managed by a board of local citizens performs in an old but fashionable resort on the northern edge of the city. These activities attract tourists as well as residents of the surrounding communities.

North City is an administrative center for a large area of northern Minnesota. The largest building in the city is the modernistic 4-story Federal Building, which houses the post office and several federal agency offices that serve the people of Cramton County and nearby counties. These agency offices include the Agricultural Stabilization and Conservation Service, the Bureau of Indian Affairs, the district director of Internal Revenue, the Economic Development Administration, the Farmer's Home Administration, the Public Health Service Indian Health Field Office, the Social Security Administration District Office, the Soil Conservation Service, the U.S. Army Recruiting Station, and the U.S. Navy Recruiting Station.

Two blocks from the Federal Building is the Minnesota Building, where there are branch offices for the State of Minnesota Health Department and the State of Minnesota Department of Education (including an office for its Indian Division). Another building is occupied completely by a State Employment Service office that has responsibility for 4 counties and the Deer Lake Indian Reservation. Offices for the Corrections Department, Bureau of Game and Fish, Division of Lands and Minerals, and Deputy Registrar of Motor Vehicles are dispersed among a number of buildings in the business district. The State Highway Department has an office building and garages on the south side of the city. The Cramton County Courthouse, at the northwestern corner of the business district, contains not only the usual county courts and offices but also the office of the Community Action Program (CAP), serving Cramton and James counties. The Cramton County Welfare Department has its own building. Near the courthouse is the North City clinic, where the majority of the city's physicians practice. A few doors from the clinic is a mental health center for the people of Cramton and 5 adjacent counties. The center is staffed by a psychiatrist, psychologist, social worker, and assistants and is supported by funds from the 6 counties and the State of Minnesota.

Educational institutions are a major part of North City's economy. The city has one parochial and 3 public elementary schools and public junior and senior high schools. In addition to city children, pupils from the surrounding countryside (including some Indians from Mission) are bused to the North City schools. A vocational school is jointly operated by the city and the state for the benefit of high school graduates in a multicounty area of northern Minnesota. The largest educational institution is North City State College, with an enrollment of approximately 3,000 students in 1966. The college curriculum includes undergraduate studies in many disciplines and 4 master's degree programs. An elementary school is operated on the campus as a laboratory school. Also at North City State College is the University of Minnesota Agricultural Extension Service area coordinator for 6 counties in the region. A federally funded technical assistance and training center for all Indian reservations in Minnesota, Wisconsin, and Michigan was established in 1968. Almost as many people are employed in education in North City as in the retail trade (Rand McNally 1965).

North City has 2 newspapers and a commercial radio station; television reception is available on 4 channels. Three banks and a savings and loan association are located in the city. There are 17 churches; the Episcopal church sponsors a home for predelinquent teen-agers, who attend city schools. Voluntary organizations in the city include the Chamber of Commerce, American Legion, Veterans of Foreign Wars, Elks, Moose, Lions, Rotary Club, Boy Scouts, Girl Scouts, Junior Chamber of Commerce, Masons, women's auxiliaries of many of the men's clubs, various professional associations, garden clubs, a country club, labor unions, League of Women Voters, sports teams, and many religious organizations.

The municipal government is composed of a mayor, city commission, and city manager. City offices, courts, and the police station are located in the City Hall, near the Minnesota Building. One of the principal problems confronting the local government is providing public services such as street maintenance and water to large areas of the city that are thinly populated.

North City has the same economic difficulties as the surrounding area; however, these problems are generally less severe for the urban population. Median family income for Cramton County in the 1960 U.S. census was $3,949 compared to $5,573 for the state as a whole. North City median family income was $4,703, well above the county median but still considerably below that of the state.

Though relatively small, North City is in fact urban. Using Charles Stewart's distinction between urban and rural areas, North City is urban by virtue of its economy, which is based on "spatially intensive industries and occupations" rather than "spatially extensive industries and occupations" (1958:154) such as agriculture, logging, outdoor recreation, and commercial fishing. To use Wirth's terms, North City is a "relatively large, dense, and permanent settlement of heterogeneous individuals" (1938:8). An administrative and educational center, the city has a large labor force of professional and managerial people and depends economically on the countryside's need for its goods and services.

The ethnic composition of North City is mostly northern European, principally Scandinavian. There are a few people of Italian, French, or Slavic ancestry; the high school Spanish teacher is Latin American. Very few blacks live in North City. Among the college faculty there are usually 4 or 5 Asiatics. A small part of the population includes persons of Chippewa ancestry.

The Indians of North City

The site of North City was apparently occupied by Indians prior to white settlement. Evidences of an early burial mound culture found by the first North City settlers were later obliterated (Vandersluis 1963:2). One burial was discovered during excavation for the present tourist information and museum building and is displayed *in situ* beneath the museum's floor. Undoubtedly the resources of Lake Gamog were utilized by early Chippewa settled nearby in the Broken Reed Reservation area. A footpath along a section of the North City lakeshore is reputed to be an old Indian trail. An old man from the Deer Lake Reservation claims that his father used to camp at what is now a lakeshore city park. An elderly female informant stated that she knew an even older Indian woman who could recall having camped as a child at the point where the river flows into Lake Gamog, and an elderly male informant retold stories he had heard of Indians camping in the North City area.

In 1888 the site of North City was occupied by a small band of Chippewa led by *Sha-na-wish-kung* ("Walks-with-his-feet-treading-backwards"). Early settlers dubbed him Chief Gamog after the Chippewa name of the lake. One of the original white settlers is reported to have married one of Sha-na-wish-kung's daughters (Vandersluis 1963:7). The published history of Cramton County includes a photograph of Sha-na-wish-kung (Vandersluis 1963:40) and another photograph bearing the caption "Indian Camp at [North City] 1897" (Vandersluis 1963:29). Today Sha-na-wish-kung is immortalized in a painted wooden statue of a generalized Indian, which is positioned by the lakeshore each summer; the statue is locally known as Chief Gamog.

Aside from discussion of Sha-na-wish-kung, no further mention of Indians in North City is made in the history of the city until 1954. In that year the Indian agency was moved from James Lake to North City "and since that time the Indian population has grown" (Vandersluis 1963:23).

Although U.S. census reports that include North City do not specifically identify American Indians, they do distinguish between "white," "Negro," and "other races" in the city. The "other races" category probably includes mainly Indians. The numbers of people in this category in North City during the last 4 censuses preceding this study are as follows: 1930—24; 1940—39; 1950—48; 1960—224. The rather large increase from 1950 to 1960 may be partly attributed to a change in census procedure in 1960. In that census, racial classification was made by each individual rather than by the enumerators, as in earlier censuses. According to the U.S. Census Bureau, "In many areas the proportion of persons classified as 'other race' may be somewhat higher because of the procedures first used in 1960" (1961). Even so, there was a decided increase in the number of Indians in North City between 1950 and 1960.

There is at least one Indian household in every major residential section of the city, but there are no visible concentrations of Indians. No section can accurately be described as an Indian ghetto, or even an Indian neighborhood. Local people can identify parts of town as places "where quite a few Indians live"; but the places mentioned are always primarily white neighborhoods where Indians are only a small minority, with the largest Indian concentrations being clusters of 3 contiguous households.

The spatial distribution of North City Indian households in 1966, shown in Figure 7.1, clearly demonstrates that there is little territorial concentration of North City Indian dwellings, and that Indians tend *not* to live in the city's northeastern section. Most affluent whites live in this section and along the lakeshore north of the city limits.

Other studies of American Indian urbanization have reported formal voluntary associations among city Indians (Ablon 1964; Hurt 1961–62; Martin 1964; Hodge 1969), an observation that holds true for the large metropolitan areas of Minnesota. Often these associations are important in the Indians' social organization and cultural adaptation. North City Indians have not formed any voluntary associations; however, a small, fundamentalist church, the Northern Light Chippewa Mission, might be regarded as a functional equivalent.

The mission's physical structure is inconspicuous. Its meeting hall is a remodeled, corrugated-tin repair garage connected to a comfortable frame house in which the missionary resides. Working for more than 20 years on the Beaver Pelt and Deer Lake reservations before coming to North City, the missionary now receives funds from the same non-denominational, fundamentalist missionary alliance which supported her reservation work.

The missionary at the North City mission is a Mennonite and is officially sponsored by her home church in southern Minnesota. In an interview, she stated that the North City mission had been her idea. She had known that Indians from reservations had migrated to North City and had felt that the mission was needed because the Indians would be reluctant to attend the non-Indian Protestant churches of North City. She is constantly on the alert for new Indian migrants to North City, keeping informed of new arrivals through her Indian acquaintances. Her "census" is incomplete, since most of the names she lists are those of the poorer Indians. The missionary noted that she frequently visits homes, does favors for North City Indians (but avoids becoming a "soft touch"), takes toys to city Indian children at Christmas, and holds rummage sales at the mission to increase Indian attendance at the mission's religious services.

Despite the missionary's efforts, attendance at the mission's meetings is poor. During an interview she admitted that no Indians had attended the previous 2 Sunday meetings. Some whites attended— mainly as the missionary's assistants. Prominently displayed in the meeting hall, her attendance chart for January–September 1966 listed the names of everyone who had attended a meeting, with a star for each subsequent attendance. Most were children; of the Indian adults, only 3 appeared to have attended regularly.

At best, the mission brings together some of the city's poorer Indians and serves as an occasional meeting place for some of the small children. Because the Indians play no role in directing or managing the mission, it cannot be considered a formal voluntary association of North City Indians. The only other organization for Indians in the city is the American Indian students' club on the state college campus. Composed of 35 American Indian students, this organization is not a voluntary association among city Indian residents either, since it is confined to the college campus.

Indians tend to congregate informally at several places in North City. One of 2 municipally operated liquor stores is known among local whites as "the Indian bar," in contrast to the other, larger bar, "Number One," or "the Muny" (from "municipal"). As a matter of fact, Indians patronize both; but middle-class whites avoid the Indian bar. One cafe is regarded as an Indian hangout and is indeed preferred by many Indians. According to some informants, it has been an Indian gathering place for many years. On its second floor, the cafe has rooms for rent that are sometimes used by Indians for short stays in North City. Another cafe, which serves beer, attracts many reservation Indians, particularly on weekends; however, the main clientele consists of elderly white men who live in the surrounding area.

Indians also congregate in front of the stores at the Third Street and Waters Avenue intersection (see Figure 7.1). One younger informant reported that he had often heard Waters Avenue referred to by his peers as "Indian Avenue." The discount and used goods stores along Third Street appeal to many Indians. The main lakefront, with its amusement park, tourist center, and occasional Indian dances, is also a gathering place for Indians as well as whites during the summer months.

Most of the Indian customers of small neighborhood grocery stores are residents of North City; reservation Indians coming into North City tend to restrict their shopping to the large supermarkets. Because of the dispersion of Indian households, none of the small grocery stores has very many Indian customers; most of their customers are whites.

One neighborhood grocery store is noteworthy. Alice's Grocery (see Figure 7.1) is operated by a part-Indian woman who formerly owned and managed a store on the Deer Lake Reservation. Herself a member of the Beaver Pelt Reservation, she receives considerable patronage from

North City Indians who knew her through her previous business. Besides those Indians who live nearby and frequent her store, others come from distant parts of the city. At the time this research was conducted, Alice had only recently come to North City; so it was possible that her store would eventually become a relatively important focus of North City Indian interaction.

In North City, Indians can usually be seen in "Indian places," in shops and large supermarkets, at the movies, and on the streets. However, most of these Indians are visitors from communities on the nearby reservations, contributing to the "invisibility" of the resident urban population of Indians. Furthermore, just as with the reservation Indians, some mixed-blood North City Chippewa cannot be visually identified as Indians. The residential dispersion of the city's Indians further contributes to their invisibility. Spatial dispersion, low visibility, absence of voluntary associations, and relative absence of focus for informal organization are probably all closely interrelated factors among North City Indians.

Demographic background

Cities differ demographically from rural areas. In addition to gross differences in size and population concentration, there are significant differences in sex ratios, age structures, and fertility rates. Whereas rural populations have disproportionately large percentages of dependent children, or the aged, or both, urban populations tend to have concentrations of people in the productive ages, 20 to 44 (Brunner and Hallenbeck 1955:188–209). In general, fertility rates are lower in the city than in the countryside (Brunner and Hallenbeck 1955:195–97). In some areas of the world, fertility rates have been shown to vary inversely with city size (Casis and Davis 1953:155–57). Nonetheless, Hammel (1964) has demonstrated for Peru that even though demographic characteristics of whole cities may differ from rural areas, urban slum populations may more closely resemble rural populations in some respects.

To find out whether North City Indians are demographically different from reservation Indians as well as whether they are distinct from the whole-city population, data on their age and sex distribution, fertility, and education were examined, in addition to information on places of birth, tribal enrollment, Indian blood quanta, household size and composition, and length of residence. The data analyzed were obtained from a random sample of 27 rather than 26 households, since one respondent who refused to complete the entire interview provided the necessary demographic information. Although the sampled households consisted of 106 individuals, non-Indian spouses were excluded from the analysis, reducing the total to 99. Children of interracial couples were counted as Indians. Occasionally, comparisons are made with data from the non-random sample. Most of the comparative reservation data are from random samples of households in 3 communities on the Broken Reed Reservation (see Jackson, Roufs, and Pelto in this volume).

Length of urban residence

During 1966 an estimated average of 300 Chippewa Indians lived in North City (some individuals and families frequently move in and out of the city and others occasionally have friends and relatives living with them on a short-term basis). A conservative estimate, this figure shows approximately a 33.4 percent increase over the 224 "other nonwhites" enumerated in the 1960 U.S. Census.

Information on length of residence in North City, obtained directly for interviewees and inferentially for spouses and children, was computed as length of continuous residence immediately prior to interviewing. One exception was a federal employee who had lived in North City for 5 years and then spent a one-year tour of duty in the Twin Cities only 2 years before being interviewed. The range of variation in length of residence was 1.5 to 29 years, and the median was 7. None of the interviewees nor their Indian spouses had resided continually in the city since childhood; 3 women had lived in North City as minor children, but had left the city for a number of years and returned. Only 5 of the 27 respondents had continuously resided in the city since 1955 or before. Approximately one-third of the sample had moved to North City after the 1960 census. These data on residence tend to corroborate the estimated increase in North City Indian population and to indicate that the increase was continuing.

Age and sex

Table 7.1 presents major age and sex characteristics of the North City sample and comparable information from the 3 reservation communities; it also shows figures for North City as a whole and for the United States. There are few differences between the reservation populations and the city Indian population. The North City Indian figures, however, exhibit some interesting tendencies.

All the Indian populations except James Lake had an excess of females, but North City Indians had the largest such excess. Of the 4

Table 7.1. Comparative demographic profile of North City Indians (random sample)

	North City Indians	Wicket[a] Indians	James Lake Indians	Rice Village	North City[b]	United States
Sex ratio (females per 1,000 males)	1,178	1,130	667	1,111	948	1,057
Fertility ratio[c]	1,593	1,265	1,333	2,660	549	717
Dependent children (under 15)	51.5%	43.5%	53.9%	50.0%	29.6%	26.9%
Active population (15 to 64)	41.4%	51.0%	38.9%	42.0%	58.3%	61.8%
Dependent elderly (65 and over)	7.1%	5.5%	7.2%	8.0%	12.1%	8.5%
	100.0%	100.0%	100.0%	100.0%	100.0%	100.0%

a. Figures for James Lake, Wicket, Rice Village, and the United States are taken from Roufs 1967:29.
b. Figures for North City are taken from U.S. Bureau of the Census 1961:111.
c. Children under 5 years of age per 1,000 women aged 20–44.

Indian populations, North City Indians had the second highest fertility ratio, far exceeding the ratio for the city as a whole. The fertility ratio of the total North City population was considerably lower than those of both Indians and whites in surrounding rural areas (figures from U.S. Census not shown in table).

The age distribution of the North City Indian sample shows only minor variations from that of the reservation communities. When compared to the United States and North City as a whole, all 4 Indian populations show a deficit of persons in the 15–64 age-group and a surfeit of dependent children. In short, the age distribution of the North City Indian population was very similar to that of the reservation communities and quite dissimilar to that of the city as a whole.

Table 7.2 presents more detailed information about age distribution for the random sample of North City Indians. Compared to the 1960 census data for nonwhites in 6 surrounding counties (figures not shown), the North City sample shows some curious differences: a relative excess of females aged 45–64 and a deficit of males aged 15–64. As a matter of fact, in the random sample there were no males or females aged 20–24. However, in the nonrandom sample there were 6 females and 2 males in the 20–24 age-group and larger percentages of males and females in the 15–44 age group.

Table 7.2. Age distribution of North City Indian sample

	Percent under 15	Percent 15–44	Percent 45–64	Percent 65 and over
Males	57.8	22.2	11.1	8.9
Females	46.3	31.5	16.6	5.6

Data on Indians living in Minneapolis (League of Women Voters 1968) suggest contrasts between North City Indians and metropolitan Indian populations. The data were collected from a random sample of 100 Indians (31 men and 69 women), the great majority of whom were Chippewa. Unfortunately, age data are given only for individual respondents rather than for whole families. These data show that those aged 23–40 comprised 56 percent of the adult (over 16) population, while those 65 and over accounted for only 4 percent. By comparison, North City and the reservation communities had relatively few young adults and many aged.

In summary, the North City Indian sample shows little variation from reservation populations, but it differs considerably from the population of the city as a whole. Available comparative data on fertility and age groups indicate that in this sample the North City Indians differed from reservation populations in the opposite direction of that indicated by gross differences usually found between rural and urban population.

Education

Since current data were not available for comparison of the educational levels of North City Indians and reservation Indian communities, 1960 census information had to suffice.

In the total sample population, the median number of years of formal schooling completed was 6. The median for those aged 25 and over was 8.5; the range was 0–14. The median number of school years completed by interviewees was 8.

By comparison, among Cramton and James County nonwhites aged 25 and over the median numbers of school years completed were 8.8 and 7.8 respectively; the median for all persons in North City aged 25 and over was 11 (U.S. Census). In the Minneapolis survey 47 percent of the Indian respondents had completed 11 or more school years (League of Women Voters 1968).

Again, the North City Chippewa sample appears to differ little from reservation populations, but it shows greater variance from the North City population as a whole (and from Indians in Minneapolis).

Birthplace and tribal enrollment

Tables 7.3 and 7.4 present the data on place of birth and tribal enrollment for the North City Indian samples. All of the persons born in North City or Minneapolis–St. Paul were dependent children at the time of the study; likewise, most of those born in "other places" were children. Therefore, the bulk of the North City Indian adults (and, incidentally, quite a few of the children) were born on one of the 3 surrounding reservations, establishing that North City drew most of its Indian population from reservations in the immediate area. A few members of other tribes (for example, the Dakota and the Flathead) were employed by the federal government and lived in North City; but they were a very small minority of the city's Indian population. Even Chippewa born on the other 4, more distant reservations in Minnesota constituted only a tiny portion of the North City Indian population.

The percentages of persons in the North City Indian sample born on each of the 3 nearby reservations were approximately proportionate to

Table 7.3. Place of birth of North City Indians (random sample)

	Number	*Percentage*
Deer Lake Reservation (population, ca. 2,650)	20	20.2
Broken Reed Reservation (population, ca. 2,400)	19	19.2
Beaver Pelt Reservation (population, ca. 2,350)	13	13.1
Other reservations	3	3.0
North City	24	24.2
Minneapolis–St. Paul	8	8.2
Other places	12	12.1
Total	99	100.0

the populations of those reservations, with the largest deviation being the low percentage for the Beaver Pelt Reservation. This deviation is partially explained by the number of children of Beaver Pelt parents born at the James Lake Indian Hospital on the Broken Reed Reservation. In the Minneapolis sample 27 percent of the respondents were born on the Beaver Pelt Reservation, 16 percent on the Deer Lake Reservation, and only 6 percent on the Broken Reed Reservation; the remaining 51 percent came from a variety of places in Minnesota, Wisconsin, the Dakotas, and elsewhere (League of Women Voters 1968).

Not all persons eligible for tribal enrollment, particularly young children, were in fact enrolled. Respondents enrolled in the Minnesota Chippewa Tribe usually reported the reservation from which they and their children were enrolled, but a few gave only the Chippewa Tribe as their enrollment. The enrollment figures shown in Table 7.4 proportionately correspond even more closely than place of birth to the 3 principal reservation populations.

Table 7.4. Tribal enrollment of North City Indians (random sample)

	Number	*Percentage*
Deer Lake Reservation (population, ca. 2.650)	22	22.2
Broken Reed Reservation (population, ca. 2,400)	17	17.2
Beaver Pelt Reservation (population, ca. 2,350)	20	20.2
Other reservations	3	3.0
Other Minnesota Chippewa[a]	10	10.1
Unenrolled	27	27.3
Total	99	100.0

a. Includes all those enrolled from other reservations and those interviewees who did not specify the reservation of their enrollment.

Indian blood quanta

Interviewees were asked to state the percentage of Indian ancestry (Indian blood quantum) of themselves and other members of the household. The percentages thus obtained were later compared with the official Indian blood quanta recorded by the Bureau of Indian Affairs. The differences between respondents' statements and the records were minimal, indicating a high degree of reliability of interviewees. Where there were any differences, figures in the official records were used for computation. In a few cases it was necessary to estimate the Indian blood quanta of children for whom there was inadequate information regarding the biological father.

In the random sample, the known Indian ancestry of all but 6 individuals was Chippewa only. The only other tribe represented in the sample was Wisconsin Oneida. One man was an enrolled Oneida, but he was married to a member of the Deer Lake Band; and one woman's mother was an Oneida, but the woman herself and her children were enrolled in the Deer Lake Band.

The Indian ancestry of the sample household population ranged from 18.7 to 100 percent; the median Indian ancestry was 50 percent. Cursory examination of Bureau of Indian Affairs records suggests that this distribution was fairly representative of all enrollees from the 3 main reservations. Among the persons interviewed, the median Indian ancestry was 58.9 percent. In this characteristic, North City Indians were quite similar to Minneapolis Indians, "over half of the 100 reported being one-half or more Indian in ancestry" (League of Women Voters 1968:4).

Household size and composition

The range of household size (including non-Indian spouses in the households) in the random sample was from one to 8 members; the mean was 3.9 and the median was 3. There was little difference between the random and the nonrandom samples. In the nonrandom sample the range of household size was from one to 7 members; the mean was 3.6 and the median was 3.0.

The composition of North City Indian households was quite varied. Only 14 (51.9 percent) of the domestic units in the random sample were nuclear family households, but 2 of these included children who were not the common offspring of the conjugal pair. Five of the households (18.5 percent) were comprised of single elderly people (2 females and 3 males). Eight of the households (29.6 percent) were "consanguineal" (see Solien de Gonzales 1965).

The composition of the nonrandom sample of households was much the same as the random sample. Sixty percent of the households were basically conjugal; 3 (15.2 percent) were single individuals living alone; and the remainder were consanguineal.

Summary

The rate of Indian migration to North City increased rapidly in the late 1950s and continued to the late 1960s. The majority of North City Indians were born on the 3 closest reservations, each of which has approximately proportional representation among the city's Indians.

Certain demographic characteristics of North City Indians are very similar to those of reservation populations but unlike those of the city as a whole. Fertility and sex ratios of North City Indians correspond closely to those of selected reservation communities. The educational level of North City Indians appears to be more similar to those of reservation populations than to either that of the city as a whole or that of Minneapolis Indians. The age structure of the North City Indian population is much like that of reservation populations in its excess of children and its deficit of young adults. In short, North City Indians are demographically more similar to rural than to urban populations

Dowling (1968) has found a similar situation among the Wisconsin Oneida. Even though the Oneida reservation merges with the city of Green Bay (population, 125,000), the age structure of the Oneida population is "rural." Young Oneida migrate to larger and more distant cities like Milwaukee for employment rather than seek local employment, despite the availability of appropriate jobs in Green Bay. Dowling attributes this phenomenon to the Oneida's perception of anti-Indian sentiments among Green Bay whites. Given the much smaller size and poorer economy of North City when compared to Green Bay, the demographic findings on North City Indians are not so anomalous in view of Dowling's work.

Why, then, are there any Indians at all here? Apparently, special circumstances lead to the eventual relocation of some Chippewa to North City.

Marriage and social marginality

In their pioneering work, Ritzenthaler and Sellers (1955) suggested that city Indians exhibited a significantly larger percentage of interracial marriages than did reservation Indians. Following their lead, it may be hypothesized that North City Chippewa are more racially exogamous than Indians on nearby reservations. (My usage of "exogamy" and "endogamy" is not intended to carry any implication of formal rules for marriage; the terms are used alternatively with the more neutral but cumbersome "out-marriage" and "in-marriage.") The hypothesis may be expanded if it is assumed that (1) interracial marriage is only one instance of the more general phenomenon of marriage between members of ordinarily endogamous categories of persons, and (2) among Indians of the North City region, tribe and reservation (as well as race) tend to be endogamous. (The Minnesota Chippewa Tribe and the Deer Lake Band of Chippewa Indians are separate political bodies [see Chapter 1].) To rephrase the hypothesis, North City Indians exhibit higher percentages of interreservation, intertribal, and interracial marriages than do Chippewa living on the reservations.

Data available on the 44 then current or most recent marital unions of North City Indians (10 persons were widowed and 8 separated or divorced) show that only 18 percent were between Chippewa originating from the same reservation. In comparison, the percentages of reservation-endogamous marriages in the Indian communities of James Lake, Wicket, and Rice Village were 52.6, 58, and 76 percent, respectively. In the 3 communities combined, 80 percent of the marriages were between members of the Minnesota Chippewa Tribe. Similarly, almost all of the Indians of the Deer Lake Reservation were members of the band.

Marriage data for North City Indians are presented in greater detail in Table 7.5. In 5 of the 8 marriages between members of the same reservation, one or both of the partners were offspring of reservation-exogamous marriages. In addition, in 23 of the 36 cases of reservation out-marriages, one or both of the partners were offspring of individuals who also married outside their home reservation.

The hypothesis is supported; North City Indians do exhibit a high degree of reservation out-marriage compared to reservation populations. This finding might be explained as the result of greater opportunity (afforded by residence in North City) to meet potential marriage partners from other reservations. Ritzenthaler and Sellers (1955) produce evidence that there is such a causal link among Indians living in Milwaukee. However, among North City Indians all except 3 of the 44 unions were established *before* relocation to North City. Moreover, the parents of many North City Chippewa also selected marriage partners from outside

Table 7.5. Ethnic affiliation of spouses in North City
Indian marital unions

Marital unions between:	Random sample	Others
1. Members of same reservation	4	4
2. Members of different reservations in Minnesota Chippewa Tribe	5	1
3. Member of Deer Lake Band and member of Minnesota Chippewa Tribe	6	5
4. Members of any other combination of Indian groupings[a]	3	1
5. Indians and whites	9	6
Total	27	17

[a] Included here are, among others, a Deer Lake Chippewa married to a Wisconsin Oneida and a Wisconsin Chippewa whose husband was also a Wisconsin Chippewa but from a different reservation. All couples in this category have at least one Chippewa member.

their home reservation. While it is true that some North City Indians met their spouses in larger cities, many of the partners met while one or both still resided on a reservation. For North City Indians the relationship between urban residence and out-marriage is not one in which North City residence "causes" selection of reservation outsiders as marriage partners; the relationship is analytically more complex.

First, whereas marriage between two Indians from the same reservation usually multiplies their mutual kinship and other ties to that particular reservation, marriage to an outsider fails to produce these additional social ties to the home reservation. Indeed, such an out-marriage establishes a new set of ties away from the home reservation. Second, over time a reservation-exogamous marriage may tend to weaken the ties of the partners to their respective communities. Third, if an exogamously married couple resides in one partner's home community, this may produce social, economic, or psychological strains on one or both of them. Finally, while out-marriage may have a profound effect on an individual's status in his or her own community, it need not weaken his or her attachment to the general vicinity of the home reservation, particularly if marital partners originate from nearby reservations.

Informants offered insight into difficulties arising from out-marriage. The Caucasian wife of a man from Mission remembered being frightened and anxious when the couple lived on the reservation many years ago. A James Lake Indian man married to a white woman from North City stated that he moved to North City in order to assist his wife's aged mother; his own mother lived on the reservation, but he managed to see her several times a week.

Problems of reservation out-marriage seemed especially apparent on the Deer Lake Reservation. Men married to Deer Lake women frequently told of the difficulties they encountered in seeking employment on the wife's home reservation. A Beaver Pelt man married to a Deer Lake woman said of his experience on her reservation, "You could just feel it—that they didn't like you being there." (The Deer Lake tribal chairman once stated that available jobs on the reservation would be offered to band members in preference to Indians from other reservations.) One Broken Reed Reservation woman who married a Deer Lake man established a consensual union with another member of the Deer Lake Reservation after her husband died. Her consensual mate's cousin reported that eventually the couple was told that if they didn't marry, the woman would have to leave the reservation. She moved to North City, and the man remained on the reservation and traveled to North City to maintain the relationship. Likewise, an informant originally from the Broken Reed Reservation lived on the Deer Lake Reservation for many years with his Deer Lake wife. Apparently he received special consideration from the former tribal secretary-treasurer (see Chapter 1), who had been a classmate of the informant's father at an eastern boarding school in the 19th century. After the political change of 1958, the informant's trapping and fishing privileges on the reservation were gradually curtailed. When his wife left the reservation to live with her children in Chicago, he moved to North City. In 1968, he was removed from the Deer Lake Fourth of July Committee, of which he had been a member for many years—even after moving to North City. The relationship between out-marriage and North City residence may best be summarized by the Broken Reed wife of a Deer Lake man: "He didn't want to live on my reservation, and I didn't want to live on his, so we came to North City—'bout half way in between."

The overall condition of marriage to a reservation outsider may be described as "social marginality." That is, in contrast to the individual whose consanguineal and affinal kin are all Indian members of the same reservation, the out-married person has those ties divided between 2 different reservations, tribes, or races and is thus not as tightly integrated into either community as are in-married persons in each of the 2 groups.

The concept of social marginality has much in common with the "marginal man" concept (cf. Shibutani 1961:574–81). However, the marginal man theory focuses on such questions as the consequences of conflicting loyalties in complex societies. The concept of social marginality, in contrast, directs attention to the structural parameters of marginality and does not deal directly with the psychology of persons "caught on the boundary of 2 or more cultures" (Shibutani 1961:577).

Other factors in social marginality

A surprisingly large number of North City Indians have personal and family occupational histories that include unusual kinds of employment compared to that of most Chippewa Indians. Several informants or their parents or both were employed by federal agencies on reservations as foremen, interpreters, or skilled and semiskilled workers. Four respondents had either owned or had parents who owned entrepreneurial establishments on reservations. Two of these cases were among the few reservation-endogamous marriages in the city. One of these is particularly noteworthy. A Deer Lake man who migrated to North City after the death of his Deer Lake wife was the son and part heir of one of the few native grocers on the reservation. His father had worked for the government as an interpreter, and the old man himself had been the Deer Lake chief of police many years before. He remarked, "Most of what I know I learned from the white man." Two other elderly North City Indian men were the sons of Indian policemen.

Another North City Indian married to a member of his own reservation, Deer Lake, appeared to have been forced into a marginal position by his father's religious conversion. When the informant was still a boy, his father converted from Catholicism to a fundamentalist sect of which few local whites and virtually no other Indians were members and forced him to attend proselytizing meetings in nearby white towns. Meanwhile, his uncle urged him to continue his Catholic devotion. The informant finally rejected formalized religion in general, as well as his father's demand that he become a conscientious objector in World War II. The informant said of his now deceased father, "People up there [on the reservation] thought he was some kind of kook."

Finally, unique circumstances have placed some people in an anomalous position in reservation society. Accidents of birth and death may leave individuals with weakened ties to the reservation community. Perhaps Mrs. Fish is the best example. Born in the late 1800s on the Deer Lake Reservation, her father was Caucasian and her mother was from Nisishin. Her mother died at an early age, and her Indian kinsmen who raised her would not allow her father to visit his offspring. When she was still quite young, Mrs. Fish established a consensual union with Mr. Fish and later married him. He took her from Nisishin across the lake to his home at Windy. In those days travel between the 2 communities was difficult and infrequent. In time the relationship between the young couple deteriorated, and Mr. Fish began abusing his wife by overwork and beatings. The husband's grandfather tried to help; Mrs. Fish recalled the old man's lecture to her husband: "'You mustn't do that to this girl, although she don't have any relations that would care for her, but that good enough you pick her up [sic] . . . if she had a mother and father why they would get after you if you 'busing [abusing] her or anything like that. But you shouldn't do this to her. . . .' It didn't stop him." Eventually they were divorced. For a time Mrs. Fish maintained a consensual union with another man. In recent years Mrs. Fish has moved back and forth between North City and the reservation. She has cut posts, fished, brewed illegal whiskey, and performed many other tasks in order to support herself and her children; she said, "I work just like a man."

Explicit reasons for migration

Social marginality notwithstanding, North City Indians gave a variety of explicit reasons for migrating. When asked why they initially emigrated from the reservation of their birth for another destination, respondents expressed reasons based on general economic, educational, or familial considerations as well as specific dissatisfactions or misfortunes. Some responses included 2 or more of these 4 factors; "dissatisfaction" was implied in most responses in the other 3 categories. Economic reasons included finding work. Educational reasons primarily focused on a need to leave to continue formal education (for convenience, enlistment in military service was included in this category). Familial reasons were given mainly by persons who were taken from the reservation as dependent children when their parents emigrated. The "dissatisfaction and misfortune" category included a variety of responses perhaps best explained by examples:

Well, I'll tell you . . . I and the boss had it out over there in the mill . . . He tell me do what you want . . . I took my cant hook . . . found another job . . . there's nothing in there anyway . . . not a thing . . . drive everybody away, sell wood [for heating] too high . . .

. . . my father did farm work and I had no mother. Went to the Indian [boarding] school. He died while I was there . . . when I was 15.

Welfare people told mother to move into town or they were going to take us kids away . . . Old man drunk, wouldn't fix house.

In 1958 . . . broke legs . . . stayed at [North City] Hospital.

When asked why they eventually came to North City, respondents gave reasons centering around jobs, kin ties, education, and the city's intrinsic attraction. Most who were concerned about work had already obtained employment in North City before immigrating. The "kin ties" category includes those responses describing the primary immigration motive to be the presence of a kinsman already in the city. Educational responses indicated that relocation to the city was to facilitate obtaining education for self or chidren. Intrinsic attractiveness refers to responses that contrasted North City with other possible residential locations on the basis of cost of living, access to material comforts and services, geographical location, or climate. Some responses combined several of these factors: "Well, 'bout the first reason would be employment . . . 'bout the second would be they have a good school system . . . then, it's centrally located . . . not too far from her [wife's] folks [at Deer Lake], not too far from mine [on the Beaver Pelt Reservation]." This response, it should be noted, explicitly and clearly acknowledged one of the adaptive advantages that North City residence afforded reservation-exogamous couples.

Respondents' reasons for migration are listed in Table 7.6. The responses were sorted on the basis of what appeared to be the respondent's most important reason for migration. Only if 2 or more factors seemed to have equal weight in a response was it placed in the "combination of factors" category. An "other" category is included for responses such as "Just wanted to roam around . . . not unsatisfied though."

Only a small portion of the interviewees indicated that they came to North City to find employment. (In contrast, 47 percent of the respondents in the Minneapolis survey gave employment as their reason for going to the city [League of Women Voters 1968:6].) The most common responses attributed migration to North City to various kinds of intrinsic attractions. Conversely, a common reason for emigration was that of general dissatisfaction or specific misfortune in the home community. In several instances of reservation-to-city migration, the intrinsic attractiveness of the city was the alleviation of a misfortune in the home community; for example, in 2 cases of permanently crippling injuries, respondents felt they could be better treated in the North City hospital than on the reservation. These statements are indicative of the relative

Table 7.6. Explicit reasons for migration

Emigration from home reservation	Random sample	Others
Economic	8	3
Educational	3	5
Familial	8	2
Dissatisfaction and misfortune	6	7
Other	2	3
Total	27	20

Immigration to North City		
Occupational	5	5
Kin ties	6	1
Educational	2	2
Intrinsic attractiveness	9	9
Combination of factors	3	1
Other	2	2
Total	27	20

unimportance of North City as a place to which Indians migrated in the hope of economic betterment. Residence in North City appears to have represented to these Indians an attractive alternative to reservation life, but one which did not require disengagement from the home territory.

Summary

North City Indians are distinguished from reservation populations by the prevalence among them of reservation out-marriage. The city Indians are socially marginal to reservational societies; however, they are not necessarily disengaged or excluded from reservation society. Other factors, such as occupational histories, have contributed to their social marginality; they are also geographically marginal to their home reservations. Thus North City Indians, rather than being separated from reservation societies, might be more accurately described as being on the reservation societies' outer boundaries.

North City does not appear to exert any powerful pull on reservation Chippewa in search of a job. Interviewees' explicit reasons for migration support this contention. North City has other attractions which seem to appeal most to the socially marginal. The marginal status of North City Indians provides the basis for a conceptual linkage between reservation societies and the urban Indian population. While North City Chippewa might be only loosely integrated into the reservation societies from which they originate, they are still very much a part of the general social network of northern Minnesota Indians.

North City Indian households and wider social networks

Households are the largest social groups which may be clearly identified among North City Indians. There is no *community* of North City Indians—that is, no community in the sense of a group which has a self-conscious social identity and is recognized by nonmembers as a distinct entity. Nonetheless, Chippewa residing in North City incidentally provide important links in the wider social network of the northern Minnesota Indian community. This function is evidenced in the sometimes rapidly changing membership of some North City Indian households.

Changes in household composition may be illustrated by the following extreme case. Mrs. Fish, age 75, left the Deer Lake Reservation and rented one of a cluster of about 20 cabins (owned by a local white businessman) located south of the business district. Within a few weeks after her arrival in North City, she was left with 5 grandchildren to care for when her daughter, who had been living in James Lake, was hospitalized after a fight with her husband (who was a member of the Broken Reed Reservation). When Mrs. Fish's daughter was released from the hospital, she joined her mother in North City. Eventually the daughter and her husband were reconciled and together occupied Mrs. Fish's cabin, and the old lady moved to a smaller cabin next door. For several months this arrangement continued.

Among the cabins was that of Mr. LeJon, originally of the Beaver Pelt Reservation; his cabin was more spacious than most of the others. (For some time LeJon had had a young friend from Beaver Pelt staying with him.) When Mr. LeJon suddenly died, Mrs. Fish's daughter and family moved into his place. In the meantime, Mrs. Fish's friend, Mrs. Wing, moved from the Deer Lake Reservation and rented a cabin in the same area. Mrs. Fish left for the summer to stay with one of her sons in Washington state. When Mrs. Fish returned, she rented the cabin next door to Mrs. Wing. Within about 2 months Mrs. Fish's youngest son returned from Minneapolis in order to seek a job in the area, hunt deer, and collect wild rice. He brought with him his 3 children and his legal wife's sister, with whom he had established a consensual union. These relatives stayed with Mrs. Fish for several days, until the son found a suitable house to rent. Mrs. Fish was then left alone again.

Mrs. Fish's daughter eventually gave birth to her third child by her present mate (she had 4 children with her from a former marriage). The father was enrolled in a job training program, and the family was able to rent a larger and more substantial house several blocks away. At about the same time Mrs. Fish moved back to Deer Lake, after an 18-month absence during which she had played a key role in the establishment of at least 2 new Chippewa households in North City. Presumably, Mrs. Fish at last found solitude and the "time to do my beading."

The flow of Indian "traffic" through North City contributes to the complexity of North City Indian households, which may frequently acquire new members on a temporary basis because of the central location of the city to the reservations and its intermediary status between reservations and larger, more distant cities. The presence of Indian relatives and friends in North City serves an important "way station" function for both Chippewa living on reservations and those who have migrated beyond North City. This function is fulfilled at the minimal level by the overnight accommodations that North City Indian households may provide for reservation friends and relatives who come to North City. One incident serves to illustrate the phenomenon. At about 10:00 a.m. I called on a young North City Indian couple to conduct an interview in their 2-room apartment. The wife had arisen and prepared breakfast for her 2 small daughters. In the back bedroom the husband and his sister from the reservation were sleeping in a double bed; in the kitchen the husband's brother, who is a regular member of the household, and a cousin from the reservation were sleeping on a narrow bed. Apparently the wife and children had slept with the husband and his sister in the double bed during the previous night.

Overnight "visits" by reservation Indians are not always welcomed by North City Indians, particularly in the case of inebriated persons stranded in North City without money. An elderly man vividly described leaping from his bed one night to bolt the door of his small room to prevent a transient Indian from spending the night, commenting in general on the trouble one has with "sleepers" if he is not vigilant.

In addition to overnight visitors, North City Indian households may acquire relatively long-term, temporary members — for whom the way station metaphor is perhaps most appropriate, since they are usually in transition to or from one of the local reservations. A good example is Mr. LeJon's son, who had married a Deer Lake woman. The couple lived on the wife's reservation in a small cabin owned by her parents. There were occasional instances of friction between the man and his parents-in-law. When the wife was killed in an automobile accident, major hostilities erupted, and young LeJon was ultimately pressured by his late wife's parents into leaving the Deer Lake Reservation. Having nowhere else to go, he lived with his father in North City for several weeks before reestablishing himself on the Broken Reed Reservation, where he had lived prior to his marriage. Similarly, a Deer Lake man who had been working in the West returned to Minnesota after marital difficulties and stayed for two weeks with a North City Indian friend before reentry to his home reservation, Deer Lake.

Occasionally a North City Indian household may be a brief stopping-off point for reservation Indians who eventually migrate to larger cities. Four interviewees in the random sample reported that in the preceding year they had had friends or relatives living with them for periods of a week and a half to three months before moving on to Minneapolis or Chicago. Conversely, five respondents reported that people then residing on one of the reservations had spent a period staying in their household during the preceding year. For example, the elderly mother of a North City Indian man regularly lives with her son during the winter months and returns to the reservation during the spring and summer.

Even though the households of North City Chippewa do not constitute a community, each household is not a totally isolated Indian unit within the city. Through the interconnections of personal social networks, most of the Indian households of North City are linked to many other Chippewa in the city, as they are similarly tied to reservation and Twin Cities Indians and, in fact, to whites in North City and elsewhere (see Paredes 1973). Indeed, given the small size of North City, it is conceivable that each resident Indian could know and frequently interact with all the others. However, this is not the case. The majority of the Indians of North City cannot even provide an accurate estimate of the number of Indian households in the city. Territorial dispersion, the absence of voluntary associations, and "invisibility" are largely responsible for this situation.

Differences in reservation of origin may also tend to impose social barriers between North City Indians. Occasionally, informants who were asked to identify other Indians in the city would provide a name with the comment, "He's from another reservation." Asked to name all the North City Indians they knew, informants named primarily people originating from the same reservation as themselves. One informant originally from the Broken Reed Reservation stated that members of the Deer Lake Band are generally "conceited," and that if one of them asks him where he is

from, he evades possible friction by simply saying, "I live in North
City." Yet, several of his close friends and relatives in North City are
married to Deer Lake women. Indeed, the general North City Indian
characteristic of reservation exogamy necessitates considerable social
contact between North City Indians originating from different reservations, despite cleavages which may exist along those lines.

Finally, differences in socioeconomic status among North City
Indian families circumscribe social boundaries around various types of
households. For example, territorial separation between the affluent and
the poor is often — but not always — greater than that between Indians
of the same economic status.

Economic adaptation

So far the relation of North City Indians to certain generalized aspects of
their social environment has been explored. We will now examine the
differences among North City Indians in adapting to various specific
environmental components, beginning with economic adaptation—its
relationship to the relocation of Chippewa to North City and its range of
variation among North City Indian households. Levels of economic
adaptation will then be compared with adaptation to other environmental
elements.

Sources of income

Income and sources of income for the 27 random sample households are
presented in Table 7.7. Slightly less than half of the households receive
their annual income from regular employment of the household head,
spouse of head, or both. The majority of the others receive the bulk of
their income from public welfare payments.

State, federal, and local government agencies, institutions, and
programs are the major employment source for the North City Indian
work force. As already observed, much of North City's total work force
is employed by various public institutions. Among the 13 regularly
employed Indians represented in the random sample, 7 are employed by
some branch of government, one by the state and 6 by the Bureau of
Indian Affairs (BIA). An elderly man and his non-Indian wife, retired
"Indian Service" employees, are also included in the sample. The Indian
Division of the Public Health Service employs a number of North City
Indians, but none of them appears in the random sample. Other North
City Indian government employees not represented in the sample in-
clude an instructor at the vocational school, an elementary school

Table 7.7. Occupations and incomes of North City Indians
(random sample)

House-hold	Sex of house-hold head	Occupation of household head or primary source of income	Total annual income	Occupation of spouse
1	M	BIA[a] employee	$12,000	Secretary (BIA)
2	F	BIA employee	12,000	No spouse
3	M	BIA employee	10,000	Telephone operator[b]
4	M	State employee	9,000	Dental assistant
5	M	BIA employee	7,800	Housewife
6	M	Bricklayer	7,750	Housewife[b]
7	M	Retired, BIA (Social Security, Federal Retirement)	4,800	Retired (BIA)[b]
8	M	BIA employee	4,000	Housewife[b]
9	M	Title V trainee	4,000	Housewife
10	F	Welfare (ADC)[c]	3,204	No spouse
11	M	Veteran's pension	3,000	Nurses' aide[b]
12	M	Welder[b]	2,880	Housewife
13	F	Welfare (ADC)	2,844	No spouse
14	M	Forest worker	2,000	Welfare (ADC)
15	M	Painter[b]	2,000	Housewife
16	M	Lumberyard worker	2,000	Housewife
17	M	Title V trainee	1,548	Housewife
18	F	Welfare (ADC)	1,488	No spouse
19	F	Social Security and welfare (OAA)	1,080	No spouse
20	F	Insurance claim and welfare (OAA)	1,000	No spouse
21	M	Welfare (OAA)	912	No spouse
22	M	Welfare (OAA)	912	No spouse
23	M	Social Security and welfare (OAA)	800	Housewife
24	M	Welfare (OAA)	650	No spouse
25	F	Social Security and welfare (OAA)	NR[e]	No spouse
26	F	Welfare (ADC)	NR	No spouse
27	F	Social Security and veteran's benefits	NR	No spouse

a. Bureau of Indian Affairs.   d. Old Age Assistance
b. Not of Indian ancestry.   e. Not reported.
c. Aid to Dependent Children.

teacher, 2 women who work in food service at North City State College, a city clerk, a retired school janitor, and several additional BIA employees.

Not all Indians who work for government agencies and programs in North City reside there; a few live in James Lake and commute daily to their jobs in the city. Conversely, some North City Indians who are employed by agencies with headquarters in the city do most of their work on reservations. For example, an urban Indian who is employed by the State Employment Service is assigned to the Deer Lake Reservation, to which he commutes daily by automobile.

Following the enactment of the Economic Opportunity Act of 1964, a Title V job retraining program was established in North City. Participation in this program is regarded as employment by most of the participants and for purposes of this study. Some of them attend classes that are designed to help them qualify for a high school equivalency certificate. Others receive on-the-job training; North City training sites include the city hall, the county courthouse, the county agent's office, the public library, and the state college. A number of North City Indians are enrolled. At least 2 Indians who had originally come to North City to attend high school equivalency classes were subsequently transferred to training sites on the Broken Reed Reservation, but they continued to reside in North City. Several urban Indian enrollees in the Title V program had lived in North City prior to participation in the program. Many of the female participants in the program formerly received public welfare.

Some relatively long-term Indian residents of North City moved away from the city after completing the training. For example, one 28-year-old man had periodically lived in North City with or near his parents since 1959. He had had a series of unskilled and semiskilled jobs and from time to time had received welfare benefits for his own family. His experience in the Title V program provided him with a high school equivalency certificate and the desire to pursue further study at North City State College. Because of his age and the size of his family (6 dependents) he was unsuccessful in obtaining the financial support necessary for becoming a student. He declined to accept BIA's plan to train him in Minneapolis as an X-ray technician; after some difficulties he finally obtained a paraprofessional post with the legal aid program in James Lake. For a while he commuted to James Lake, eventually moving to James Lake, which was near his original reservation home, Mission.

Only a small number of North City Indians are regularly employed in the private sector, primarily because North City has no major industry that needs many unskilled and semiskilled workers. Additionally, the jobs for which most male Indians are usually best suited from experience, such as logging and manual labor, are more accessible in reservation areas. Finally, Indians are usually unsuccessful in competing with whites for North City's available jobs. Since long-term white residents of North City have greater geographical and informational access to job openings in North City than do Indians living on reservations, Indians usually move to North City only after they have secured a position there.

Contributing to the Indian's difficulty in finding employment in North City is the white stereotype of the "typical" Indian: that he or she is unreliable, lazy, and likely to miss work and quit without notice. Although some Indians exhibit such behavior often enough to reinforce the stereotype, some whites patronize Indians (for example, by lending them money that they can't pay back), again reinforcing the stereotype. A similar pattern of "reciprocal exploitation" has been noted for the Cree by Braroe (1965).

Many Indians suspect that they are discriminated against by whites. According to a North City woman who migrated from the Broken Reed Reservation, "Before I came to [North City] I didn't know whether to move here or not. It seemed like they [whites] disliked the Indians." She said that she wished some of the local whites would spend some time in the South to become acquainted with the volatile racial situation there: "Let 'em have a taste of that and maybe they'd think different." On one occasion, she continued, her cousin's Caucasian-looking daughter, who worked at the now defunct shirt factory in North City, had suggested that she and her cousin, the girl's mother, apply for work at the factory. When the 2 women did so, "they just took one look at us and said, 'We don't need no help.' So we just left. [The cousin's daughter] said that it was a lie. They were crying for help. But we couldn't go back down there."

A North City woman married to a white also pondered the question: "I wonder, if I really wanted to work some place, [whether] they'd hire me. That question always comes to mind . . . you wonder, if they didn't hire you, [whether] it was because you were Indian or [because you] didn't come up to the job." Similarly, a North City man suspected that his supervisor at work was prejudiced against Indians, since "the boss" would not promote him after many years of service.

At meetings of the local Human Relations Commission, initially established to resolve a conflict between North City leaders and reservation leaders, an often-discussed issue was job discrimination against Indians in North City and in other nearby white communities. During one meeting the manager of the North City telephone company stated that he had always been willing to hire Indians but that none had ever applied. To this the superintendent of the Deer Lake Reservation, an Indian from Wisconsin, replied that Indians characteristically were uncertain as to how hard they were going to have to push in order to get in. Consequently, he said, employers had an obligation to let Indians know they are welcome to apply. The Chippewa present at the meeting enthusiastically agreed. At the same meeting, representatives of the North City State Employment Office proudly reported on their new policy of hiring Indians as employment counselors on local Indian reservations to ensure equal access to new job openings. Because of the efforts of the Human Relations Commission and the new employment policy, it was hoped that more Indians would be seeking employment in the private businesses of North City, and that both Indians and whites would become more aware of the relative lack of Indian employees in North City businesses.

Some Indians are employed in North City's private businesses in spite of the difficulties in obtaining such jobs. One 23-year resident moved to North City with his white wife and their children from Mission. Before relocating, he had worked as a telephone cable splicer in a number of places, including James Lake. After coming to North City, he worked for a few years in a local hardware store. Later he acquired his present job at the telephone company, a job that requires him to spend much of the year in southern Minnesota and northern Iowa. An Indian woman who has lived in North City since childhood because her mother did not want her children to grow up in a reservation environment is a respected employee of a local dress shop. A Beaver Pelt Reservation man married to a white woman works for a local construction firm. After being trained as a bricklayer in a Bureau of Indian Affairs boarding school, he worked in Denver, Colorado, and other parts of the country briefly before settling in North City. His frequent work out of town is usually within commuting distance.

Aside from these people, most other North City Indians employed in private enterprise work primarily as common laborers. A few are truck drivers. One man, who drives semitrailers between Port City and the West, is particularly successful; but even he experiences occasional periods of unemployment during the slack seasons.

A few nonworking Indians in the city derive their income from social security and/or veteran's benefits.

Many households receive some form of public welfare payments; 40.7 percent of the households in the random sample were recipients of welfare at the time of interviewing. Aid to Dependent Children (ADC), Old Age Assistance (OAA), and occasional, short-term "general relief" payments account for most of the public welfare assistance received by North City Indians.

Dependence on public welfare is indirectly responsible for the migration of some Indians to North City, especially those residing on the Deer Lake Reservation or in the western portion of the Broken Reed Reservation (both areas are within the jurisdiction of the Cramton County Welfare Department). For example, the adult daughter of a Mission female migrant to North City stated, "Our house [at Mission] wasn't good . . . welfare people told mother to move into town or they were going to take us kids away." The mother added that her "old man" was a drunk and wouldn't fix the house. Similarly, a young welfare mother and her mother moved to North City after their house burned down—a move encouraged by the welfare agent, who saw the move as therapeutic for the young woman's social and psychological problems.

An elderly man from the Broken Reed Reservation who had lived with his wife on the Deer Lake Reservation decided to move when his wife began to spend most of the year living with their children in Chicago. He selected North City as his new residence partly because of increased welfare payments: "I [asked] about welfare . . . if I get a raise if I live here. They said yeah. Otherwise, I go to Trotter, I get nothing. I got a house there." This man also illustrates the shrewd thrift with which elderly welfare recipients manage their small income. When the Welfare Department encouraged him to participate in a food stamp program rather than receive his monthly allowance of $87 in cash, he refused, explaining that if he did so, he would be restricted to the store that accepted the stamps and therefore could not use them for such money-saving devices as buying stale bread. Another elderly man purchases only one issue of the local newspaper each week—the one with the weekly grocery sales advertisements. This man keeps all of his money in a cigar box, returning even small change to the box in order to avoid spending carelessly and lending money to his acquaintances.

North City Indians augment their incomes through a variety of minor economic activities. Some of the women interviewed earned extra money by making and selling craft items, such as braided rugs, blankets, and beadwork. On one occasion I interrupted Mrs. Fish as she was scraping deer hide for buckskin. She was working indoors in her small cabin in North City. One end of a basswood log was resting on her thigh;

the other end was wedged under a chest of drawers; the hide was spread over the log as she scraped away hair and fat with a large butcher knife. Other women did occasional babysitting in return for cash, goods, or services. One retired man made and sold wooden birdhouses. An elderly man earned extra cash by singing for powwows at Deer Lake and in Chicago when he visits his children. A man in his eighties worked part-time as an agricultural laborer on nearby potato farms. A few households received additional income through labor of their younger members; for example, teenage girls in 2 households have worked as part-time waitresses at small North City cafes.

The middle-aged son of one of the elderly women living in North City did a variety of things to augment his meager welfare income. In his early 50s and crippled by polio since childhood, he resided (when he was in the city) with his mother in a low-rent apartment house. In addition to performing small repairs on clothes and electrical appliances and cutting hair for other tenants, he made and sold craft items, having worked at one time in a shop near James Lake that produced miniature totem poles and other souvenirs.

Five of the households in the random sample received cash income from collecting wild rice during the season that immediately preceded interviewing, earning $50 to $300 for the season. Four respondents in the random sample reported that they had earned some money from wild rice collection since migrating to North City, but not during the immediately preceding season. In both the random and the nonrandom sample, only 2 individuals stated that they had kept wild rice from the preceeding season for their own use. Although most North City Indians go to reservation areas to collect wild rice, 3 men reported that they had collected rice from a small bed in Lake Izzy, which bounds the city to the Southwest. One of these men said that his trip to Lake Izzy was the only time he had gathered rice. Another said that he wanted to show his young sons how to gather rice; he collected approximately 20 pounds in one day and kept all of it. At the time of the initial interview the rice was still "green" (unprocessed), since neither he nor his wife had yet removed the chaff.

Annual incomes and material style of life

The annual incomes of North City Indian households varied from $650 to $12,000. Those with the lowest incomes were single elderly welfare recipients; those with the highest were couples in which both husband and wife were fully employed (see Table 7.7). In the random sample, median annual household income was $2,862. North City Indians as a whole were more prosperous than Indians in James Lake and Rice Village (which had median annual household incomes of $1,950 and $1,584 respectively) but not as affluent as Wicket Indians, whose higher median income of $3,500 is attributable to the high rate of employment, especially in mining, of Wicket men.

The North City Indian median annual income was well below that of the city as a whole ($4,703). About half the city's Indian households had to survive on meager incomes from public welfare.

Although cash is the primary consideration in economic adaptation, budgeting, buying patterns, perceived utility of specific goods, and available housing also affect adaptation to American material culture. Interviewees were asked about the possession or presence in their households of certain material items. By using the Guttman scaling technique, households were systematically ranked in terms of standard of living and items were ranked to indicate regularities in the acquisition of material goods.

Kay (1964) applied the Guttman technique to Tahitian consumer behavior. He emphasizes that the technique reveals regularities in behavior (acquisition of certain goods) and that "objects" (households) may be ranked into a series of types with reference to the behavior, but that the scalability of a body of data is not a "theory" explaining the regularities. He suggests that his data may be explained by a combination of 2 major factors, cost and utility, but that "scale errors" (deviations from the ideal model) may be produced by unique circumstances in some Tahitian households. The following data on North City Indian consumer goods were treated in essentially the same manner.

Table 7.8 presents a Guttman scale based on the presence or absence of 15 material items among the 26 households in the random sample. The scale measures an aspect of economic adaptation that may be referred to as "material style of life" (Schensul 1965). A number of items were eliminated from the scale either because they had an identical frequency distribution and thus did not discriminate a separate scale type or because there were too many errors in the items. The second reason appears inadmissible; but since this scale was not constructed to test a specific hypothesis, all items did not have to be included (Goodenough 1963b:240–41). Arguments for the legitimacy of similar procedures have been advanced by Carneiro (1962:161–62). The items that did not "scale" are probably confounded by variables other than those that produce the regularities in the scalable items. What is most important for

Table 7.8. Scalogram of material style of life of North City Indians (random sample)

Household	Scale type	A	B	C	D	E	F	G	H	I	J	K	L	M	N	O
4	16	x	x	x	x	x	x	x	x	x	x	x	x	x	x	x
12	16	x	x	x	x	x	x	x	x	x	x	x	x	x	x	x
1	15		x	o	x	x	x	x	x	x	x	x	x	x	x	x
2	15		x	x	x	x	x	x	x	x	x	x	x	x	x	x
7	15		x	x	x	x	x	x	x	x	x	x	x	x	x	x
6	14			x	x	x	x	x	x	x	x	x	x	x	x	x
5	13				x	x	x	x	x	x	x	x	x	x	x	x
8	13				x	x	x	x	x	x	x	x	x	x	x	x
3	12					x	o	x	x	x	x	x	x	x	x	x
18	12					x	o	x	x	x	x	x	x	x	x	x
20	11						x	x	x	x	x	x	x	x	x	x
11	10							x	x	x	x	x	x	x	x	x
25	9								x	o	x	x	x	x	x	x
26	8									x	o	x	x	x	x	x
10	7						(x)				x	o	x	x	x	x
22	7										x	o	x	x	x	x
14	6								(x)			x	x	x	x	x
19	6											x	x	x	x	x
9	5												x	x	x	x
15	5												x	x	x	x
17	5												x	x	x	x
13	4													x	x	x
21	3													x	o	x
16	2														x	o
23	1										(x)					
24	1											(x)	(x)			

Key to scale items

A. More than one bathroom
B. Automatic clothes washer
C. Food freezer
D. Power lawn mower
E. Life insurance
F. Automobile, 1960 or newer
G. Clothes washer, any type
H. Bathtub or shower
I. Telephone
J. Hot running water
K. Indoor toilet (excluding communal toilet in apartment building)
L. Running water
M. Range
N. Radio
O. Refrigerator

Coefficient of reproducibility = .96

purposes of this study is that the scale produces a systematic typological ranking of the households along a single dimension. No assumptions are made about individual values or aspirations in reference to material goods, nor is it assumed that position on the scale is the result of the operation of a single variable. Rather, scale types provide a measure of the extent to which households have completed the myriad necessary activities and conditions antecedent to the acquisition of each item.

Households are assigned the same number in Table 7.8 as in Table 7.7. By comparing the positions of households on the 2 tables one can see that cash income and possession of material goods are generally related but not identical. Owning a house, as opposed to renting, closely corresponds to the higher types on the material style of life scale.

Other researchers in northern Minnesota have constructed similar "material style of life" scales for other populations. Pelto (in this volume) has done so for a random sample of whites and Indians in James Lake, and Schachter (1967) has done so for North City whites. The Schachter scale is based on 2 random samples of whites, one from a lower-class neighborhood and one from an upper-middle-class neighborhood; thus an approximation of the total range of variation in material style of life among North City whites is covered. Since information about the items in the Pelto and Schachter scales was also obtained from North City Indians, one can determine if the city Indians will "fit" into either or both of these scales. In fact, the North City Indians' possession of material goods is scalable with acceptable coefficients of reproducibility on both scales.

Pelto has found that James Lake whites tend to be higher types on her scale than are James Lake Indians. When North City Indians are compared to James Lake Indians on this same scale, there is a significant tendency ($p < .02$) for the city Indians to cluster in the top half of the scale as do James Lake whites; James Lake Indians, contrarily, tend to be in the bottom half of the scale. When North City Indians are placed on the North City whites scale, Indian households tend to be in the bottom half of the scale, though not at an acceptable level of significance ($p < .20$). These findings are evidence that North City Indians as a whole have a material style of life much like that of whites in a racially mixed reservation town, which is in turn higher than that of Indians in the same community. However, available evidence, including median incomes, suggests that North City Indians are in about the same position relative to North City whites as James Lake Indians are to James Lake whites.

This situation is similar to the one described by Grindstaff (1968) among southern Negroes. Grindstaff has demonstrated that although Negroes in certain southern cities experience absolute gains over rural Negroes in education, income, and occupation, urban Negroes are further below urban whites in these measures than rural Negroes are below rural whites. Thus, while North City Indians may have an economic adaptive advantage over Indians in at least one reservation community, as a total population their position relative to the whites in their own community is probably not much different.

Traditional economic activities

Chippewa residents of North City engage in a number of traditional activities of economic significance. Most rice collection is for cash return, although some North City Indians "go ricing" primarily as a recreational activity. Other traditional Chippewa economic activities pursued by North City Indians are hunting, fishing, and wild berry collecting, activities that provide families with a dietary supplement. For some families, the wild foods supply little more than occasional variety in the menu; for other families, however, several pounds of fish, a whole deer, several game birds, and 2 or more gallons of berries are a sizable supplement to their food needs.

On the whole, interviewees appeared reluctant to discuss at length the amount of game they had taken, probably because of their awareness of strict game laws. One Beaver Pelt migrant reported having brought in a total of 9 deer during the year, explaining that on his wife's reservation, Deer Lake, he could hunt in both summer and winter; apparently he was oblivious to the illegality of bringing game off the reservation. A recent migrant from the Broken Reed Reservation responded to the question "How often do you go hunting?" with the statement "Whenever I need meat on the table."

Extensive taking of game was not an activity of low-income families only. One of the most affluent families in the sample reported having taken and consumed 2 deer, 7 pheasant, and large amounts of fresh fish the previous year. Recalling his childhood on the Deer Lake Reservation, the head of the family described his father's attitude toward hunting: "It got too much like work. After a while, my father would say, 'We've got to kill at least 12 deer this fall so we have enough for winter, and we're going to start hunting now.' And he'd take 2, 3 weeks off from work, and we would hunt every day until we got the quota—till we got what was set out."

A few individuals and families derive small amounts of cash from the sale of wild berries. Berries are collected primarily as an excuse for an outing or to provide an occasional treat in the form of pies or sauce. Much of the interviewees' berry collecting was done close to the city and much less frequently on reservations than were hunting, fishing, and wild rice collecting.

Indians who migrate to North City from the nearby reservations continue to hunt, fish, and collect wild foods in their former home areas. These activities are much more accessible for Indians in North City than for those in larger and more distant cities and can thus be pursued without loss of time from jobs and with only small costs of time and money for travel. Even those who do not or cannot hunt or fish often receive gifts of game and fish from friends and relatives.

Interaction with national, state, and city systems

Data on North City Indians may be analyzed to demonstrate inferentially the significance to them of national, state, and city sociocultural systems and the extent of their participation in these components of their environment.

National and state systems

The Indians of North City have, in general, been surprisingly mobile. Interviewees were asked to identify all the communities in which they had resided. Including the original reservation, North City, and boarding schools, and excluding military assignments, the mean number of places of residence was 5.5. Each interviewee was coded for the most distant city in which he had lived; the distribution for the random sample is displayed in Table 7.9. A number of those who had lived in the more distant metropolitan areas had also lived in the Twin Cities or Chicago. Half of the respondents had resided in a metropolitan area at least as far away as Port City, Minnesota, or Fargo, North Dakota. Some respondents had resided in a metropolitan area for only a year or two; others had spent nearly half of their lives in one or more metropolitan areas. Apparently North City is not simply an initial off-reservation residence for Chippewa who eventually migrate to larger, more distant cities; for about half the resident Indian population, North City is a return point from more distant urban areas.

Even though approximately half of the sample respondents had never resided in a metropolitan area, only one, a middle-aged woman,

Table 7.9. Previous places of residence of North City
Indians (random sample)

Has lived in the Twin Cities	3
Has lived in other Minnesota-Dakota metropolitan area	1
Has lived in other metropolitan area of Midwest	2
Has lived in metropolitan area of Far West	7
Has lived in other metropolitan areas	1
Has never lived in metropolitan area	13
Total	27

moved directly to North City from her natal reservation without prior
residence in other communities. Two men who migrated directly from a
reservation to North City had served abroad in the military. One of these
men originally came to North City to attend the state college; after
establishing residence in the city, he served 4 years in the Navy. The
other joined the service while living on the reservation and returned to
the reservation after completing his tour of duty. He moved to North City
several years later after being hospitalized there following a severe
automobile accident; he married a white employee of the hospital. Two
women came to North City when very young—one with her mother and
the other with her adult sister; later, both married whites and lived in a
variety of places outside the state, ultimately returning to North City.
One of these women attended an Indian boarding school in Wisconsin
for 3 years prior to her relocation to North City. Another woman had
moved when she was 8 years old from her original reservation, Beaver
Pelt, to the Broken Reed Reservation, from which she migrated directly
to North City as an adult. Two elderly men from Deer Lake Reservation
and one middle-aged woman had had only minimal off-reservation
residential experience before relocating to North City.

The small number of persons migrating directly from their reservation to North City is more evidence that North City is not primarily a first
destination of reservation Chippewa who eventually migrate to more
distant cities. Although some Chippewa move to cities such as Minneapolis after an initial period in North City, many more migrate to
Minneapolis, Chicago, or Los Angeles directly from reservations.

Eleven individuals in the sample had never resided outside the region surrounding North City. All but 2 of the respondents who had never resided in a metropolitan area had also never lived outside the North City region. Nevertheless, the majority of North City Indian adults had had at least minimal experience as members of communities other than their home community, preceding migration to North City. However, slightly over half of the respondents who had lived away from their natal reservation (including prior periods of residence in North City) had returned to one of the 3 Chippewa reservations in the vicinity before finally moving to North City.

Many North City Indian men have had the opportunity to view the national system as military servicemen. Nine of the 16 male respondents had been in the military. Six of these respondents were among the interviewees who had never resided in a metropolitan area; however, their military experience may be taken as a kind of functional equivalent to metropolitan residence.

Indians of North City make brief trips to larger cities. Respondents were asked to state the frequency of trips to Minneapolis–St. Paul. The Twin Cities area was chosen for 3 reasons: it is the state's largest urban area, it can be reached by automobile in less than 5 hours, and it has the largest Indian population of any nearby metropolis. Respondents' answers were coded for frequency spans, producing the distribution shown in Table 7.10.

Table 7.10. Frequency of visits by North City Indians to Twin Cities (random sample)

More than once per year	7
Once per year	12
Once every 2 or 3 years	5
Less than once every 3 years	3
Total	27

Even though some individuals had never resided in a metropolitan area, most visited the Twin Cities at least once every 3 years. (Only 2 of the 13 who had never lived in a metropolitan area visited there less frequently.) Typically, the visiting Indians stay for a period of a few days to a week, although some stay for a month or more. They usually spend their time visiting relatives and shopping, occasionally attending a professional baseball game, and, in the case of government employees, handling business affairs. Because many Minnesota Indians have migrated to Minneapolis–St. Paul, North City Indians frequently have relatives there who can accommodate them with food and lodging.

North City Chippewa have relatives in a variety of American cities and towns. The adults in the random sample had a total of 70 children not living in the household. All the interviewees together had a total of 110 living siblings (2 of the respondents were full siblings, so their siblings were only counted once). These children and siblings are widely scattered over the United States. Table 7.11 presents data on the location of siblings and children not living in North City households.

In general, North City Indians' visits to kinsmen living beyond the range of Chicago are infrequent. However, the geographically more distant relatives return to northern Minnesota for visits somewhat more often. In addition, the Chippewa of North City exchange letters and telephone calls with their children and siblings living in distant places. North City Indians also maintain fairly regular communication with other types of consanguineal relatives and with affines living far away.

Using the data in Table 7.11, generalizations can be made about the geographic locations of North City Indians' siblings and adult children. First, most of the adult children of North City Indians did not live on reservations; after having relocated to North City with their parents, many children migrated still further when they reached maturity. (Five of the 10 North City children in the sample, as shown in Table 7.11, are minor children in foster homes.) Not all the children had resided in North City; some had migrated directly from reservations to more distant

Table 7.11. Location of North City Indians' siblings
and children not living in household
(random sample)

	Children	*Siblings*
1. North City	10	10
2. Home reservation of either interviewee or spouse	10	33
3. Minneapolis–St. Paul	18	23
4. Other Minnesota areas	6	8
5. Chicago	7	2
6. Other metropolitan areas of Midwest and Far West	10	18
7. In military service	2	3
8. Other areas	7	13
Total	70	110

communities. Second, Table 7.11 shows that the North City Indians were not unique among their siblings in having moved away from the reservation: less than a third of the total population of siblings resided on the home reservations. Nearly twice as many siblings had migrated beyond North City as had remained on the reservations. Only 3 of the city Indians had all of their siblings residing on reservations. Although North City Indians' parents, many of whom were deceased, were excluded from this analysis, the data on kinsmen presented in Table 7.11 provide a contrast to Ablon's information for San Francisco Indians, which indicates that the "majority" of Bay Area Indians' close relatives live on reservations (1964:297).

Although only a few North City Indians, by virtue of their occupational roles (e.g., BIA employee), receive specialized information concerning state and national systems, all of them are exposed to the cultural influences of mass media. Within the random sample, 74 percent of the households had television sets, and 88 percent had at least one radio. In at least one kin-linked set of 3 households, only one had a television set, but individuals in all 3 households frequently used it. Interviewees' preferences in television programming tended toward game shows, westerns, variety programs, and sports.

Interviewees were asked about their attendance at motion pictures and their utilization of reading material. The responses to these inquiries were found to be amenable to Guttman scaling.

Table 7.12 ranks North City Indians according to their exposure to print and film media; respondents were assigned the same numbers as in Table 7.7. They were most familiar with the local newspaper, published daily except Sunday. It emphasizes stories of local interest but also carries national and state news from the wire services and syndicated columns and features. Morning, evening, and Sunday newspapers from Minneapolis–St. Paul and Port City and a variety of magazines were also utilized by respondents, and some attended North City's one indoor movie theater and 2 drive-ins, which show films within a year or so of their release. In constructing the scale in Table 7.12, "regularly" was liberally interpreted to include such responses as "once a week" and "as often as I can." Magazines and newspapers that were "read regularly" but were not subscribed to were either purchased by single issue or received as gifts from subscribing friends and neighbors, who pass on newspapers and magazines once they have finished reading them.

It is difficult to determine what variables might be responsible for the results of the mass media scalogram. Income, reading ability,

Table 7.12. Scalogram of North City Indians' exposure to mass media
(random sample)

Inter-viewee	Scale type	A	B	C	D	E	F	G	H	I
2	10	x	x	o	x	x	x	x	x	x
7	10	x	x	x	x	x	x	x	x	x
12	10	x	x	o	x	x	o	x	x	x
3	9		x	x	x	x	x	x	x	x
5	9		x	x	x	x	x	x	x	x
1	8			x	x	o	x	x	x	x
4	8			x	o	x	x	x	x	o
6	8			x	x	x	x	x	x	x
8	8			x	x	x	x	x	x	x
20	8			x	x	o	x	x	x	o
9	7				x	x	x	x	o	x
13	6					x	o	x	x	x
14	6	(x)	(x)			x	o	x	x	o
11	5						x	x	x	x
15	5						x	x	o	x
18	5						x	x	x	x
19	5						x	x	x	o
25	4							x	x	x
10	3				(x)				x	x
24	3								x	x
17	2					(x)				x
21	2									x
16	1									
22	1									
23	1							(x)		
26	1									

Key to scale items

A. Goes to movies more than 3 times per year
B. Goes to movies more than once per year
C. Subscribes to more than one magazine
D. Subscribes to local newspaper
E. Goes to movies at least once per year
F. Reads more than one magazine regularly
G. Reads at least one magazine regularly
H. Reads a metropolitan newspaper regularly
I. Reads local newspaper regularly

Coefficient of reproducibility = .92

recreational interests, interethnic relations, public awareness, and the diligence of neighborhood newsboys probably all play a part. Whatever the variables that produced the scale, it may be taken as one measure of North City Indians' informational articulation to city, state, and national systems.

City involvement

North City Indians conduct most of their economic transactions within the city, although not all their buying is done within North City. Some purchase children's clothing by mail order from companies such as Montgomery Ward. Eleven out of 27 interviewees in the random sample bought automobiles outside North City, and 2 interviewees reported purchasing furniture and appliances outside the city. Most nonlocal purchases are made in the Twin Cities, in racially mixed reservation towns, and in predominantly white towns in the vicinity. Comments from informants indicated that "finding the best deal" and personal ties to sellers largely account for these divergencies in buying patterns.

Noneconomic forms of participation in city life were scaled using the Guttman technique, as shown in Table 7.13. Because of the variety of items, individuals' positions would probably not be altered on related city-involvement scales. Some of the items are derived from open-ended questions rather than yes-no questions. Levels of adaptation to the city may be operationally defined as the behaviors characterizing each scale type (see Paredes 1971).

The variation among North City Indians ranges from those who did

Table 7.13. Scalogram of North City Indians' city involvement (random sample)

Inter-viewee	Scale type	A	B	C	D	E	F	G	Key to scale items
3	8	x	x	o	o	x	x	x	A. Belongs to more than one voluntary association in the city
4	8	x	x	o	x	x	o	x	
8	8	x	x	x	x	x	x	x	B. Belongs to one voluntary association in the city
1	7		x	x	x	x	x	x	C. Has voted in a city election
6	7		x	o	x	o	x	x	D. Attends or has attended school activities (e.g., PTA, ball games)
7	7		x	x	o	x	x	x	
2	6			x	x	x	x	x	E. Has current voter registration in the city
5	6			x	x	x	x	x	
13	6			x	x	x	x	x	F. Considers self to be a member of some church in the city
15	6			x	x	x	x	x	
18	6			x	x	x	x	x	G. Seeks medical service in the city
19	6			x	o	x	x	x	
25	6			x	x	o	x	x	
14	5				x	x	o	x	
11	4					x	x	x	
12	3						x	x	
16	3						x	x	
24	3						x	x	
9	2							x	
10	2							x	
17	2							x	
20	2							x	
26	2							x	
21	1		(x)						
22	1								
23	1								

Coefficient of reproducibility = .94

not utilize even medical services in the city to those who had multiple memberships in the city's white-dominated voluntary associations. Although Indians were technically ineligible for Public Health Service treatment after one year of off-reservation residence, some North City Chippewa stated that they returned to their reservation when they needed medical attention. However, more than half of those in the random sample stated that they utilized the services of a North City physician. Similarly, the majority of the interviewees were at least nominal members of a North City church; however, some considered their church membership still to be on their home reservation.

The city involvement scale represents a pivotal departure from the way in which other researchers have dealt with adaptation to the city. Most studies of American Indian urbanization maintain or imply that the city is an alien, stressful environment for the newcomer. Adaptation to the city is then seen as a process of "adjustment" or "accommodation," and judgments are made about the relative success of individual adjustments. Consequently, such studies are concerned with the psychological orientations and reactions of urban in-migrants and less interested in describing their simple behavioral differences. The method used in this study provides a solid, empirical basis for rigorous specification of relationships between urban adaptation and other dimensions of the adaptation of individuals to the *total* environment.

"Indian culture"

Individual Chippewa of North City have, in their cultural repertoire, standards for behavior that can loosely be labeled "Indian." Indeed, "Indian culture" may dominate a person's self-image and tend to obliterate awareness of other equally important conceptions that are frequently employed as "operating cultures." For example, in the course of a year North City Indians will make purchases in shops, fulfill duties as employees (or deal with public welfare personnel), travel to Minneapolis, observe national holidays, watch children take part in school activities, attend a city church, and engage in other activities that require conceptions about expected behavior. It is difficult to see how these kinds of perceived expectations could be construed as distinctly "Indian." As a matter of fact, whether they perceive it or not, most North City Indians' behavior is guided by conceptions that have little relationship to traditional Chippewa culture.

Although to Indians and whites alike such routine activities as buying groceries or playing bingo at the VFW (Veterans of Foreign

Wars) hall are not ordinarily thought of as being "culture," certain other activities and behaviors are explicitly conceptualized as "Indian culture." For both Indians and non-Indians, this term represents a set of beliefs and behaviors that are peculiar to persons of American Indian descent. Belief in traditional Chippewa myths and supernatural cures and the manufacture of certain artifacts are readily identified as elements of Indian culture by both Indians and whites; however, in matters that involve attitudes and values, there is much less agreement about what is a cultural attribute and what is a flaw in character, behavior, or mentality. On the whole, whites ascribe less of an Indian's behavior to his or her "Indian culture" than do other Indians. Whereas a white might perceive an elderly Chippewa woman's drab clothing as slovenliness, the Indian woman might say, "I've never fixed myself up to look like white people."

A fairly common attitude of northern Minnesota whites toward modern Indians is that they are "cultureless," unlike the colorful Indians of 50 or 60 years ago, who displayed many overt traits of traditional culture (cf. James 1961:731). A recent modification of the more obvious "Indians have no culture" view is the notion of "cultural deprivation," a concept particularly popular with teachers and social workers; perhaps, as the Waxes (1964) have argued, it provides them with an acceptable rationalization for failing to effect the cultural changes with which they are charged.

Indians have their own conceptions of Indians in general and of how one should behave toward them. Such conceptions are derived from intensive interaction with other Indians since birth instead of interaction in specialized and restricted contexts, as in the case of most whites. For many whites face-to-face interaction with Indians is almost nonexistent; their conceptions are derived from conversational routines with whites about Indians rather from extended interaction with Indians. The Indian who successfully functions in the "white world" is usually regarded by whites as an exception, but the Indian ancestry of such an individual is still a crucial element in whites' perceptions of him or her—if for no other reason than contrast with other Indians.

Indians execute thousands of behaviors—waiting for the traffic light to change, selecting a pair of shoes, reading the newspaper, asking for a particular brand-name product—that imply detailed knowledge of non-Indian culture and exemplify the identical cultures of Indians and whites *in certain situations*. The cultural differences between Indians and whites are based on the extent to which they meet the criteria for acceptance into their respective communities and social groups, and the degree to which they manifest appropriate behavior in different contexts. Thus, in North City, Indians and whites share a number of similar cultures associated with a variety of groups, including voluntary associations, church congregations, places of employment, North City citizens, and United States citizens. Other subcultures cannot be shared by Indians and whites, such as those associated with childhood friendship groups in their respective home towns. In transitory groups to which both may be admitted, such as the audience at a PTA meeting or the audience at a reservation powwow, Indians and whites frequently exhibit differential performances of roles. These differences are the consequences of the extent to which conceptions about performance are well formed and rehearsed and match the conceptions of the majority of others in the situation (whites in the case of the PTA, Indians in the case of the powwow).

The term "Indian" rather than "Chippewa" has been used advisedly. Among local whites the term "Chippewa" is seldom employed except in formal politico-legal contexts or to contrast Chippewa with members of other tribal groups. If a finer distinction is necessary, one refers to the person's home reservation: "He's a Deer Lake Indian." The Indians themselves employ terminology that is much the same: "My mother talks Indian real good" or "They had an Indian wake when the old man died." Local Indians also use "Chippewa" for precise political identification, such as when they boast good-naturedly about how their ancestors "beat the hell out of the Sioux" and drove them from Minnesota.

Chippewa speakers have a variety of racial and ethnic identification terms that they use in their own language and interject into English conversations. Caucasians are known as *chimúkama*, which some speakers delight in informing their listener means "big knife" but cannot be analyzed as such in their Chippewa vocabulary. (Characters used in spelling native terms have approximately the same phonetic value as in English words, with the following specifications: *ch* is pronounced as in "*ch*urch"; *sh* as in "*sh*oe"; *zh* as in "gara*ge*"; *a* in an unstressed syllable represents a shwa; *i* in an unstressed syllable represents *ɨ*.) Negroes are referred to as *makadéwias* (variously translated as "black meat" or "tar paper"). Chippewa also have terms for various American Indian tribes. One of the most commonly heard terms is *pwan* ("Sioux"). An added *-ish* makes any of the terms mean "embodying all the negative qualities of the group." This form is sometimes used to tease those who have some familiarity with the language, for example, by calling them *chimukamánish*.

In referring to themselves, some Chippewa speakers use the word *ochípwe*; more commonly, they use *anishanábe*. Sometimes, particularly when speaking in English, speakers shorten the form to *shanábe* or even *shnáb*. In some contexts the shortened form *shanábe* connotes "any American Indian regardless of tribal affiliation." Thus, even in the native language the conceptual boundaries between "Chippewa" and "Indian" are blurred.

To understand North City Indians' total environmental adaptation, their acquaintance and interaction with "Indian culture" must be examined. For analytic purposes, we may look upon Indian culture as a composite of 3 interlocking systems: (1) traditional Chippewa culture, as described in the ethnographic literature; (2) modern reservation cultures, containing some elements of traditional culture and some unique elements developed over time through interaction between Indian society and the larger American society; and (3) the emergent intertribal culture, Pan-Indianism. In this context the word "culture" refers not so much to standards for perception and behavior, but to "artifacts" of behavior, "public culture," and "culture pools," to use Goodenough's terms (1971).

Traditional culture

Frederica de Laguna has remarked, "Even for the bewildered individual who hesitates between two worlds, the past of his fathers must be understood as part of him though he tries to reject it" (1968:470). North City Indians stand midway between the world of the reservation and the world of modern urban America. Though some Chippewa traditions are only memories, others are elements of most North City Indians' environment just as are the many facets of city, state, and national life. Further, some *do* try to reject the "Indian" part of themselves. One affluent North City man said, "The Indian part of me is something I usually try to keep in some dark corner of my mind."

Many bits and fragments of traditional Chippewa culture survive in the lives of North City Indians. Nearly all adults know some of the Chippewa language. Many remember, from their childhood, tales of Ojibwa mythological characters. For some, the power of dreams and malevolent witchcraft continues to have unsettling reality. Traditional, though fragmented, forms of social organization and behavior persist in joking relationships and in fictive kinship ties to *wíyen* ("namesakes"); a few adults recall the earlier importance of the *dódem*, or *dódaim* ("clan"). Most have participated in at least a Christianized Chippewa wake; some have witnessed "pagan" wakes and are familiar with the Grand Medicine Society or its adherents. Many recall pleasant memories of camping out along rice lakes or in maple sugar groves when the time had come in the traditional annual cycle to "make rice" or "make sugar."

All the North City Indians I encountered could speak English. Even in the most conservative Chippewa communities of the area, only a very few old people were monolingual in the native language—although some elderly Chippewa had only a minimal reading and speaking knowledge of English. Many of the older Indians learned English as a second language in school; some recall vividly the punishments meted out at boarding schools if they were discovered "talking Indian." Others spoke English first and then learned Chippewa or were bilingual from the time they began to speak.

An anecdote told by one old North City Chippewa about another illustrates the difficulties some have with English. Bill was a "quarter-blood" who had worked for the Bureau of Indian Affairs for many years; he was also an amateur ethnologist. One day a distant cousin, Tom, came to visit. Bill wanted to show Tom his prized copy of an antique Ojibwa grammar (Baraga 1853). While looking for the book, Bill said, "I want to show you this Chippewa grammar I have." His cousin queried, "*Nikomis*?" ("Grandmother?"), thinking Bill had said "gran'ma" in English. Interviews with Tom reaffirmed that he could understand only the simplest English.

Not all native Chippewa speakers in North City are elderly. One interviewee in his early thirties, who was orphaned at an early age and placed in the care of his grandmother, said that, according to his boarding school teachers, when he had first arrived at the school he could speak no English. Another man in his early forties was somewhat anxious about his knowledge of Chippewa. As a child, he said, his family spoke a mixture of English and Chippewa, and he understood both. However, when he spoke Chippewa, his family laughed at him: "I don't know why . . . my pronunciation or something . . . always seemed to come out funny." His father sent him to stay with his aunt during the summers to improve his Chippewa. Despite his difficulties with the native language, he remembers once being sick at school and frantically trying to think of the word "vomit," remembering only the Chippewa equivalent. Today, he says, he likes to go to Indian gatherings and "eavesdrop" on Chippewa conversations to "test myself."

Many North City Indians are native English speakers, having less proficiency in Chippewa than in English. Interviewees were asked to rate their own ability to speak and understand Chippewa, as well as that of others in the household. Excluding white members of households and infants under 3 years of age, Table 7.14 shows the Chippewa proficiency of the total random sample population. As might be expected, most of those in the "speaks none, understands none" category were children; however, not all small children were in this category, and it includes some adults. Adding the item "native speaker," to the data of Table 7.14 enabled the construction of a nearly perfect Guttman scale of the respondents' Chippewa language proficiency (Table 7.15).

Table 7.14. Proficiency in Chippewa of North City Indians (random sample)[a]

Speaks	Understands	Number
None	None	37
None	Some	15
Some	Some	9
Some	Well	5
Well	Well	20
Undecodable response		4
Total		90

a. Children under 3 have been excluded.

Interviewees were asked when they would be "most likely to use Chippewa." The older, fluent speakers gave responses that indicated their preference for the native language; in general, they use Chippewa whenever they encounter someone else who speaks it, especially their contemporaries. Slightly younger fluent speakers frequently converse in Chippewa with older people and specific relatives. Still others who understand the language well but are less fluent speakers stated that they usually speak Chippewa for humorous effect: "Just goofing around...just in a humorous mood, I guess, is the best way to say it;" or, "I don't know...probably just when I'm being silly."

Of the many elements of Chippewa folklore and religion, only a few were selected as subjects for systematic inquiry. Individuals were asked if they had ever heard various Indian stories, including *Nanabúshu*

Table 7.15. Scalogram of Chippewa language proficiency of
North City Indians (random sample)

Inter-viewee	Scale type	A	B	C	D	E		Key to scale items
11	6	x	x	x	x	x		A. Native speaker of Chippewa
16	6	x	x	x	x	x		B. Speaks Chippewa fluently
17	6	x	x	x	x	x		C. Understands Chippewa well
20	6	x	x	x	x	x		D. Speaks at least a little Chippewa
21	6	x	x	x	x	x		E. Understands at least a little
22	6	x	x	x	x	x		Chippewa
23	6	x	x	x	x	x		
24	6	x	x	x	x	x		
26	6	x	x	x	x	x		
3	5		x	x	x	x		
4	5		x	x	x	x		
7	5		x	x	x	x		
9	5		x	x	x	x		
10	5		x	x	x	x		
18	5		x	x	x	x		
25	5		x	x	x	x		
2	4			x	x	x		
14	4			x	o[a]	x		
6	3				x	x		
12	3				x	x		
13	3				x	x		
15	3				x	x		
5	2					x		
8	2					x		
1	1							
19	1							

Coefficient of reproducibility = .99

a. While this scale error appears suspicious, it must be included to be consistent with the general "rule" of taking interviewees' assessments of their language ability at face value.

and *windigo*. They were also asked about attendance at and participation in Grand Medicine Society and other shamanistic performances, as well as about attendance at wakes "where Indian songs were sung." Since migrating to North City, 45 percent of the respondents had returned to a reservation to attend an "Indian-style" wake. Recently, a wake had been conducted for a North City Indian couple who had perished in a house fire; several North City families attended the wake, which took place at Mission. The couple was given a "pagan" burial at the Mission graveyard, but their graves serve as neat examples of Chippewa religious syncretism. The grave houses were made of commercial lumber, which was painted with commercial paint. In addition to the traditional grave post set in the ground and a food shelf attached under a small "spirit hole" in the front of the house, each grave was adorned with plastic flowers and marked by a bronze plaque from the North City funeral parlor that had prepared the bodies for internment.

Interviewees mentioned only one wake that had been performed in North City. When the aged father of 3 middle-aged North City Indians died, his body was placed in a North City funeral parlor. His children and other relatives gathered together from distant places across the nation and met for several nights in the North City home of the man's only daughter. There they sang Christian songs in Chippewa from hymnals in the native language, as the old man had requested. The daughter implied that they would have had his body present but that the casket "wouldn't fit through the door." This case dramatically demonstrates that North City Indians can and do continue traditional practices within North City. That 3 of the old man's children and several of his grandchildren live in North City (none of his 6 children live on his original reservation) is probably an important circumstance in explaining why the wake was held in the city rather than on the reservation.

Nanabushu, or *Winibuzhu* (Nanabushu being preferred usage in the Deer Lake dialect, Winibuzhu in the Broken Reed and Beaver Pelt dialects), and *windigo* are important personages in Chippewa folklore. Nanabushu is an important symbol of traditional cultural identity among contemporary Chippewa. An older North City Indian—Bill, the amateur ethnologist—hypothesized that the Chippewa greeting *bazhú* is a shortened form of Winibuzhu (rather than a borrowing from the French *bonjour*) and means, "We are fellow Chippewa." North City Indians vary in their attitudes toward these legendary beings. At one extreme is Mrs. Fish, who as a girl was deeply troubled by dreams of windigo and who regarded Nanabushu's behavior as a prototypic explanation of such aberrations as father-daughter incest. In contrast are those to whom windigo is simply "some kind of bogey man," or even a buffoon, and Nanabushu merely an entertaining character to tell stories about.

Some of the tales told about these Indian characters have included elements from European culture. For example, one elderly informant reported that Chippewa workmen used to exchange tales in which Nanabushu plays pranks around lumber camps. One such story ends when Nanabushu is revealed as the one who stole sugar from the camp kitchen because he has sugar on his whiskers; to this story a listener is supposed to respond, "But Nanabushu doesn't have a beard" (since he is an Indian). In the tales of one North City Indian man, windigo and Winibuzhu have become merged—both are tricksters and often seem interchangeable. In these accounts both characters are sometimes equipped with such artifacts as motorcycles and cigarette lighters. In one story windigo is playing baseball!

Nanabushu is sometimes compared to figures in Euro-American folklore, in remarks such as "He's the Indian Paul Bunyan," or "When I was little I used to think he was the Indian Santa Claus." Even those who regard Nanabushu with reverence sometimes make such comparisons. Mrs. Fish reported that one of her contemporaries thought that "maybe he's Jesus." Mrs. Fish's grandchildren, who attend the Indian mission in North City, objected to this interpretation, referring to some of the "obscene" acts of Nanabushu and saying, "Jesus would never do anything like that." A few Indians indicate disbelief in these characters. One old man said, "They told me that [as a child] I didn't believe 'em."

North City Indians do not typically transmit these elements of traditional Chippewa culture to their offspring. Only a few older respondents reported having told Nanabushu or other Indian folktales and myths to their children, although some said their children had heard the stories from grandparents. Frequently, respondents said they had not told their children the stories because the children could not understand Chippewa, indicating a prevailing attitude that these stories can be appreciated only in the native language. Much of the humor in Nanabushu stories is thought to be lost in translation. The head of one consanguineal family stated that she does warn her grandchildren that windigo will "get them" if they don't behave.

With few exceptions, the Indians of North City are self-identified Christians. Roman Catholics and Episcopalians predominate, the former comprising 53 percent of the total random sample population and the latter, 14 percent. Even so, some of the adults had witnessed traditional rituals such as tent-shaking ceremonies, Midéwiwin initiations, and funeral rites. Some recount experiences of close relatives who had been "grand-medicined," that is, had suffered from the effects of malevolent witchcraft. For example, one woman from a Catholic family described her husband's affliction, which occurred soon after their marriage in the early 1900s:

> ...he said he was going to play cards. I didn't really know what he went for, but when he got back he said what he was doing [selling bootleg whiskey]. He must have been gone 3 days and when he left, he left on a horse and returned the same way. As soon as he walked in the house he fell; so we, my Ma and I, put him on the bed; ... and

my mother sent for an old lady...to see what was wrong with him. She knew what it was right away: he was grand-medicined. So, she went and got some medicine and he drank it. He was really out, he was sick, out of his head. He could talk but he didn't know anything. I really got scared. My goodness, I heard what they can do, it can kill you. So my mother brought out the candles, put up the rosaries, and sprinkled holy water on him.... That is powerful for Catholics.

Finally, members of the family successfully warded off the supposed medium of injury, a "fireball," by shooting at it with firearms. (Again, notice the combination of Euro-American cultural traits and traditional beliefs.) The informant surmised that her husband was bewitched because he had offended a shaman by not selling him any more whiskey. Similarly, a 41-year-old man recalled the mysterious conversation of his parents when (as he learned later) his father was bewitched by his hunting partners because of his consistent hunting success, seemingly at the expense of his partners' luck.

Aside from the more formalized elements of Chippewa supernaturalism, a few North City Indians maintained their belief in the efficacy of spirit helpers. An elderly man said that he was "born a Catholic and will die a Catholic," yet he felt that as a young man he must have had "somebody back of me helping me;" otherwise, he said, he would not have won so much money at poker and at moccasin game. This man also kept a crucifix on his bedpost to ward off "bad dreams" and sadly recalled that his failure to follow instructions in one dream caused the death of one of his sons. Mrs. Fish recalled the miraculous manner in which she used the telephone for the first time—without instructions, during a dire emergency. "Somebody must have been helping me," she explained. Even young adults are willing to accept the possible efficacy of native magico-religious phenomena. A college graduate (not in the random sample) related an incident in which his grandmother successfully divined a death on the basis of omens, adding "You'd like to think it was coincidence, but...."

North City Chippewa seemed most likely to accept the effectiveness of traditional Chippewa practices in the area of medical treatment, including both herbal and magical cures. "I wouldn't have believed it myself, but he helped me," said a devout Catholic woman about an "Indian doctor's" successful treatment of her laryngitis. For nonbelievers, such treatment was often regarded as a last resort, but not necessar-

ily inconsistent with belief in Christianity and modern science. Their
attitude was essentially pragmatic: "If it works, it must be true; those old
Indians probably knew things which we don't understand today." Although there were few real shamans remaining in the area, herbal cures
could be obtained from knowledgeable old people.

The term *jíbik* is used to describe several herbal concoctions presumed to have magical properties; however, it is most commonly known
as "love medicine." This medicine may be used to obtain sexual partners
or (by a spurned suitor) to exact vengeance. Familiarity with *jíbik*
appears to be fairly widespread among modern Chippewa, including
those of North City. A jest by an elderly North City woman illustrates the
integration of traditional beliefs with values of modern American society: "If I had some *jíbik*, I'd get me a banker."

A number of North City women continue to manufacture traditional
(though not necessarily aboriginal) crafts, such as beadwork, buckskin,
and braided rugs. (One young woman used the plastic bags from store-
bought bread to braid rugs.) Other North City Indians collect and
preserve Chippewa artifacts, or even books, photographs, and newspaper clippings describing traditional material culture. A North City man
who had kept his grandfather's Catlinite pipe for many years chuckled
about the many times his children had taken it to North City schools to
show to their classmates.

More than one older woman reported that her oldest child was kept
in a *dikanágan* ("cradleboard"). Today, even in the most remote areas of
the reservations, cradleboards are not used. However, in North City
itself the use of rope and blanket hammocks for infants was observed in 2
Indian households. In both cases the houses were small and crowded and
the young parents explained the use of the hammocks as a matter of
practicality. In one of the houses, the child's hammock was suspended
directly over the parents' bed.

Modern northern Minnesota Chippewa are generally known by
their Christian names or by nicknames. The nicknames are sometimes
derived from the native language, but more often from English; occasionally, the nicknames are not readily assigned to either language.
Additionally, quite a few Chippewa possess seldom-used "Indian
names." These names are given to individuals in infancy by adults
outside the nuclear family who either request or are asked by the parents
"to have the child" as a namesake. Traditionally, the naming is accompanied by a ceremony, where tobacco is given to invited witnesses. In
recent times the naming is accompanied by little ceremony beyond the

parents' agreement to "give the child" to an older person as a namesake. Sometimes, frequently used Indian nicknames are acquired in a similar manner. Ideally, a person has a special interest in his or her namesake, or *wiyen* (a term that is self-reciprocal), overseeing the socialization of the child and presenting gifts from time to time.

Interviewees in the random sample were asked whether they or any of their children had Indian names. Six stated that they had Indian names (although some were uncertain of the proper pronunciation or meaning); 3 reported that one or more of their children had Indian names; one stated that he had an Indian nickname.

Traditional economic pursuits (hunting, fishing, and the gathering of wild rice and berries) have been discussed already; most North City Indians engage in these activities at least sporadically. Unlike the other traits discussed here, these are also characteristic of a great many non-Indians. Sometimes Indians make contrasts between their skills and those of whites in execution of the activities, particularly rice collection.

North City Indians' knowledge and practice of traditional religion, folklore, and other nonlinguistic traits are more erratically distributed than their knowledge of the native language. However, some of these items were regular enough in the random sample to permit constructing a Guttman scale of familiarity with Chippewa customs, presented in Table 7.16. Although the scale has a respectable coefficient of reproducibility, it is in some ways the least acceptable of all the scales presented. Complicating factors were the apparent anxiety of some interviewees in responding to the religious items, possible prevarication, and language difficulties. Thus, the scalogram should be considered as only an approximation of the typological ranking of North City Indians in terms of one dimension of "traditionality."

Table 7.16 shows that the typical North City Indian adult has been a participant in at least a Christianized Indian wake and has collected wild rice at some time in his or her life. More than half heard Nanabushu tales as children, and over a fourth have at least witnessed a Chippewa shamanistic performance.

Chippewa Indians bring to North City a wide range of knowledge of and experience with traditional culture. Although a few manifestations of traditional culture within the urban setting have been cited, on the whole the Indians do not perpetuate traditional practices within the city. Instead, they maintain and reinforce their identification with the traditional past through participation in reservation life. Often the Chippewa child of North City would have no direct exposure to

Table 7.16. Scalogram of North City Indians' familiarity with
Chippewa customs (random sample)

Inter-viewee	Scale type	A	B	C	D	E	F		Key to scale items
18	7	x	x	x	x	x	x		A. Has employed services of native
25	7	x	x	x	x	x	x		medical practitioner
26	7	x	x	o	o	x	x		B. Has witnessed some form of
10	6		x	x	x	o	x		"pagen" supernaturalism
11	6		x	x	x	x	x		C. Has heard windigo tales
15	6		x	x	x	o	x		D. Has heard Nanabushu tales
2	5			x	x	o	x		E. Has collected wild rice at some
3	5			x	x	x	x		time in the past
8	5			x	x	x	x		F. Has attended a wake where
9	5			x	x	x	x		songs were sung in Chippewa
12	5			x	x	x	o		
17	5			x	x	x	x		
23	5			x	x	x	x		
24	5			x	x	x	x		
4	4				x	x	x		
5	3					x	x		
6	3					x	x		
14	3					x	x		
16	3					x	x		
22	3		(x)			x	x		
7	2						x		
13	2						x		
21	2						x		
1	1				(x)				
19	1								
20	1								

Coefficient of reproducibility = .95

traditional culture were it not for interaction with those still living on the reservation.

Modern reservation culture

The description by Bernard James of a contemporary Wisconsin Chippewa reservation as a "poor white type" subculture is generally applicable to the reservations in the North City area. The "socio-economic status differential" (James 1961:744) (in the comparison of the reservation with the larger white society)—which James sees as a crucial requirement for the existence of such subcultures—is present to some extent on all of the reservations in the North City area. Some of the behaviors James regards as psychological consequences of this situation are matched almost point for point by northern Minnesota Chippewa.

However, with the possible exception of Beaver Pelt, the reservations surrounding North City have not experienced a "deculturation" (James 1961:728), or loss of traditional traits, as extensive as that reported for the reservation described by James.

In the absence of unique culture traits by which differences in North City Indians' knowledge of reservation culture can be identified, the Indians' social relations to the "reservation culture" component of their environment are examined here. Data were collected from interviewees concerning the frequency and location of interaction with relatives living on reservations and the kind and frequency of return trips to reservations. These data permitted the ranking of individuals into types along a dimension of "reservation contacts," as seen in Table 7.17.

Item F appears inconsistent with the others; however, it too is a "frequency" item. An attempt was made to incorporate participation in a wake since relocation to North City, but this item did not fit empirically or logically into this scale, since such participation is contingent on special factors, such as death, over which the respondent has no control.

According to the scale, the minimal level of social interaction with reservations was one visit per year. Two of the 3 individuals who had had less contact than this were the aged daughter of a nonreservation Chippewa from northwestern Minnesota and the only adult in the sample who was brought to North City as a preschool-aged child. The presence of these rather unusual individuals in Type 1 supports the general validity of the scale. At the opposite end of the scale were those who had weekly contact with members of reservation communities. All the individuals in Types 11 and 12 had kinsmen living at Mission, the geographically closest reservation community. The large number of errors for Interviewee 5 may be accounted for by the fact that his job with the Bureau of Indian Affairs required him to make almost daily trips to James Lake; his mother resided there when she was not staying in North City with him.

To document the nature of the contacts between North City Indians and reservation kinsmen, the following directly observed instance is cited at length. This example illustrates the importance of interaction with the reservation in maintaining traditional culture and the effects of acculturation on Chippewa rituals.

Ben came to North City from an isolated community on the Broken Reed Reservation to participate in the Title V training program. His wife was from Deer Lake, and they had several young children. Traditionally, his kinsmen have gathered at the grave sites of their immediate ancestors on Memorial Day to remove weeds, place flowers and gifts (usually food

Table 7.17. Scalogram of reservation contacts of
North City Indians (random sample)

Inter-viewee	Scale type	A	B	C	D	E	F	G	H	I	J	K	Key to scale items
9	12	x	x	x	x	x	x	x	x	x	x	x	A. Visits a kinsman living on a reservation once per week
14	12	x	x	x	x	x	x	x	x	x	x	x	
													B. Is visited by a reservation kinsman once per week
16	11		x	o	x	o	x	x	x	x	x	x	
18	11		x	x	x	x	x	x	x	x	x	x	C. Visits a reservation kinsman more than once per month
26	11		x	?ᵃ	x	?ᵃ	x	x	x	x	x	x	
													D. Is visited by a reservation kinsman more than once per month
4	10			x	o	x	x	x	x	x	x	x	
17	10			x	x	x	x	x	x	x	x	x	
22	10			x	x	x	x	x	x	x	x	x	E. Visits a reservation kinsman more than once every 2 months
3	9				x	x	x	x	x	x	x	x	
6	8					x	x	x	x	x	x	x	F. Hunts, fishes, or collects wild rice or berries on a reservation
10	8					x	x	x	x	x	x	x	
21	7						x	x	x	x	x	x	G. Is visited by a reservation kinsman more than once every 2 months
11	6	(x)		(x)				x	x	x	x	x	
23	6							x	x	x	x	x	H. Is visited by a reservation kinsman at least once every 2 months
15	5								x	x	x	x	
20	4									x	x	x	I. Is visited by a reservation kinsman more than once per year
25	6									x	x	x	
5	3	(x)		(x)		(x)					x	x	J. Visits a reservation more than once per year
8	3										x	x	
													K. Visits some reservation in the region at least once per year
2	2											x	
7	2					(x)						x	
12	2											x	
24	2											x	
1	1												
13	1												
19	1												

Coefficient of reproducibility = .96

a. Uncertainty in interpretation of data; counted as an error.

and tobacco) on the graves, and eat a picnic lunch together. The second year that Ben lived in North City, I accompanied him (and his children, but not his wife) to this annual ritual.

Arriving at the grave site of his mother and other relatives, we found about 6 people already busily attending the graves. Ben was instructed by one of his senior kinsmen to "brush" his mother's grave. After the graves were cleaned, an elderly woman offered prayers in Chippewa, and several people arranged offerings of food and tobacco on the graves. (Ben stated that if the deceased used tobacco in life, one should place on the grave the brand of tobacco he or she had used.) Ben placed an offering of bread in the earth over his mother's grave.

The group then seated themselves on blankets and ate the food they had brought. Some of the younger men who had arrived late sat on top of some grave houses. During the meal there was much jovial conversation, almost all of which was in Chippewa.

When everyone had finished eating, the dishes were repacked, and the oldest woman present poured the remaining drink at the head of 3 of the graves. She placed the margarine tin that she had used as a cup upside down on one of the graves. Several of the graves were marked with cups, plates, and glasses from previous "picnics." Soon afterward we left, taking with us a large box of leftover food.

All but 2 of the participants in this Memorial Day celebration were Christians, yet all were involved in the "pagan" ritual. In remarking on the paradox, Ben explained that the ritual would no longer be conducted when the older relatives had died. I asked if he would then continue coming back to care for his mother's grave. He replied, "Yeah, I suppose so," as though he had never thought of the matter in these terms.

Ben was back at his North City home a scant 5 hours after we had left it that morning. During those few hours he and his children had reentered a social setting in which Chippewa was the common language and old people led the young in a traditional ritual. The next day Ben returned to his training as an electrician, and his older children to study with their white classmates at a North City public school.

The scale in Table 7.17 actually understates the frequency of contacts with reservation Chippewa. North City Indians interact socially with acquaintances and types of kinsmen for which data were not systematically elicited. Frequently these encounters may be rather casual, such as a momentary conversation on the streets of North City, where both urban and reservation Indians meet. Whatever the "true" frequency of interaction, the data at hand are sufficient to demonstrate that the Indians of North City continue to maintain social ties with the reservations.

Because they are the nearest fish, game, and wild rice areas with which North City Indians are familiar, the reservations also serve as a kind of ecological reservoir. Migrants from the Deer Lake Reservation have the additional attraction on their reservation of the absence of legal restrictions on the taking of game and fish by members of the band.

One might expect North City Indians would maintain contacts with reservation life through political participation, for example, by voting in tribal elections. In fact, only a third (9) of the North City random sample interviewees had ever voted in a tribal, band, or village election. There were 6 Deer Lake respondents in this group. The other 3 were a Wisconsin Chippewa who voted in the early 1960s, a former officer of the Minnesota Chippewa Tribe who voted in a tribal election in 1964, and one Beaver Pelt enrollee who said she had voted once "about 25 years ago." Clearly, while North City members of the Deer Lake Band continue to maintain political interest in their reservation, urban members of the Minnesota Chippewa Tribe, with but a few exceptions, are not and have never been politically active in tribal affairs. Information from other sources indicates that even on the Minnesota Chippewa reservations participation in political affairs is generally limited to a few people (cf. Pelto, Chapter 6 in this volume).

Finally, attendance at and participation in powwows reinforce the cultural and social ties of North City Indians to reservation life. More important, powwows provide a bridge between modern reservation society and Pan-Indianism.

Pan-Indianism

Although Pan-Indianism in northern Minnesota is less developed than in Oklahoma, for example (cf. Howard 1965), several aspects of modern Chippewa reservation life—especially powwows—can best be described as "Pan-Indian."

Powwow celebrations are an important symbol of Indian identity. Through them, Indian communities and individuals reassert their cultural distinctiveness in a manner that has positive, or at least neutral, value in the larger white society. Powwows bring together dancers, singers, and spectators from reservations in the Dakotas, Iowa, Wisconsin, Ontario, and Montana, as well as from all the reservations in Minnesota. In addition, Indian migrants to Chicago and Minneapolis–St. Paul frequently return for these events; North City Chippewa have only a short distance to travel, by comparison. (In North City and Trotter, white businessmen sponsor short powwows for the benefit of tourists. Unlike celebrations in Indian communities, which last for several days, the tourist powwows last around an hour and attract Indians only from the nearby Chippewa reservations.)

Although distinctive tribal styles of powwow singing, dancing, and dress may be identified at powwows, intertribal borrowings often blur these distinctions. For example, in recent years Chippewa singers have begun to wear straw cowboy hats like those of northern Plains tribes.

Chippewa beadworkers have started fashioning Oklahoma-style dance suspenders—but they bead them in the traditional floral motifs of Chippewa. Part of the impetus for this acculturation comes from returning Chippewa who have migrated to large cities and participated in intertribal activities at metropolitan Indian clubs.

On the whole, northern Minnesota Chippewa do not appear to appreciate fully the Pan-Indian significance of powwows. Some informants commented on the opportunities provided by powwows for "seeing how other tribes dance and what kind of outfits they have" and for meeting Indians from other tribes. However, for Chippewa who participated in powwows only as spectators, the powwow seemed to function principally as an arena for interaction with old friends and acquaintances and for aesthetic and emotional gratification.

In an attempt to determine how often North City Indians attend powwows, interviewees were asked to name by place the powwows they had attended; Table 7.18 shows the distribution of their responses. Deer Lake, with the most elaborate celebrations, was the most popular. Surprisingly, the commercial Indian dances at the North City waterfront were frequently mentioned, albeit sometimes with the rejoinder "I don't really call that a powwow." However, despite crass commercialism, these dances are the only organized public expression of Indian culture within the city, making their attractiveness somewhat more understand-

Table 7.18. Powwow attendance by North City Indians (random sample)[a]

Does not attend	4
Attends only North City powwows	5
Attends powwows at North City and Deer Lake[b]	8
Attends powwows at Deer Lake and elsewhere (Trotter, Wicket, Nisishin)	3
Attends powwows at Deer Lake, North City, and elsewhere	2
Attends powwows only at Deer Lake	3
Other responses	2

a. Information from partially completed interview included.

b. An interviewee's inclusion in a category does not necessarily imply that he or she annually attends powwows in all the places listed for that category, although most do.

able. As shown by the table, the majority of North City Indians interviewed also attended powwows conducted on reservations. Since the North City dances are fairly well attended and many who attend the Deer Lake celebrations are not from that reservation, powwow attendance appears to represent more than merely a desire to return to the home community. Possible explanations for this interest are, again, the emotional gratification derived from witnessing the performances and the opportunities provided for associating with other Indians.

Peyotism is the religious counterpart of powwows in the Pan-Indian "movement" (Howard 1965:159–61). Northern Minnesota represents a hiatus in the distribution of the peyote cult, having only one small settlement of Peyotists (see Jackson, Chapter 4 in this volume). However, when the informants in the North City random sample were asked a series of questions to ascertain the extent of their knowledge of peyote, approximately half indicated having some knowledge of peyote. Most said that they had "heard of it," but disclaimed detailed knowledge; only 2 persons said they had actually seen peyote buttons. Probably more of the interviewees were familiar with the plant, but (1) could not recall the name of the plant (several pronunciations of *peyote* were used in questioning to try to avoid this problem); (2) had negative feelings about the plant (some informants referred to the plant as "dope"); or (3) were uncertain as to the possible legal consequences of claiming knowledge of the plant. An interviewee who initially stated that he had never heard of peyote later discussed a drink made from a thing "like a dried peach, with . . . cotton inside. . . . It makes them crazy," he said, but "that's a religion, too." He said that he had never been to a meeting but had heard the singing; however, he described the passing of the drum and had a fairly accurate idea of where peyote buttons were obtained. Apparently, most of his knowledge of peyote was based on his familiarity with Rice Village.

At the time of this study, North City was an arena for political Pan-Indianism, as more and more Indians were being drawn there to participate in federal programs designed to "help the Indian." A program of particular importance was the technical assistance center established at North City State College and directed by a Chippewa originally from the Beaver Pelt Reservation. Other Indians were also directly employed by the center. Many men and women in such positions, including some Bureau of Indian Affairs employees, were developing a keen sensitivity to the need for cooperation among reservations and tribes in order to deal with government bureaucracy. They were becoming more and more outspoken on "Indian problems." In the late 1960s there existed in North City the possibility of the emergence of a local Indian administrative elite made up of the highly educated Indians who manage these government programs. Such a group could well make North City a regional focus of political Pan-Indianism just as the city has been an administrative and trade center for Indians during recent decades.

Relationships among dimensions of adaptation

The Chippewa of North City constitute a heterogeneous population, with wide ranges of variation among individuals along a number of dimensions of adaptation. It is important to recognize that many of these variations are not random, but are patterned in terms of the cumulation of traits or items—that is, they conform to a Guttman scale distribution.

Guttman scale analysis of some rather simple kinds of data has produced six separate typologies of North City Indians. Theoretically, each typology is based on a single dimension. The ordinal arrangement of types is an important distinguishing characteristic of this kind of typology. In this study, different levels of adaptation to the several systems comprising the North City Chippewa's sociocultural environment are operationally defined as the scale types; they may be compared to determine what associations, if any, may exist among the several scales. The random sample interviewees' types on all scales are presented in Table 7.19.

Two other kinds of data for the sample are also presented. Formal education is generally assumed to be an important variable in the adaptation of native peoples to Western civilization. Therefore, years of school completed are included in Table 7.19. Additionally, in the absence of a more exact measure of Pan-Indianism, interviewees were ranked for this dimension in terms of powwow attendance.

To determine any patterns in the association of levels of adaptation with various components of the environment, a statistical measure was applied to discover to what extent an individual's position on one scale or measure can be predicted from his or her relative position on another. The statistic utilized is a coefficient of rank-order association known as *gamma* (Freeman 1965:79–88). The gamma coefficient represents the percentage of agreements over inversions (+ value), or inversions over agreements (− value), between relative positions of the same cases on 2 ordinal measures. For example, a gamma of .5000 means that there are 50 percent more agreements (in relative position on the 2 measures) than

Table 7.19. Scale types, formal education, and powwow attendance
of interviewees (random sample)

Inter-viewee	FE	MSL	MME	CI	CLP	FCC	RC	PWA	Key to abbreviations
1	13	15	8	7	1	1	1	1	FE – Formal education
2	14	15	10	6	4	5	2	3	(years of school com-
3	14	12	9	8	5	5	9	1	pleted)
4	12	16	8	8	5	4	10	3	MSL – Material style of
5	6	13	9	6	2	3	3	1	life
6	12	14	8	7	3	3	8	2	MME – Mass media
7	8.5	15	10	7	5	2	2	3	exposure
8	12	13	8	8	2	5	3	3	CI – City involvement
9	8	5	7	2	5	5	12	2	CLP – Chippewa lan-
10	8	7	3	2	5	6	8	3	guage proficiency
11	8	10	5	4	6	6	6	1	FCC – Familiarity with
12	8	16	10	3	3	5	2	3	Chippewa customs
13	11	4	6	6	3	2	1	2	RC – Reservation con-
14	8	6	6	5	4	3	12	3	tacts
15	13	5	5	6	3	6	5	3	PWA – Powwow atten-
16	0	2	1	3	6	3	11	3	dance: 1= does not
17	9	5	2	2	6	5	10	3	attend; 2= attends in
18	8	12	5	6	5	7	11	3	North City only; 3=
19	8	6	5	6	1	1	1	3	attends on reserva-
20	7.5	11	8	2	6	1	4	3	tions
21	7	3	2	1	6	2	7	2	
22	5	7	1	1	6	3	10	3	
23	8	1	1	1	6	5	6	3	
24	7	1	3	3	6	5	2	3	
25	9	9	4	6	5	7	4	2	
26	6	8	1	2	6	7	11	3	

there are inversions. Values for gamma have been tested for significance using a procedure described by Freeman (1965:162–75). Because of difficulties in interpreting absolute values of gamma, the statements that follow concerning "relative strength" of associations should be regarded as tentative.

A matrix of gamma coefficients among the 6 scales, formal education, and powwow attendance is presented in Table 7.20. Associations among amount of formal education and the scales for material style of life, mass media exposure, and city involvement are strong, positive, and significant. Thus, a close correspondence is seen among an individual's levels of adaptation to the several "white culture" elements of the sociocultural environment. For example, those individuals who are at a high level of adaptation to the city are also very likely to be high in amount of formal education and on the scales for material style of life and mass media exposure.

Table 7.20. Associations among scales and other indices

	MME	*CI*	*FE*	*FCC*	*RC*	*PWA*	*CLP*
MSL	.6433[a]	.5173	.3231	(−.0339)	(−.2070)	(−.1377)	−.3920
MME		.5988	.4821	−.2000	−.3428	−.3043	−.5696
CI			.6385	(−.0677)	−.2500	−.3108	−.6444
FE				(.0656)	−.2222	−.2418	−.5087
FCC					.2923	.1586	.2405
RC						.1515	.4262
PWA							.2971

MSL: Material style of life scale   FCC: Familiarity with Chippewa customs scale
MME: Mass media exposure scale   RC: Reservation contacts scale
CI: City involvement scale   PWA: Powwow attendance
FE: Formal education   CLP: Chippewa language proficiency scale

a. All associations except those enclosed in parentheses are significant at the .01 level or better; those in parentheses do not even approach the .05 level of significance.

Even though it is significant, the association between formal education and material style of life appears weak, despite the commonly assumed importance of "getting an education" in order to "get ahead." Formal education by itself, however, appears not to be an exceptionally powerful factor in determining the standard of living of North City Indians.

Levels of adaptation to "Indian culture," as reflected in powwow attendance and in the scales for familiarity with Chippewa customs, reservation contacts, and Chippewa language proficiency, are significantly and positively associated with each other. However, the associations are not nearly as strong as in adaptation to white elements of the environment. There is probably greater functional economic interrelatedness among the white elements than among the Indian ones. Moreover, with the exception of formal education, all the white elements of the environment converge in a synchronous nexus at North City; the Indian elements have several loci. All North City Indians reside in the same white community, but they represent different Indian communities, or reservations.

For the most part, levels of adaptation to Indian elements of the environment are inversely associated with adaptations to white components. Chippewa language proficiency consistently shows the strongest negative association with each of the 4 white measures. The greatest inversion is between Chippewa language proficiency and city involvement; conversely, Chippewa language proficiency with reservation contacts is by far the strongest positive association among elements of Indian culture. Despite uncertainties in assessing the importance of numerical values of gamma, this pair of findings suggests that language abilities are of extreme significance in North City Indians' patterns of adaptation.

In general, there are negative associations between Indian and white dimensions of adaptation. However, familiarity with Chippewa customs is negatively associated with only one of the white-culture measures, mass media exposure. The absence of significant associations with other white scales and indices suggests that adaptations to white elements of the overall environment are unaffected by the extent of North City Indians' acquaintance with certain formalized traits of traditional culture. Conversely, it has been shown that Chippewa fluency is strongly and inversely associated with levels of adaptation to white culture. Thus, while the participation of the Chippewa in the "mainstream" of American society may be conditioned by their language abilities, their experience with certain nonlinguistic traits of traditional culture is not directly relevant to the kinds of adaptation they make to the larger society. The significant, but relatively weak, inverse relationship between the scales for mass media exposure and familiarity with Chippewa customs may mean that the cosmopolitan character of the world view transmitted by mass media is difficult to reconcile with the tribal life-style implicit in traditional culture traits.

Material style of life is not significantly related to familiarity with Chippewa customs, reservation contacts, or powwow attendance. There is a significant negative correlation between material style of life and Chippewa language proficiency, but it is the weakest of such negative associations. The absence of significant associations between material style of life and dimensions of Indian culture means that an individual's level of familiarity with Chippewa customs, level of reservation contacts, and extent of powwow attendance cannot be predicted on the basis of his or her material style of life.

Since no significant patterns are apparent in the way economic adaptations are associated with nonlinguistic elements of Indian culture, this is evidently an area of flexibility. Residence in North City may be a strategy by which northern Minnesota Chippewa simultaneously maximize both the material advantages of urban centers and the social and emotional advantages of reservation society. Life in North City offers a compromise between the lack of material advantages on reservations and the potential cultural deprivation that may result from settling in a distant metropolis. Other data that support this interpretation are the superior economic position of urban Indians as compared with residents of certain reservation communities, and the relative ease with which North City Indians may pursue traditional economic activities in the surrounding lakes and forests. From this perspective North City resembles what Hodge terms "transitional communities" (1969:26–28) on the Navajo reservation. These communities (for example, Shiprock, New Mexico), according to Hodge, offer some of the material advantages of cities without the social and emotional disadvantages; at the same time, they provide the opportunity for participation in reservation life. Hodge states that many of the "anglo-modified" Navajos of Albuquerque hope to return to the reservation and live in such transitional communities (1969:27). Since many North City Chippewa lived in larger cities before coming to North City, it appears that this Minnesota community serves the same function for a segment of the Chippewa population as the "transitional communities" serve for "Anglo-modified" urban Navajos.

Summary of conclusions

Usually, northern Minnesota Chippewa do not migrate directly to North City from their home communities. The economic structure and race relations in North City discourage extensive immigration of young adult Chippewa in search of employment opportunities. These Indians are more likely to migrate directly from reservations to large cities, as did many North City Indians earlier in their lives. Consequently, the age structure of the North City Indian population is more like that of rural communities than that expected in urban situations. Most North City Indians had established an economic tie to the city prior to relocation.

An important distinguishing characteristic of North City Indians is their social marginality. Reservation out-marriage and unusual occupational history are the major manifestations of marginality. Although a North City Indian may be marginal to a specific reservation society, he or she is not necessarily marginal to the general sociocultural Indian milieu of northern Minnesota; thus, North City is an ecologically advantageous habitat for the socially marginal. Furthermore, the interreservational marriages of North City Chippewa and the "way station" function of North City Indians' homes appears to make North City a nexus for the social network integration of the several reservations into a regional Chippewa social order, analagous to the tribal integration of 19th-century Mescalero Apache (Basehart 1967)—much as North City is a trade, administrative, and political center for Indians, and others, in the surrounding countryside.

The geographic context of North City has facilitated examination of resident Indians' adaptations to several environmental elements outside the city. Including these elements in the analysis has produced a more accurate representation of the total adaptive process than if we considered adaptation only in terms of the city element of the environment.

In general there are significant positive associations among levels of adaptation to elements of "white culture" as well as to elements of "Indian culture." The two kinds of adaptations are negatively associated on the whole, but economic adaptation is unrelated to nonlinguistic measures of experience with Indian activities. This absence of association has been interpreted as an indication that residence in North City affords northern Minnesota Chippewa the opportunity for a wide range of individual variation in "maximizing" the benefits of disparate elements of their overall environment.

8
Anishinabe, a People

J. Anthony Paredes

In view of the great diversity of historical, social, economic, and cultural characteristics of contemporary Chippewa life described in the preceding chapters, the question becomes: how can one identify a contemporary Chippewa social entity in northern Minnesota?

Before answering this question, we should emphasize that while the studies in this volume comprise a fair sample of current Chippewa diversity, they are only a sample. Several of the Indian communities on the Broken Reed Reservation are mentioned only briefly here. The people of the Beaver Pelt Reservation are included only tangentially in some of the research, and the Deer Lake Reservation is represented primarily by Rynkiewich's specialized study of powwows. Additionally, thousands of Chippewa, or Ojibwa, reside on 4 other Minnesota reservations, several reservations in Wisconsin, Michigan, North Dakota and Montana, and many reserves in Canada; and there are many metropolitan Chippewa in such cities as Minneapolis, St. Paul, Chicago, Los Angeles, and San Francisco. Thus "the Chippewa" are a widely dispersed and diverse group (undoubtedly, the same could be said of many modern American Indian "tribes"). Because the generalizations made in this chapter are derived from only a small sample of that diversity, these statements are not necessarily applicable to other Chippewa. Nonetheless, the range of variation among the communities studied is wide enough and the methodology of the studies sufficiently rigorous to make these summary conclusions useful guides to an understanding of current Chippewa life.

Patterns and variations among contemporary Chippewa

The Chippewa of Minnesota are far from being a homogeneous population. Therefore, description must be approached initially in terms of intercommunity and interindividual ranges of variation along common dimensions—a more complex, tedious approach than the customarily qualitative ethnographic statements made about tribal or peasant peoples, but one that avoids the flat, stereotypic picture that would emerge from attempting to compress the data into a description of the "typical" modern Chippewa of Minnesota. Conversely, qualitative description linked with analyses of interrelationships among quantitatively described variables also avoids the weaknesses of superficial cataloging of statistics of malnutrition, substandard housing, and alcoholism so common in popular descriptions of American Indians.

The Indians of northern Minnesota, as a broad demographic category, are economically disadvantaged by state or national standards. They live in an area that has been designated overall as economically depressed; the population as a whole is poorer than the state and nation, and many white communities as well as Indian have family incomes well below state and national medians. But median incomes and standards of living among the Chippewa vary from community to community, depending upon a complex of such factors as proximity to employment opportunities, availability of public services, size of community, and general patterns of relationships with whites. Moreover, as most clearly demonstrated in the chapters by Jackson, Roufs, Pelto, and Paredes, within each community there are wide ranges of variation among Indian households in cash income and material style of life. Each community has members, including both families and individuals, living in poverty by any American standard, but at least a few Chippewa in nearly every community have a standard of living surpassing median levels for the general northern Minnesota population. Even in North City many families substantially augment their incomes through hunting and fishing and their cash through sources likely to be overlooked in ordinary economic surveys of modern Chippewa. As a result, any blanket characterization of modern Chippewa as "poverty-stricken" must be regarded somewhat skeptically as a generalization, unless one wishes to define only the poverty-stricken as "real Indians." This should not be taken to mean, however, that Minnesota Chippewa typically live in affluence.

Because the population of northern Minnesota as a whole falls below national standards of economic well-being, it is not surprising that the Chippewa, who constitute approximately 10 percent of that population, are also below national economic standards. More important, even though economic conditions of local whites as well as Indians are depressed, the Chippewa as a group are below even the *local* white economic levels. While support for this statement is not as complete as one would like, together the studies by Pelto and Paredes demonstrate that in absolute terms the economic position of North City Indians is superior to that of Indians in James Lake, but when compared to whites in their own communities, the relative positions of North City and James Lake Indians are much the same. Although the Indians of Wicket, when compared with some white communities studied by the Upper Minnesota Research Project, have a higher median income, a more meaningful comparison would be with white towns in similar proximity to the Iron Range. Unfortunately the data for such a comparison are not available, but in all probability the level of Indian incomes in relation to those of whites in the same situation would be much the same as in the case of James Lake or North City. In the economic comparison of Chippewa and whites, relative deprivation is not absolutely categorical but is rather a situation of overlapping ranges of variation: some Chippewa high in economic measures fall within the white range and some whites low in these measures fall within the Indian range.

A common assumption is that crime, school truancy and dropouts, illegitimacy, and family instability rates are correlates of poverty. No systematic data on these indices are included here, but the parameters of the modern Chippewa situation in these respects probably closely parallel those that are strictly economic. However, Pelto's work obliquely suggests that these social-problem behaviors are more susceptible to exacerbation by any overt or subtle discrimination by whites that may exist. Furthermore, the association between material style of life and other elements of white culture demonstrated by Paredes indicates close connections between economic variation and middle-class behaviors among Chippewa.

Much has been made of the individualistic character of traditional Ojibwa society, and some of the authors in this book have directly examined the question of Chippewa individualism. Although no data in these studies deal directly with psychological aspects of individualism, the studies do reveal that among modern Chippewa, individualism as a feature of social interaction is subject to conditioning by a variety of situational factors. Rice Villagers appear to have developed a tightly knit, informally cooperative, closed society based on ties of kinship and exclusive commitment to the distinctive beliefs and practices of Peyotism. Wicket residents demonstrate the capacity of Chippewa communities (given an adequate economic base and external support) to override consciously longstanding patterns of interpersonal mistrust and pursue communal goals systematically. Even the relatively atomistic James Lakes Chippewa have been somewhat successful in undertaking temporary, concerted political actions when presented with a sufficient stimulus or, perhaps more accurately, irritant. Moreover, Pelto's data suggest that the Chippewa evince more day-to-day sociability, particularly with kinsmen, than do many of their white neighbors. While data on the Chippewa of North City might superficially provide support for the idea of a basic Chippewa proclivity for individualistic orientations, it is extremely difficult to sort out what is distinctly Chippewa and what is inherent in the prerequisites of town life. Furthermore, data on North City Indians' varying rates of interaction with reservation Chippewa support the view that the extent of individualism among present-day Chippewa is itself an individual matter. Finally, as Rynkiewich has shown, powwows, with their roots in the traditional past, are a powerful institutional mechanism for fostering and perpetuating a sense of separate, corporate identity in certain reservation communities. Thus, any discussion of individualism among contemporary Chippewa must take into account specific historical, economic, social, and political conditions in particular communities. (Such a discussion should also take into consideration the self-professed individualism of the rural whites, particularly Scandinavian descendants, among whom the Chippewa have lived for over 70 years.)

An argument for a Chippewa predisposition to individualistic adaptations may be made simply on the basis of economic data presented in the preceding chapters. Agents of social betterment frequently decry the "Indian" pattern of sharing limited resources among friends and relatives, thus depressing the overall economic condition of that group as well as discouraging the ambitious individual. Plenty of evidence indicating communal sharing of goods and services in the contemporary Chippewa communities (most pronounced in Rice Village and least pronounced in North City) has been presented. Yet all communities show wide ranges of variation among households in cash income and acquisition of major goods, despite relatively closed social networks of kinsmen and friends (even in North City, although such data are not included here). It may be argued that all these data are evidence of highly individual modes of adaptation to present-day economic conditions. But it would be extremely difficult, and perhaps not worth the effort, to assign relative weights to covert cultural patterning derived from the Ojibwa past and contemporary survival requirements as causative factors in the economic individualism of modern Chippewa families. It is interesting—in the light of extended anthropological discussion of the individualism of Ojibwa and their passive acceptance of white domination—that from the ranks of metropolitan Chippewa have come some of the most militant leaders of recent Indian activities, as in the American Indian Movement and in the disruption of Columbus Day festivities in California in 1968.

"Traditional culture" shows essentially the same patterns of variation seen in economics and individualism. For example, in studying Chippewa native language ability, one finds important intercommunity differences in the proportion of native speakers but overlapping ranges of individual variation in fluency. Although the data presented in these studies are incomplete, the situation is much the same for other traits, such as possession of an Indian name, knowledge of folklore, and religious beliefs. Wild rice gathering presents special problems due to its relatively recent transformation from an aboriginal subsistence practice to a small but well-integrated part of the state and national economy. The monetary transformation of wild rice notwithstanding, the same pattern emerges: intercommunity differences in economic importance and intracommunity differences in frequency (ranging from those who seldom, if ever, harvest rice to those who rely heavily on it as a source of income). In addition, as Berde has shown, involvement in ricing activity seems to be directly correlated with socioeconomic status in the larger society.

Indeed, one of the most interesting results of this set of studies is the rather unexpected relationships discovered between contemporary manifestations of "Indianness" and economic adjustment. Of the communities studied, Wicket has the highest overall economic level; it is also the only community that has engaged in conscious, concerted efforts to maintain and promote a traditional heritage, principally through its powwow. These data suggest that, in the modern context, organized community expressions of Chippewa identity are partially dependent upon minimal levels of economic success. Objections to this interpretation might be raised on the grounds that the powwow is a modern, synthetic creation. However, Rynkiewich has shown that the modern Wicket powwow is modeled on historically modified, ethnological complexes perpetuated and/or remembered by some Wicket residents. At the individual level, Pelto's sketches of various Chippewa leaders in James Lake reveal no particular relationship between economic or traditional practices and involvement in "Indian politics." Likewise, Paredes shows that, among North City Indians, although adaptation to the American economy is closely related to other indices of middle-class white behavior, the reverse is generally not true. With the exception of native language fluency, North City Indians' economic adjustment and involvement in distinctly "Indian" activities seem to vary independently. So it may be tentatively concluded that degree of "Indianness" cannot accurately be predicted from individual levels of economic adjustment.

Chippewa identity

In view of the complex and highly variable situation among Minnesota Chippewa today, what justification is there for conceptualizing "the Chippewa" as a distinct social entity? Certainly in much of their daily behavior they differ little from their white neighbors. Many Chippewa know little of native language and lore. They no longer constitute a tribal culture in the anthropological sense. Their independence as a political entity is severely limited by the state and nation. Their lives are bounded by the same social, economic, and political forces that shape the behavior of other Americans. Nonetheless, within the context of national political and economic supremacy and immersion in the mass culture of the United States, they can be differentiated on 3 closely related bases: structure, culture, and ideology. Discussion of these factors must be prefaced with a brief consideration of biological distinctiveness.

Chippewa social differentiation rests upon, and is in part derived from, the biological descent of the Chippewa from a discernible aboriginal population. However, genes and social identity are only partially correlated. There are a few "full-bloods," and many "mixed-bloods" display an Indian phenotype; but the processes of white admixture and acculturation have produced a situation in which some individuals regarded as "Indian" by both whites and Indians may have more European-derived ancestry than Chippewa. Others can "pass for white," but are identified by themselves, their kinsmen, and their associates as Indians. A few with predominantly Indian ancestry have come to be accepted in white communities as "good people" but still "Indians."

A great many Chippewa with varying degrees of white ancestry bear key physical characteristics that immediately mark them as "Indian" in the eyes of both Indians and whites, and they are treated accordingly. Among these characteristics are brown eyes, straight dark brown or black hair, and any skin color darker than "fair." Two of the researchers, Jackson and Paredes, have those traits and are of the opinion that this may have contributed to their acceptance by and rapport with some Chippewa. These two individuals may have been regarded as "Indians" by non-Indians as well. (Anecdotally, a local, white research assistant reported to Paredes that when she and a girlfriend happened to pass by a basketball game in which Paredes was playing with a group of Indians, the girlfriend made a casual reference to "all those Indians out there"—to which the research assistant replied, "That's no Indian, that's my boss.") Thus, while genetic history may be a basic starting point for understanding current Chippewa social identification, biology has become only incidental to the processes by which the continued social existence of the Chippewa is maintained. Conversely, nonbiological factors have prevented complete intermarriage and have thereby preserved a Chippewa biological population, such as it may be.

The structural separateness of the Chippewa from other Americans is quite explicitly maintained by local representation of national institutions specifically designed to serve Indians, such as the Bureau of Indian Affairs, the Indian Division of Public Health, and the Indian missions of various churches, both on and off the reservations. The general exclusion of Indians from other white organizations, such as the social clubs in James Lake, whether intentional or not, serves to maintain structural boundaries between whites and the general Indian population. The structural integrity of specific Indian communities, as well as whole reservations, is maintained in the same way as that of other communities: through territorial delineation, exclusive rights of political participation, and control of communal resources. Since all of these communities are comprised primarily of individuals who are locally categorized as "Indian," their separation is interwoven with the maintenance of broad racial boundaries as well.

Selection of marriage partners from one's own community, although not supported by formal sanctions in northern Minnesota, appears to be a particularly important aspect of the maintenance of community and racial boundaries. This is negatively reflected in the special case of the high proportion of reservation-exogamous marriages among the off-reservation Chippewa in North City.

The economic differential between Indians and whites is an especially powerful factor in the structural delineation of a Chippewa social category. Despite (1) local white income averages that are below state and national levels, (2) considerable overlap between white and Chippewa standards of living, and (3) continuing increase of goods and services for both groups, median incomes and material life-styles of Chippewa and whites remain sufficiently divergent to support generalized characterizations of the Chippewa as poor and the whites as affluent. Interpretation and evaluation of this perceived difference varies, of course, from "Indians are basically lazy" to "whites are prejudiced and take advantage of Indians," depending upon the social identity and individual personality of the observer. In the local context it matters little that other minorities in the United States and some foreign peoples may be more economically disadvantaged than the Chippewa, or that some northern Minnesota whites live in extreme poverty while some Chippewa maintain a middle-class standard of living. Generally speaking, for both Indians and whites poverty tends to be identified with "being Indian," while relative affluence and its attendant social advantages become defining characteristics of "being white."

In theory, at least, none of these structural bases for discriminating a Chippewa ethnic category are dependent upon fundamental, qualitative differences in cultural content. Indeed, Hicks and Kertzer (1972) have argued that for such fully acculturated Indians as the "Monhegans" of New England, Indian identity can be maintained even in the absence of clear-cut structural boundaries. However, the structural differentiation of Chippewa (and other) individuals and communities as a distinct *social* category in itself can be powerful enough to imply a *cultural* difference, whether one exists or not. This presumed cultural difference serves as a stimulus for many kinds of studies—governmental, educational, and anthropological—that appear to be predicated on the assumption that the Chippewa are indeed "different." Such studies reinforce the mutual perceptions of "differentness" held by Indians and whites. These perceptions are the cognitive underpinnings of the structural separation of Chippewa from other northern Minnesotans. Thus, the mere fact of conducting the researches reported in this volume has contributed to the maintenance of Chippewa distinctiveness. Such studies probably also indirectly serve to strengthen any actual cultural differences that may exist. Nonetheless, research on Indians can engender hostility toward such investigations ("The Indians have been studied to death") because of apparent disregard by researchers for the "real problems" faced by Indians. Fortunately this kind of hostility was seldom, if ever, encountered by the authors in this volume; as a matter of fact, on at least one occasion an informant explicitly contrasted research reported here as being "different" from the numerous government studies that he personally found so objectionable. Often it seemed clear that individuals saw this research as being to their advantage, even though they knew no direct rewards were forthcoming.

There are in fact some qualitative cultural factors that differentiate Chippewa from other northern Minnesotans and thus further reinforce and complement the structural distinctions of the Chippewa. These cultural differences are not simply "ethnographic survivals" from the aboriginal past; they are historically derived products of the interplay of Indian and European traditions. Some show considerable Euro-American influence and others manifest little; but all have been modified to some extent over time.

Despite individual and community variation in retention of native Chippewa practices and beliefs, at least 2 major cultural institutions distinguish Chippewa from the general population: wild rice gathering and powwows. Chippewa from all the communities studied participate in these activities. Although there are important local variations, which can serve as foci for intercommunity rivalry, Chippewa representing the entire spectrum of individual variation described here engage in some form of these activities. While it is true that some whites take part in them as well, their mode and degree of participation is different from those of Indians. Moreover, even in the absence of complete statistical documentation, it is safe to say that the majority of northern Minnesota Chippewa have participated in these activities, while only a small minority of northern Minnesota whites have done so. Thus, participation in powwows and ricing are major points at which contemporary Chippewa can be behaviorally distinguished from whites. Furthermore, powwows and wild rice gathering are the primary public expressions of cultural differences that serve to buttress the structural boundaries between whites and Indians. Powwows explicitly display the differences, and rice harvesting has become a focus of opposition between the Indian community and state government. Powwows seem to function primarily in supporting local Chippewa identity; but they also play an important role in linking the Chippewa to the larger American Indian network of the region and nation.

A third distinguishing Chippewa cultural institution that should perhaps be included is the wake. However, compared to powwows and ricing, wakes are less public, more closely paralleled by native white practices, and more variable in form—ranging from "pagan" to heavily Christianized, and including the peyote wake. Nevertheless, in Wicket, opposition to "Indian wakes" was an important factor provoking initial efforts for social change. In general, participation in Indian wakes is another measure by which the majority of Chippewa can be culturally differentiated from the majority of whites. Like the other 2 activities, wakes involve overlapping white and Indian ranges of individual variation in extent of participation, analogous to "racial" overlap in population genetics.

Besides powwows, ricing, and wakes, numerous other elements of more or less traditional Chippewa culture—language, supernatural beliefs, oral literature, and handicrafts—are still to be found among the modern Chippewa. However, they are not nearly so widespread among the Chippewa as is participation in ricing, powwows, and wakes. Furthermore, the opportunities for social expression of these other beliefs and behaviors are limited, since they tend to be individual rather than group traits. In contrast, powwows, ricing, and wakes provide opportunities for participation in Indian activities regardless of whether an individual can speak Chippewa, believes in grand medicine, or can tan a deer hide. Nonetheless, Chippewa who do not have these other elements of traditional culture in their own personal cultural repertoires frequently have kinsmen who do. Often, nontraditional Chippewa were brought up in an environment where native practices were commonplace. Nearly all Chippewa know that these traits "came from our ancestors." Thus, these ethnographic "survivals" belong to all the Chippewa, even if only by association. Finally, a vast array of motor habits, attitudes, personality configurations, value orientations, and other implicit cultural patterns of which neither Chippewa nor whites are ordinarily conscious may exist and may categorically distinguish the Chippewa. Research is needed in this area to provide a fuller understanding of the bases for maintaining personal and social boundaries between Indians and whites.

A third set of factors, which may be ultimately the most important, completes the picture of contemporary Chippewa social identity. These are the ideological factors, the symbols by which modern Chippewa consciously identify themselves as a *people* and that they manipulate in order to perpetuate their continued existence as a distinctive element of society. Symbols, of course, are classically included under the rubric of "culture." However, the term "ideological" is introduced here to differentiate conscious symbolization of Chippewa identity in the modern national context from tribal symbols directly derived from the traditional past, which tend to be simply experienced rather than consciously conceived and manipulated.

Nonetheless, the "ideological" is closely connected with the "cultural" and "structural" as these terms have been used here. Many of the structural and cultural parameters of current Chippewa identity acquire symbolic value. Reserved lands, special status with the federal government, economic deprivation relative to whites, usage of native language, powwow attendance, and wild rice gathering serve not only as structural and cultural supports of the Chippewa entity but also become transformed into symbolic devices for explicit furthering of ethnic distinctiveness. Paradoxically, these symbols may also be employed in reducing structural forces that have segregated the Chippewa and, thus, in better articulating the Chippewa to the larger society. Historically these modern symbols have emerged as a result of the impending possibility of the loss of structural support of tribal integrity provided by federal protection and services; the gradual erasing of cultural distinctiveness through acculturation and political pressure; and, with greater articulation to national culture, increasing frustration over perceived social and economic inequalities between Indians and whites. As the symbols of Chippewa identity become established, they serve as rallying points for organized actions designed to strengthen the Chippewa position in the modern world. For example, the Wicket community development effort was centered around combating the new priest's threats to local institutions (such as wakes), reviving the powwow, and reducing the disparity between white and Indian housing facilities. Likewise, the Chippewa of James Lake mobilized support for their civil rights activities on the basis that the common lot of the Chippewa was one of discrimination. Similarly, but less spectacularly, the studies by Rynkiewich and Berde mention numerous explicit statements by Indians that indicate conscious conceptualization of powwows and ricing as contemporary symbols of Indian identity.

One of the most potent symbols of Indian identity is land, although it can also be a point of conflict between Indian groups (as in debates over whether Deer Lakers should be permitted to rice in Minnesota Chippewa Tribe waters). There are several bases for the power of this symbol:

(1) Aboriginal ownership of the land differentiates American Indians from other U.S. minorities.

(2) Historically, land has been the primary issue in Indians' official dealings with whites; thus, it underlies another important symbol, broken treaties.

(3) In recent decades the threat of the U.S. government's withdrawal of its guardianship of existing Indian lands and subjection of the land to state jurisdiction, i.e., "termination," as well as the establishment of the U. S. Indians Claims Commission, have stimulated even more interest in land.

(4) Land represents the major resource with which Indian leaders hope to overcome the economic differential between Indians and whites.

(5) Tribal lands and reservation areas are the locus of Indian social and cultural resources and the home base to which off-reservation Indians can retreat from the "white man's world."

Most important, land is the major link between the present and the past, providing Chippewa with a sense of historical experience. With increasing articulation to the national society and participation in mass culture, the knowledge of being a people with a separate history is crucial to the Chippewa's creation of a unique position in national life.

In the hierarchy of Chippewa symbols, the most inclusive is "the Indian way of life." Although the Indian, or tribal, way of life is becoming a national symbol that transcends political divisions of American Indians, in the local context of northern Minnesota it serves primarily to cement the identity of the Chippewa. The Indian way of life is supported by all the structural, cultural, and ideological factors presented here, as well as by a widely shared assumption that Indians think and feel differently from whites in some pervasive way, external appearances notwithstanding. The mystique of the Indian way of life is becoming the quasi-mythical charter for the processes by which the Chippewa and other Indians are accommodating to the national society—not by reinforcing structural boundaries or by being assimilated in the larger society but by incorporating into the national culture as an entity whose distinctiveness is maintained by an ideology of what Deloria has called "peoplehood" (1970:44). At the present time, even though the Chippewa are highly acculturated and greatly mixed with whites, structural and cultural factors alone are sufficient for distinguishing the Chippewa from other northern Minnesotans. Nonetheless, it is the ideology of peoplehood that gives Chippewa identity its distinctly modern cast and through which the Chippewa are brought into consonance with other elements of the contemporary United States.

Ideologies of peoplehood appear to be the principal means by which the members of so-called plural societies sort themselves into the various components of the society. Indeed, the separate identity of certain groups, such as some of the Indians of the eastern United States, appears to be maintained almost solely on the basis of ideology in the absence of real structural and cultural differentiators. While peoplehood is usually associated with race and/or ethnic or national origin, this is not always the case. Common occupational background can be a starting point for developing an ideology of peoplehood, as in "farm people" and "working people." In certain cases regionality has produced full-blown ideologies of peoplehood, complete with the "way of life" symbol, as in "the southern way of life." While it is tempting to think of all the ideologies of peoplehood as being neatly subsumed and articulated under the grand symbol of "the American way of life," dissident elements in the society have come to regard that symbol as having been unfairly appropriated by an amorphous segment of the nation that cross-cuts regional, occupational, ethnic, and religious lines.

All of these ideologies have as their essential features (1) the notion of common genealogical descent from a parent population distinguishable by race, religion, region, or occupation, (2) belief in a unique historical experience of that population and its descendants, and (3) belief in structural forms and cultural patterns by which that people may be differentiated from all others, even though such structural and cultural differentiators actually no longer exist as universal group traits. In addition, ideologies of peoplehood are sustained and reinforced through nonmembers' acknowledgment of adherents as distinctive components of the society. Such acknowledgment is perhaps most evident during national elections, when politicians explicitly vie for "the black vote," "the Jewish vote," and so on. Although all the forms of peoplehood known thus far are directly or indirectly linked to parentage, there appear to be incipient forms of peoplehood that need not be genealogically based, as in "educated people," "concerned people," and, most problematic of all, "young people."

In addition, then, to the distinct local communities of Chippewa maintained by structural forces and a core of cultural traits that generally distinguish Chippewa from whites, contemporary Chippewa social identity is sustained by a modern ideology that emerges from a historical experience of discrimination and dispossession and a recognition of a cultural heritage different from that of all other Americans. Similar ideologies developing among other Indian groups are producing simultaneously a renewed pride in specific "tribal" identity and an emergent continental ideology of American Indian or, in some quarters, "native American" peoplehood transcending tribal and national boundaries. In the usage of modern Indian leaders, "Indian Country" is a concept that is not bound by mere geography.

A sure indication of the current type of Chippewa social identity is their widespread preference for "Indian people" as the term to use in referring to them. The Chippewa and other American Indians appear to be increasingly conscious of the importance of maintaining an identity in the modern world that is not based merely on the white man's categorizations of them all simply as Indians, but rather emphasizes the continuity of the modern Indian people with a historical tradition that precedes and is independent of whites in North America. Thus, a Minnesota Chippewa writer has proposed recently "to relume the tribal identity of the woodland people by changing the tribal name back to *Anishinabe*" (Vizenor 1971:16).

So, after 350 years of acculturation and intermarriage with whites and despite a complex array of individual and community adaptations to 20th-century America, the Chippewa endure—no longer an aboriginal tribe, not even simply a racial minority, but a people. *Anishinabe* means "the people."

References Cited

Aberle, David F.
1966   The Peyote Religion among the Navajo. Viking Fund Publications in Anthropology, No. 42. New York: Wenner-Gren Foundation for Anthropological Research, Inc.

Ablon, Joan
1964   Relocated American Indians in the San Francisco Bay Area: Social Interaction and Indian Identity. Human Organization 23(4):296–304.

Adair, John, and Evon Vogt
1949   Navajo and Zuni Veterans: A Study of Contrasting Modes of Culture Change. American Anthropologist 51:547–61.

Baraga, Friedrich
1853   A Dictionary of the Otchipwa Language, Explained in English. Cincinnati: Jos. A. Hemann.

Barnouw, Victor
1950   Acculturation and Personality among the Wisconsin Chippewa. American Anthropological Association Memoirs, No. 72. Menasha, Wis.: George Banta Publishing Co.
1961   Chippewa Social Atomism. American Anthropologist 63:1006–13.
1963   Culture and Personality. Homewood, Ill.: Dorsey Press.

Barrett, S. A.
1911   The Dream Dance of the Chippewa and Menominee In-
        dians of Northern Wisconsin. Milwaukee Public Museum,
        Bulletin 1(4):251–406.
Basehart, Harry W.
1967   The Resource Holding Corporation among the Mesca-
        lero Apache. Southwestern Journal of Anthropology
        23:277–91.
Basso, Keith H.
1970   The Cibecue Apache. New York: Holt, Rinehart and
        Winston.
Bennett, John W.
1944   The Development of Ethnological Theory as Illustrated by
        Studies of the Plains Sun Dance. American Anthropologist
        64:162–81.
Bock, Phillip K.
1966   The Micmac Indians of Restigouche: History and Contem-
        porary Description. National Museum of Canada, Bulletin
        213, Anthropological Series, No. 77. Ottawa: Queen's
        Printer.
Boggs, Stephan T.
1956   An Interactional Study of Ojibwa Socialization. American
        Sociological Review 21:191–98.
1958   Culture Change and the Personality of Ojibwa Children.
        American Anthropologist 60:47–58.
Boissevain, Ethel
1963   Detribalization and Group Identity: The Narragansett In-
        dian Case. Transactions of the New York Academy of
        Sciences, Ser. II, 25(5):493–502.
1965   Tribes, Clubs, and Factions among Contemporary Southern
        New England Indians. Paper presented at the 64th Annual
        Meeting of the American Anthropological Association.
Braroe, Neile W.
1965   Reciprocal Exploitation in an Indian-White Community.
        Southwestern Journal of Anthropology 21(2):166–77.
Brunner, Edmund de Schweinitz, and Wilbur C. Hallenbeck
1955   American Society: Urban and Rural Patterns. New York:
        Harper and Row.
Bushnell, John H.

1968 From American Indian to Indian American: The Changing Identity of the Hupa. American Anthropologist 70:1108–16.

Carneiro, Robert L.
1962 Scale Analysis as an Instrument for the Study of Cultural Evolution. Southwestern Journal of Anthropology 18(2):149–69.

Casis, Ana, and Kingsley Davis
1953 Traits of the Urban and Rural Populations. *In* Readings in Latin American Social Organization and Institutions. Olan E. Leonard and Charles P. Loomis, eds. East Lansing: Michigan State University Press.

Caudill, William
1949 Psychological Characteristics of Acculturated Wisconsin Ojibwa Children. American Anthropologist 51:409–27.

Chance, Norman A.
1966 The Eskimo of North America. New York: Holt, Rinehart and Winston.

Copeland, Priscilla
1949 An Analysis of Peer Groups among the [Deer] Lake Ojibwa. Master's thesis, University of Chicago.

De Laguna, Frederica
1968 Presidential Address—1967. American Anthropologist 70(3):469–76.

Deloria, Vine, Jr.
1970 We Talk, You Listen: New Tribes, New Turf. New York: Macmillan.

Densmore, Frances
1913 Chippewa Music II. Bureau of American Ethnology, Smithsonian Institution, Bulletin 53, Washington, D.C.
1918 Teton Sioux Music. Bureau of American Ethnology, Smithsonian Institution, Bulletin 61. Washington, D.C.
1929 Chippewa Customs. Bureau of American Ethnology, Smithsonian Institution, Bulletin 86. Washington, D.C.
1932 Menominee Music. Bureau of American Ethnology, Smithsonian Institution, Bulletin 102. Washington, D.C.

Dowling, John H.
1968 A "Rural" Community in an Urban Setting. Human Organization 28(3):236–40.

Downs, James F.
    1966   The Two Worlds of the Washo: An Indian Tribe of California
              and Nevada. New York: Holt, Rinehart and Winston.
Dozier, Edward
    1951   Resistance to Acculturation and Assimilation in an Indian
              Pueblo. American Anthropologist 53:56–66.
Dunning, R. W.
    1959   Social and Economic Change among the Northern Ojibwa.
              Toronto: University of Toronto Press.
Eggan, Fred
    1954   Social Anthropology and the Method of Controlled Com-
              parison. American Anthropologist 56:743–63.
    1966   The American Indian: Perspectives for the Study of Social
              Change. Chicago: Aldine.
Embree, John F.
    1950   Thailand—A Loosely Structured Social System. American
              Anthropologist 52:181–93.
Finney, Joseph C., ed.
    1969   Culture Change, Mental Health, and Poverty. Lexington:
              University of Kentucky Press.
Fletcher, Alice, and Francis L. La Flesche
    1911   The Omaha Tribe. Bureau of American Ethnology, Smith-
              sonian Institution, 27th Annual Report, pp. 15–672.
              Washington, D.C.
Freilich, Morris
    1958   Cultural Persistence among the Modern Iroquois. An-
              thropos 53:473–83.
Friedl, Ernestine
    1956   Persistence in Chippewa Culture and Personality. American
              Anthropologist 58:814–25.
Freeman, Linton C.
    1965   Elementary Applied Statistics: For Students in Behavioral
              Science. New York: John Wiley.
Gardner, Peter M.
    1966   Symmetric Respect and Memorate Knowledge: The Struc-
              ture and Ecology of Individualistic Culture. Southwestern
              Journal of Anthropology 22(4):389–415.
Goodenough, Ward Hunt
    1963a   Cooperation in Change: An Anthropological Approach to

Community Development. New York: Russell Sage Foundation.

1963b   Some Applications of Guttman Scale Analysis to Ethnographic and Cultural Theory. Southwestern Journal of Anthropology 19:235–49.

1971   Culture, Language, and Society: A McCaleb Module in Anthropology. Reading, Mass.: Addison-Wesley Publishing Company.

Graves, Theodore D.
1970   The Personal Adjustment of Navajo Indian Migrants to Denver, Colorado. American Anthropologist 72:35–54.

Grindstaff, Carl F.
1968   The Negro, Urbanization, and Relative Deprivation in the Deep South. Social Problems 15(3):342–52.

Guttman, Louis
1944   A Basis for Scaling Qualitative Data. American Sociological Review 9:346–58.

Hallowell, A. Irving
1940   Aggression in Saulteaux Society. *Reprinted in* Culture and Experience, pp. 277–90. A. Irving Hallowell, ed. Philadelphia: University of Pennsylvania Press, 1955.

1942   Acculturation Processes and Personality Changes as Indicated by the Rorschach Technique. Rorschach Research Exchange 6:42–50.

1945   The Rorschach Technique in the Study of Personality and Culture. American Anthropologist 47:195–210.

1950   Values, Acculturation, and Mental Health. American Journal of Orthopsychiatry 20:732–43.

1952   Ojibwa Personality and Acculturation. Proceedings of the 29th International Congress of Americanists, pp. 105–12. Chicago.

1955   Acculturation and the Personality of the Ojibwa. *In* Culture and Experience. A. Irving Hallowell, ed. Philadelphia: University of Pennsylvania Press.

Hammel, Eugene A.
1964   Some Characteristics of Rural Villages and Urban Slum Populations on the Coast of Peru. Southwestern Journal of Anthropology 20(4):346–58.

Hays, H. R.

1958   From Ape to Angel. New York: Alfred A. Knopf.
Hickerson, Harold
  1960   The Feast of the Dead among the Seventeenth-Century
              Algonkians of the Upper Great Lakes. American An-
              thropologist 62:81–107.
  1962   The Southwestern Chippewa: An Ethnohistorical Study.
              American Anthropological Association Memoirs, No. 92.
              Menasha, Wis.
  1963   The Sociohistorical Significance of Two Chippewa Cere-
              monials. American Anthropologist 65:67–85.
  1965   The Virginia Deer and Intertribal Buffer Zones in the Upper
              Mississippi Valley. In Man, Culture and Animals: The Role
              of Animals in Human Ecological Adjustments, pp. 43–65.
              Anthony Leeds and Andrew P. Vayda, eds. Washington,
              D.C.: American Association for the Advancement of Sci-
              ence.
  1966   The Genesis of Bilaterality among Two Divisions of Chip-
              pewa. American Anthropologist 68:1–26.
  1967   Some Implications of the Theory of the Particularity or
              "Atomism" of Northern Algonquins. Current Anthropol-
              ogy 8(4):313–43.
  1971   The Chippewa of the Upper Great Lakes: A Study in
              Sociopolitical Change. In North American Indians in His-
              torical Perspective, pp. 169–99. Eleanor Burke Leacock
              and Nancy Oestreich Lurie, eds. New York: Random
              House.
Hicks, George L., and David I. Kertzer
  1972   Making a Middle Way: Problems of Monhegan Identity.
              Southwestern Journal of Anthropology 28:1–24.
Hilger, M. Inez
  1951   Chippewa Childlife and Its Cultural Background. Bureau of
              American Ethnology, Smithsonian Institution, Bulletin
              146. Washington, D.C.
Hodge, William H.
  1969   The Albuquerque Navajos. Anthropological Papers of the
              University of Arizona, No. 11. Tucson: University of
              Arizona Press.
Hoebel, E. Adamson
  1941   The Comanche Sun Dance and the Messianic Outbreak of
              1873. American Anthropologist 43:301–3.

1966   Anthropology: The Study of Man. New York: McGraw-Hill.

Hoffman, W. J.
1891   The Mide'wiwin or "Grand Medicine Society" of the Ojibwa. Bureau of American Ethnology, Smithsonian Institution, 7th Annual Report, pp. 143–300. Washington, D.C.
1896   The Menominee Indians. Bureau of American Ethnology, Smithsonian Institution, 14th Annual Report, pp. 3–328. Washington, D.C.

Honigmann, John J.
1949   Culture and Ethics of Kaska Society. Yale University Publications in Anthropology, No. 40. New Haven.

Howard, James H.
1951   Notes on the Dakota Grass Dance. Southwestern Journal of Anthropology 7:82–85.
1955   The Pan-Indian Culture of Oklahoma. Scientific Monthly 28:215–20.
1965   The Ponca Tribe. Bureau of American Ethnology, Smithsonian Institution, Bulletin 195. Washington, D.C.
1966   The Henry Davis Drum Rite: An Unusual Drum Religion Variant of the Minnesota Ojibwa. Plains Anthropologist 11:117–26.

Hunter, A. E.
1965   County Work Force Estimates: 1965. St. Paul: Minnesota Department of Employment Security, March, 1966. Mimeographed.

Hurt, Wesley, R., Jr.
1961–62 The Urbanization of the Yankton Indians. Human Organization 20(4):226–31.

James, Bernard
1954   Some Critical Observations Concerning Analyses of Chippewa "Atomism" and Chippewa Personality. American Anthropologist 56:283–86.
1961   Social-Psychological Dimensions of Ojibwa Acculturation. American Anthropologist 63:721–46.
1970   Continuity and Emergence in Indian Poverty Culture. Current Anthropology 11(4–5):435–43.

Jenks, Albert E.
1900   The Wild Rice Gatherers of the Upper Lakes: A Study in

American Primitive Economics. Bureau of American Ethnology, Smithsonian Institution, 19th Annual Report, pp. 1013–37. Washington, D.C.

Kay, Paul
    1964   A Guttman Scale Model of Tahitian Consumer Behavior. Southwestern Journal of Anthropology 20(2):160–67.

Kluckhohn, Clyde
    1966   The Ramah Navajo. Bureau of American Ethnology, Smithsonian Institution, Bulletin 196, pp. 327–77. Washington, D.C.

Kupferer, Harriet Jane
    1966   The "Principal People," 1960: A Study of Cultural and Social Groups of the Eastern Cherokee. Bureau of American Ethnology, Smithsonian Institution, Bulletin 196, pp. 215–325. Washington, D.C.

La Barre, Weston
    1964   The Peyote Cult. Hamden, Conn.: The Shoe String Press.

Landes, Ruth
    1937   Ojibwa Sociology. New York: Columbia University Press.
    1937–38 The Personality of the Ojibwa. Character and Personality 6:51–60.
    1939   The Ojibwa Woman. Columbia University Contributions to Anthropology, No. 31. New York.
    1968   Ojibwa Religion and the Midéwiwin. Madison: University of Wisconsin Press.

Leacock, Eleanor B.
    1954   The Montagnais "Hunting Territory" and the Fur Trade. American Anthropological Association Memoirs, No. 78. Menasha, Wis.

League of Women Voters of Minneapolis
    1968   Indians in Minneapolis. Mimeographed.

League of Women Voters of Minnesota
    1962   Indians in Minnesota. Minneapolis: State Organization Service, University of Minnesota.

Leighton, Alexander H.
    1959   My Name is Legion. New York: Basic Books.

Levine, Stuart
    1965   The Indian as American: Some Observations for the Editor's Notebook. Midcontinent American Studies Journal 6:3–22.

Levine, Stuart, and Nancy Oestreich Lurie
  1968   The American Indian Today. Deland, Fla.: Everett Edwards.

Lewis, Oscar
  1961   The Children of Sanchez: Autobiography of a Mexican Family. New York: Random House.

McConnell, Campbell R.
  1960   Elementary Economics: Principles, Problems, and Policies. New York: McGraw-Hill.

McFee, Malcolm
  1968   The 150% Man, a Product of Blackfeet Acculturation. American Anthropologist 70:1096–1107.
  1972   Modern Blackfeet: Montanans on a Reservation. New York: Holt, Rinehart and Winston.

MacGregor, Gordon
  1946   Warriors Without Weapons: A Study of the Society and Personality Development of the Pine Ridge Sioux. Chicago: University of Chicago Press.

Martin, Harry W.
  1964   Correlates of Adjustment Among American Indians in an Urban Environment. Human Organization 23(4):290–95.

Mead, Margaret
  1932   The Changing Culture of an Indian Tribe. New York: Columbia University Press.
  1966   The Changing Culture of an Indian Tribe *with* A New Introduction on the Consequences of Racial Guilt. New York: Capricorn Books.

Merriam, Alan P.
  1967   Ethnomusicology of the Flathead Indians. Viking Fund Publications in Anthropology, No. 44. Chicago: Wenner Gren Foundation for Anthropological Research.

Merton, Robert K.
  1949   Social Theory and Social Structure. New York: The Free Press.

Michelson, Truman
  1923   On the Origin of the So-Called Dream Dance of the Central Algonkians. American Anthropologist 25:277–78.
  1924   Further Remarks on the Origin of the So-Called Dream Dance of the Central Algonkians. American Anthropologist 26:293–94.

1926 Final Notes on the Central Algonquian Dream Dance. American Anthropologist 28:573–76.

Miller, Frank C.
1966 Problems of Succession in a Chippewa Council. *In* Political Anthropology. Marc J. Swartz, Victor W. Turner, and Arthur Tuden, eds. Chicago: Aldine.
1967 Humor in a Chippewa Tribal Council. Ethnology 6(3):263–71.

Miller, Frank C., and Douglas D. Caulkins
1964 Chippewa Adolescents: A Changing Generation. Human Organization 23(2):150–59.

Minnesota Department of Conservation
1965 Minnesota Outdoor Recreation Preliminary Plan. St. Paul.

Minnesota Governor's Human Rights Committee
1965 Minnesota's Indian Citizens. St. Paul.

Mittleholtz, Erwin F.
1957 Historical Review of the [Deer] Lake Indian Reservation. Bemidji, Minn.: General Council of [Deer] Lake Band of Chippewa Indians and Beltrami County Historical Society.

Nicholas, Ralph W.
1966 Segmentary Factional Political Systems. *In* Political Anthropology. Marc J. Swartz, Victor W. Turner, and Arthur Tuden, eds. Chicago: Aldine.

Noon, John A.
1949 Law and Government of the Grand River Iroquois. Viking Fund Publications in Anthropology, No. 12. New York: Wenner Gren Foundation for Anthropological Research.

Oliver, Symmes
1965 Individuality, Freedom of Choice and Cultural Flexibility of the Kamba. American Anthropologist 67(2):421–28.

Opler, Marvin K.
1941 The Integration of the Sun Dance into Ute Religion. American Anthropologist 43:550–72.

Paredes, J. Anthony
1965 Community Celebrations in Northern Minnesota. Paper presented at the 64th Annual Meeting of the American Anthropological Association.
1971 Toward a Reconceptualization of American Indian Urbanization: A Chippewa Case. Anthropological Quarterly 44:256–71.

1973 Interaction and Adaptation among Small-City Chippewa. *In* American Indian Urbanization. Jack O. Waddell and O. Michael Watson, eds. Institute for the Study of Social Change, Purdue University, Monograph 4, pp. 51–73. Mimeographed.

Paredes, J. A., T. Roufs, and G. Pelto
1973 On James' Continuity and Emergence in Indian Poverty Culture. Current Anthropology 14:158–67.

Pelto, Pertti J.
1962 Individualism in Skolt Lapp Society. Kansatieteellinen Arkisto 16. Helsinki: Finnish Antiquities Society.
1968 Differences between "Tight" and "Loose" Societies. Transaction 5:37–40.
1970a Research in Individualistic Societies. *In* Marginal Natives: Anthropologists at Work, pp. 251–92. Morris Freilich, ed. New York: Harper and Row.
1970b Anthropological Research: The Structure of Inquiry. New York: Harper and Row.

Peterson, William
1961 Population. New York: Macmillan.

Polgar, Steven
1960 Biculturation of Mesquakie Teenage Boys. American Anthropologist 63:217–35.

Radin, Paul
1916 The Winnebago Tribe. Bureau of American Ethnography, 37th Annual Report, pp. 35–55. Washington, D.C.
1963 The Autobiography of a Winnebago Indian. New York: Dover Publications, Inc. (Originally published in 1920.)

Rand McNally Commercial Atlas and Marketing Guide.
1965 Richard L. Forstall, ed. 96th edition. Chicago: Rand McNally.

Redfield, Robert
1950 A Village That Chose Progress: Chan Kom Revisited. Chicago: University of Chicago Press.

Redfield, R., R. Linton, and M. J. Herskovits
1936 Memorandum for the Study of Acculturation. American Anthropologist 38:149–52.

Ritzenthaler, Robert E.
1953 The Potawatomi Indians of Wisconsin. Milwaukee Public Museum, Bulletin 19, No. 3, pp. 99–174.

Ritzenthaler, Robert E., and Mary Sellers
    1955   Indians in an Urban Situation. The Wisconsin Archeologist,
            N.S. 36, No. 4:147–61.
Rohner, Ronald P., and Evelyn C. Rohner
    1970   The Kwakiutl Indians of British Columbia. New York:
            Holt, Rinehart and Winston.
Rohrl, Vivian
    1967   The People of Mille Lacs: A Study of Social Organization
            and Value Orientation. Ph.D. dissertation, University of
            Minnesota.
Rottsolk, James E.
    1960   Pines, Mines and Lakes. [Big Run], Minn.: County His-
            torical Society.
Roufs, Timothy G.
    1967   Social Structure and Community Development: An
            Analysis of a Chippewa Case. Master's thesis, University
            of Minnesota.
    1974   A Note on Myth in Method: Some Further Observations on
            James' "Continuity and Emergence in Indian Poverty Cul-
            ture." Current Anthropology 15:307–10.
    1975   The *Anishinabe* of the Minnesota Chippewa Tribe. Phoenix:
            Indian Tribal Series.
    1976   Early Indian Life in the Lake Superior Region. *In* Duluth:
            Sketches of the Past. Ryck Lydecker, Lawrence J. Sommer,
            and Arthur Larsen, eds. Duluth: Duluth Legacy Series.
            Reprinted in Minnesota Archaeologist 37(4):157–96.
Rubel, Arthur J.
    1966   Across the Tracks: Mexican-Americans in a Texas City.
            Austin: University of Texas Press.
Sasaki, Tom T.
    1960   Fruitland, New Mexico: A Navajo Community in Transi-
            tion. Ithaca: Cornell University Press.
Schacter, Jay Kliman
    1967   Family Interaction Patterns in Two Neighborhoods of North
            City. Paper presented at the Meeting of the Central States
            Anthropological Society. Chicago.
Schensul, Stephen L.
    1965   Lakewood: An Ethnographic Analysis of a Northern Min-
            nesota Community. Master's thesis, University of Min-
            nesota.

Schensul, Stephen L., J. Anthony Paredes, and Pertti J. Pelto
  1968   The Twilight Zone of Poverty: A New Perspective on an
          Economically Depressed Area. Human Organization
          27(1):30–40.
Service, Elman R.
  1955   Indian-European Relations in Colonial Latin America.
          American Anthropologist 57:411–25.
Shibutani, Tamotsu
  1961   Society and Personality. Englewood Cliffs, N.J.:
          Prentice-Hall.
Shibutani, Tamotsu, and Kian M. Kwan
  1965   Ethnic Stratification: A Comparative Approach. New York:
          Macmillan.
Shimony, Annemarie Anrod
  1961   Conservatism among the Iroquois at the Six Nations Re-
          serve. Yale University Publications in Anthropology, No.
          65. New Haven: Yale University Department of Anthropol-
          ogy.
Siegal, Sidney
  1956   Nonparametric Statistics for the Behavioral Sciences. New
          York: McGraw-Hill.
Skinner, Alanson Buck
  1916   Political Organization, Cults, and Ceremonies of the Plains
          Ojibway and Plains Cree Indians. *In* Societies of the Plains
          Indians. Clark Wissler, ed. Anthropological Papers of the
          American Museum of Natural History 11:475–542.
  1923   A Further Note on the Origin of the Dream Dance of the
          Central Algonkian and Southern Siouan Indians. American
          Anthropologist 25:427–28.
  1925   Final Observations on the Central Algonkian Dream Dance.
          American Anthropologist 25:340–43.
Slotkin, James S.
  1952   Menomini Peyotism: A Study of Individual Variation in a
          Primary Group with Homogenous Culture. Transactions of
          the American Philosophical Society 42, pt. 4, pp. 565–700.
          Philadelphia.
  1957   The Menomini Powwow: A Study in Cultural Decay. Mil-
          waukee Public Museum Publications in Anthropology, No.
          4.
Smith, M. G.

1956 On Segmentary Lineage Systems. Journal of the Royal Anthropological Institute 86, pt. 2:39–80.

1960 Government in Zazzau, 1800–1950. International African Institute. London: Oxford University Press.

Solien de Gonzales, Nancie L.

1965 The Consanguineal Household and Matrifocality. American Anthropologist 67(6, pt. 1):1521–49.

Spicer, Edward H.

1940 Pascua: A Yaqui Village in Arizona. Chicago: University of Chicago Press.

1961 Perspectives in American Indian Culture Change. Chicago: University of Chicago Press.

Spindler, George D.

1955 Sociocultural and Psychological Processes in Menomini Acculturation. University of California Publications in Culture and Society, Vol. 5. Berkeley: University of California Press.

Stewart, Charles T.

1958 The Urban-Rural Dichotomy: Concepts and Uses. American Journal of Sociology 64(2):152–56.

Stewart, Omer

1944 Washo-Northern Paiute Peyotism: A Study in Acculturation. University of California Publications in American Archaeology and Ethnology, No. 3, 40:63–141.

Tanner, Helen Hornbeck

1976 The Ojibwas: A Critical Bibliography. The Newberry Library Center for the History of the American Indian Bibliographical Series. Bloomington: Indiana University Press.

Tanner, John

1830 Thirty Years Indian Captivity of John Tanner. Reprint. Edwin James, ed. Minneapolis: Ross and Haines, 1956.

Teit, J. A.

1930 The Salishan Tribes of the Western Plateaus. Frans Boas, ed. Bureau of American Ethnology, Smithsonian Institution, 45th Annual Report. Washington, D.C.

Thomas, Robert K.

1965 Pan-Indianism. Midcontinent American Studies Journal 6:75–83.

U.S. Bureau of Indian Affairs

1963 Minnesota Indians. Unpublished report.

1965a   Minnesota Indians. Mimeographed.
1965b   Minnesota Agency. Mimeographed.
U.S. Bureau of the Census
  1901   Twelfth Census of the United States: 1900. Population, Vol. 1, pt. 1. Washington, D.C.: U.S. Census Office.
  1921   Fourteenth Census of the United States: 1920. Population, Vol. 1. Number and Distribution of Inhabitants. Washington, D.C.: U.S. Government Printing Office.
  1932   Fifteenth Census of the United States: 1930. Population, Vol. 3, pt. 1. Washington, D.C.: U.S. Government Printing Office.
  1943   Sixteenth Census of the United States: 1940. Characteristics of the Population, Vol. 2, pt. 4. Washington, D.C.: U.S. Government Printing Office.
  1952   U.S. Census of Population: 1950. Characteristics of the Population, Minnesota, Vol. 2, pt. 23. Washington, D.C.: U.S. Government Printing Office.
  1961   U.S. Census of Population: 1960. General Population Characteristics, Minnesota. Final Report PC(1)-25B. Washington, D.C.: U.S. Government Printing Office.
U.S. Weather Bureau
  1961   Climatography of the United States. No. 86-17, Decennial Census of the United States Climate. Climate Summary of the United States, Supplement for 1951–1960: Minnesota. Washington, D.C.: U.S. Government Printing Office.
Vandersluis, Charles W.
  1963   A Brief History of [Cramton] County. [North City], Minn.: [Cramton] County Historical Society.
Vizenor, Gerald
  1971   The Anishinabe. The Indian Historian 4(4):16–18.
Wallace, Anthony F. C.
  1956   Revitalization Movements. American Anthropologist 58:264–81.
  1956   Mazeway Resynthesis: A Biocultural Theory of Religious Inspiration. Transactions of the New York Academy of Science 18:626–38.
Wallerstein, Immanuel, ed.
  1966   Social Change: The Colonial Situation. New York: John Wiley.
Wallis, Wilson D.

1952   The Canadian Dakota. Anthropological Papers of the American Museum of Natural History. 41:1–226.

Warner, William Lloyd
1962   An American Sacred Ceremony. *In* Reader in Comparative Religion, pp. 169–80. William A. Lessa and Evon Z. Vogt, eds. Evanston, Ill.: Harper and Row.

Wax, Murray, and Rosalie Wax
1964   Cultural Deprivation as an Educational Ideology. Journal of American Indian Education 3(2):15–18.

Wirth, Louis
1938   Urbanism as a Way of Life. American Journal of Sociology 44(1):1–24.

Wissler, Clark
1916a   Societies and Ceremonial Associations in the Oglala Division of the Teton-Dakota. *In* Societies of the Plains Indians. Clark Wissler, ed. Anthropological Papers of the American Museum of Natural History 11:1–99.
1916b   Societies and Dance Associations of the Black Foot Indians. *In* Societies of the Plains Indians, Clark Wissler, ed. Anthropological Papers of the American Museum of Natural History 11:359–460.
1916c   General Discussion of Shamanistic and Dancing Societies. *In* Societies of the Plains Indians. Clark Wissler, ed. Anthropological Papers of the American Museum of Natural History 11:853–76.

Wissler, Clark, ed.
1916   Societies of the Plains Indians. Anthropological Papers of the American Museum of Natural History, Vol. 11.

Wolcott, Harry F.
1967   A Kwakiutl Village and School. New York: Holt, Rinehart and Winston.

Wolf, Eric
1957   Closed Corporate Peasant Communities in Meso-America and Central Java. Southwestern Journal of Anthropology 13:1–18.

Woodward, John
1968   The Anniversary: A Contemporary Diegueño Complex. Ethnology 7(1):86–94.

Index

Nelson Amendment. *See* Antipoverty programs
Noncooperation, 143, 186, 302–3, 309, 312, 317. *See also* Antagonism and hostility; Conflict
North American Indian groups: Algonquian, 2, 7, 40, 109; "Antlers," 3; Apache, 169, 170, 182 (Lipan, 161, 162, Mescalero, 161, 162, 169, 396); Arapaho, 170;   Assiniboin, 7, 8, 76; Blackfeet, 4; Canadian Chippewa, 109, 137, 304; Canadian Dakota, 35; Comanche, 162; Cree, 7, 8, 36, 76, 357; Crow, 1; Dakota (Sioux), 7, 8, 16, 34–35, 37, 38, 44, 62, 71, 72, 74, 75, 76, 92, 93, 94, 98, 133, 164, 250, 289, 314, 316, 340, 374; "Eastern," 409; Flathead, 35, 340; Hopi, 184; Iowa, 38; Iroquois, 1; Kaska, 307; Kiowa, 162, 178; Kwakiutl, 1; Menomini, 36, 37, 38, 182; Mesquakie (Fox), 38, 100; Navajo, 3, 182, 184, 324, 395; northern Ojibwa, 305; Osage, 38; Ottawa, 109, 110; Pawnee, 34; Pima, 62; "Plains," 33, 34, 35, 36, 71, 162; Plains Cree, 40, 92; Plains Ojibway, 6, 38, 40; Potawatomi, 37, 38, 44, 109; Shawnee, 38; Shoshone, 313; Tewa, 184; Ute, 62; Winnebago, 38, 44, 90, 163–64, 165, 169, 170, 173; Wisconsin Chippewa, 38, 109, 300, 301, 384, 388; Wisconsin Oneida, 342, 343; Zuni, 1, 184. *See also* Intertribal relations
Nuclear family. *See* Households, nuclear families; Kinship

Occupations, 139–40, 149, 157–59, 203–4, 210–13, 255, 279, 354–57, 359–60; comparisons of, 256, 264; forest-related, 14, 16, 136, 137, 139, 145, 149, 150, 208, 211, 213, 255, 289 (attitudes about, 149, 255). *See also* Employment; Income; Welfare recipiency
Office of Economic Opportunity. *See*

Antipoverty programs

Pan-Indianism, 97, 98, 388, 389, 390–91, 405. *See also* "Indianness"; Intertribal relations
Personality. *See* Psychology
Peyotism, 22, 28, 29, 127, 137, 140, 144–48, 161–63, 187, 390, 400; attitudes of non-Peyotists toward, 144, 148, 162, 173, 175, 390; role of Bible in, 164, 168–69, 175; food in, 170, 172, 180; functionaries in, 166–67, 171, 172–73, 175, 176, 177, 178, 179, 180; history of, in Rice Village (pseud.), 163–65, 182–83; ideology of, 162, 163, 169, 170, 173, 178, 182, 192; meetings, 141–42, 146, 165–66, 169, 173, 179, 181, 183, 406; paraphernalia of, 166, 167, 168, 169, 171, 172, 175, 176, 177, 178, 179, 180, 183; and use of peyote plant, 161, 167, 169, 171, 173, 175, 176, 177, 178, 181, 182; ritual in, 128, 131, 158, 162, 165, 170–73, 176, 177–79, 180, 183; songs and singing in, 166, 169, 170, 172, 177, 178, 179, 180–81, 183. *See also* Native American Church
Police, 19, 22, 23, 44, 51, 56, 62, 68, 69, 77, 86, 233, 242, 250, 256, 258, 259, 284–87, 289, 347. *See also* Conflict; Political organization
Political behavior, 141, 144, 149, 230, 243, 244, 298, 310–13, 321–22; activism, 5, 112, 208, 227, 229, 242, 259, 284, 285, 286, 287, 289, 290–91, 311, 321, 322, 401; factionalism, 52–53, 222, 227–28, 230, 237–41; leaders and leadership, 139, 144, 166, 194–95, 207, 208, 226–27, 229–30, 236, 241, 245, 279, 282, 283, 289, 290, 294, 296, 297, 317, 320, 401 (attitudes toward, 227, 279–80, 282, 283, 289, 290, 294–96, 297, 303, 310, 311, 317, 319–20); "Indian politics," 29, 244, 276, 278, 279, 402; meetings, 50,